There are numerous books on ancient Greek warfare which focus on tactical and strategic problems. This book, however, concentrates on the experiences of the soliders who did the fighting, not on their generals, nor on logistics, tactics, or strategy, which were, after all, for much of Greek history deliberately secondary considerations.

The essays comprising *Hoplites* explore the pragmatic concerns of Greek infantry. In part two, 'The Men and their Equipment,' for example, three essays discuss the problems of wearing bronze arms and armour in battle conditions: why was the spear alone the favoured weapon of attack? How were armoured corpses identified, stripped, and returned? How did infantry maintain the great weight of the three-foot hoplite shield? In part three, 'The Environment of Battle,' scholars address the actual mechanics of phalanx advance and retreat, the atmospherics and role of battle music, and the place and activity of the hoplite commander. The fourth part, 'Hoplite Tradition and Practice,' covers fortification in Greek battle and the peculiar absence of artillery siegecraft. The dedication of spoils – and the effect of such trophies on the soldiers themselves – is treated in detail, as is animal sacrifice in the graphic context of the battlefield.

Hoplites is an important book, the first to give this topic comprehensive *scholarly* treatment.

HOPLITES

The Classical Greek Battle Experience

Edited by
Victor Davis Hanson

London and New York

First published 1991
First published in paperback 1993
by Routledge
11 New Fetter Lane, London EC4P 4EE

Simultaneously published in the USA and Canada
by Routledge
29 West 35th Street, New York, NY 10001

Reprinted 1994

Typeset in Garamond by Witwell Ltd, Southport
Printed and bound in Great Britain by Mackays of Chatham,
Chatham, Kent

British Library Cataloguing in Publication Data
A catalogue record for this book is available from the British Library

Library of Congress Cataloging in Publication Data
A catalog record for this book is available from the Library of Congress

ISBN 0-415-09816-5

To
John Keegan
for
The Face of Battle

It is wickedness to clothe
Yon hideous grinning thing that stalks
Hidden in music, like a queen
That in a garden of glory walks,
Till good men love the thing they loathe
Art thou hast many infamies,
But not an infamy like this.
O stop the fife and still the drum,
And show the monster as she is.

Richard Le Gallienne
(1866–1947)

CONTENTS

ILLUSTRATIONS

MAJOR GREEK BATTLES

Battle	*Date* (BC)	*Combatants*
Hysiae	669 (?)	Argive victory over Sparta
Sepeia	494	Spartan defeat of Argos
Marathon	490	First Greek conquest of Persia
Thermopylae	480	Persian defeat of Greeks
Plataea	479	Greek victory over Persia
Dipaia	471	Spartan defeat of Arcadians
Tanagra	458	Spartan–Theban defeat of Athens
Oinophyta	457 (?)	Athenian victory over Thebes
First Coroneia	447	Theban defeat of Athens
Delium	424	Theban defeat of Athens
Amphipolis	422	Spartan allied victory over Athens
First Mantineia	418	Spartan victory over Athenian allies
First Syracuse	415	Athenian defeat of Sicilians
Assinarus River	413	Final Sicilian defeat of Athens
Haliartus	395	Boiotian defeat of Spartans
Nemea River	394	Spartan victory over allied Greeks
Second Coroneia	394	Narrow Spartan defeat of Thebans
Tegyra	375	Theban defeat of Spartans
Leuctra	371	Dramatic Theban victory over Spartans
Second Mantineia	362	Theban–Spartan standoff
Crimesus	339	Sicilian defeat of Carthage
Chaironeia	338	Macedonian conquest of Greece

THE CONTRIBUTORS

J.K. Anderson is well known as a classicist, historian and archaeologist and holds the Chair of Classical Archaeology at the University of California, Berkeley. Besides numerous journal articles on Greek art and history, Professor Anderson has written several books on topics as diverse as warfare, ancient horsemanship, hunting, and Xenophon. He is perhaps best known to military historians for his classic *Military Theory and Practice in the Age of Xenophon* (California, 1970).

Victor Davis Hanson teaches Greek and Latin as a Professor of Classics at California State University, Fresno, and farms near Selma, California. He is the author of *Warfare and Agriculture in Classical Greece* (Pisa, 1983), *The Western Way of War. Infantry Battle in Classical Greece* (New York, 1989), and articles concerning Greek history.

Alistar H. Jackson, archaeologist and historian, teaches Ancient History at the University of Manchester. He has published various articles on Greek military history, piracy, the economics of warfare, and Greek arms and armor.

Michael H. Jameson, classicist, historian and archaeologist is Edward Clark Crossett Professor Emeritus at Stanford University. The discoverer of the "Themistocles Decree," he has written a wide variety of articles on Greek religion, history, agriculture, and epigraphy. Professor Jameson directed the excavations at Halieis for the University of Pennsylvania and initiated the Argolid Exploration Project.

Peter Krentz has written articles on Greek military, diplomatic, and political history in addition to Greek epigraphy. He is the author of *The Thirty at Athens* (Cornell, 1982), an editor of Xenophon's

Hellenika I–II.3.10 (Warminster, England, 1989), and is currently an Associate Professor of Ancient History at Davidson College, Davidson, North Carolina.

John Lazenby, after taking "Greats" at Oxford in 1956, spent the better part of three years in Greece, researching on prehistoric topography, but also indulging his love of battlefields. In 1959 he was appointed Lecturer in Ancient History in what is now the University of Newcastle upon Tyne, and is currently Reader in Ancient History and Head of the School of Humanities. In addition to numerous articles, he is co-author of *The Catalogue of Ships in Homer's Iliad* (Oxford, 1970), and author of *Hannibal's War* (Warminster, England, 1978) and *The Spartan Army* (Warminster, England, 1985).

Josiah Ober is a Professor of Ancient History at Princeton University. He has written *Fortress Attica* (Leiden, 1985), *Mass and Elite in Democratic Athens* (Princeton, 1989) and is co-author of *The Anatomy of Error* (New York, 1990). In addition to numerous articles and reviews on Greek history, archaeology and topography, he has conducted extensive surveys of forts and other fortifications in the Greek countryside.

Pamela Vaughn received her Ph.D. in Classics in 1988 from the University of California, Berkeley. Currently, she is Assistant Professor of Classics at California State University, Fresno, where she directs the Classical Studies Program.

Everett L. Wheeler teaches Classics and Ancient History at Duke University, Durham, North Carolina. The author of articles on Greek and Roman history, strategy, terrorism, and various entries on ancient tacticians in *The International Military Encyclopedia*, he has also written *Stratagem and the Vocabulary of Military Trickery* (Leiden, 1988). Along with Walter J. Renfroe, he has translated three volumes of Hans Delbrück's *The History of the Art of War within the Framework of Political History* (Westport, Conn., 1980–85).

PREFACE

Over twenty years ago *Le Centre de Recherches comparées sur les Sociétés anciennes* published a collection of seventeen essays on Greek warfare under the direction of Jean-Pierre Vernant, entitled *Problèmes de la guerre en Grèce ancienne.* This present volume on hoplites differs in at least three fundamental ways from that earlier important study. First, our collection focuses primarily on the Archaic and Classical Periods, the great age of hoplite battle between 650 and 338 BC; Mycenaean, Dark Age and Hellenistic warfare are therefore *excluded* entirely. Those battles were among Greeks, and often in Greece, but otherwise they were quite different phenomena. Moreover, we have also deliberately ignored all types of conflict other than purely infantry battle; there is little here concerning cavalry, chariots, naval warfare, artillery, archers, or other missile troops. All such fighting presupposed specialized skills, where mastery of technology, rather than muscular strength and unshakeable nerve, was essential, not incidental, for military success. Lastly, whereas the former book studied Greek warfare from a variety of approaches – tactical, strategic, religious, and sociological – we have, as the title of this book suggests, a very narrow angle of vision: the view of fighting from the eyes of the Greeks who did the actual killing and dying. Our volume, then, is not merely an English updated version of earlier work; only by narrowing the confines of our military history can we hope to widen understanding of the true nature of Greek warfare.

Yet, it is also quite different from a number of recent illustrated accounts and anthologies published in the United Kingdom, France, and America, and primarily aimed at the so-called (and elusive) general audience. While we hope these essays are enjoyable for scholar and non-scholar alike, they seek to incorporate research found primarily in academic journals and especially in ancient sources –

literary, iconographic, epigraphic, and archaeological – not always accessible to most readers. Consequently, the success or failure of these articles will depend not only on their ability to interest the uninitiated in a legacy of the Greeks often either unknown or forgotten, but also in turning scholarly discussion on to the killing field itself.

My editorial intervention has been reasonably limited, mostly restricted to setting limits upon length, standard methods of citation, and the more mundane task of collecting the essays before a publisher's deadline. While I have selected the contributors, assigned the broad areas of investigation, read carefully these essays and made suggestions, all chose their own precise topics and exercised control over the final product. My chief contribution has been a plea at each stage to direct all investigation from the vantage point of the hoplite infantrymen; how else could there be justification for yet another study of Greek warfare? I have also provided an introduction, the notes on the contributors, a select bibliography of Greek battle, indices, and a brief epilogue. Citations in parentheses in the text or in the notes *may* refer to the secondary works listed in full in the bibliography by name (and date) alone; otherwise we have followed the stylistic guidelines present in the *American Journal of Archaeology*. Abbreviations of Greek and Roman authors and their works follow those found in the *Oxford Classical Dictionary* (second edition). Greek words and quotations have nearly all been translated and are not found in Greek script. No effort has been made to impose on the contributors consistency in the spelling of Greek names and places.

Following Part I, my brief introduction, the nine essays have been grouped into three thematic and sequential parts. J. K. Anderson introduces Part II, 'The men and their equipment', by reviewing various offensive arms in an effort to imagine how hoplite weapons were worn and employed under the actual conditions of shock battle. P. Vaughn follows, but now reverses the angle of vision: given the nature of such edged instruments, and the protective cover of bronze armor, wounds to the head were sometimes so hideous that the very identification of the dead – crucial to the Greeks – must have been difficult and therefore deserving of inquiry. I conclude with a description of the shield and butt-spike, suggesting that the unique attributes of the hoplite panoply for massed fighting must be seen as a technological *response* to improving *preexisting* phalanx tactics.

In Part III, 'The environment of battle,' J. Lazenby provides a proper introduction to the section (and, in some sense, the book) with a synopsis of a 'typical' hoplite battle. He leads us from the initial charge to the final burial, but more from the viewpoint of those who actually fought than from a strategic or tactical approach. P. Krentz narrows that focus considerably, concentrating on the acoustics of the killing field – specifically, the use of the trumpet in battle and thus the nature of its usage in command and communication. E. L. Wheeler complements the previous two essays with a long and extensive account of generalship in battle. He does not, as is often done, trace the tactical vision of a few notables, but rather for the first time describes the situation that all the hoplite commanders were faced with and attempts to refine considerably the notion – argued by myself and others – that hoplite commanders customarily exercised leadership only through example.

The fourth section, 'The rules of the game,' despite its title, is really not a deviation from our stated intention of focusing on actual battle. J. Ober, for example, explains the peculiarly limited role of obstacles, fortifications, and siegecraft itself in set battle, but through a pragmatic understanding of the hoplite agonistic tradition. M. H. Jameson similarly discusses in explicit detail the mechanics of another rite, the prebattle sacrifice, its practical ramifications – and difficulty – for the armed men of the battlefield who were waiting to fight. A. H. Jackson concludes the section with an essay on dedications, not merely their visual spectacle, but the emotional and inspirational power of such symbols as well – understandable only through the minds of the hoplites who experienced the combat ordeal.

I should like to thank Richard Stoneman of Routledge. His initial interest in and real enthusiasm for the project made this volume possible. Professors Mark Edwards and Michael Jameson of Stanford University freely offered their characteristically valuable advice to a former student. I owe special gratitude to my four more established colleagues in this endeavor, Professors Anderson, Jackson, Jameson, and Lazenby, who all graciously allowed a junior scholar, one with less expertise and experience than they, to act as general editor. In a collective sense, all scholars of Greek military history owe a special debt of gratitude to Professor W. K. Pritchett; his five-volume study of the *Greek State at War* – as frequent references in this book illustrate – is now the cornerstone of all research concerning Greek warfare. Jennifer Heyne – now of University of California, Santa Cruz – and Kathleen Page of California State University, Fresno both helped with typographical responsibilities. My wife, Cara, read all the essays and assured our three children, ages 3, 7, and 9, of the 'importance' of this work. Perhaps, it might seem presumptuous for an editor to offer an anthology to a specific individual, inasmuch as my own contribution has been so small. However, I believe that John Keegan's *The Face of Battle* has affected all classical military historians; it has taught us to look at Greek warfare in a novel and far more rewarding fashion. To his ingenuity, then, I offer this book as very small thanks.

V. D. H.
Selma, California
January 1, 1990

Part I
INTRODUCTION

[War is] a sweet thing to him who does
not know it, but to him who has made
trial of it, it is a thing of fear

Pindar

THE IDEOLOGY OF HOPLITE BATTLE, ANCIENT AND MODERN

Victor Davis Hanson

Here is a volume of essays about classical Greek battle, rather than warfare, a view of combat seen largely from the vantage point of the hoplite infantrymen who did the actual fighting. This approach is entirely sensible for three reasons, one of incidental importance, the other two fundamental to our very understanding of the Greeks. In the first place, few previous scholarly studies have been devoted exclusively to the military experience of the hoplite, the feel of armor, the manner of inflicting and receiving wounds, the occurrence of the atypical and bizarre in battle, the look of the dead, the pragmatics of hoplite sacrifice and commemoration. Thus, the essays in this book (none of them published previously) raise new questions and bring in fresh evidence. Secondly and more importantly, it is essential to remember that conflict between the classical Greek city-states for over two centuries (ca 650–431 BC) usually focused – at least on land – on one encounter, a day's collision between phalanxes of heavily armed infantry. It was a single battle, then, not war as we know it, and was so recognized by the Greeks themselves – thus 'battle' rather than 'war' in this book's title reflects more than the mere contents of the collection. Finally, no military history should ever avoid the human element: it is men, after all, who fight, wound, kill, and die; it is men alone who deserve our attention, incite our imagination, earn our empathy. True, often in classical scholarship – the nature of its evidence usually being fragmentary and circumstantial – there is a tendency to identify and then elevate a particular trend into 'The Trend.' Study of Greek battle, emphasis on the infantrymen who fought and the environment of their struggle, however, is not trendy and surely avoids that danger: battle is not a mere truism of military history, but its central, its only truth.

The extended campaign where episodic fighting breaks out instantaneously, accidentally, or unknowingly between either soldier or civilian, in the guise of horseman, archer, skirmisher, guerilla, or terrorist, was relatively absent in Greece on a large scale from the rise of the city-state until the later fifth century. Many scholars believe this and are surely correct on this count to discuss the 'ritualized' nature of early and classical Greek battle – provided they refer primarily to its predictable sequence of action, often identically replayed, regardless of the place, or time, or the particular Greek combatants present. For example, after the ordered columns of armored infantry squared off, the 'general' – battlefield leader is a better term – gave his brief harangue, a sheep or goat was sacrificed before the front line, and then, as Xenophon said of Koroneia, the men charged, collided, pushed, collapsed, killed, and died. By Hellenic tradition, and also because of the rarity of skilled cavalry and the ubiquity of nearby rough terrain, real pursuit of the defeated was limited. Instead, there was usually a mutual acknowledgment, often unexpressed, to abide simply by the decision of the battlefield dead, to view and then exchange their corpses, to allow the victors to erect a battlefield trophy, and to permit the losers to mope home in defeat and dejection. In the mind of the hoplite, what would be the point of further hostilities, when the losing combatants had no grounds for complaint over the location, time, and circumstance of battle, nor over the number, equipment, generalship, and tactics of their foe, no complaint at all over the outcome other than their own failure of bodily strength and loss of nerve?

'Strategy' for the army of the invading hoplite landowners was largely the science of collecting and deploying the various contingents of the alliance, choosing the route and time of invasion, and, if need be, organizing a provocative, rather than a destructive, attack on the farms and agricultural installations of the defenders. For those attacked, it could occasionally be a case of riding it out safely behind the municipality's walls (siegecraft at this time still being in its infancy), thus wisely, but less courageously, allowing a brief, and usually relatively benign, ravaging of their farms, as the invader grappled with the myriad tasks of destroying cereals, vines, and olives on any wide scale. Yet, far more often men wished to fight. The decision was quickly made to assemble the farmers, to preserve their pride and the sanctity – rather than the viability – of their ancestral plots, to march out in columnar formation and to meet the trespassers in a single, pitched battle.

In the battle's aftermath, permanent occupation of the defeated's prime lands, absolute destruction of his rural infrastructures, murder, rape, and enslavement of his people – the whole repetitious nightmare of the 'campaign' of modern warfare – rarely followed in the Archaic and early Classical Periods. That belongs more to those terrible, final years of the Peloponnesian War (431–404 BC) when the agriculturalists' absolute monopoly and control over conflict vanished. Then much that was found tried and true by two prior centuries of landed amateurs – their arcane rules, their ethos of battle, which limited infantry conflict in a social, economic, chronological, and even spatial sense – was finally cast away, repudiated, through the steady and barbaric escalation of twenty-eight years of war. The combatants, Sparta and Athens, were, to employ a cliché, atypical societies; diametrically opposed in spirit, they were ironically similar in their relative independence from the dominance of free agriculture and thus immune both from the traditional requirements of farm work and from the confining regulations of hoplite battle, which was so agrarian in outlook and practice. They were 'free' instead, unlike most other smaller Greek *poleis*, to wage among themselves a new war so akin to the agony of our own. Butchery in the streets of Plataia and Mykalessos, skirmishing at Aitolia, Sphakteria, and Sicily, abject murder on Corcyra and Melos, all widened the scope of battle far beyond the old afternoon killing-fields of the past.

'Tactics', too, from 650 BC to the later fifth century were deliberately as banal and one-dimensional as strategy. They consisted mainly of determining the proper, albeit elusive, ratio between the breadth and depth of the phalanx, a few rudimentary flanking movements, and the placement, always somewhat political, of the particular allied troops on the proper wings. By design, little – very little – was left to chance. With the accompanying absence of reserves, specialized units, the surprise attack, the night engagement, and the concealed ambush as decisive encounters, there was no desire for elaborate, pre-battle tactical planning. Nor, then, was there reason for any other to enter infantry battle except the owners of small farms, the wearers of bronze armor. The landless, rootless poor who could act either as light-armed skirmishers or guerillas in difficult, mountainous terrain were unwelcome and thus they were relegated to rowing in the fleet or occasional harassment, mopping-up and scavenging before and after battle. After all, in the great age of the hoplite their presence on a wide scale could only prolong war (and cost money), endangering the very economy, the very purpose of pitched battle, by blending D-Day into nightmarish Vietnamization, war into cold war, by creating an overall climate of farming, but no farming. Besides, the elevation of such 'trash' into real militiamen might bring along with it their dangerous ideas about land redistribution and the radicalization of democracy. And in the Greek mind – the landowning Greek mind at least – there was a somber pathos to the notion that skirmishers could kill from afar their social betters, without recourse to hand-to-hand combat and the burden of hoplite armor. Yet, hoplite snobbery was of a peculiar sort: on the other social extreme, chateau generals and indeed generalship itself, as we know it, were also virtually non-existent. Such plumed officers and other assorted military intellectuals and planners were not only unneeded, but disliked and unwanted as well. The elite cavalry likewise played an insignificant role, one more of mutual posturing and prancing than real charging into the ranks of armed men; whatever their claims to martial virtue, they were nearly as irrelevant in battle as their impoverished opposites on the social scale.

Consequently, the often noted 'paradoxes' of Greek warfare – the ravaging of cropland, but the accomplishment of little lasting agricultural damage; the decisive hoplite clash without extensive battle fatalities; the choice of level battlefields rather than the garrisoning of defensible, mountainous passes; the adoption of heavy, bronze armor under the summer, Mediterranean sun; the exclusion not merely of the very poor, but of the very rich as well – must not be seen at all as true incongruities. All are explicable in light of the small farmers' utopian agenda: free men who arose out of the Dark Ages as independent landowners intent on creating and preserving an exclusive society, an *agrotopia*, in their own image. Hoplite battle – itself most often arising over a struggle for disputed borderlands – for over two centuries was real war in an artificial climate – the private domain of a rural, middle class where all of like circumstance could fight and yet never really endanger their mutual agricultural prosperity. For one of the few times in history, bloodletting served in the long run to spare, rather than to expend, lives. In short, Greek warfare for over two centuries was a wonderful, absurd conspiracy.

Although it was clear to the vast majority of the Greeks that the collision of men, always stumbling and grappling in the melée of infantry battle, was their only image of war, it has not necessarily been so in the minds of their modern successors. On the contrary, all too little has been written about the environment of a Greek battle, unique though it surely was. Yet, we see fallen hoplites on the public panorama of extant monumental sculpture from many temples, spear-thrusting on a great number of red- and black-figure vases, and descriptions of fighting throughout all varieties of Greek literature; this suggests, does it not, that most Greeks were disinterested in the parade, the May-Day march, and things quasi-military, resigned instead to the notion that war was only the few minutes of fighting and dying? That the claim of modern scholarly 'neglect' of the Greek battle phenomenon is no exaggeration is clear from recent controversy over the very nature of hoplite fighting; some, for example, have sought to argue against the pushing of crowded ranks, as if phalanx combat was instead relatively fluid, characterized by individual skirmishing, not a concentrated, massed thrusting of shields. The significance of this 'controversy' is not the persuasiveness of the argument (it is demonstrably false), but rather, at this late date, its very existence, for its presence is surely symptomatic of our own intrinsic misunderstanding of the battlefield experience of the Greek hoplite, misunderstanding of what Greek battle was, and thus, too, what Greek battle was *for*.

Instead, scholars for over 150 years have concentrated on the very three areas of warfare which were not so important to the great class of small landholders who comprised the hoplite infantry of most Greek city-states. Strategy, tactics and the 'sociology' of Greek warfare tell us very little about the fighting experience in the life of these citizens of the *polis*. Nor can this lack of interest in battle reflect a scarcity of information in our written, pictorial, or archaeological sources. Ancient historians, it is true, concentrated mostly on the campaign. Even when they do turn to factual, rather than rhetorical, descriptions of key battles, there is more emphasis on rudimentary tactics and deployment than on the fighting itself. Nevertheless, because hoplite battle was a common, shared experience to most men of the city-state, bits and pieces of the true story emerge in nearly all Greek literature, from the poetry of Tyrtaeus to the comedies of Aristophanes. The constant finds of hoplite arms and armor and the frequency of battle scenes on Greek vases and in sculpture reinforce this picture drawn from literature. Consequently, if there is any interest, we can present a confident account of the nature of hoplite battle. True, recent scholarship devoted to most Greek social and economic history has often been less than positivist, in the sense that classicists long ago discovered what we could 'know' with certainty about the Greeks, and left it to us to fill in the gaps through less certain testimonia and (sometimes faulty) modern analogy. Yet, the study of Greek battle is surely an exception; this volume, it must be confessed, could have been composed many years ago at the very dawn of Classical scholarship. The real reason for these traditional (and repetitive, if not misguided) approaches to Greek warfare that resulted in neglect of the battlefield is to be found *not* in the primary sources: the fault lies with the peculiar nature of classical scholarship in general, and with the predilections of military historians in particular.

Classicists have most often framed the study of Greek warfare from their own individual training and interests – uniformly originating out of the university and thus long study in archaeology, philology, and history. Battle was to be political history, battle was to be Greek philology, battle was to be historiography. And so, for example, they have chronicled the military 'strategy' of a Pericles, Agesilaos, or Epameinondas, but only as an ancillary to a larger, historical interest in the rise of Athenian, Spartan, or Theban hegemony. Even when individual battles were studied – their number always small and static – it was usually through the process of 'reconstruction': key Greek words were to be analyzed and re-analyzed, inferior, pedantic, tactical manuals of much later ages consulted, passages in original sources questioned and rejected, numbers of faceless combatants surmised, sterile wings and contingents of men moved and removed – all like chess pieces on some ivory board, as if this approach alone could ever explain why or how one group of men collapsed and fled the battlefield. Similarly, arms and armor, ironically the most tangible of all evidence for hoplite fighting, were discussed largely as an offshoot of archaeological excavation; that is, their shape, form, construction, and finish were seen (as other decorative bronzes and sculpture) as works of art, rather than heavy, cumbersome tools to protect real men from awful arrow, spear, and sword attacks. Usually, then, their actual weights, the effectiveness of their protection, and the difficulty inherent in their very construction and usage were less well studied. Instead, like pots and temples, discussion of arms, of tools of mayhem and slaughter, centered on date, origin, type, and aesthetic quality and was more often introduced in the manner of a museum catalog or the slide show of an art history class, than in the proper framework of frightful killing and dying.

The rise of sociology and psychology in the twentieth century as legitimate 'sciences' has also led the more creative in Classics to envision Greek infantrymen as everymen, primeval warriors or young adults engaged in a universal rite of passage into manhood, thus seeing the undeniably ritualistic nature of Greek warfare as something other than a deliberate, contrived contest between small farmers. Their pitched battle, in this more recent and fashionable view, is the arena where society showcases these initiations – characteristic of all cultures and thus not unique to the classical Greeks – as part of larger religious and civic obligations; the hoplite dance, group war-cry, and trophy, are all, then, sure evidence for the predictable social expression of like individuals of roughly any time or place. Yet, there was something very real, very exclusively murderous to all involved in Greek battle which is often forgotten here by anthropologists and other social scientists, something more than a mere nexus for social and religious study. Does not such an effort to explain conflict in universally 'human' terms inevitably become inhuman? The Greeks' experience was always the bloody pit of the ugly cock fight, not the posturing of the banty rooster; in short, the battlefield of Greece was often a deliberate mini-holocaust, predicated on very precise physical and mental criteria and a moral imperative specific to hoplite infantrymen, and thus far removed from the tribal give and take found in other preindustrial societies.

Military historians of Greek warfare – originally an odd breed of nineteenth-century German nationalists – while out of favor now, have been far more pragmatic than classicists and, in that narrow sense at least, therefore more successful in revealing what ancient battle was 'like'. For example, in the work of Johannes Kromayer and his numerous associates, Greek strategy and tactics were at least predicated upon close attention to topography. They explored the Greek countryside and calibrated the size of ancient battlefields, always seeking to understand whether the armies of Herodotus, Thucydides and Xenophon might actually fit the physical conditions of the (albeit modern) landscape. Hans Delbrück went even further. His idea of *Sachkritik* (the effort to comprehend 'the reality of the thing') was all important, as if Greek warfare could not be understood unless drill, maneuver, and even equipment were explicable through analogy to the common practice of the German army. The fault, however, with these scholars, the first scientific military historians to categorize Greek warfare into neat compartments – arms, logistics, tactics, and strategy – was not their ethnocentric demand for practical references to the conditions of real, though contemporary, warfare. Indeed, that particular interest was their chief strength. Rather, it was their marked distance, not merely in time, but, more importantly, in spirit, from the combatants of the ancient battlefields. Rife snobbery is present in their handbooks and at times obnoxious. In truth, most were either officers themselves or civilian 'consultants' who mingled intimately with the upper civilian and military strata of society. Either way, the result was predictably the same: they gazed down on the Greek battlefield from the 'proud tower' of their own privilege, naturally searching in vain for similar kindred spirits of an ancient officer class or military intelligentsia, who practiced 'operational control' and exercised 'articulation' – a class which they never realized did not exist. 'Theaters,' 'Fronts,' 'Flanks,' and 'Salients,' after all, are nonsensical terms when applied to the Greek battlefield.

Military historians' influence, then, on balance, also has been often detrimental, since it ignores most battle experience. It is a misreading of ancient realities by faulty modern analogy whose influence is still felt today; it has imposed an artificial, glamorized separation between hoplite and commander, fighting and tactics; it is an amoral view of the phalanx from without, which tells us very little, at the expense of the picture from within, which reveals so much more about the mind of the Greeks. Indeed, the very notion of a brief collision of uniformly armed equals – little tactics, little strategy, little generalship – must have disturbed these men and so they did their best to reinvent Greek warfare into something that it was not. Their legacy in some sense is the generation of 1914, when a classical education, drawing the wrong lesson from a selective reading of ancient texts, contributed to, rather than assuaged, that madness.

Clearly, classicists and professional military historians alike have not been so interested in the experience of Greek battle. The former have seen battle theoretically, as an intellectual exercise from the extremes of textual exegesis to psychoanalysis, dry and devoid of relevance to the how and why of killing and dying; the latter, pragmatists *par excellence*, squandered the capital of their military expertise, such as it was, by their social distance from, and careful disdain for, the great middle classes who invariably provide the landed infantry of any citizen combative force. The mind of these soldiers alone experienced, analyzed, and preserved for us the true (hideous) nature of pitched battle, and so inevitably became the sole repository of the Greek combat ordeal, and thus the key to Greek military history. In the past, we scholars have not done our job and so as a profession we bear no little responsibility for the promulgation of *dulce et decorum est pro patria mori*, for the corresponding neglect of Tyrtaeus, 'His white head and grey beard breathing out his strong soul in the dust, holding in his dear hands his groin all bloody' (10.24–5).

This small collection, I believe, is part of a healthy trend, current in classical scholarship recently, to investigate the 'ordinary' in Greece; only this way can we appreciate the achievements of the extraordinary – the extraordinary who nearly all experienced frequently the horrors of a hoplite battle. On a variety of fronts, archaeological, epigraphic, and linguistic, be it through the use of field-surveys, computer techniques, or expanded prosopographical study, we are learning a great deal about farming, sexuality, food supply, demographics, the accumulation, use, and abuse of wealth, the ratios between rich and poor: life, then, as it was lived, among the vast majority of the Greeks. Whatever the conventional arguments for the need of each new generation of classicists to 'reinterpret' for us the traditional canon of Greek literature, the limits of literary theory – psychoanalytic, feminist, structuralist, deconstructionist, minimalist – surely have now been reached. It is not so much the sheer overabundance (and faddishness) of literary work on the major authors – although any brief look at current American Ph.D. thesis topics in Classics or casual perusal of the learned journals will bear this out – as much as their culpability for the subsequent neglect of the mundane and practical. Literary theorists' appropriation – confiscation, to use a better word – of a Greece, which was not and is not their own, has left us often with a counterfeit empty Greece, sophisticated as it is sterile, with little to offer any outside the university. Perhaps these few essays on the nature of hoplite battle will help to restore in a larger sense what the Greeks all along wished to instill as their sole military, their moral, legacy: that warfare is simply battle, that battle is only fighting, that fighting is always killing and dying, nothing more, nothing less.

Part II

THE MEN AND THEIR EQUIPMENT

It will be easier to defeat them
in battle than to strip away their
armor once they are dead.

Plutarch

1

HOPLITE WEAPONS AND OFFENSIVE ARMS

J. K. Anderson

The great round shield, the *hoplon* from which the hoplite derived his name, cannot be omitted from an account of 'offensive arms,' partly because it determined the conditions under which spear and sword were used; partly because it was used not merely passively, to ward off the enemy's blows, but actively pressed forward in the pushing (*othismos*)[1] that decided the battle when two phalanxes met face to face. 'Set foot against foot; strain shield against shield, crest upon crest, helmet upon helmet; breast to breast close with your man and fight him, grasping your sword's hilt or long spear-shaft' (Tyrtaeus 8.31–4). This exhortation to Spartans engaged in the Second Messenian War (first half of the seventh century BC?) is undoubtedly influenced by two famous passages in the *Iliad* (13.130–3 and 16.215–17). But the heroes of the Trojan War are described as packing closely together with their own friends, so that shield touches shield, helmet helmet – exceptionally, since Homeric battles are normally affairs of heroes moving about the field in chariots, from which they alight for single combat. What is new in Tyrtaeus is the shield pressed against the enemy's shield.

The fighting that Tyrtaeus describes is not that of the fully developed phalanx, in which each man takes his appointed place in the file, with the best soldiers forming a 'cutting edge' in front (Xen. *Hell.* 3.1.23; *An.* 3.4.42; 5.2.26; 5.4.22) and the remainder, like the iron that gives weight to a blade (Arr. *Tact.* 12.2), carrying the leaders forward. The young men whom Tyrtaeus addresses may stay shirking out of weapon-shot if they choose, though 'those who dare boldly to stand by each other and come to grips, fighting in the front rank, lose fewer dead and save the people behind them' – the 'naked' folk, who, after the poet has sufficiently encouraged their betters, are told to 'crouch here and there under shield, and pelt the enemy with big stones, or shoot at them with polished javelins, standing close to the fully armored men' (Tyrtaeus 8.28; 11–13; 35–8). This mingling of the fully equipped with men who might have no equipment at all, to say nothing of the reliance on the individual's sense of shame rather than on discipline, is foreign to hoplite warfare as it eventually developed. But one cannot suppose that the Spartans would have paid any attention to a lame, feeble-minded Athenian schoolmaster (so Tyrtaeus is described, no doubt fancifully: scholiast on Pl. *Leg*. 629a) whose exhortations were completely irrelevant to their own battlefield experience. His description of battle, problematic to us, must have been true to reality in his own day.[2] At least the individual, biting his lip as he braces his straddled feet firmly on the earth and brandishes his mighty spear in his right hand, is recognizable as the ancestor of the hoplite, though the shield whose 'belly' covers him from shin to shoulder seems larger than the hoplite shield as we know it from other literary and archaeological evidence.[3] The combination of armored spearmen and light-armed missile throwers may reflect guerilla warfare in the mountains of Messenia; or the storming of enemy strongholds;[4] alternatively, there may have been a transitional period during which hoplite armor and weapons, as known in later times, were carried by at least some individuals, but the phalanx in its later technical sense was still evolving from Tyrtaeus' opposed groups of front-line fighters. Against this view is the suitability of the shield to the tactics of the phalanx, since it covered a man's left-hand neighbor as well as himself (Thuc. 5.71) and was used, unlike other armor, 'for the sake of the whole line' (Plut. *Mor*. 220A).[5] But in favor of a time of development, extending perhaps from the first to the third quarter of the seventh century BC, is the fact that works of art from this period frequently show hoplites carrying a second spear.[6] This would appear to be an inheritance from the equipment of the chariot-borne warriors described in the epic poems and shown in the art of the late eighth century BC. (Whether poetry and art depict the actual warfare of any period, and if so of which, is controversial and need not be discussed here.) But the two spears of the epic hero are used indifferently for throwing or for thrusting; it is the use of the first spear for throwing that renders a second spear necessary for thrusting at close quarters.[7] The hoplite in seventh-century art is never actually shown throwing a spear, though the possibility that he may have done so requires further discussion. He often carries two spears on the march; in action, like Tyrtaeus' young soldier, he almost invariably wields a single spear in his right hand.

An early picture of a hoplite carrying a second spear in battle is on a small oil-bottle (*aryballos*) painted at Corinth early in the seventh century BC.[8] A soldier, dressed in a loose tunic without body-armor but wearing a high-crested 'Corinthian' helmet and carrying a large round shield, strides from left to right. His left arm is flung forward, and the arm-band (*porpax*) and hand-grip (*antilabe*) of his shield are clearly visible. He carries a spear, somewhat longer than his own height, in his right hand, just above waist level. His hand and arm are drawn back for the thrust, with the elbow sharply bent. A second spear, apparently rather shorter and with its head bent to the front in order to accommodate it within the picture, appears to be tucked between his shield and the back of his left wrist. His opponents, also helmeted and without body-armor, charge from the right. The first two brandish at shoulder level large spears in their right hands, and carry shields of the indented 'Boeotian' shape, covered with small bosses. A third man throws his Boeotian shield behind him as he draws his straight sword; a fourth has no shield, stretches his left arm forward at shoulder height, with the fingers of the hand extended, and is probably about to throw the spear that he holds in his right hand, drawn back and also at shoulder height. Two more spears appear on each side of the leading warrior with the Boeotian shield. Their shafts are at a slight angle to the vertical; their heads point upwards. They have presumably been thrown, though by whom or at what target is not clear. Behind the hoplite a naked archer is about to shoot to the right – in support of the hoplite? Or attacking him treacherously from behind? In either case, his intentions are frustrated by a naked man who from behind seizes the archer's hair with his left hand, while his right plunges a straight sword clean through his victim's body.

If this scene represents a contemporary battle and not an episode from a lost epic,[9] it seems to portray the state of affairs already deduced from Tyrtaeus – the intermingling of armored and unarmored men and the use of missile weapons, including the bow and arrow, which Tyrtaeus does not mention. The hoplite's second spear may be for throwing – but why is he apparently charging home without throwing it first?

Bows and slings (more effective than hand-flung stones, but requiring more space for free action) are mentioned by Archilochus (fr. 3), Tyrtaeus' approximate contemporary. They will not long be stretched forth, once the 'mill of Ares,' the war-god, is assembled in the plain, 'but there will be grievous work of swords, for skilled in this warfare are the spear-renowned lords of Euboea.' Since the poet, quite exceptionally, gives the sword preference over the spear for close action,[10] it is not clear that hoplites are involved; nor is the passage necessarily connected with a treaty banning missile weapons which the Euboean cities of Chalcis and Eretria are said by a late source (Strabo 10.1.12) to have concluded at about this time.[11]

Of his own personal equipment, Archilochus (fr. 2) 'emphatically says that his weapon is the spear – the single spear – no one could sing quite in that key about a pair of throwing-spears.'[12] He sums up the life of a seventh-century soldier of fortune as follows: 'In my spear-shaft is my kneaded barley-meal; in my spear-shaft is my Ismaric wine; leaning on my spear-shaft I drink.'[13] It is further inferred that he was a hoplite because he abandoned his shield when running away, instead of flinging it over his back to protect his shoulder-blades; 'he would hardly have left his shield behind him if it had been anything but an encumbrance; moreover, if no discredit had attached to the incident, he would not have troubled to make a song' (fr. 6) 'about it.'[14]

Yet the second spear may have sometimes been found as part of the hoplite's equipment after the development of the regular hoplite phalanx, from which light-armed or unarmored missile-throwers were excluded. The evidence is a painting, perhaps the finest of all pictures of hoplites marshalled in formation and on the point of joining battle, on the small wine-jug known nowadays as the Chigi vase.[15] This vase was made at Corinth possibly about the middle of the seventh century BC, and shows two opposed armies, each consisting of a first and second rank of hoplites. Those advancing from the right show the emblazoned faces of their shields. The insides of their opponents' shields are turned to the viewer, with each man's left hand grasping the hand-grip (*antilabe*) and the arm bent at the elbow, with forearm horizontal, implying the existence of an arm-band (*porpax*). The *porpax* was in fact originally depicted in paint applied over the 'glaze' with which the figures are portrayed in silhouette, but this paint can now only be made out with difficulty on the shields of the final figures of the second rank.[16] The soldiers of the front ranks of both armies poise spears held shoulder high at the point of balance in their right hands. The point is aimed slightly downwards for the deadly thrust over the shield at the throat. Second spears, whose points break the upper margin of the picture, slope backwards at an angle of about 30 degrees above the warriors' heads. The lower shafts are visible among the legs of the army advancing from the right, but cannot be seen in the left-hand army. The rear-rank soldiers of the left-hand army have only one spear each, carried at the slope on the right shoulder. The rear rank of the right-hand army have brought their first spear down, so that the heads project at about waist level into the gap between the ranks (possibly an intermediate movement between the slope and the raising of the spear to shoulder level). Second spears appear at the slope above the soldiers' heads.

The second spears have been interpreted as 'ghosts,' 'intended to indicate that each man had a second spear in reserve, carried by his servant.'[17] But this would contribute nothing to his own safety or the strength of the line if the first spear broke. Meriones in the Trojan War, after breaking one spear, could hasten off to the camp by the ships to retrieve his second (Hom. *Il.* 13.159–68). But the soldier in the closely ordered phalanx must abide in his place and defend himself as he could with the splintered truncheon. One might suggest as an alternative that the artist wishes to combine two moments in time in a single picture – the front-rank men carried their spears at the slope during the approach, and brought them to the thrusting position just before closing with the enemy. Or, again, the extra spear-points might be intended to multiply and crowd the weapons on both sides, and give an added impression of numbers (the empty space between the ranks, which in the right-hand army is filled with the projecting spear-heads, in the left contains a flute-player, to whose music his companions have advanced).

But the simplest explanation, that the men (though why not those of the left-hand army's second rank?) actually do have two spears, seems the most acceptable. They must be supposed to be carried at the slope on the left shoulder, and grasped (together with the shield-grip) by the left hand, and indeed traces of two spears carried in this way were still visible at the time the drawings were made for the original publication.[18] They are clearly reserves, suggesting a system of tactics in which the first spear was thrown just before the armies closed, and the second was then grasped for thrusting. Two spears, one smaller than the other, appear above a stack of arms behind the rear rank of the second army, and these have attached to their shafts loops intended to give extra purchase when the spear is thrown.[19] So do the two spears of a man who is arming himself still further to the rear. On the other hand, no such loops appear on the spears of the men who are in action on both sides; the front ranks are apparently too close to throw before taking their reserve spear; there are no thrown spears in the field (such as appear on the *aryballos* of a generation earlier); the levelled first spears of the rear rank of the right-hand army are clearly not about to be thrown; and the rear-rank men of their opponents have first spears only, and are making no attempt to throw them. Indeed it would be difficult for either rear rank to throw without hitting their own leaders. Perhaps therefore the second spears are intended to replace breakages. In any case, second spears evidently proved more nuisance than they were worth. They do not appear in later art, and the helplessness of the hoplite whose one spear breaks is stressed, more than two centuries after the painting of the Chigi vase, by Euripides (*HF* 190–203); the hoplite is the slave of his weapons, and if his comrades prove wanting in courage he himself perishes through the cowardice of those by his side. If he breaks his spear, he cannot with his body ward off death, since he has but the one resource. In all this the archer, who keeps himself out of danger and deals death blindly with his myriad arrows, has the advantage. Strange sentiments these, even in the context of the mortal enmity between the archer-hero Herakles and the villainous King Lycus, to win favor with an audience which had grown up believing that the spear successfully opposed to Persian archery had saved Greece from enslavement (Aesch. *Pers*. 813, 1001–3).

Needless to say, in classical times the hoplite seldom threw his spear (which none the less could prove an effective missile) except as an act of desperation before running away. Men who intended to stand and put up a fight had better uses to which to put their 'one resource.' Agesilaus of Sparta, fighting his way out of the mountains of Acarnania in 389 BC, stormed a position from which his men were being harassed by the enemy's light-armed troops.

> On the summit were the hoplites of the Acarnanians drawn up in order, and the greater number of their peltasts, and they waited for the Spartans there. They discharged their missiles, and, shooting their spears like javelins, wounded some cavalrymen and killed a number of horses. But when they were almost come to grips with the Spartan hoplites they gave way, and there were killed of them that day about three hundred.
>
> (Xen. *Hell.* 4.6.11)

Again, in 377 BC, Agesilaus, campaigning in Boeotia, turned the Thebans' position and forced them to retire hurriedly. 'While they were running past, some of the polemarchs [Spartan regimental commanders] charged them at the double with their regiments. However the Thebans threw their spears like javelins from the ridges, so that Alypetus, one of the polemarchs, was actually killed, shot by a spear. All the same, the Thebans were routed from this ridge too'

(Xen. *Hell.* 5.4.52). On the other hand, when the Athenian democrats were defending Munychia against the Thirty Tyrants and their supporters in 404 BC, their leader Thrasybulus encouraged them by pointing out that the enemy, charging uphill, could make no use of missiles for fear that those who threw them from behind would hit their own leaders. 'But we, letting fly spears and javelins and stones downhill, will reach them and wound many of them' (Xen. *Hell.* 2.4.15). Thrasybulus' men were not, of course, a regular hoplite phalanx but a scratch force using improvised equipment.

Missile weapons seem, in fact, to have been comparatively ineffective against the hoplite phalanx, or even against hoplites marching in good order on level ground. At Marathon in 490 BC (Hdt. 6.112) and at Cunaxa in 401 BC (Xen. *An.* 1.17–20) hoplites charged successfully at the double against Persian archers, whose bows were probably not powerful enough to penetrate Greek shields. At Cunaxa the 'barbarians' had no confidence in the stopping power of their archery, but gave way and ran before the Greeks came within bowshot. Nor were Persian archers and slingers able to overwhelm the Greeks during their long march up the Tigris (Xen. *An.* 3.1–18); and, more remarkably still, a raiding party of 'about six hundred men,' after it had failed to surprise its intended victim and the countryside had been raised against it, was able to make good its retreat by keeping a circular formation, with shields turned to the enemy arrows and slings. Certainly the Greeks suffered severely, nearly half of them being wounded; but there were apparently few or no fatal casualties (Xen. *An.* 7.8.8–19). Of all the nations whom Xenophon and his 'Ten Thousand' encountered on their march through Asia, only the Carduchi, the ancestors as it would seem of the modern Kurds, had missiles that would penetrate Greek armor – 'bows nearly three cubits long, and arrows of more than two cubits, which went through shields and breastplates. The Greeks used them as javelins when they took them' (Xen. *An.* 4.2.28).

The triumph of the Greek spear over the Persian arrow had in fact been decided at Plataea in 479 BC, where the Persians shot for a long time (perhaps for hours) against a stationary target of thousands of Spartan hoplites sitting patiently behind their shields. They inflicted casualties: Callicrates, 'the most handsome man in the Greek host,' regretted, as he was carried off the field mortally wounded by an arrow in his side, not that he was dying for Greece but that he had shown no deed worthy of himself, as he had desired (Hdt. 9.72). But the Spartans were not seriously weakened by a total of ninety-one dead (Hdt. 9.70), while the Persian army was destroyed with the loss of many thousands.

In the campaign of Plataea the Athenians, alone among the Greek allies, were assisted by a corps of archers, who did good service against the Persian cavalry in the first part of the campaign (Hdt. 9.21.3–23.2) and whom the Spartans would gladly have borrowed during the battle itself (Hdt. 9.60.3).[20] Archers, including horse-archers, continued to be a valuable part of the Athenian military establishment, but we hear nothing of their use in pitched battles. Hoplites who were defeated by light-armed troops armed with missiles – notably the Spartans by the Athenians on Sphacteria in 425 BC (Thuc. 4.30.4–4.37.5) and the Athenians themselves in Aetolia in 426 BC (Thuc. 3.94.3–98.5) – were generally overwhelmed by superior numbers on rough ground where it was impossible to maintain a regular formation. A great victory of peltasts, armed with javelins, over a regiment of Spartan hoplites on level ground was indeed won in 390 BC by the Athenian Iphicrates; but the peltasts were supported by a large Athenian hoplite and cavalry force (Xen. *Hell.* 4.5.12–17).

To sum up, the hoplite weapon was the spear, used for thrusting at close quarters, with the sword as a secondary adjunct. Hoplites might have to fight against, or in combination with, light infantry and cavalry in skirmishes and mountain warfare, and in fact their tactics and armor were modified with this possibility in mind during the centuries of hoplite warfare. But these modifications did not affect the form of spear and sword, and so need not be discussed here.

A description of the spear may begin with the wooden shaft. Naturally no complete specimen has survived, but the pictorial evidence suggests that the spear was generally rather longer than the height of the bearer. 'Traces of the wooden shaft connecting the head and small iron butt of a spear were found in a grave in Macedonia dating from the early Iron Age.' This particular specimen had a total length of 'just over 7 ft 3 in. (2.2 m), but its evidence is not directly applicable to hoplite warfare. Some at least of the spears given to hoplites by the vase-painters seem to be longer – perhaps 8 ft (2.4 m). The 'Pelian ash,' on which Achilles leans in the picture that has given the 'Achilles Painter' (c.450–440 BC) the name by which he is known today, seems longer still.[21] Ash-wood was used for the spear of Homeric heroes; Achilles inherited from his father the 'Pelian ash spear' that the Centaur Chiron had gathered on the peak of Mount Pelion (Hom. *Il.* 19.390) and old Priam's warlike youth is recalled by the epithet 'of the good ashen spear' (Hom. *Il.* 4.47 etc.). Cornel was preferred for the sarissa, the great pike of the Macedonian phalanx that eventually overcame the hoplite; according to Theophrastus (*Hist. Pl.* 3.12.2) the length of the sarissa was limited to 12 cubits (18 ft) by the limited growth of the cornel. Neither wood is very readily available in southern Greece; perhaps the use of less tough substitutes is one reason why the broken spear was such a hazard of hoplite warfare. We are not told what those substitutes may have been. Grattius Faliscus, who wrote a Latin poem on hunting about the beginning of the present era, gives a list of woods suitable for the shafts of hunting spears (*Cynegeticon* 127–49). These include cornel from the Hebrus Valley, far away in Thrace; myrtle, the plant of Venus; 'Termes' (a smooth leafless branch cut from a tree, but here, where a particular variety is demanded by the context, perhaps wild olive: cf. Hor. *Epod.* 16.45); yew; pine; broom; and even frankincense. He is thinking (line 147) of light javelins only 5 ft (1.5 m) long, but pine and wild olive at least might have made infantry spears. Another tree with fragrant gum, the styrax, growing on the tops of the Taurus mountains, is said by Strabo (12.7.3) to furnish shafts for javelins (*akontismata*), which are similar to shafts made of cornel-wood. Clearly hoplite spears are not in question, and there is no need to imagine the Greek city-states importing spear-shafts from the Taurus. The connection between the tree's name and the use of the words styrax or styrakion for the butt of a spear or javelin is obscure (Th. 2.4.3; Xen. *Hell.* 6.2.19; Pl. *Lach.* 183E). To the woods used for spear-shafts Virgil (*Aen.* 11.543) adds oak hardened in the fire; but none of these seems as suitable as ash, when it was available. Spokeshaves for trimming shafts are listed by Xenophon (*Cyr.* 6.2.32) among the tools that should accompany an ideal army, suggesting that replacements might have to be provided in the field, using whatever wood was available.

On the metal parts of the spear we are better informed, thanks to dedications from the great sanctuaries. Iron spear-heads had replaced bronze after the collapse of Mycenaean civilization, and continued to be used during and after the development of hoplite warfare, from the seventh century BC onward. They are socketed, and were further secured to the shaft by rivets. There is no simple standard type, but a narrow and leaf-shaped blade with a strong central rib is usual. The length also varies: often from about 8 in. (20 cm) to over 1 ft (30 cm). Bronze, already long in normal use for articles, like helmets and cuirasses, that required to be carefully shaped, is reintroduced for spear-heads in the sixth and fifth centuries, without completely supplanting iron. Very large spear-heads, with decorated blades a metre in length, have been found at the great sanctuaries and are believed to come from Sicily or Southern Italy. Their purpose may well have been ceremonial rather than practical.[22]

A butt-spike or 'lizard killer' (*sauroter*), generally made of bronze, was a feature of the classical hoplite spear. The earliest appearance of the word is in the *Iliad* (Hom. *Il.* 10.153), in a passage describing soldiers asleep with their heads pillowed on their shields and their spears standing upright, with the sauroter driven into the ground. As so often with Homeric evidence, it is not easy to decide whether these spears belong in the heroic age, as their bronze heads, gleaming from afar, suggest, or to some later period.[23] At all events, the sauroter disappears from the archaeological record in southern Greece after the end of the Bronze Age, and reappears possibly during the seventh century, though it remains 'a rarity before the sixth century.'[24] It is usually cast solid, a four-sided spike on occasion 'no less than seventeen inches' (40 cm) long,[25] but usually perhaps half this length. It is socketed, to receive the end of the spear-shaft. Its primary purpose was probably always to enable the spear to be stuck upright in the earth when not in use; but it might also have served for a downward thrust to finish off a fallen enemy, and square holes in pieces of armor found at the great sanctuaries were, it has been suggested, made with the *sauroter*.[26] But there is also a possibility that dedicated armor may have been fixed to boards with spikes; perhaps not all of these holes were made in battle.

For shafted weapons with slashing blades, like the medieval halbert, there was simply no room in the crowded files of the phalanx. Plato (*Lach.* 183D) describes, and makes fun of, a 'spear-sickle' (*dorudrepanon*) designed to cut the enemy's rigging in a sea-fight. When the inventor's galley grappled with a merchantman, the blade became entangled in the rigging, and as the ships passed on opposite courses the man had to run the whole length of his own deck, hopping ridiculously when someone threw a large stone at his feet, in order to hang on to his weapon. In the end he had to let go, and the enemy ship went off with the shaft wagging from her rigging. The 'spear-sickle,' many centuries later, enabled Julius Caesar (*B.G.* 3.14) to win a decisive naval battle against the ocean-going sailing-ships of the Gauls. But in classical Greek naval warfare it played no further part. A few Attic vases of the second half of the fifth century BC show what may be the dorudrepanon, but in the hands of barbarians, not of Greeks. It is represented as a spear, below whose head a sickle-shaped blade curves forwards and downwards. Held by the bodyguards of eastern monarchs, its function seems to be purely ceremonial, though it is once wielded in battle by an Amazon. This curious weapon is not an actual Asiatic halbert; at least, no text or work of art from the Persian empire provides evidence for it.[27]

Nor did the battle-axe find a place in the hoplite phalanx – again, presumably, because there was no room to swing it. The Greeks were aware of a light battle-axe (*sagaris*) used by mounted tribesmen like the Massagetae (Hdt. 1.215.1) and Sacae (Hdt. 7.64.2). It is frequently depicted in Greek art, often in the hands of Amazons; indeed Xenophon (*An.* 4.4.16) talks of 'a sagaris such as the Amazons have.' This belonged to a Persian captive; Xenophon is perhaps expressing contempt of the feeble weapons (including also a 'Persian bow and quiver') of the enemy. The sagaris is generally depicted as having a small axe-blade backed with a short spike or a rounded butt. The butt of a splendid ceremonial axe found in 1903 at Kelermes in South Russia is ornamented with heraldic animals.[28] A sacred axe, supposedly fallen from heaven, was among the treasures of the Scythian royal house (Hdt. 4.5.3).

Homer (*Il.* 13.611–12; 15.711) gives battle-axes to the Trojans twice. He uses the names *pelekus* and *axine*; the ancient commentators suggest (without warrant in the poet's text) that the axes might have been intended to break up the Greek ships, rather than for fighting. But the poet certainly speaks of them as weapons. A modern scholar sees 'a contrast between the Greek with his gentleman's weapon' (the sword) 'and the Trojan with his barbaric and ineffectual tool.'[29]

There is evidence also for the use of a heavy double-bladed battle-axe as an infantry weapon in Italy in the seventh century and later. A helmet in the University of California museum collection bears marks that may have been caused by a battle-axe, which, though it failed to break through the bronze armor, might well have concussed the wearer.[30]

The sword, then, was the hoplite's only secondary weapon. And it was quite definitely secondary; there is no classical Greek word for swordsman, and the Greek speaks of plunder, captives, and lands 'won by the spear,' where we might say 'by the sword.' A straight, two-edged cut-and-thrust with a small cross-guard appears in archaic and classical works of art. The blade normally swells slightly from the hilt to reach a maximum width at about two-thirds of its length, before tapering to a point, and appears to be strengthened by a slight mid-rib. The length of the sword varies, but seems seldom to exceed about 2 ft (60 cm). Surviving specimens, always of iron, confirm the pictorial evidence; for example, a sword from a warrior's grave in Western Locris had a total length of about 20 in. (48 cm) and a hilt of 3.3 in. (8.5 cm).[31] This grave contained also a slashing sword (length 53 cm; about 22 in.), a large and a small iron spear-head, a bronze *sauroter*, and a short dirk, probably the dead man's total armoury of offensive weapons. A thrusting spear and a javelin might have been carried together; but two swords never.[32] The slashing sword was not necessarily longer than the cut-and-thrust. A fine specimen of the latter from Olympia measured about 27 in. (68 cm) as preserved, and may originally have been as much as about 32 in. (80 cm) long. When not in use, the sword is shown carried in a scabbard slung from a baldric passing over the right shoulder.[33]

A single-edged slashing sword becomes common during the fifth century BC. Sometimes the back is nearly straight, as is that of the Locrian example already mentioned,[34] and the cutting edge is curved so that the maximum width of the blade is near the tip. Much more often the back of the blade is curved also. The hilt ends in a hook, curved towards the cutting edge of the blade and often ending in a finial shaped like the head of a bird of prey.[35] This seems to be the weapon known to the Greeks as the *machaera* (scimitar) or *kopis* (cleaver). A smaller blade of this shape is used by the cook who chops up the meat for the banquet of Eurytios on a Corinthian krater of about 600 BC in the Louvre.[36] Xenophon (*Eq.* 12.11) recommends the *machaera* rather than the sword (*xiphos*) for the cavalryman, because the blow of a cleaver (*kopis*) will be more effective than that of a sword when delivered from above. In vase-painting the *machaera* is frequently given to barbarians or to Amazons as well as to Greek hoplites, or to heroes of the epic past, armed as hoplites. There cannot have been much room to wield it in the press of battle; its use must have come after the ranks were broken. (Compare Polybius (17.30.7–8) on the comparatively loose order of the Roman infantry, which made it possible for them to swing their cutting swords.) The terrible effect of Roman slashing weapons – 'bodies maimed by the Spanish sword, with arms cut off along with the shoulder; heads separated from bodies with the whole neck cut away; entrails laid bare and other revolting sights' – was demonstrated in a cavalry action at the beginning of the Second Macedonian War (Livy 31.34.4). The Macedonians, who were used to the less hideous puncture wounds inflicted by spears, arrows and lances, were severely shaken in their morale.

The Spartans, by contrast, used in the classical period a short stabbing sword – a juggler's sword, easily swallowed, said their enemies. 'Yet the Spartans reach their enemies with these swords' was the reply (Plut. *Mor.* 191E); and the shortness of the Spartan sword gave rise to several of the sayings that were recorded as illustrations of the stern, self-sacrificing bravery of the Spartans and their women. 'Add one step forward' to the length of your sword, a Spartan mother told her son when he complained of his blade's shortness. 'We use short blades because we fight close to our enemies,' said Antalcidas, a Spartan general and diplomat of the early fourth century (Plut. *Mor.* 217E, 241F).

It must in fact have been for close fighting that the sword was designed. Its effectiveness when men were closely packed together was unhappily confirmed when the murderers of Dion of Syracuse (354 BC), unable to strangle their victim, called for a sword, and were passed one which was 'short, like the Spartan swords' (Plut. *Dion* 57–8; *Mor.* 553D). Such a sword appears on an Athenian gravestone of the late fifth century, now in the Metropolitan Museum, New York. An Athenian hoplite, shield flung forward, spear uplifted, strides forward to give the final blow to a fallen opponent, wearing the Spartan *pilos*, who props himself on his left elbow and stabs upwards with a short, straight-bladed sword in his right hand.[37]

In passing, it should be noted that the Spartan sword was not the sickle-shaped object called *xyele*, which formed part of the equipment of young Spartans, apparently in place of the strigil, used elsewhere in Greece to scrape off oil, sweat and dust after athletes had finished exercise.[38] 'Scraper' is indeed the translation of *xyele*; the word is also used for the 'spokeshaves' for trimming spears mentioned earlier (p.23). The belief that the Spartan sword was curved (most unsuitably for sword-swallowing!) and called *xyele* arises chiefly from two passages in Xenophon's *Anabasis* (4.7.16; 4.8.25). In the first, the Chalybes, a savage tribe living just south of the Black Sea, are said to have carried at their belts a small sabre (*machairion*) 'as big as a Laconian *xyele*, with which they butchered whoever fell into their hands. They cut off their heads and carried them as they went along, and sang and danced when the enemy were going to see them.' (Their principal weapon was a pike 15 cubits long.) The second passage mentions a Spartiate Dracontius, 'who had been exiled from his home as a boy, for the involuntary manslaughter of another boy, whom he struck with his xyele.' Plutarch (*Mor.* 233F) has another story of how Spartan boys fought with sickles (*drepana*). One was mortally wounded, but would not let his friends avenge him, because he would have done as much to his opponent if he had got his blow in first. These passages prove that Spartan boys did indeed possess a curved object which could be used as a weapon, and a deadly one. But the *xyele* is never called a sword (*xiphos*) – the word used for the Spartan sword. Nor is it associated with grown men. Iron sickles dedicated in the Roman period by Spartan boys on reaching manhood may represent the classical *xyele*.[39]

The average citizen soldier probably received little training in handling his weapons. At Athens, according to Aristotle (*Ath. Pol.* 42.3) the ephebes (youths entering upon manhood at the age of 18) spent a year in garrison at the Piraeus, during which trainers elected by the people taught them 'to fight with hoplite weapons, archery, javelin-throwing and discharging the catapult.' After a year's training, dining in a common mess paid for by public money, they gave a display of drill (*ta peri tas taxeis*) to the people in the theatre and received from the city shield and spear – the essential equipment of the hoplite. Aristotle's testimony may refer only to the late fourth century, when the Athenians reorganized their defences in the vain hope of once more making their city a great power. Certainly the catapult did not come into use at Athens much earlier, and the training in javelin-throwing and archery, though useful for garrison troops, had nothing to do with hoplite warfare as such. In its later history, the Athenian ephebeia appears as a sort of military academy, for rich young foreigners as well as for a minority of wealthy Athenians, in which philosophy and literature were taught as well as the martial arts. Perhaps it had already begun to change into something of the sort in Aristotle's time.

Xenophon (*Cyr.* 2.1.16–18) makes the elder Cyrus declare that a major advantage of weapons intended for close combat over bows and javelins (servile weapons, fit only for mercenaries!) is that it is impossible to excel with the latter except by constant practice, whereas with the former there is no fear of missing a blow. Peasants called up to fight beside their masters will thus be at no disadvantage, if they are as bold and as physically robust. One such peasant boasts that, just as animals know by nature how to use tooth and claw, so he himself from childhood has needed no teacher to show him how to strike out with his fists, or with a *machaera*. 'It was not merely natural, like walking and running, but seemed to me naturally delightful as well.' This sort of fighting is 'a work of enthusiasm rather than of art' (Xen. *Cyr.* 2.3.8–11). It is true that the peasants of the *Cyropaedia* are imaginary Persians, equipped with oriental scimitar (*machaera*) or battle-axe (*sagaris*). But Xenophon himself had seen armies of newly enfranchised helots (*neodamodeis*) turned into good hoplites by their Spartan masters, and no doubt intended his readers to apply his words to the Greek spear and sword, as well as to oriental stage properties. What the peasant recruits did have to learn was how to march and fight in organized formation, not as a mob.[40]

It is true that an art of fencing with hoplite weapons was developed, and in the later fifth century was being taught at Athens by professional instructors, some of whom also offered instruction in formation drill.[41] But this training was not for the general mass of citizens. Plato counts these teachers among the sophists; and like the other sophists they addressed themselves to rich young men who had leisure to perfect themselves in the arts of political and military leadership and money to pay handsomely for instruction. Plato (*Lach.* 181E–183D) begins a discussion of the nature of courage with comments on a demonstration of this new-fangled art of hoplomachia that has just been witnessed by an Athenian audience, including the distinguished gentleman-soldier Nicias and the more hardened professional Laches.

To Nicias, it appears that this art will have value chiefly as an exercise, and only secondarily in actual warfare. It will give some advantage when one is fighting in formation, but will be chiefly useful when the ranks are broken and the battle has resolved itself into individual combats of pursuer and pursued. In such circumstances the expert will always defeat a single adversary, and perhaps several at once. To this Laches replies that if this art were any use it would not be completely neglected by the Spartans, who devote their whole lives to the discovery and practice of whatever is advantageous in war. The teachers of *hoplomachia* do not so much as set foot on Spartan ground, but look for honor and reward elsewhere, especially among people who freely acknowledge their own military inferiority.

The value of armed dances as military training, in which different movements with shield and weapons were mimicked, also appears to be limited. Certainly such dancing, even more than the exercises of the gymnasium, would promote physical fitness, an essential object of the individual's training.[42] And this art at least was not neglected by the Spartans, whose children from the age of 5 up danced the Pyrrhic dance, using fennel stalks instead of spears (Ath. 4.631a). Grown men would become accustomed to real armor and weapons – 'get the feel of them,' as we say nowadays. But citizen armies contained their proportion of the physically unfit, whose fat bellies needed three or four shields to cover them (Plut. *Mor.* 192C–D). Perhaps not many of these men had been dancers in their youths; clearly they neglected, at the peril of their lives, physical fitness and good discipline well before they reached the age of discharge from military service (Xen. *Mem.* 3.12.1–8). In a long imaginary conversation between Socrates and the younger Pericles, Xenophon (*Mem.* 3.5.1–28, especially 21) criticizes the want of good order and military discipline among the Athenians, which has brought them to fear invasion from the Boeotians, whose territory they themselves used to invade. The dramatic date is earlier than 406 BC, when Pericles was put to death for alleged misconduct at the battle of Arginusae, but the criticism applies to the situation shortly before 362 BC.

Even men in good condition can hardly have reproduced the figures of the dance in actual battle. Probably the most famous description of such dances is given by Xenophon (*An.* 6.1.1–13). These included a sham combat performed by two Thracians to the sound of the flute; a Thessalian 'harvest dance,' in which a robber fought a ploughman for his oxen, with victory going now to one, now to the other; a Mysian dance, in which a single performer clashed light shields in time to music, and a processional display by 'certain Mantineans and other Arcadians.' Finally came a Pyrrhic dance, danced amid great applause by a girl with a light shield – 'these were the ones who beat back the Great King from the camp,' as the Greeks assured their barbarian guest. One may, without denying what has been said already about the value of the dance as an exercise, agree that 'the dances described by Xenophon appear to have little practical value. They are pantomimes, processional marches, or simply entertainment.'[43]

Some movements with spear and shield the hoplite was undoubtedly required to perform as a drill. When he was standing still, he would put down his heavy shield as often as possible. But in the presence of the enemy he would not lay it flat on the ground but lean it against his knees, ready to be picked up instantly, while holding his spear upright. The smartness with which a force of mercenaries under the Athenian general Chabrias performed the movement showed the Spartan king Agesilaus that their discipline was to be respected, and dissuaded him from attacking them (Diod. Sic. 15.32–3; Polyaenus *Strat.* 2.1.2; Nep. *Chabrias* 1).[44] When standing 'at attention,' rather than 'at ease,' the hoplite carried his shield on his left arm, but continued to hold the spear vertically, with the butt resting on the ground.[45]

On the march, including the final approach, as shown on the Chigi Vase and other works of art,[46] the spear was carried at the slope on the right shoulder, at an angle of perhaps 30 degrees behind the vertical, with the spear-head upwards. 'Slope spears!' as a drill movement, carried out in unison at the word of command, appears in a story about the famous early fourth-century Athenian mercenary general Iphicrates (Polyaenus, *Strat.* 3.9.8). On one occasion he declined battle, though his army was larger and the omens were good, because his undrilled men could not throw their shields forward in unison and upon the order 'Slope spears!' the clash of arms was drowned out by the chattering of teeth. (This must have been an occasion when Iphicrates was in command of a force of citizen hoplites, not his own highly trained mercenary peltasts.) Held at the slope, the spear would have some value in deflecting missiles falling from above,[47] but would not have covered the heads of the front ranks, as did the great Macedonian sarissa, carried in both hands, sloping forward (Polyb. 18.29–30). When two hoplite armies met, protection from missiles was not, of course, important.

From the slope, the spear could be brought straight down to an underhand thrusting position. The force of the underhand thrust, delivered at a run, has rightly been emphasized.[48] Charging at the double against a mob of demoralized Asiatics, the Greeks at Cunaxa (401 BC) evidently carried their spears in this way, since some of them beat their spears against their shields in order to frighten the Persian chariot-horses (Xen. *An.* 1.8.18). The underhand thrust might also have proved useful when the younger soldiers were ordered to break ranks and pursue light-armed troops (Xen. *Hell.* 3.4.24; 4.5.14, etc.). It is sometimes shown in pictures of heroic combat.[49] But when two hoplite phalanxes met face to face and it was important to preserve the coherence of rank and file, the lowering of the spears was merely a preliminary to raising them again to an overarm position above the right shoulder. (As noted earlier (p.19), this is apparently what the soldiers in the rear rank of the right-hand army on the Chigi vase are doing.) Before bringing the spear up, it is necessary to reverse the grip. Not much practice or dexterity are needed to do this by tossing the spear upwards a few inches and catching it again with the grip reversed.[50] Alternatively, as Professor Lazenby suggests in chapter 4 of this volume, 'the change-over could have been effected by sticking the spear in the ground, then picking it up again with the hand reversed.' This does seem to involve a check in the forward movement of the phalanx, and lacks the warrant of even such slight ancient evidence as the Chigi vase supplies for the other method. The overarm thrust would be directed in the first place at the enemy's throat, which might be left bare if his left arm grew tired and he dropped his guard. But especially in archaic vase-painting it is sometimes aimed more sharply downwards, against the thighs or buttocks below the cuirass, which is generally worn at this period, or against the back of a collapsing enemy.[51] In these circumstances the underhand thrust is the weak retort of the defeated, who turns back as he retreats and jabs at the enemy in the hope of finding an unprotected spot.[52]

Apart from the imprecise references to *hoplomachia* mentioned above, there is no ancient evidence for sword-drill. Some of the movements shown in works of art, such as the backhand cut with the machaera carried back above the left shoulder, are found in modern drill-books,[53] but this of course does not prove that they were taught, rather than used instinctively, in antiquity. In works of art, the machaera is usually used for a downright slash, either the backhand or directly from above the right shoulder. The straight sword is often used for thrusting, sometimes through the back, as already noted, or, against a kneeling enemy, vertically through the base of the throat.[54] Often a swordsman seems to be using his weapon defensively, to parry an enemy's spear or cut through its shaft.[55] Pictures of Asiatics defending themselves with sword against spear, dating from the generation after the Persian invasion, may refer directly to the Greek victory at Plataea in 479 BC, though Herodotus (9.62.2) speaks of the barbarians catching hold of and snapping the Greek spears, rather than cutting or parrying them with their swords.

Pictorial evidence makes up for the want of verbal descriptions of the wounds inflicted by sword and spear in hoplite battle. The classical historians do not describe in detail, as Homer does, the path of spear or arrow through the right buttock into the bladder, or the sword-stroke that breaks the skull above the nose so that the eyes start out (Hom. *Il.* 5.66–7; 13.615–18; 13.650–2). This is in accordance with the concept of hoplite battle, in which the exploits or sufferings of the individual are submerged in the triumph or disaster of the whole army. Even when a great commander is killed or wounded, what matters (apart from the extent to which the battle is decided by the loss of a leader) is the moral example rather than the exact clinical details of the wound. Epameinondas at Mantinea (362 BC) receives a mortal spear-thrust in the chest, but who struck the blow remains doubtful, and our attention is drawn from the wound itself to the hero's comportment in the face of death. The death of Brasidas is contrasted with the ignoble end of his opponent Cleon and set in the context of his achievements and posthumous honors (Thuc. 5.10.8–11.1). But we are told only that he was wounded in his right side and lived long enough to know that his men had conquered. The details of the wound are unimportant. Occasionally Xenophon is shocked into describing some particular wound; the description of how Nicarchus the Arcadian brought to the Greek camp the news that the generals had been arrested by Tissaphernes, 'wounded in the belly and holding his entrails in his hands' (Xen. *An.* 2.5.33) is as grim as anything in Homer. However this is not hoplite battle but a sudden attack on unarmed men who thought themselves protected by a truce. Xenophon's description of the aftermath of hoplite battle is not less intense, but is more general and impersonal – 'the ground empurpled with blood at the place of conflict, the corpses lying, friend mingled with foe, shields pierced, spears shivered, daggers unsheathed, some on the ground, some in the bodies, some still in the hands of the slain' (Xen. *Ages.* 2.14). It is notable that though this passage comes from an encomium of the victor, the Spartan king Agesilaus, the king's own wounds are merely said to be 'many,' not described. What does deserve description is his pious respect of the right of sanctuary after he learns that a party of the enemy has taken refuge in a nearby temple, and the display with which he demonstrates to friend and foe the fact of victory, rather than its cost.[56]

Poetical descriptions of two duels, set in the heroic past but reflecting the historic development of the art of fencing, may conclude this account of hoplite weapons and serve as reminders that it was to single combat (*monomachia*) that fencing (*hoplomachia*) was generally applicable. In the first, Euripides (*Phoen.* 1380–420) tells how the feud of the two sons of Oedipus, Eteocles and Polynices, was resolved by mortal combat. The trumpet sounded; the champions advanced. Each aimed with his spear at his adversary's eyes, which barely showed above the rim of his shield. Neither guard was broken, until Eteocles stumbled upon a rock, and, before he could recover, his brother pierced his left leg. Now Polynices left his own breast bare for a thrust; but the spear of Eteocles broke (apparently after penetrating the cuirass, though the armor is not specifically mentioned). Springing back, the hero picked up a great stone and broke his brother's spear. Both took to their swords, and Eteocles, deceiving Polynices by the 'Thessalian Trick' of a feigned retreat, dealt him a mortal blow in the entrails. (Again the cuirass is not actually mentioned; but it may be supposed that Eteocles struck below its edge, in the spot 'between navel and privy parts,' where, as Homer remarked centuries earlier (Hom. *Il.* 13.568) death comes most painfully to wretched mortals.) Now Eteocles stood triumphant over his dying brother; but the hatred of Polynices gave him strength for a last blow upwards, and the brothers died together.

It is clear that both adversaries were using their spears in the overhand position during the first part of the fight. The fact that one particular feint had apparently acquired a name that was recognizable to the audience – or some of it – indicates that the hoplomachia was indeed known at Athens at the time when the play was produced (411 BC; the 'dramatic date' of Plato's *Laches* must be some years earlier, since Laches was killed at the battle of Mantinea in 418 BC).

The effort by which Polynices avenges his own death looks at first sight like a rather implausible attempt by the poet to reconcile his own evident wish to represent Eteocles as the winner with the traditional story, which required the death of both brothers. But Euripides' version is perhaps not so far-fetched. A little less than a century after this play was produced, Eumenes of Cardia was hurt in the groin under the cuirass by a sword-stroke from his enemy Neoptolemus, whom he had mortally wounded and was stripping of his arms. This injury however was only slight (Plut. *Eum.* 7.6–7).

The second example is the fight of Castor and Lynceus for the daughters of Leucippus, as described by Theocritus (*Id.* 22. 183–204). Lynceus thrusts at Castor with his spear 'below the rim of his shield' (i.e. underhand). Castor thrusts back; both spears break in the shields, but without pause the heroes draw their swords and strike against each other's helmets, whose crests they can barely reach above the shields. Lynceus attempts a side-stroke against Castor's left thigh, but Castor escapes the blow by pulling back his leg and shears away his opponent's finger-tips. Lynceus drops his sword and turns to run, but Castor overtakes him and drives his sword clean through him, from back to navel. 'And Lynceus, bowing down, lay there, and a heavy sleep came upon his eyelids.'

This description, as carefully orchestrated as the duel at the end of a good production of *Hamlet*, was written early in the third century BC. Gladiatorial combats were not, to the best of my knowledge, exhibited in the Greek world until about a century later, when they formed part of a gigantic spectacle produced by Antiochus IV of Syria (Ath. 5.195c). Theocritus may therefore have been inspired by the bloodless demonstrations of the professors of hoplomachia. Both Euripides and Theocritus bear out the criticisms directed by Laches against the art. In hoplite battle the front-rank fighters of the 'cutting edge,' carried forward by the mass behind them, would have had little opportunity for feints and withdrawals, which would in any case have opened gaps in the line. Their duty was to hold their position until they conquered or died.

NOTES

I am indebted to Miss Elizabeth Sutherland, not only for the care with which she has typed this chapter but for several valuable suggestions about form and content, which have greatly improved it.

1. Victor Davis Hanson, *The Western Way of War: Infantry Battle in Classical Greece* (New York, 1989) 28–9, 132–77.
2. On Tyrtaeus as 'the most perplexing witness among the poets,' H. L. Lorimer, 'The Hoplite Phalanx with special reference to the poems of Archilochus and Tyrtaeus,' *BSA* 42 (1947) 121–4.
3. Hanson (*supra* n. 1) 158 notes the 'unusual size and bowl-like shape' of the hoplite shield; cf. Lorimer (supra n. 2) 122 on the 'hollow' hoplite shield of Tyrtaeus 1.11.6; but also has doubts on the great size of Tyrtaeus' shield: (*supra* n. 2) 122–7.
4. So N. G. L. Hammond, 'The Lycurgean Reform at Sparta,' *JHS* 70 (1950) 51 n. 50. Anthony Snodgrass, *Early Greek Armour and Weapons* (Edinburgh, 1964) 181 finds in Tyrtaeus 'contradictions that are reminiscent of Homer,' some of which may be resolved if 'the context is one of siege warfare, in which hoplite tactics would of necessity be modified.'
5. Lorimer (*supra* n. 2) 128 . . . 'The porpax shield, which implies hoplite tactics.'
6. Snodgrass (*supra* n. 4) 138. Snodgrass has persuaded me to modify my former complete acceptance of Miss Lorimer's views: J. K. Anderson, *Military Theory and Practice in the Age of Xenophon* (Berkeley and Los Angeles, 1970) 15. For the second spear carried on the march, e.g. Lorimer (*supra* n. 2) 90 fig. b; 97 fig. 8 b, c.
7. That the second spear at least was a reality is confirmed by the presence of pairs of spearheads in graves; Snodgrass (*supra* n. 4) 136–9.
8. Snodgrass (*supra* n. 4) 138 and pl. 15 b, c. We should probably understand, as Snodgrass does, that the hoplite's second spear is in his left hand. D. A. Amyx, *Corinthian Vase-painting of the Archaic Period* (Berkeley and Los Angeles, 1988) 25 and pl. 6 – 'Near the Huntsmen Painter.'
9. Compare Lorimer (*supra* n. 2) 93–5 and fig. 7 for a similar mixture of arms and equipment in a roughly contemporary picture convincingly identified as the death of Achilles at the hand of Paris.

10. Lorimer (*supra* n. 2) 115.
11. Lorimer (*supra* n. 2) 114 represents what is probably the majority view – that the treaty is genuine. But see the very pertinent criticisms of Everett L. Wheeler, 'Ephorus and the prohibition of missiles,' *TAPA* 117 (1987) 157–82.
12. Lorimer (*supra* n. 2) 115.
13. David A. Campbell, *Greek Lyric Poetry* (London, 1967) 141–2 notes the difficulties of this seemingly straightforward couplet. He offers the interesting suggestion that the poet's rations might have been 'in a knapsack slung from his spear in the Mycenaean manner,' but prefers the interpretation 'my spear provides my bread and wine.'
14. Lorimer (*supra* n. 2) 114–15.
15. Amyx (*supra* n. 8) 32 no. 3. 'By the Chigi Painter.' Amyx (*supra* n. 8) 397–434 discusses the difficulty of establishing an absolute chronology and offers (p.428) a system 'closely comparable to that originally proposed by Payne' – which has been orthodox for the past half-century.
16. Compare the drawings of the original publication (*AD* II (Berlin 1901) fasc. 4 pl. 44) with the best recent photographs, those by Max and Albert Hirmer, in Erika Simon, *Die Griechischen Vasen* (Munich, 1976) pls. VII, 25.
17. Lorimer (*supra* n. 2) 83.
18. Snodgrass (*supra* n. 4) 138. The second spear was assumed to be really there by the scholar who originally published the vase (Georg Karo, *AD* II fasc. 4 p. 8).
19. For the throwing-loop (*aiganee*), Hans-Günter Buchholz, Gerhard Jöhrens and Irmgard Maull, *Jagd und Fischfang: Archaeologica Homerica* Band I Kapitel J (Göttingen, 1973), J83–J96.
20. This force – possibly Cretan mercenaries: Ctesias, *Persica* 26 – seems to be distinct from the Scythian archers shown in friendly association with hoplites on Athenian black-figured vases of the last generation of the sixth century; M. H. de Vos, *Scythian Archers in Archaic Attic Vase-painting* (Groningen, 1963). See A. M. Snodgrass, *Arms and Armour of the Greeks* (London, 1967) 83–4, 98–9.
21. Snodgrass (*supra* n. 20) 38. For the Achilles Painter's 'namepiece,' J. D. Beazley, *Attic Red-Figure Vase-Painters* (2nd edn: Oxford, 1963) 987 no. 1.
22. Snodgrass (*supra* n. 4) 133.
23. H. L. Lorimer, *Homer and the Monuments* (London, 1950) 261.
24. Snodgrass (*supra* n. 4) 133.
25. Snodgrass (*supra* n. 20) 80.
26. Snodgrass (*supra* n. 4) 56. Cf. Polyb. 6.25.6–9.
27. Margaret C. Miller, 'Midas as the Great King in Attic fifth-century vase-painting,' *Antike Kunst* 31 (1988) 82.
28. Thomas Hoving *et al.*, *From the Lands of the Scythians* (New York, 1973) pl. 7; E. H. Minns, *Scythians and Greeks* (Cambridge, 1913) 72–3. Minns, while noting other examples, comments on the comparative rarity of the battle-axe in Scythian graves.
29. Lorimer (*supra* n. 23) 305–6.

30. Caroline Weiss, 'An unusual Corinthian helmet,' *California Studies in Classical Antiquity* 10 (1977) 195–207.
31. A. D. Keramopoullos, '*Taphos polemistou en tois ozolais Locrois*,' *AE* 1927–8, 109 fig. 66γ. Cf. also Snodgrass (*supra* n. 20) 84–5 and pls 51–2.
32. A hero (Memnon), with a sword in his hand and a second, scabbarded, by his side, appears on a krater by the Berlin Painter in London. (Beazley (*supra* n. 21) 206 no. 132.) This must be a mistake by the painter; there is no second scabbard. Anderson (*supra* n. 6) 37.
33. Examples, Anderson (*supra* n. 6) pls 2, 3, 8, 9.
34. Keramopoullos (*supra* n. 31) 109 fig. 66ε.
35. Snodgrass (*supra* n. 20) 97 and pl. 50, compares this sword with the modern Gurkha kukri.
36. Amyx (*supra* n. 8) 147 no. 1; for the cleaver, see also the list of men 'cutting up carcase,' 'chopping meat,' and 'cutting up a tunny,' T. B. L. Webster, *Potter and Painter in Classical Athens* (London, 1972) 247–8.
37. Anderson (*supra* n. 6) 32 and pl. 10. Miss G. M. A. Richter (quoted in Anderson, page 278 note 99) first identified the sword as Spartan.
38. J. Boardman, 'Sickles and strigils,' *JHS* 91 (1971) 136–7: J. K. Anderson, 'Sickle and xyele,' *JHS* 94 (1974) 166.
39. K. M. T. Chrimes, *Ancient Sparta: A Re-examination of the Evidence* (Manchester, 1949) 255: Anderson (*supra* n. 6) 38.
40. Anderson (*supra* n. 6) 84–5.
41. E. L. Wheeler, 'The Hoplomachoi and Vegetius' Spartan drillmasters,' *Chiron* 13 (1983) 1–20.
42. W. K. Pritchett, *The Greek State at War* II 210–16.
43. E. L. Wheeler, 'Hoplomachia and Greek dances in arms,' *GRBS* 23 (1982) 230.
44. J. K. Anderson, 'The Statue of Chabrias,' *AJA* 67 (1963) 411–13.
45. e.g. the flanking figures on Side A of the calyx-krater by Euphronios in New York (D. von Bothmer, *BMMA* 1973 no. 15).
46. e.g. the reverse of Euphronios' Amazonomachy krater in Arezzo: Beazley (*supra* n. 21) 15 no. 6.
47. Hanson (*supra* n. 1) 75–6.
48. Hanson (*supra* n. 1) 84.
49. e.g. Anderson (*supra* n. 6) pl. 2b.
50. Anderson (*supra* n. 6) 88.
51. e.g. Amyx (*supra* n. 8) pl. 60.1; Lorimer (*supra* n. 2) 102 fig. 10.
52. Lorimer (*supra* n. 2) 103.
53. B. B. Shefton, 'Some iconographic remarks on the Tyrannicides,' *AJA* 64 (1960) 174 n. 13. Cf. Snodgrass (*supra* n. 20) pl. 44.
54. As on the 'namepiece' of the Penthesilea Painter, Beazley (*supra* n. 21) 879 no. 1.
55. Shefton (*supra* n. 53) 174. Compare Snodgrass (*supra* n. 20) pl. 46.
56. For 'the killing-field' and 'the wounded,' cf. Hanson (*supra* n. 1) 197–218.

2

THE IDENTIFICATION AND RETRIEVAL OF THE HOPLITE BATTLE-DEAD

Pamela Vaughn

'For many of the Trojans and Achaians alike were that day stretched out side by side with faces in the dust' (*Iliad* 4.543–4). Homer's scene, while perhaps from a context of pre-hoplite warfare, nevertheless succinctly describes the mix of bodies which would have confronted any army that fought in mass array. After the crush of battle, after the victor had routed the vanquished and taken possession of the field, after the defeated had regrouped and acknowledged defeat by asking for a truce to recover the bodies of the dead, the grim misery of sorting and identifying the hoplite casualties began. Besides the emotional pain of hoplites seeing their friends and kinsmen lying among the dead, there was the additional practical difficulty of identification to consider; in the carnage following a hoplite battle such identification could at times be nearly impossible. Xenophon, for example, described the chaotic aftermath of a hoplite battle at Koroneia (394 BC): 'the earth stained with blood, friend and foe lying dead side by side, shields smashed to pieces, spears broken asunder, daggers drawn from their sheaths, some on the ground, some in bodies, others still gripped by hand' (Xen. *Ages*. 2.14). The image, then, of tangled bodies and weapons on a field reeking of carnage is abundantly clear: corpses had to be separated and cataloged somehow, regardless of the condition of the actual remains.

Identification was difficult, not only because the bodies of friend and foe were frequently mingled, but also because corpses were often found stacked in piles, due to the very crush of the initial hoplite confrontation and the subsequent pressure generated by the pushing of the ranks to the rear.[1] Homer, for example, envisions Sarpedon lying almost hidden among the dead, 'for many had fallen upon him' (*Iliad* 16.661). At Leuktra (371 BC), too, the Spartan king Kleombrotos perished while fighting 'and a great mound of corpses' piled up around his body (Diod. 15.55.5). If we can believe Plutarch,[2] the Theban Pelopidas, sinking upon a pile of corpses belonging to both friend and foe, might well have perished among them (and those who, in their turn, fell upon him) during a skirmish had not Epameinondas, his great friend, found and defended his compatriot until both were rescued by the Spartan king Agesipolis (Plut. *Pel.* 4.5).[3] In such circumstances, the great weight of the hoplite panoply (approximately 70 lbs/31 kg), coupled with that of the infantryman himself, made suffocation beneath a mound of corpses or near-dead a real possibility for any hoplite felled in the crush of pitched battle. Wounded or dead, ally and enemy would lie piled together; consequently, there was little chance that, at the conclusion of a hoplite battle, corpses could easily be known merely by their position on the battlefield. Very few hoplite armies had elite contingents who fought and died exclusively as a group and whose corpses thus could be identified on the field; the notable exception, of course, was the 150 paired dead whom Philip of Macedon easily identified as the remains of the Theban Sacred Band at Chaironeia (Plut. *Pel.* 18, *Mor.* 761a–d).

Difficult as it would have been for the survivors to separate armor-encased enemy soldiers from their own forces, pursuit of routed troops often led to bodies being strewn over a much wider area, creating a task of collection and sorting almost as difficult as that in the center of the battlefield. At Kynoskephalai (364 BC), for example, after Pelopidas, commander of Theban and allied Thessalian forces, had fallen fighting against Alexander of Pherai, his cavalry chased the entire enemy phalanx for a considerable distance, slaying more than 3,000 and filling up the countryside with corpses (Plut. *Pel.* 32.7); thus, the recovery of the enemy dead must have been a logistical nightmare. It was therefore, from such a mass of lifeless humanity – concentrated and entangled or solitary and scattered – that all Hellenic forces were accustomed to recover their dead in order to administer proper and necessary funeral rites.

Why was it so important that the war fatalities of the Hellenic states receive such special, almost ritualistic, attention? The physical evidence of the ancient war monuments, burial sites, casualty lists, epitaphs, vase paintings, as well as confirmation found in the literary sources, proves the existence of such reverence, and virtually all surviving evidence points to the unusual homage and commemoration accorded to the battle-dead.[4] Therefore, after the battle, when either victory or defeat was usually absolute and unquestioned, established custom dictated that Greek armies were faced with the very real task of sorting, collecting and identifying, as accurately as possible, the corpses of each side. This was absolutely crucial because, within such a context, the funeral ritual and burial, whatever forms they might take, fulfilled the obligations to the fallen warrior, while reassuring the survivors as to their own future treatment. The identification process, then, was a necessary means to that end, a crucial first step that acknowledged the critical link between military and civilian life by reaffirming the basic belief in the sanctity of the dead. Men would be identified and accorded proper funerary rituals, either at home or on the battlefield, never allowed to rot where they fell nor to be thrown anonymously into a collective pit.

Hoplite commanders exhorted their men to victory by reminding them of the civic honors and glory which would attend their death: 'fortunate also is he who may die, for no one even if wealthy will acquire for himself a monument so glorious' (Xen. *Hell.* 2.4.17). This same sentiment was phrased eloquently by the seventh-century BC poet Tyrtaios at the very dawn of the hoplite era:

And he who so falls among the champions and
loses his sweet life,
so blessing with honor his city, his father, and
all his people,
with wounds in his chest, where the spear that
he was facing has transfixed
that massive guard of his shield, and gone
through his breastplate as well,
why, such a man is lamented alike by the young
and the elders,
and *all his city goes into mourning* and grieves
for his loss.
His tomb is pointed to with pride, and so are
his children,
and his children's children, and afterward all
the race that is his.
His shining glory is never forgotten, his name
is remembered,
and *he becomes an immortal*, though he lies under
the ground,
when one who was a brave man has been killed by
the furious War God
standing his ground and fighting hard for his
children and land.

(12.23–34; Lattimore translation, emphasis added)

Besides the more mundane assurance that each hoplite would be accorded proper funeral ritual, he also would have known that the dead, in particular those who had sacrificed their lives for their country, were deserving of special recognition; society at large, then, provided further reinforcement to stand fast and fight hard for 'children and land.' The sacrifice of life for country was a laudable one, and one by which others could measure the value of a man's life: Solon, for example, tells Croesus that one man, Tellus, was the most fortunate of men, in part because he died bravely on the field of battle and was given a public funeral, and thus earned wide recognition by the Athenians (Hdt. 1.30). Plutarch relates that Solon also was credited for various reforms involving the funeral ritual at Athens, including a law which forbade speaking ill of the dead, which all praised since 'it is pious to regard the deceased as sacred, and just to spare those who are absent, and politic to rob hatred of its perpetuity' (Plut. *Sol.* 21).

Socrates, himself an old hoplite veteran, even if he disapproved of the principle of public eulogy, still recognized that the commemorative elevation of the war dead was a fact of Athenian life: 'To fall in battle, Menexenus, indeed seems to be a splendid thing in many ways. For a man obtains a splendid and magnificent funeral even though he be at death a poor man; and though he be worthless, he wins praise at the hands of skilled men who do not praise at random, but have prepared their words a long time beforehand' (Plato, *Menex.* 234C).

The respect and homage, therefore, paid to the battle-dead is a common enough theme in Greek literature, and the pervasive feeling is that the tradition somehow derived from divine ordinance and sanction. Naturally, such respect was predicated on the practice of mutually returning (and thereby distinguishing) enemy-dead for proper observances, a tradition first attributed variously to Theseus or Herakles, which attests to its antiquity (Plut. *Thes.* 29; Ail., *VH* 12.27).[5] Depending on the sources, Theseus is portrayed either as mounting an armed assault against the Thebans in order to retrieve the Argive dead from their city and thus to preserve the custom of 'all Greeks' (Eur. *Supp.* 526–7, 538–40), or as establishing the first truce for the collection of the dead (Plut. *Thes.* 29.4).[6] Either version quite clearly shows that respect for war fatalities is deep-seated in Greek society. The pre-Socratic philosopher Herakleitos also observed that 'gods and men honor those who are killed in battle' (B24). Homer, too, reminds us that when Achilles killed the Trojan Hektor and persisted in his attempted desecration of the body, the gods not only took every effort to preserve Hektor's body from corruption, but also ordered Achilles to return Hektor's body to his family or risk the wrath of Zeus (*Iliad* 24.134–7).[7] The preservation of Hektor's corpse in a pristine condition emphasizes how disconcerting the very thought of mutilating even an enemy's corpse was to the Greeks.

In a similar attempt to fulfill the obligation due to the fallen kindred warrior, Antigone risked death to bury her brother Polyneikes in spite of Kreon's edict expressly forbidding such action. She explained her reasons by stating simply that a mortal's decree cannot transcend the unwritten and unassailable rules of the gods (*agrapta k'asphale theon nomima*) which have been in effect through all time (Soph. *Ant.* 450–7). Dire consequences befall Kreon's city because of his edict, once again demonstrating the anger of the gods when such violations of custom occur (id. 1016–30). Such literary evidence reveals the common, near-religious fervor for proper burial rites, the antiquity of the practice, and the real concern in the Greek mind for any anonymous, decaying corpses of warriors.[8]

Archaeological and epigraphical evidence, including that reported by ancient authorities and extant remains,[9] corroborates the literary sources and again demonstrates that the intent to honor the dead was commonplace and almost always fulfilled. For example, Pausanias records many monuments for Athenian war-dead which show that Athens recorded the names not only of citizens who fought and died on her behalf, but also those of allies, slaves, and even foreign mercenaries (1.29). The location of the monuments, of course, varied with the city-state involved, but usually burial took place in one of three general areas: at home, on the battlefield, or in allied territory. Athenians from various battles would most commonly be buried in the *Demosion Sema*, but at Marathon Pausanias noted the unusual case of two separate tombs commemorating that famous battle (490 BC): one for the Athenian dead, another for the Plataians (1.32.3). Battlefield entombment, although common for the Spartans, was less so for the rest of Greece. Frequently, if it was neither practical nor feasible to bring the dead home for burial, they would be buried in regions which would treat them with respect; the Argive dead from Hysiai (ca 669 BC), for example, were transported to Kenchreai so that they could be buried in allied territory (Paus. 2.24.7).[10]

Cult status was also frequently accorded the dead and further reflected the concern over proper interment. Moreover, it was not even necessary that the fallen be those of one's own state; nor is this surprising, given the general panhellenic acceptance of the practices and customs surrounding warfare and its attendant rituals. At Phigaleia, for example, a polyandrion was erected of those 'chosen Oresthasians' who helped to force a Spartan garrison from the area (ca 659 BC?); Pausanias further noted that the Phigaleians sacrificed to these Oresthasians as heroes every year (8.41.1).[11] The Plataians, too, undertook an annual sacrifice to honor all the dead Greeks[12] who had fallen and were buried on the field there; interestingly enough, this particular ceremony was still carried out in Plutarch's time, nearly six hundred years after the battle of 479 BC (Plut. *Arist.* 21). At the entrance to the city were separate graves for the Lakedaimonians and Athenians who fell fighting the Medes; elegies of Simonides were carved upon the tombs, commemorating both groups (Paus. 9.2.5).[13] Thus, heroic feats on a panhellenic scale were, naturally, worthy of remembrance by all Greeks. Herodotus was proud to relate that he had learned the names of the 300 Spartans who gave their lives at Thermopylai, information which most surely must have come from the battlefield inscription detailing the names of the dead (7.224); Pausanias also related a similar story of diligent commemoration: he claimed that the names were listed on a pillar at Sparta as well (3.14.1),[14] again suggesting that a careful inventory of the fallen had taken place.

Monuments, cults, and rituals such as these, of course, were intended to honor one's countrymen who died in the achievement of some noteworthy victory on behalf of the state. However, it becomes just as clear that such commemoration could also be a source of honor for the adversaries of the fallen. As Hektor's speech in *Iliad* 7 (89–90) shows, the surviving victorious enemy often found some pride in such a monument: 'this is the grave mound of a man who died long ago, whom once in the midst of valor glorious Hektor slew.' It is precisely for this reason that the Lakonian dead buried in the Athenian Kerameikos at a time when Athens was under quasi-Spartan rule eventually – and ironically – became a witness of Athenian valor (Lys. *Epitaphios* 63; Xen. *Hell.* 2.4.33).[15] Similarly, the magnanimity of Philip II was well illustrated by his return of the bodies after Chaironeia (338 BC) (Diod. 16.86.5–6; Polyb. 5.10.4, 22.16.2; Plut. *Pelop.* 18, *Mor.* 849A). Pausanias reports that the Lion monument near Chaironeia marked a common grave of the Thebans (9.40.10): 'no inscription is carved on the tomb, but a lion is placed on it, perhaps in allusion to the spirit of the men.' The geographer Strabo also refers to the 'public tombs of those who fell in the battle' (9.2.37) which were erected near the battlefield.

Whether Philip himself erected the monument out of respect for the Theban Sacred Band or allowed it to be erected by Thebes,[16] his actions regarding the fallen at Chaironeia came to be counted among his own merits – at least in the judgment of the Hellenic world – and the magnificent Lion added to his own glory, as well as to the respect due the dead.

Finally, the evidence of engraved casualty lists again shows the attention given to the identification and the recording of war casualties *by name* and the overall importance of such commemoration in the life of the state at large. In spite of the fragmentary nature of most lists, it is clear enough that they followed the general pattern evident in the muster rolls by listing names, often with patronymics, by tribe.[17] That such commemorative lists were far more than mere sources of public information is evident to any who have gazed on the black granite engravings of the Vietnam war-dead in Washington, DC, a monument whose arrangement by year of death bears a haunting resemblance to the yearly Athenian stone lists of casualties, men who likewise were killed far from home. For both such memorials it was essential to obtain an exact list of the war-dead, involving an ongoing and difficult process of identification, as perhaps the frequent additions of names on both the ancient and modern stones attest.

Just as the observance of custom and ritual for the war-dead could bring honor to them and to their states, so too the failure to perform funeral rites or to retrieve the bodies for burial could be a source of particular shame, as experienced, for example, by those generals who fought at the sea-battle off Arginusai (406 BC) and failed to bring back either the wounded, the battle dead or the drowned (Xen. *Hell.* 1.6.35, 1.7.30, 2.3.32, 35; Diod. 13.100–2; Paus. 6.7.7; Athen. 5.218A; cf. Pritchett, *War* 4, 204–6). The repercussions of such a shocking disgrace could be felt long after: in one instance, Chabrias, during a hotly contested action at Naxos in 376 BC, 'being mindful of Arginusai,' did all in his power to retrieve the bodies of his own soldiers (Diod. 15.35). Similarly, the stigma of Aigospotamoi (405 BC) apparently followed the Spartan general Lysander, not merely because he cowardly massacred the prisoners of war, but also because he refused burial to the Athenians.[18] Again, we see – here by looking at infrequent occasions of non-observance of custom – the panhellenic acknowledgment that all warriors were deserving of funerary rituals befitting their heroism on the battlefield.

Failure to comply with burial rites protected under the customary battle truce could also prove risky for the recalcitrant side. Philomelos, after he seized Delphi and plundered the territory of the Lokrians (355/4 BC), was refused the bodies of the twenty or so men he had lost in battle. The argument proffered by the Lokrians was that the dead had been sacrilegious temple-robbers; Philomelos, in turn, railed against the Lokrians' own blasphemy in their refusal of burial, and eventually he employed military force to recover his own (Diod. 16.25.2–3).

If Hellenic armies were forced to abandon their dead, the situation was always desperate: at Sicily, for example, in 413 BC (Thuc. 7.75.3) the Athenians were forced by the impending absolute destruction of their forces to neglect the burial of friends and relatives. The soldiers could see in their midst the faces of the fallen and hear too the cries of the sick and wounded who had to be left behind. It was an emotionally wrenching scene, and one which Thucydides, who took an avid interest in chronicling the increasing erosion of Hellenic customs during the course of the Peloponnesian War, no doubt deliberately employed to portray poignantly the extreme despair of the army. Indeed, whenever casualties were left unburied for any reason, Greek writers went to great lengths to explain the phenomenon, either in terms of cruelty (e.g. Aigospotamoi), dereliction of duty (e.g. Arginusai), or simply abject despair (e.g. Sicily). Thus, when an Ambrakiot herald fails to complete his mission and obtain a burial truce, Thucydides emphasizes the utter shock and horror which the herald experienced when he learned that both the initial force of the Ambrakiotes and the reinforcements had been annihilated (Thuc. 3.113).[19]

In spite of these rare failures, the Greeks nevertheless must have encountered certain practical difficulties in collecting and identifying their dead. Not only was there the universal problem of rapid corruption under the summer sun, but the unprotected areas of the armored hoplite – in particular the face and neck – could receive disfiguring wounds which would hamper identification. That the Greeks in most cases apparently did identify their corpses cannot be disputed, but the general silence as to the exact procedures arouses our curiosity. Their methods must have been commonplace in the Hellenic world and, therefore, like so many other ubiquitous and mundane practices of the Greeks, did not require discussion in our sources.

The Athenians, of course, recognized that it was not always possible to recover all war-dead. For example, in the introduction to

Perikles' famous funeral oration, Thucydides describes the general public procession attending the burial:

> The bones of the departed lie in state for the space of three days in a tent erected for that purpose, and each one brings to his own dead any offering he desires. On the day of the funeral coffins of cypress wood are borne on wagons, one for each tribe, and the bones of each are in the coffin of his tribe. One empty bier, covered with a pall, is carried in the procession *for the missing whose bodies could not be found for burial.*
>
> (2.34.2–3, Loeb translation, emphasis added)

This last statement is very revealing, since it obviously implies that the Athenians at least knew for whom they were searching, and were able to compare the number of bodies actually retrieved against some master list of the original number of men sent out. Such a list was available, of course, in the hoplite *katalogos* which was posted at Athens by tribe, each list being affixed to the statue of the eponymous hero of that tribe (Arist. *Ath. Pol.* 53.7, cf. 26.1; Ar. *Pax* 1181–4, *Eq.* 1369–72). Each taxiarch would have kept the service lists for his own tribe and made out the muster rolls for each campaign from that service list. Such lists were used to call roll at the beginning of an expedition (Ar. *Pax* 354; Andoc. *Myst.* 45), and since they were in the possession of the taxiarch during the campaign (Lys. 15.5), they would have been the primary source against which to check the names of the missing and dead.[20] The procedure, even if duplicated outside of Athens, was not without difficulty, however, since the process of identification and retrieval was not immune to external influences. What, then, were some of the obstacles which could hinder the collection and identification of war fatalities?

In the first place, if we concentrate on infantry casualties and lay aside the real possibility that many of the missing in such yearly tallies of war fatalities were drowned in sea battles, the initial problem in any retrieval and subsequent identification would center on the conduct of the victorious army. Each conqueror not only had control of the battlefield and the right to set up a trophy, but also enjoyed a monopoly over the fate of the vanquished dead: the exchange of bodies, then, always was predicated on the benefaction and piety of the conqueror. The usual order of events would have required the winning side to set up a trophy to claim its victory, collect its own dead, and then strip the armor and weapons from the fallen enemy. The haphazard looting and plundering of bodies by individuals in the very midst of ongoing fighting that one can see in Homer was simply not a practical endeavor during pitched hoplite battles; true, the Spartans frequently could be found fighting a desperate battle to protect the body of a fallen king from being seized by the enemy (e.g. Xen. *Hell.* 6.4.13; Diod. 15.56.1),[21] but this had more to do with their unique reverence for their own royalty (a holdover of sorts from the monarchy of the Dark Ages) than with any desire for plunder. Instead, in the hoplite age, looting of the dead was usually an aftermath of battle, and thus burial crews were relatively free from enemy attack.

During the time the conqueror was collecting his own dead, and viewing and plundering the bodies of the enemy,[22] the defeated army would have regrouped and sent a herald to ask for a truce in order to collect its fallen. By the time the defeated force was allowed to retrieve its own men, virtually all possible identifying tokens of any value – shields, helmets, cloaks and the like – would surely have been stripped by the other side; the dead, then, were usually returned to the losing army absolutely nude, and thus apparently without specific identifying markings (e.g. distinctive clothing, jewelry, personal documents).[23] It was an irony of Greek warfare that the defeated army had to rely on the good will and sense of religious propriety of its conquerors in order to collect its own dead. The victorious side, of course, because they were in sole possession of the battlefield, governed the collection of nearly all the corpses of *both* sides. Outside of Homer, few, if any, hoplite dead of the winners ever would have been dragged away by the defeated army in its retreat. As a result, even in the face of a technical defeat on the field of battle, the retrieval of bodies without asking for a truce signified some sort of moral victory and perhaps created ambiguity over the actual significance of the outcome as well. In a skirmish at Phrygia with Boiotian cavalry (431 BC), for example, the Athenians and Thessalians were forced to retreat, leaving a few bodies behind, but they were able to recover them on the same day without asking for a truce (Thuc. 2.22). Clearly this would have been possible only where a few died, or where the fallen could be retrieved relatively easily; otherwise significant numbers of corpses would require nothing short of another pitched battle – virtually taboo in Greek practice – to regain them without a truce. Again, the importance to the Greeks of possession and interment of the dead is emphasized: in cases of ambiguous outcomes, the technical verdict of defeat or victory frequently hinged on which side had control of the war dead.

The dilemma that this situation could present is illustrated again by the experience of the Spartan king Pausanias at Haliartos (395/4 BC): there, he arrived at the battle site only to discover that Lysander and many of his fellow Spartans had already been slain. During the post-battle council to decide whether to ask the Thebans for a truce (of course, implying inferiority, if not total defeat), or once more to fight a pitched battle, some of the older Spartans rejected outright the idea of a truce, wishing instead to fight for the body of Lysander, in order to bury it as if they were indeed victors. However, clear evidence of the superiority of the victorious Theban forces, as well as the more mundane fact that the bodies actually were close to the walls of the Theban towers, eventually suggested to Pausanias that he wisely seek a truce (Plut. *Lys.* 29; Xen. *Hell.* 3.5.22–4). Xenophon adds a wrinkle to the story, stating that the Thebans were only willing to give back the Lakedaimonian dead if the Spartans left Boiotia, which they promptly agreed to do. In this instance, one can see that the dead became part of a strategy to force the hand of an occupying army. Moreover, although both sides ostensibly followed the dictates of Hellenic custom, in the harsh reality of the battlefield and in the aftermath of the general erosion of hoplite rituals during the Peloponnesian War, any army could have its own respect and devotion for its fallen comrades turned against it. Indeed, at Delion (424/3 BC),[24] the Boiotians put up a trophy, collected their own dead, stripped the bodies of the Athenian dead and put a guard over them. The Athenians, who apparently could not proceed without their fallen, were thus forced to retreat from Boiotian territory altogether in order to gain possession of their own dead (Thuc. 4.97–101). Nor is the image of corpses as hostages such an arcane notion; one need only recall in modern times the reluctance of the Vietnamese to return American war-dead or, more recently, the intense, drawn-out wrangling with Iran over the fate of a few American corpses (from a nation of millions), that were left behind after the failed rescue attempt in 1980.

Frequently, such a strategy could work toward a virtual stalemate, if both armies were in a position to acquire some of the dead of each; that is, if no one party had absolute control of the environs of the battlefield. At Mantineia (362 BC), for example, all participants expected some final resolution to come from the battle, but the situation was such that both sides set up victory trophies, neither hindering the other; the two armies gave back the fallen under truce, both acting in a sense as victor and vanquished simultaneously (Xen.

Hell. 7.5.26–7). As Xenophon tells the story

> When these things had taken place, the opposite of what all men believed would happen was brought to pass. . . . Neither was found to be any better off, as regards either additional territory, or city, or sway, than before the battle took place; but there was even more confusion and disorder in Greece after the battle than before.
>
> (7.5.26, 27, Loeb translation)

Diodoros tells roughly the same story and provides the telling reasons for this ambiguous outcome: the Boiotians had decided against an extensive pursuit, preferring instead to acquire first the bodies of the dead. (The use of the neutral term 'the dead,' without any suggestion of possession clearly shows the intent to recover the bodies as a means to ensure the claim of victory.) The Athenians, in turn, had bodies of their own, the Euboian dead (15.87.3), while the Boiotians had possession of Lakedaimonian corpses. In this confusing scenario, neither side would move, until finally the Lakedaimonians resolved the issue by sending a herald to ask for a general truce (15.87.4). At that point the bodies were returned to each party for appropriate burial. Thus, no clear-cut victory was apparent, in large part because each side had some of the corpses of the other, and so neither army could claim absolute sovereignty over the battlefield. Although the Spartans were the first to ask for a truce, there is no indication that either side required the other to abandon its own victory trophy. In such rare instances where hoplite fighting was uncharacteristically indecisive, there was a disruption in and, in fact, a reversal of the natural process: the return of the corpses in itself became tantamount to an acknowledgment of victory, defeat, or stalemate, rather than a mere reflection of the customary practice regarding retrieval and identification of the battlefield dead.

The situations just mentioned, however, raise another, more pragmatic issue which is more germane to our central interest in the actual mechanics of such a practice of collection and burial: delay. After the battle, each army surely would need time to gather its remaining forces, to collect its equipment where possible, and to regroup; brief delays would be natural and would neither imply any neglect of the responsibility each army had for its own dead, nor at that point necessarily raise problems of simple identification and burial. Indeed, initially this time could be quite useful, since it would afford an opportunity either to check those surviving hoplites against the muster rolls of the entire army kept by the taxiarchs (as at Athens), or simply to call roll. This action could be either beneficial or demoralizing, of course, depending on the relative successes and losses of the army. At Kromnos (365 BC), for instance, the Arkadians had the upper hand against the Spartans, who became disheartened when they saw their king Archidamos wounded and when they heard later the names of the dead, all of whom were among their bravest men (Xen. *Hell.* 7.4.24). Apart from the general demoralization arising from the defeat, the losses were substantial; thus the troops were discouraged sufficiently for the Spartans to seek a characteristically un-Spartan truce rather than to continue to fight (*Hell.* 7.4.25).[25] In the close quarters of the phalanx, both during and between battles, it seems that an unofficial (i.e. word-of-mouth) roll-call of the dead would keep the men generally aware of their relative circumstances, as informal story-telling would quickly produce some details of battle casualties. Indeed, it seems unrealistic to think that the hoplites would be completely unaware that very many of their number were missing and unaccounted for.[26] This ability to ascertain such a situation quickly may in fact actually be illustrated by the extraordinary Athenian action at Solygeia (425 BC, Thuc. 4.44). After a victory there, the Athenians had already stripped the corpses of the enemy dead, retrieved their own casualties, and set up a trophy to commemorate the victory. When Corinthian reinforcements appeared, the Athenians, under Nikias, were forced to retreat, leaving behind in the process two bodies which, as our sources tell us, they were unable to find. Total casualties were known to have been somewhat less than fifty, and so the Athenians must have been able to confirm the actual body count, if not to complete the identification of individual corpses.[27] Later, when the enemy was in possession of the territory, the Athenians were compelled to return in order to ask for a truce to recover the remaining two bodies. This incident raises a couple of interesting points. In the first place, the tale is used to illustrate the piety of Nikias, the general who preferred 'to abandon the honor and reputation of his victory than to leave unburied two of his fellow citizens' (Plut. *Nik.* 6). Second, besides providing clear evidence again of both the concern for burial and the strategic importance of recovering bodies, the incident demonstrates the relative precision involved in the Athenians' reckoning of battle casualties.[28]

This well-defined ability to reckon casualties was neither limited to Athenian forces,[29] nor confined to the arena of the battlefield. A preliminary tally of battle casualties could reach the home cities in advance of the soldiers' actual return, especially if losses were significant enough to warrant a call for reinforcements. For example, after the famous Spartan disaster at Leuktra (371 BC), the names of the fallen (numbering some 1,000) were sent on to their kinsfolk, but the women were under strict orders not to make any public outcry, but instead to bear the disaster in silence (Xen. *Hell.* 6.4.16). Meanwhile, the *ephoroi* made the necessary proclamation of those who were to be included in the next service levy (Xen. *Hell.* 6.4.17). Such an efficient system of determining the dead once again must have been based upon a strict attention to accounting, to rosters, to prompt reporting of battle casualties (see, for example, n. 33) – in short, to the necessity of identifying all the dead immediately after battle.

Any natural delays in interment caused by the necessity of accounting or by disputes over principles of exchange, by their very nature, however, could wreak havoc upon the corpses of the dead, left exposed to the elements and the process of decay and thus preventing specific association of name with body. That exact problem is the basis for Menander's *Aspis*, in which the faces of the corpses after battle are bloated beyond recognition. The poet tells us that, when the servant comes to identify his master, the fallen warriors have been in the sun for three days (69–72), a period not at all uncommon, given the time necessary, as previous examples have indicated, to regroup and dispatch heralds. Remember, too, that hoplite battles were usually fought in summer, when Mediterranean temperatures in the range of 90–100° F (32–37° C) could cook flesh in a few hours and consequently expand the corpses into grotesque caricatures of human beings. Further risks of attack by carrion – the infamous birds and dogs of Greek tragedy and earlier epic – were sure to increase the longer the corpses lay exposed; indeed, such images can actually be found in ancient reliefs and on vases (e.g. Vermeule 1979 103–7, figs 20–3, 26). Finally, moisture, whether in the form of rain, blood, or humidity arising from fertile fields, hastened the natural corruption of the flesh. In the *Anabasis* (6.4.9), for example, Xenophon reports on a small debacle where some Arkadians were isolated and then butchered. When Xenophon and his men were finally able to backtrack and recover the bodies, five days had passed. Xenophon notes that obviously it was then not possible to cart off the corpses and so they had to be buried, such as they were, where they lay. He does mention, however, that some bodies on the road could be gathered, while others simply could not be found. This suggests two things: first, once more it implies that, based on their ever-present muster rolls, the armies knew exactly whom to seek among the dead. Second, in sharp contrast to the other multifarious risks attendant upon the rotting bodies – 'ripe' is the word modern soldiers use – lying in the open terrain, the dry, hard road caused far less deterioration in the corpses lying there; they at least were apparently intact enough to be handled and perhaps gave off a less overpowering stench. Most bodies, however, would not rest on roads, and thus the fate of the more decayed corpses of Xenophon's men would be more typical of Greek warfare in general.

Indeed, any lack of decomposition and corruption would have been most unusual and taken on mythic proportions, as illustrated in Plato's tale of a bold warrior, Er, son of Armenios, of the race of Pamphylos. He once was slain in battle, and when the corpses were taken up on the tenth day already decayed, was found whole' (*Rep.* 10, 614B). A similar wondrous story is related about Alexander's body: during the many days of dissension among his commanders after Alexander's death, his corpse, although it lay without any special care and in places moist and stifling, showed no signs of corruption, but remained pure and fresh (Plut. *Alex.* 77.3). Given the normal damage delay could inflict on all but immortal corpses, it seems most amazing to consider that the Boiotians were even able to give back the Athenian dead at Delion after seventeen days (Thuc. 4.101.1); that those bodies had not only some rudimentary form of care from their Boiotian guards, but also some protection from the animals and the elements seems to be the most likely explanation. Even today, the problems engendered by delay are still a relevant issue; it is a task with which the Red Cross recently struggled in Lebanon, after that organization finally had been given permission to gather bodies of the rival Christian forces – dead which had been lying in the streets and abandoned rubble of Lebanese cities for several weeks and which were therefore, in all likelihood, unrecognizable.

In addition to the forces of time and nature, the typical blood and gore created by the use of edged and pointed weapons during battle also hindered identification of the bodies. For example, during a truce in the Trojan War to allow for collection of the dead, Homer portrays both sides working side by side, roaming the battlefield to collect their respective slain comrades. It was difficult, the poet tells us, to know each man, but then they washed the blood from them (*Iliad* 7.423–6). Although Homer does not specifically draw the connection, it seems clear that with the washing came recognition, for all wept as the bodies were loaded into their respective carts. While disfiguring facial wounds themselves, or even decapitation, would seem to be the chief obstacles to identification, especially since much of the face and neck of the hoplite was unprotected, few such detailed cases are reported with any frequency in our sources. Instead, disfigurement seems more likely to have come either from the inevitable trampling during phalanx battle or from occasional, deliberate secondary mutilation (e.g. Ducrey 1985: pl. 170, 174) than from the give and take of spears and swords in the collision of pitched battle.[30]

Moreover, we should not forget the role of the hoplite panoply in the deterioration of the dead, for it too could only add to the intrinsic problems of identification and collection. For example, armor, especially the breastplate and helmet, would maintain or even elevate to some degree body temperature and thus increase the initial process of decomposition. In addition, should the corpse not be stripped immediately, *rigor mortis* would make that task even more difficult; perhaps a good deal of mutilation could ensue in the course of plundering the armor of the dead, since the flesh or limbs could have been torn in the attempt to acquire booty. It is perhaps in this context that we can interpret the statement of the Roman commander Lucullus who, when he realized that his men feared especially the soldiers in full armor, reportedly bid them not to be afraid, as it would be 'harder work to strip them than to defeat them' (Plut. *Mor.* 203A2).

In any case of nearly complete disfigurement, it would be natural, perhaps crucial, to turn to secondary forms of identification, but oddly none of the hoplite's traditional equipment would have been truly reliable in identifying individuals. In the first place, shields and other armaments (even if normal looting did not occur) would be notoriously unreliable as a form of personal identification, even though there is some evidence that panoplies were occasionally modified and thus reflective of individual taste (cf. Hanson 1989: 55–88). After all, shields can be dropped or lost (cf. Alkaios, fr. 428) – or more likely thrown down – in a pitched battle or rout (e.g. Archilochos, fr. 6; cf. Hanson 1989: 65–71). On occasion a hoplite would also pick up another's weapon or any shield close to hand if his own was no longer available; certainly, then, deception and confusion over ownership, whether intentional or not, were always a possibility. Patroklos, in the armor of his friend Achilles, set the Trojan forces trembling when they were convinced that the hero himself had returned to the fray (*Iliad* 16.278–83). The entire comic plot of Menander's *Aspis*, as so often in New Comedy, revolves around misidentification;[31] in this case, the corpses of soldiers, as mentioned earlier, were bloated beyond recognition from exposure to the sun. As a result, the servant of Kleostratos (wrongly) identified his master by his shield, buckled and bent by the body. As we learn later, however, the 'dead' Kleostratos had marched out of camp equipped with borrowed armor and apparently unrecognized by others (lines 106–13).

In another instance, a desire for deliberate deception inspired the Spartan cavalry to take up the shields of their allies, the Sikyonians, and to advance against the Argives who remained unafraid, naturally thinking that those who bore those 'Sigmas' were inferior Sikyonians, not the dreaded Spartans. Then, so the story goes, the Spartan commander Pasimachos said 'by the twin gods, Argives, these Sigmas will deceive you' (Xen. *Hell.* 4.4.10). In similar fashion, Arkadian hoplites once painted clubs on their shields, 'as though they were Thebans' (*Hell.* 7.5.20). Yet such shield devices, even when recognizable as Spartan 'Lambdas,' Sikyonian 'Sigmas,' or Messenian 'Mus,' would usually be of service only in identifying forces in a collective sense – perhaps in pinpointing the general area where a number of Spartans or Messinians lay dead. As the determining factor, however, in identification of specific, individual corpses, they were usually utterly without value.[32] For instance, even the occasional occurrence of such striking shield emblems as the Eros with thunderbolt that Alkibiades carried (Plut. *Alk.* 16), the purple and gold of Nikias (Plut. *Nik.* 28), or the fly on the shield of an anonymous Spartan (Plut. *Mor.* 243C) would be of little use: if it were found lying on a battlefield, even attached to a warrior's arm, one could still say only that it was the shield of a certain hoplite, not necessarily the man himself, who, if dead, may have lain distant from his armor and weapons. Clearly there must have been some more effective mechanism of identification that could not be so easily confused, lost, or exchanged. Remember, too, that although arms and armor occasionally may have proved to be of some help for the victorious army, such equipment usually would have been unavailable for the defeated force, as they were stripped away by the victor and piled anonymously together.

Weapons in possession of the conquering army occasionally can, on the other hand, have some limited value as an indication of the general number, rather than identity, of casualties. As referred to previously (p.45), when a herald from the Ambrakiotes arrived to ask for a truce to bury the bodies of those killed in the first of two encounters with the Akarnanians (426/5 BC), he noticed immediately the pile of weapons taken from the defeated hoplites. This caused some confusion, since the stack was far more extensive than would have been warranted by the number of troops sent out to the first encounter. As Thucydides tells the story,

> he was amazed at their number, for he did not know of the recent disaster, but thought that the arms belonged to the men of his own division. And someone asked him why he was amazed, and how many of his comrades had been slain, the questioner on his part supposing that the herald had come from the forces which had fought at Idomene. The herald answered, 'about two hundred.' The questioner said in reply, 'these arms, though, are clearly not those of two hundred men, but of more than a thousand.' And again the herald said, 'then they are not the arms of our comrades in the battle.' The other answered, 'they are, if it was you who fought yesterday at Idomene.' 'But we did not fight with anyone yesterday,' he responded; 'it was the day before yesterday, on the retreat.' 'And it is certain that we fought yesterday with these men, who were coming to your aid from the city of the Ambrakiotes,' came the reply. When the herald heard this and realized that the force which was coming to their relief from the city had perished, he lifted up his voice in lamentation and, stunned by the magnitude of the calamity before him, departed at once, forgetting his errand and making no request for the dead.
>
> (3.113.2–5, Loeb translation)

Both the herald's initial judgment and his final horror were based on the amount of armament plundered from the dead. Note that, as a final note to his despair, and as an incident which Thucydides uses to illustrate the depth of his shock, the herald returned to the Ambrakiotes without asking for the burial truce he originally came to obtain.

Similarly, at Epipolai in Syrakuse (413 BC), after the Athenians' ill-fated night attack, the 'arms taken were out of proportion to the dead, for while some of those who were forced to leap down the bluffs were destroyed, others were saved' (Thuc. 7.45.2). Unlike the case of the Ambrakiot herald, the Athenians could take some small comfort in the fact that their casualties, although numerous, were fewer than the number of weapons retrieved would have indicated. Again, however, it is clear that abandoned weapons were unreliable evidence of actual battle-dead.

With such confusion and misinterpretation possible, we must search for more reliable tokens – name tags of some sort, perhaps – which would have ensured unequivocal identification even in the worst of circumstances. Not surprisingly, what little evidence exists for such forms of identification is associated with the Spartans, the only professional soldiers in Greece. On one occasion at least, when the Spartans were about to go into battle with the Messenians, they supposedly wrote their names on small pieces of wood (a *skytalis*) and wrapped these (with leather thongs, perhaps?) around their left wrists, so that their kinsmen (that is, their fellow hoplites within the ranks, since Spartan soldiers traditionally were not returned home for burial)[33] would know who they once had been.[34] Since these *skytalides* were not intrinsically valuable pieces, they were unlikely to be taken as plunder by the enemy in the event of a Spartan defeat. It is interesting also to observe that this most clever idea for these apparent 'dog tags'[35] – a practice which itself would not reappear in the west on any uniform scale until the First World War – seems to have come from the soldiers themselves, who knew better than any the real hazards of war, the likelihood of disfigurement, and the Spartan emphasis on proper identification of corpses for burial; there was, after all, if we can believe Plutarch (*Lyk.* 27), a tradition that only Spartan men who died in battle, in addition to women who died in childbirth, were deserving of monuments with names inscribed on them. We hear of even further distinctions accorded to some of the Spartan hoplite dead: Aelian (*VH* 6.6), for example, asserted that those few who had especially distinguished themselves in battle were buried in their red cloaks, while others were laid among olive branches (cf. Plut. *Lyk.* 27.1–2, *Mor.* 238d). The sheer practicality of these markers and the general uniformity of hoplite battle throughout Greece should suggest some such similar practice of body identification elsewhere; yet, there seems no evidence outside Sparta for this particular usage, nor any confirmation that this use of 'dog tags' was ever uniformly carried out even by all Spartans. Certain stamped emblems (see, for example, n. 32) apparently only identified state-issued armaments; other clay tokens, stamped with the names of Athenian military commanders stationed in various areas outside of Athens, seem to have been employed as credentials (*symbola*). Indeed, these particular tokens have been convincingly identified as 'passports' carried by state couriers or others on official business to certain commanders in outlying areas.[36] As yet, to my knowledge, there has been no suggestion that any engraved clay or inscribed lead pieces have been found in excavations which might be associated with military identification tags during battle. Until such evidence is found, or reassessed and linked to hoplite battle practice, our Spartan *skytalides* remain unique. Thus, we are left in the end with a dilemma of sorts: we know disfigurement or loss of corpses and subsequent misidentification could occur, and yet we hear of no standard methodology for precise identification which could explain the Greeks' apparent facility in reckoning individual battle casualties. Perhaps the relatively small losses (in modern terms) in battle (e.g. Krentz 1985, 13–20), the accuracy of muster lists, and the presence of family and close friends in the ranks usually allowed for a rough 'process of elimination' which left only a few hoplite dead positively unidentified.

We have considered the *katalogos* and the muster rolls carried by the taxiarch, roll-calls, personal recognition, armaments, and hoplite initiative – all of which could work in concert to help determine the number of casualties and ensure identification of the dead. But with whom, then, did ultimate responsibility lie for the gathering up and identification of the dead? Hellenic society clearly assumed that responsibility lay with the commanding general; the rationale for this practice is nicely summarized in the following passage from Onasander, which may well have applied to the earlier Archaic and Classical Periods:

> The general should take thought for the burial of the dead, offering as a pretext for delay neither occasion nor time nor place nor fear, whether he happen to be victorious or defeated. Now this is both a holy act of reverence toward the dead and also a necessary example for the living. For if the dead are not buried, each soldier believes that no care will be taken of his own body, should he chance to fall, observing what happens before his own eyes, and thereby judging of the future, feeling that he, likewise, if he should die, would fail of burial, waxes indignant at the contemptuous neglect of burial.
>
> (*Strategikos* 36.1–2, Loeb translation)

Yet, in spite of this more formal delegation of responsibility to officers, the performance of which undoubtedly involved muster lists and roll-calls, it seems equally clear that each hoplite on the field would have felt an obligation to those with whom he served, not only to aid him during the onslaught of battle, but to protect and treat him when wounded and to retrieve and identify him when fallen (e.g. Ducrey 1985 pl. 146); the use of tokens by the Spartans perhaps suggests as much, that the real concern for proper identification came from the hoplites themselves, who knew best what spear, sword, looting and decay could do to flesh. Depending on the number of casualties, both hoplites and their servants would have been employed in the physically and emotionally unpleasant process of gathering the bodies of the dead – in some cases friends, brothers, fathers, and sons – always after having taken part in an exhausting battle.

The participation of the army in this battlefield ritual of retrieval and identification of the dead – like the battle sacrifice and trophy – marked yet another strong affirmation of the unique, integrated nature of Hellenic military and civil life in the Classical Period. As we have seen, the war dead were lionized by the living and were held up as monuments, both literally and figuratively, to the greatness and glory of a particular state. The efforts of comrades – and even enemies – to ensure that the bodies of the fallen were given their due without shameful desecration or neglect demonstrate the strength of the shared beliefs of the Hellenic community, and the near-conspiratorial composition of hoplite armies from a landed class of like individuals, originally small farmers all.

Euripides' sentiment that robbing the dead of their rightful dues would 'unman even heroes' (*Suppl.* 538–41), implying as it does that no warrior would be brave were he not secure in receiving proper funeral rites, at first glance might seem to ignore the intensity of the battle experience and to suggest that, on occasion, this was not the natural responsibility of fellow hoplites. However, the real force of the passage is one of reassurance, to reinforce the truth that the state was obligated to the soldier, even in cases of awful and bizarre circumstances, such as the prolonged delay at Delion or the Spartan débâcle at Leuktra. Such universal custom and knowledge became a comfort which the hoplite carried with him, consciously or not, that in a larger sense his service to the state would not go unrewarded. Furthermore, the hoplite had this promise from both the man at his side and his community at large, and he had seen this mystique come to fruition for those who had died before: that the dead really did live on in glory forever. No words here can substitute for those of Thucydides in the famous funeral oration of Perikles:

> For the whole world is the sepulchre of famous men, and it is not the epitaph upon monuments set up in their own land that alone commemorates them, but also in lands not their own there abides in each breast an unwritten memorial of them, planted in the heart rather than graven on stone.
>
> (2.43.3)

There would have been few missing in action, few 'unknown soldiers,' few skeletons on the battlefield like those Herodotus saw at Plataia years after the Persian disaster (Hdt. 9.83). This eternal commemorative meant that the Greek hoplite, though fallen, would continue to be part of his community, not separated from it by death. Furthermore, memorializing the dead always involved, lest we forget, the particularly unpleasant task of removing and identifying the decomposing remains of family and friends. Individual recognition – for the living and the dead – and glory in war really did work together, like so many other aspects of Greek society, to reinforce the unity of all the citizens of the city-state.

NOTES

I would like to thank my colleagues at California State University, Fresno, Dr Victor Hanson and Dr Bruce Thornton, who both read early drafts of this paper and offered many helpful suggestions. The final result has been immeasurably improved by their able assistance, and naturally any omissions or shortcomings are mine alone. Works referred to by author alone or with short title or date are cited in full in the Bibliography to this volume.

1. One sees this portrayed early in Greek art as well; see, for example, several plates in Ahlberg 1971: 6, 57, 87–90. See also the discussion in Hanson 1989 ('The Killing Field,' and in particular pp.199–204) regarding the appearance of the battlefield after hoplite warfare.
2. Who apparently and mistakenly (?) associates the incident with the battle of Mantineia in 418 BC; despite the apparent apocryphal nature of such a story, designed to affirm the friendship and loyalty between Pelopidas and Epameinondas, the depiction of the danger to Pelopidas seems quite accurate.
3. This situation also illustrates the great risk to the wounded once they fell among the crush of dead and dying. In one instance the Spartans thought that their commander, Hippagretos, had died at Sphakteria (425 BC), but he was actually lying wounded among (and possibly hidden beneath) the many corpses (Thuc. 4.38).
4. Of course, it is neither the intention here to reopen any discussion regarding the well-known controversy pertaining to the Athenian *patrios nomos* nor to presume to expand on the extensive and invaluable material in W. Kendrick Pritchett's several volumes on *The Greek State at War*, (1971–85) especially his fourth, and in some sense, his most valuable treatment of hoplite battle.
5. Cf. Plut. *Thes*. 36.1–3, *Kim*. 8. Kimon, according to Athenian legend, was able to echo the spirit of Theseus' undertaking on behalf of the Argive dead, for he returned to Attika Theseus' own bones from hostile territory (cf. Paus. 1.17.2).
6. Plutarch disputes Euripides' portrayal, which shows the Thebans flouting panhellenic tradition, and cites Philochoros as his source for Theseus'

truce. Herakles, in some sources, is also credited as the first to establish the practice of a truce for retrieval of the dead (Plut. *Thes.* 29.5; Ail. *VH1 12.27).*

7. In the *Odyssey*, too, respect is shown for the bodies of the dead suitors, when they are all returned (properly identified?) to their families for burial (24.418).
8. Obviously, such concern for the dead was not limited to the field of battle, as the previous note indicates. Ultimate responsibility for all dead – civilian and military – lay with the state (Dem. 43.57–8). Cf. Ail. *VH* 5.14, for the Athenian law requiring all who saw an unburied body to cast earth upon it, which of course assumes that corpses could occasionally not be given over for burial.
9. For a complete analysis of the material, see generally Pritchett, *War* 4.
10. See Pritchett, *War* 4.152 regarding the distance of transportation in this case, and generally *War* 4.145–53 regarding the monuments in detail.
11. This particular *heroon* is apparently quite old according to Pritchett (*War*, 4.152), perhaps from the seventh century BC, and thus further evidence of the antiquity of the notion of reverence to the dead, even accorded to those from outside the immediate community.
12. But certainly not the Persians, who for their effrontery in invading Greece were left to lie where they had fallen (cf. Hdt. 9.83).
13. The Plataians, remember, at the beginning of the Peloponnesian War, were able to appeal to the Lakedaimonians for mercy on the basis of the Spartan dead from the battle of 479 BC still interred at Plataia. They believed (wrongly) that devotion to those glorious fallen warriors might cause the Spartans to prevent Thebes from taking over Plataia, thus putting Spartan dead in enemy hands (Thuc. 3.58–9). But, like so much of hoplite ritual and practice during the barbarism of the Peloponnesian War, the old rules simply no longer applied.
14. Showing both names and patronymics; cf. Pritchett, *War* 4.168–73 and notes cited there.
15. See, for example, the discussion in L. Van Hook, 'On the Lacedaimonians buried in the Kerameikos,' *AJA* 36 (1932) 290–92.
16. I, like most others, find extremely persuasive Pritchett's argument that, in spite of the lack of an inscription, the joint testimony of Strabo and Pausanias should be decisive. His analysis of the excavations, including the evidence of the skeletons buried in the Theban tomb, seems conclusive. 'Observations on Chaironeia,' *AJA* 62 (1958) 307–11. For an opposing view, see N. G. L. Hammond, 'The two battles of Chaironeia (338 BC and 86 BC),' *Klio* 31 (1938) 186–218. Regarding the Athenian epigrams, see Pritchett, *War* 4, 223–6.
17. For treatment of the lists (the majority of which are Athenian) and the usual problems and controversies involved, see generally G. Smith, 'Athenian casualty lists,' *CP* 14 (1919) 351–64; D. W. Bradeen, 'Athenian Casualty Lists,' *CQ* 63 (1969) 145–59; Pritchett, *War* 4.139–45; C. W. Clairmont, *Patrios Nomos* (Oxford, 1983) 179ff.
18. If one believes Pausanias, 9.32.9; cf. also Plut. *Lys.* 13; Xen. *Hell.* 2.1.31; and (especially) the discussion in Pritchett, *War* 4.238–9 (with notes).

19. On unburied dead, both during and after the Classical Period, see generally Pritchett, *War* 4.235–41.
20. Regarding the *katalogos*, see references also in Thucydides 6.31.3; 6.43; 8.24.2; Plutarch *Nik.* 14; Xenophon *Hell.* 2.3.20; *Mem.* 3.4.1, cf. *Hipp.* 1.2. See further G. Smith, 'Athenian Casualty Lists,' *CP* 14 (1919) 351–64, especially at 351–4; A. Andrewes, 'The Hoplite Katalogos.' M. H. Hansen's contention ('The number of Athenian hoplites in 431 BC,' *SO* 56 (1981) 19–32) that there was *no* central *katalogos* drawing exclusively from the hoplite census in no way affects the idea that military commanders always had master lists of the men in the field.
21. It was a Spartan custom to bring the bodies of kings (who, apparently, were always easily identified) home for burial (e.g. Plut. *Ages.* 40; cf. Xen. *Hell.* 5.3.19, Diod. 15.93); consequently it was a great disgrace to let the body fall into enemy hands (Paus. 9.13.10).
22. 'Let us slay the men, then at leisure you will plunder the corpses lying on the ground,' as Nestor told the Argive forces (Homer, *Il.* 6.70–1). On viewing hoplite dead, cf. *supra* note 1.
23. Was it a particular mark of courtesy between fellow citizens that, after the battle against the Thirty at the Peiraieus, the bodies of the dead were returned with their tunics still on (Xen. *Hell.* 2.4.19)? Perhaps this suggests that in most cases even undergarments were stripped away, with nudity thus adding to the anonymity of the corpses in some cases.
24. For additional information regarding both the battle and the topography of the area, see Pritchett, *Topography* 2. 31–2; 34–6.
25. Polyainos, in his traditional eulogistic fashion, records that Archidamos, although wounded himself, sought the truce in order to save his own men (1.41.4).
26. See, for example, the well-known story related in Polyainos 2.3.11, in which Epameinondas was reluctant to draw up his troops because they would have been disheartened to see the number of dead friends missing from their ranks, which might imply, too, that there was some element of delay between the end of battle and visual recognition and identification of the fallen. Otherwise, the men would have already known the outcome from their own inspection of the corpses.
27. See once more the discussion in Pritchett, *War* 4.190.
28. It must be noted that Thucydides does not say that these two corpses were unidentified, merely that they could not be found. It is entirely possible, therefore, that their identity was already known through visual recognition or surmised from lacunae during roll-call before Nikias and the army were forced to withdraw.
29. Although, admittedly, there is less information available about the mechanics of, for example, the Spartan methods, the use of muster rolls is implicit in the sources. Cf. Lazenby 1985: 12–14.
30. See again, generally, discussion in Hanson 1989: 175–7.
31. 'The alert spectator will realize that a man is less certainly recognized by his shield than by his face,' A. W. Gomme and F. W. Sandbach, *Menander, A Commentary* (Oxford, 1973) 68. For the Roman practice of writing names on their shields, cf. Vegetius *Epit.* 2.18.
32. The bulk of the evidence for such state shield blazons is classical. See

Chase 1902: 75–7, 81–3; L. Lacroix, 'Les "blazons" des villes grecques,' *Et. Arch. Class.* 1 (1955) 89–116; Anderson 1970: 17–20, 262–3; Snodgrass 1967: 55 and 64–7, fig. 22. The evidence also shows that Athens, by the Hellenistic period at least, may have begun to use on state-owned armor a similar state emblem. Cf. Kroll, 'Some Athenian Armor Tokens,' *Hesperia* 46 (1977) 141–6, pl. 40. The arms and armor from the panhellenic sanctuaries which are inscribed with a name represent dedicatory or votive offerings, where such identification is a post-battle phenomenon.

33. See, for example, Polyainos 1.17; Diod. 8.27.2; cf. Pritchett, *War* 4. 243–6. The word *skytalis*, of course, is a diminutive form of the *skytale* ('stick'), and often associated with the famous Spartan device for sending coded messages through enemy lines. See an early discussion in J. H. Leopold, "De Scytala Laconica," *Mnemosyne* 28 (1900) 365–91 (esp. pp. 381–2 on *skytalis*). One wonders whether the smaller identity 'bracelets' of the Spartan troops, as described in Polyainos and Diodoros, were similarly coded so that they could only be read by fellow Spartans. Perhaps one-half of the *skytalis* was left on the body, the other removed by the *enomotarch* or *lochagos* to be collated with others against a master list. Dog tags in both world wars were worn in duplicate or more, to allow both constant identification of the remains in the field and simultaneous recording at the rear.
34. The need for additional methods was felt in spite of the distinctive long hair (e.g. Hdt. 1.82.8; Plut. *Lyk.* 22.1) and red cloak (e.g. Xen. *Lak. Pol.* 11.3; Plut. *Lyk.* 27.1) of the Spartan soldier which, after all, would only identify them collectively, not individually. Nor could Spartiate dead even be distinguished from the corpses of *perioikoi*, who were apparently often outfitted similarly (Anderson 1970: 39).
35. See discussion in Hanson 1989; 206–7.
36. See the complete discussion in J. H. Kroll and F. W. Mitchel, 'Clay tokens stamped with the names of Athenian military commanders,' *Hesperia* 49 (1980) 86–96.

3

HOPLITE TECHNOLOGY IN PHALANX BATTLE

Victor Davis Hanson

INTRODUCTION

From the research since the early 1960s a clear picture of the Greek hoplite panoply has emerged. Archaeological finds of helmets, breastplates, swords, greaves, shield remnants, and spearheads and butts from the major sanctuaries have been carefully collated; from these, taken together with the evidence of painted vases, the few remains of the pertinent Lyric poets, and anecdotal remarks from the Greek historians and much later military manuals, we have learned a great deal about the first appearance of hoplite arms, their composition and methods of fabrication, regional and stylistic variations, and also the chronological development of and transformation in their use from the mid-seventh to the late fourth century BC. Only a few controversies remain, yet they are fundamental to the very study of Greek history: there is no consensus about and often little interest in, the circumstances of the panoply's introduction into Greece or the ensuing ramifications (military, social, and political) of its adoption for the tactics of phalanx warfare. This controversy has arisen in part because many have often ignored the most practical (and important) of all considerations: the battlefield experience of the men who wore the panoply. For example, even at this late date there is no agreement concerning the actual *weight* or suitability of hoplite armor and offensive weapons.[1] Neither can we obtain any accurate idea about the limits of physical endurance of men under arms and thus the very length of hoplite battle itself.[2] Nor do we appreciate how specific elements of the panoply were exclusively advantageous for the particular environment of fighting in close array.

This last omission is especially regrettable because the very conditions of battle (in this case, phalanx fighting) usually explain (that is, predate) the peculiar nature of weapons (e.g. the weight, shape, and size of the hoplite panoply), seldom, I think, vice-versa. For example, it has long been generally recognized, and correctly so, that the later, steady reduction in the hoplite's arms and armor followed new attitudes and strategies in infantry fighting. By the fifth century, the use of the composite corselet and *pilos*, the loss of thigh, arm, and shoulder guards, and even the occasional omission of greaves, all illustrated a greater desire for a lighter warrior, more suitable for the challenges of ever increasing mobility and fluidity present on the rapidly changing battlefield.[3] While scholars thus agree here that the nature of infantry fighting dictates the choice and style of offensive and defensive personal equipment – in this instance, the elimination or reduction of items in the panoply – strangely they do not allow for this same phenomenon in reverse chronological order: the preference (well before 700–650 BC) for massing shock troops in close formation led to demands by combatants for new, heavier equipment.[4] In other words, there seems always to be a symbiotic relationship between ancient Greek tactics and armament; usually the former determines the latter.[5] Consequently, it is surely time to complete this historical picture of Greek warfare by admitting that a prior preference for phalanx-like tactics caused a natural transformation in equipment toward suitably heavy Greek arms and armor, just as later trends at the end of the fifth century to modify heavy infantry fighting once more resulted in changes back again toward lighter equipment.

I shall suggest therefore that the adoption of the hoplite shield and spear-butt, to narrow the focus upon only two examples, were representative of the response of technology to a preexisting practice throughout Greece to fight in massed array. Obviously, then, many current theories concerning the introduction of hoplite weapons and the phalanx into Greece are probably mistaken. Those who see no real, intrinsic connection between tactics and equipment are perhaps overly cautious; those who do, but who postulate the abrupt development of the phalanx in response to these new designs in equipment, have reversed the natural evolutionary process – discernible often throughout history – and have put the proverbial cart before the horse. Before proceeding to a discussion of the unique advantages of the hoplite shield and butt-spike to contemporary, phalanx warfare (and thus their corresponding unsuitability for individual combat of the early Dark Ages), it will be best to review briefly these two standard schools of thought on the hoplite reform.

Most agree that many components of Greek armament – helmet,

body armor, greaves, round shield, and thrusting-spear – were known in some form or another to the earlier Mycenaean and Dark Age Greeks, and also to particular Eastern and European peoples.[6] Controversy, though, arises surrounding the exact sequence and nature of events which led to the alteration, sudden or otherwise, between 725 and 675 BC, of these earlier designs into a new, codified, heavy set of bronze and iron arms and armor (double-grip, concave, shield, Corinthian helmet, bell-corselet, pliable, laceless greaves, double-pointed spear, short sword) – the so-called 'hoplite panoply' and hence a relationship to the tactics of the phalanx.

Currently the more influential hypothesis (the 'gradual change' to the phalanx school) correctly stresses that the introduction of such 'hoplite' equipment was piecemeal, a slow twenty-five-year or even longer process. Thus, the birth of the phalanx, in this view, need not be simultaneous nor necessarily interdependent; no intrinsic connection must exist between the two phenomena, separated as they were by many decades.[7] To support this thesis, it is usually pointed out that archaeological finds prove the presence of many items of hoplite equipment in the last quarter of the eighth century BC, but there is no corresponding pictorial evidence on vases or references in literature to (what this school would call 'true') phalanxes until much later, perhaps not until 650 BC at the earliest. On the other hand, the 'sudden change' to the phalanx thesis usually concentrates on the shield, arguing that the adoption (around 700 BC) of the unique double-grip, the *porpax* and *antilabe*, immediately necessitated an abrupt transformation in the very manner of fighting, with all the well-known social and political ramifications.[8]

The former school, then, sees gradual changes in weaponry, a phalanx after or around 650 BC, and no accompanying wider social revolution; the latter envision a brilliant breakthrough in technology, followed very quickly in or near 700 BC by fresh phalanx tactics, all indicative of an undeniable military surge forward of a new potent, land-owning middle class. Both schools, remember, postulate that new tactics, either around 700 or 650 BC, followed the adoption of novel equipment.

The economic, political, and social implications of this so called 'hoplite reform' need not be discussed again here.[9] But a few considerations, mostly military, arise which question the validity of both these abrupt and gradual theses and thus of the *entire* notion itself of a revolution in tactics. First, because chronology is absolutely crucial to the two hypotheses, although in diametrically opposed ways, any doubts about the evidence in dating the introduction of the phalanx must be taken very seriously. Van Wees, for example, recently concluded: 'the evidence for either 700 or 650 BC is very thin indeed. In fact, it boils down to three Corinthian vase-paintings and Tyrtaeus' exhortation to "stay together" in battle.'[10] The significance of his point surely is that there simply is not enough proof to determine whether or not the phalanx existed earlier, though unrecorded (or even undetected by us moderns) in the few contemporary genres available at the time. Second, it has long been argued that the numerous references in Homer's *Iliad* to mass fighting are historical and thus must reflect phalanx tactics of some type before the adoption of the hoplite panoply.[11] Most likely an earlier, less rigid style of massed attack (e.g. without standard depth and clear-cut, uniform files) was already commonplace in the eighth century BC. Such tactics obviously could exist apart from hoplite equipment, or as Salmon, in another context, more eloquently put it:

> The phalanx was not yet known in its later form; but early phalanx warfare might well have taken a slightly different form without being different in nature. A phalanx has two essential features: its cohesion and its relatively large size; both can be achieved without following the later canonical pattern closely.
> (Salmon 1977: 90)

This is especially understandable, and, in fact, provable, when we realize that there are plenty of references in Greek and Persian history where armies mass in column and fight as 'hoplites' without what is usually termed the hoplite panoply.[12] Pritchett, who recently reexamined the entire question in detail, in many ways confirmed Latacz's earlier, carefully argued conclusions about the entire nature of Homeric fighting: 'There is no literary evidence for a view which has gained wide currency that there was a change in tactics in the early seventh century from pre-hoplite warfare to hoplite warfare. A technical progress in arms is not synonymous with a new battle formation.' (*War* 4.49). This is not to say that some particular offensive and defensive weapons (i.e. the hoplite panoply) were not better suited to massed fighting. Indeed, I believe Pritchett may not have gone far enough: a technical progress in arms is more than merely 'not synonymous with a new battle formation,' but rather in this case surely it is conceptually a result of battle formation. For example, if it can be shown that particular elements of the panoply were difficult and expensive to fabricate, and yet also disadvantageous for fluid fighting and individual combat, why, then, would duelists pay for these novel designs that were no better (and probably a great deal worse) than their current lighter, less expensive brands? Instead, the hoplite panoply offered new advantages to phalanx warfare alone. Thus it must be seen as a specific invention aimed at improving on (and perhaps codifying) the preexisting conditions of massed warfare – evidence, then, of a technical response to a precise need, a 'better mousetrap' to meet the particular challenges of contemporary battle.

THE RESPONSE OF TECHNOLOGY: THE 'BELLY' OF THE HOPLITE SHIELD AND THE SPEAR-BUTT

The weight and clumsiness of the bell-corselet and Corinthian helmet were proverbial and obviously reduced the mobility and quickness of the wearer. Both severely limited endurance and rapidly brought on fatigue. Accordingly, it is usually acknowledged that such protection was suited primarily to the relatively brief collision of mass combat, where pushing and shoving in the midst of the 'sea of spears' required full cover for the body, rather than unfettered movement and quick agility.[13] Yet, have scholars ever granted the next logical step: the presence of both the breastplate and Corinthian helmet seems *prima facie* one piece of evidence for the existence of phalanx tactics, where men would want such vital protection, unconcerned with the drawbacks which heavy equipment could entail in individual combat characteristic of an earlier age? Examination of the configuration and efficacy of the hoplite shield and spear-butt reveals that they must have been likewise designed for the peculiar demands of contemporary battle, battle that was fought at very close quarters mainly between massed bodies of shock troops. Now much has been written about the hoplite shield, but oddly discussion has centered exclusively on one point, the suitability of the double-grip shield for phalanx tactics. For example, scholars have rightly pointed out that the employment of the *porpax* and *antilabe* curtails the mobility of the individual combatant, offers less cover for his right side, and none at all for his back – all in exchange for an enormous increase in frontal protection. The shield-bearer deliberately assumes vulnerability in every direction save directly ahead.

Many critics answer that the double-grip shield could be equally employed in single combat among loosely grouped individuals. They are, of course, correct in some sense, but they fail to see the logical extension of such an argument, that any 'shield,' of almost any size or shape, from a circle to an enormous rectangle, could on occasion be valuable for self-protection. Is not the real question one of degree: why should such ingenuity (and considerable expense) be invested in a particular design that was so poorly suited to combat between isolated individuals?[14] Consider, for example, the radical concavity of the hoplite shield, a point which is all too often forgotten, but which on examination, like the double-grip, also argues for the notion of preexisting phalanx tactics.[15] Perhaps since nearly all wood cores are lost, and thus we possess only the flat, thin outer metal blazons, or because of the tendency of many early vase painters to depict their warriors frontally or without perspective, the unusual bowl-shape of the shield is often deemphasized and unacknowledged, yet it was considerable. Circular shields are known to have existed both before and after the appearance of the hoplite shield; but why are all such Mycenaean, early Dark Age, and most later Macedonian models, conspicuously flat or nearly so? The answer must be that concavity, on balance, offered few real advantages either to individual fighters or to those who hung their shield from the neck. The extensive 'sides' awkwardly kept the surface away from the wearer's body: not only must the warrior hold its weight up, but 'out' as well, which required greater muscular strength.[16] Moreover, this lip of considerable size also restricted the angles of deflection: it inevitably first bumped into the corselet when the shield was turned either side-to-side or upward and downward. The construction, too, involved in creating a concave shape was far more intricate than the simple skills needed for flat designs. Even the additional protection which a curved surface offers (iron enters diagonally and must penetrate more wood; air space between the body and shield negates the effects of blows which just pierce the surface) apparently was of little concern to warriors both prior to and after the era of phalanx battle. Why again, one wonders, did this oddly concave, round shape accompany the novel double-grip around 700 BC?

For those who desired to fight in massed array, holding a spear in one hand, shield in the other, concavity did offer one enormous advantage quite apart from consideration of improved armor. Because the lip of the hoplite shield jutted out at nearly a 90 degree angle, its entire weight could rest on the shoulder – a frequent enough scene in both vase-painting and occasionally described in literature.[17] This allowed a shield of much greater size and hence weight than previous models – specifically, a diameter of nearly 3 ft (almost a metre) for the new demands of pushing and frontal protection. While the double-grip allowed the shield to be worn on one arm, that aided the hand, but ironically also increased the burden of the wearer, concentrating over 15 lbs (6.8 kg) on a single limb, without the chance to change arms occasionally as had been possible with earlier, single-grip shields. Concavity, however, solved the dilemma. In conjunction with the double-grip, it allowed the hoplite warrior a real respite at frequent intervals. To rest a shield stationary on the shoulder in individual combat was suicidal, and, within the later Macedonian phalanx, superfluous, given the neck strap and its smaller size, but under the peculiar conditions of the hoplite phalanx such an opportunity to save the arm was practicable and, indeed, became an absolute necessity. The rear ranks (usually the majority of fighters from row four to the back) were not exposed to initial enemy spear thrusts and thus had no need to deflect and parry incoming blows; rather their job for minutes on end was simply to hold up their shields and spears continuously and to thrust their comrades on ahead.[18] Therefore, hoplites could push on the backs of the men in front, while resting their arms until their own turn in the killing zone, when it then would become necessary to hold the shield out with the arm away from the body and deflect attack. That way their left arms were fresh until they met the enemy. Thus the double-grip saved the hand, but concavity saved the arm as well. Sometimes, too, there must have been so much pressure that fighters, once they reached the killing-zone, never had the opportunity to raise and extend their shields at all. Here the shield's enormous size and radical concavity once more offered dramatic advantages: the wearer was nearly 'absorbed' and became a human battering-ram, with 'both the chest and shoulder in the belly of the hollow shield' (Tyrt. 11.24).

This same need to relieve the weight of the hoplite shield by resting it upon the shoulder must also account for its very shape. Quite simply, why was the hoplite shield round? Few scholars have addressed this simple question either, perhaps because the answer seemed to be self-evident or again due to the usual emphasis on the novelty of the double-grip. True, a circular shape offers a more economical usage of surface area, eliminating the four corners of a rectangle that bring little additional protection at the expense of increased weight. The torso and arms in movement also form a circular zone critical to the warrior and are naturally protected well by a design without 90 degree angles, which can at times obstruct vision and snag on another's equipment. Many suggest, too, that a circular shield is wielded with greater ease, offering an increased sense of mobility; the shape constantly offers a nearly identical zone of critical protection, regardless of the particular angle in which it is deflected at any given moment. Finally, there is the undeniable force of tradition. Smaller, flat, single-grip round shields are known both in the Mycenaean and Dark Age periods and are occasionally portrayed by vase-painters of the time.[19] It makes sense that at the end of the eighth century experimentation with the hand and shield grip was first applied to traditional circular designs.

All these factors are no doubt true, but remember in hoplite battle individual skill and mobility, at least until the rout, were less critical than maintenance of rank, generation of force forward, and, most importantly, wall-to-wall frontal protection of the densely packed occupants of the phalanx. In this crucial regard, the round shape of the hoplite shield was simply no advantage. For example, it failed to cover the entire body of the infantryman. Therefore, it endangered the safety of the entire formation, due to the vulnerability of the outermost, 'naked' file on the right. Also, a wall of round shields left vital areas of the front lines unprotected; 'triangles' of exposure appeared between shields at both top and bottom. Indeed, the whole notion of a phalanx advancing with 'locked shields' is technically incorrect: it is impossible to create a continuous solid joint between curved edges, no matter how much shields overlap. Consequently, the concern which prompted early hoplites to employ a round shield of greater size and novel grip could only have been the unique suitability of such a circular design to the accompanying crucial requirement for radical concavity.

If concavity was essential to the heavily armed warrior in maintaining the unusual weight of the new shield, then square or rectangular shapes, for all their advantages in creating a solid wall of protection, became utterly impractical. After all, concavity when applied to those configurations resulted, like the Roman *scutum*, only in a cylindrical shape, useful for protecting the warriors' flanks, adding more armor-plating against some thrusts, but hardly effective in reducing weight off the hand and arm. To create the necessary flap or lip at the top of such shields would result in awkward corners, hardly compatible for insertion of the shoulder when pushing or resting the shield. Also, construction of such a lip would require a supporting framework or, even worse, perhaps accompanying side-guards down the entire length of the shield, which would impair lateral movement. Of course, such a 'shoe-box' shield could be poised only in a single position, absolutely perpendicular to the ground, flap-side always up. No such shield to my mind has ever existed at any time. The circular shape, on the contrary, always presented a natural fit for the shoulder, regardless of the shield's rotation or angle of deflection. Circularity was perfect for the application of concavity; concavity was perfect for the tactics of the phalanx.

Less dramatic, but equally innovative, was the near universal adoption of a spike added to the butt end of the thrusting spear – a device only rarely seen before the advent of the hoplite panoply and not at all on javelins or spears outside of Greece.[20] Like the concavity of the shield, it too represents a technological reaction to the increasing practice of fighting in massed array. A bronze, squared spike usually ranging from 2 to 8 ins (5 to 20 cm) in length, it has often been described rather awkwardly by modern scholars as the 'butt-spike,'[21] but to the Greeks it was commonly known as either the *sturax, sauroter,* or *ouriachos*.[22] True, the butt-spike was useful in providing a counterweight to the spearhead (or so the adjective *saurobrithes* suggests [*Trag. Adesp.* 264]), allowing the 7 or 8 ft (2 or 2.4 m) shaft to be balanced with ease. Its combined small diameter and sharp point also ensured that the spear could be reversed and conveniently stuck fast into even hard ground when not in use (e.g. Hom. *Il.* 10.153): the phrase 'spears on their butt-spikes' was proverbial – whether for inactivity or battle-readiness (cf. Dio. Chrys. 2.45.5). In addition, this bronze covering at the base stopped rot and wear of the wood there, and perhaps also reduced cracking and splintering of the shaft itself by containing fractures which originated at the base. Since the bronze spike lacked a sharp edge along its side, occasionally the butt-spike was slapped against a victim in mock combat or employed for non-lethal punishment (e.g. Xen., *Hell.* 6.2.19; Onasander 10.4).

All these considerations, however, were really secondary: it was the spike's more important function as an offensive weapon during phalanx battle (e.g. cf. the verb *sturakizo* Hsch. 732.6), which explains its growing popularity after the appearance of the phalanx. Indeed, only the critical combat advantages which might accrue to the hoplite in mass combat from the use of butt-spike justified the addition of such a potentially treacherous weapon to his arsenal, liable to contribute to the accidental wounding of one's own men (e.g. Plut. *Pyrrh.* 33). In the crowded conditions of the phalanx, hoplites in the second, third, and fourth ranks would have to contend with the dangerous butt-points of those positioned in front of them in the first three ranks. Fighting with level spears ahead, these hoplites were, of course, unaware of the exact effect to the rear of their spear strokes. The Persians, at any rate, used small spheres instead of spikes, perhaps with fear of such accidental wounding in mind (Hdt. 7.41.8).

In a great many hoplite (and later Macedonian) battles we hear that the spears of the front ranks were snapped during the initial collision (e.g. Aesch. *Ag.* 64–6; Xen. *Hell.* 3.4.14; Diod. 15.86.2; 17.100.7; 19.83; Hdt. 7.225; Plut. *Alex.* 16.4; *Eum.* 7.3). So frequent was this phenomenon that Euripides' Amphitryon is made to ask how might a man defend himself when his spear-shaft was apt to break (*HF* 193). The answer obviously is that most hoplites, if the shaft was not seriously splintered, could simply switch their grip (*ek metalepseos*) and reverse ends.[23] Since most spears probably broke between the lance-head and grip point, the hoplite might still retain 3 or 4 ft (1 or 1.2 m) of good shaft attached to the butt-spike. In the subsequent press of bodies the reduced 'spear' for a time must have made a most effective 'inside' weapon for fighting in the pushing and shoving of the first ranks. Balance, of course, was now hardly a problem for the broken shaft of reduced length, since the spike was both lighter and smaller than the original spear point. The smaller size of the broken shaft and spike therefore could allow the hoplite to jab quickly and repeatedly with great mobility and freedom of movement. Its diminished length of 3 or 4 ft also still offered an extra foot or two of striking power over the less effective, secondary weapon, the short sword. In Lucian's *Toxaris* (55.3), for example, Lonchates perhaps suffered from such a blow when he is described suffering a butt-spike wound to the thigh, presumably as he fought in the front ranks.

The value of the butt-spike as a secondary weapon once the spear head was lost is also nicely illustrated in Polybius' famous comparison between Greek and Roman armament: 'Without butt-spikes the Romans could only deliver their first blow with the point of the spear; afterwards, should the points be broken, the spears became useless to them' (6.25.6). He adds that once the Romans finally incorporated Greek-style spear-butts, they could continue to fight 'by reversing ends and striking with the butt-spike' (6.25.9). Even when the spear head remained intact, the butt-spike was also useful. Sometimes segments of the phalanx were cut off and surrounded, or found themselves too far inside the enemy's ranks – instances where the enemy might not only appear at face to face, but at the rear and side as well. Then a quick jab backward with the butt-spike could clear the way and provide a second or two of safety in which the hoplite might turn about and face the danger to the rear. Consequently, even if hopelessly surrounded, he was still to be attacked with caution, since the moving shaft could keep the enemy clear at both ends.

The most common use of the butt-spike in both literature and art, however, is in the *coup de grace*, where it is brought down – often with both hands – vertically on a prostrate, usually wounded foe. Among the first-rank fighters, after an enemy was hurt or knocked off his feet, the smaller diameter and stoutness of the spike made it the preferable weapon to penetrate the opponent's breastplate or helmet. There are examples at Olympia and elsewhere of armor pierced with square, rather than round or irregular shaped holes, suggesting the entry and exit wounds from the spike rather than the spear-head.[24] On sculpture, too, we occasionally see a hoplite aiming his butt-spike for a final blow against a defeated adversary.[25] In literature the picture is similar. Once Philopoemen had wounded Machanidas, Polybius relates that he finished him off with a two-handed stab of the butt-spike (11.18.4, cf. too Paus. 8.49.7), a blow that was often used in hunting wild animals (*AP* 6.110,111). Plutarch, remember, describes the last moments of Masistius, the Persian cavalry commander at Plataia. His unusually thick armor protected him well even while unhorsed on the ground until finally a hoplite ran him through at his helmet-visor with his butt-spike (Plut. *Arist.* 14.6.4), indicating that the spike was often the weapon of choice for dispatching prostrate, armored foes.

A second instance where hoplites found the vertical stab of the butt-spike indispensable was among the rear ranks, those men who were stationed behind the first three rows. In ranks four through eight of most phalanxes, infantry advanced in battle with raised spears. In this way accidental wounding before the encounter with enemy ranks could be minimized and hoplites could offer the phalanx some protection against missiles (e.g. Polyb. 18.29–30). The shaft also perhaps offered stabilization as the hoplite pushed and leaned into the men in front, ready, too, to step up a rank if any of those ahead went down. Occasionally, as the advance progressed, the battlefield was littered with the bodies of the dead, the wounded, and those who had simply tripped and were unable, in their armor and amid the mob, to regain their feet. As the rear ranks of the phalanx encountered these unfortunates on the ground there was a need to dispatch them quickly before they could trip up or strike out at the advancing ranks. Simple trampling of the enemy was both awkward and dangerous, and thus the best way to attack then was simply to come down hard with the already upraised spear-shaft, driving the butt-spike through their armor or exposed flesh. That way the march could continue relatively unimpeded and there was no need to reverse the spear or bend over with the short sword – impossible tasks anyway during the advance of crowded ranks. Those in the killing-zone at the front of the phalanx could rest assured that their role need not be to finish off their adversaries, but merely to wound, trip, or knock them out of the way as they went on ahead to create crucial momentum in this contest of pressure. It was the job of those hoplites to the rear to dispatch with their butt-spikes all who were passed over. The wedge construction, sharp point, and absence of barbs made the butt-spike the ideal secondary weapon, designed specifically to pierce armor (if given a stationary target) and to be withdrawn quickly with ease.

Thus, the butt-spike, too, must be seen as a weapon deliberately introduced for phalanx warfare. This inclusion of a weighted spike at the butt end of the spear illustrates that it was now seen as a thrusting, seldom a throwing, weapon; its added weight was no drawback to a warrior who had already sacrificed moveability and with it the desire for individual duelling. Moreover, the added offensive capability of the spike suggests that the prior practice of employing two spears was now superfluous, since even a broken shaft need not be discarded as 'useless.' The uniform adaptation of the butt-spike and the real advantages it brought in the melée must also account for the ever diminishing size of, and thus need for, the secondary sword, which evolved from the long, heavy weapon of the early Dark Ages to the short, slashing blade of classical times. True, the use of either end of the spear in the attack suggests a natural limitation in range: the lethal zone of assault is confined in a vertical sense to stabbing up and down, without the lateral scope the sword offers. But, again, within the confines (and safety) of dense formations there was really no need – or rather no chance – to slash sideways, but rather a need for a hoplite only to stab his foe standing at his face or dispatch him on the ground at his feet. Neither movement of the spear fouled his neighbor at his side.

CONCLUSION: A TECHNOLOGICAL, NOT A TACTICAL, REFORM

Military technology in the Greek world – despite what most scholars think – usually *reacted* to the demands of the changing battlefield in the form of new or improved weapons. The emergence of hoplite arms and armor in Greece, generally around 700 BC, was no exception to this natural process. Such equipment must be seen as part of the historical response to improve the combat efficacy of men who were currently fighting in massed array – in this case, presumably at first with a variety of 'outdated' weapons such as javelins, long swords, non-metallic armor, and flat, single-gripped shields of various shapes. There is not enough substantial evidence from Proto-Corinthian pottery or lyric poetry to convince us that phalanx tactics either emerged gradually around 650 BC, and thus somewhat independently of hoplite equipment, or, on the contrary, were a revolutionary breakthrough brought about suddenly around 700 BC, largely by the adoption of the double-grip hoplite shield.

Moreover, both theories inherently must postulate an *immediately* preceding age (at least prior to 700 BC) of widescale duelling and skirmishing, predominantly by armies of aristocratic grandees, usually mounted (for transportation rather than charging), and armed with the javelin or spear, a long sword, and light body protection. Yet, the recent research of Latacz and Pritchett on the so-called phalanx passages in the *Iliad* demonstrates that these lines probably reflect historical reality – a logical, understandable method of massed combat in practice well before 700 BC. Would not these early phalanx fighters initially employ traditional weapons?

Soon, however, the growing uniformity of such fighting must have affected the contemporary equipment of the later Dark Ages in a wide variety of different ways.[26] Some items traditionally in use such as both the small, round and the larger rectangular shields, the long sword, and the javelin – not to mention the use of the horse itself – were eventually discovered in the environment of the new battlefield to be inadequate for phalanx tactics. For example, earlier shields could not resolve the two contradictory demands of great size and supportability created by phalanx warfare; previous offensive arms also required too much room to maneuver and perhaps lacked the penetrating power necessary to force back ranks of newly armored men. Consequently, they were either abandoned outright or gradually superseded by the superior technology of hoplite weaponry. Other elements were retained, albeit drastically modified to meet new needs. For example, crested head-gear and body armor were kept (after all, they still retained advantages for men who would fight in the phalanx), but now they were considerably enlarged and reworked with heavy bronze, emerging as the so-called Corinthian helmet and bell-corselet. Both items stressed, above all, complete defensive protection for the eyes, nose, ears, mouth, chest, and back in the crowded melée, all at the expense of mobility, comfort, and visibility.

Similarly, the advantages of the spear, which had seen prior haphazard use, now became apparent for men who would thrust only in one direction – directly ahead: it was also uniformly outfitted with a bronze spike at its butt-end – something only seen rarely in the past – now uniquely useful for *both* front and rear ranks of the phalanx. In turn, little opportunity was left for sword play; the advantages the sword offered in maneuverability were negated by the confines of the phalanx. Since it lacked the crucial penetrating power and length of the spear, the sword soon evolved into a shorter secondary blade. Finally, radically new components were introduced, entirely unknown and unlike anything ever seen previously. The double-grip and concavity of the circular shield were designed specifically for the requirements of heavily armored men in close combat, most of whom needed to push with their bodies when not thrusting with the spear. Thus hoplites could save their left hands with the double-grip, their arms by resting the shield's lip on their shoulders; for most in the phalanx who pressed against bodies of their friends, not their foes, the enemy might more often be an exhausted arm than a point of iron. In short, the expense and the careful, peculiar construction of the shield were justified only by its application to this particular type of massed fighting. The concave shield and the butt-spike, then, both reflected the new needs of men who would now fight in the middle and rear ranks as well – *men who might never encounter the enemy at all face to face.*

This hypothesis of prior phalanx tactics not only accounts for the very discovery and purpose of such hoplite weapons, but also is not dependent upon the shaky evidence of vase-painting or lyric poetry, either for the exact dating of specific items of panoply or the emergence of the phalanx. More importantly, the general idea that preexisting phalanx warfare of some sort was continuously being improved or reinvigorated by the adoption of various new designs in equipment synchronizes well with later evolutionary patterns in Greek warfare. For example, already by the end of the sixth century BC, the bell-corselet itself was replaced by a composite cuirass, while crests and greaves at this time began to be omitted entirely.[27] These trends only continued in the fifth century. A desire to make phalanxes more mobile and more flexible to meet a variety of new opponents and challenges accelerated the spread of a less restrictive, conical helmet and often perhaps the very abandonment of the metal breastplate entirely.

Armament and tactics thus must be seen always as interrelated; throughout the history of Greek warfare warriors invented, adapted, or rejected specific weapon designs – constantly seeking through their own hands-on experience those best suited to contemporary fighting, often without any larger social, political, or economic implications. Thus, the growing shock tactics of phalanx warfare very soon spawned a fully armored, though awkward fighter. Nearly two centuries later he gave way to the modified figure of a hoplite without complete bronze protection, who, in turn, by the late fifth century, became a much lighter infantryman – all in technological response to continual tactical changes on the battlefield. The reverse process seldom occurred.

This belief that items of the panoply were responses to prevailing massed tactics neither proves or disproves the accompanying idea of sudden political and social changes between 700 and 650 BC – the so-called hoplite reform.[28] Some who would still believe in such a dramatic transformation in both war and society might interpret the invention and adoption of the panoply in this crucial period by growing groups of phalanx warriors as the critical impetus for their ultimate success against the 'enemy' (aristocratic knights?). According to this view, such equipment probably could have provided much needed technological superiority and uniformity – the final, successful 'edge' to the struggles of a less organized (and less successful) phalanx of past times.

My own belief, however, is that because the adoption of the panoply represented a technological, not a tactical, breakthrough, it must also be seen (alas) as a purely military, rather than a political or social phenomenon. The acquisition of new equipment on a wide scale by small landowners was *reflective*, not causative, of their economic prosperity and growing political independence. It was simply an illustration that most small farmers who fought in the phalanx had already 'arrived' and now gradually had gained the experience, expertise, and wealth to manufacture superior arms for their specialized needs as shock troops. Both the peculiarity and limitations of hoplite weaponry may suggest that phalanx warfare around 700 BC was finally becoming codified as the exclusive ritual of landed infantry men, as the only game in town. The notion that there is an intrinsic connection between hoplites and phalanxes thus must be modified: hoplites (i.e. men equipped with the panoply) were created for, and nearly always fought in, phalanxes (i.e. massed groups of shock troops); phalanxes, however (both an earlier and later phenomenon), were not necessarily always composed of hoplites. Or, to put it another way, technology more often responds to, than creates, tactics.[29]

NOTES

I wish to thank Professors A. H. Jackson, Josiah Ober, and Mark Edwards, who kindly read an earlier draft and offered many helpful suggestions.

Works referred to by author alone or with short title or date are cited in full in the Bibliography to this volume.

1. Precise estimates of all components of the panoply may be impossible since most archaeological finds show substantial corrosion of bronze. Wood shield cores and spear shafts, as well as the interior leather padding of helmets, greaves, and shields, are nearly all lost; no representative weights, then, can be confirmed. Students at California State University, Fresno, have fabricated various types of metal helmets, body armor, shields, spears, swords, and greaves. They tell me that the total weight of the entire ensemble is nearly 70 lbs (over 31 kg). A sample of (subjective) scholarly opinion follows (all weights converted to pounds): (1) total panoply: over 70 lbs (G. Glotz and R. Cohen *Histoire grecque* II, Paris, 1938: 347); 70 lbs (L. Montross, *War Through the Ages*, New York, 1946: 8); 72 lbs (J. F. C. Fuller *Armament and History*, London, 1946: 37; Delbrück 1975: 86). (2) breastplate, helmet, sword: 35 lbs (Donlan and Thompson 1976: 341 n. 4). (3) shield: 13.5 lbs (H. Blyth (1977) has a full discussion of fabrication and materials based on careful examination of a surviving wood core); 16.5 lbs (Connolly 1981: 47); 15.5–17.5 lbs (Donlan and Thompson 1976: 341 n. 4); 18 lbs (Warry 1980: 35). (4) spear: 2.2 lbs (Markle 1977: 325). (5) breastplate: 40–50 lbs (Snodgrass 1967: 123). See Hanson 1989: 55–88 for a small sampling of ancient complaints over equipment, weight, and difficulty in usage. See Connor 1988: 10 n. 30; P. McKechnie, *Outsiders in the Greek Cities in the Fourth Century* BC (London, 1989): 94 n. 12; and A. H. Jackson's chapter in this book, for estimates of the cost of arms and armor.
2. Pritchett, *War* 4.46–51 has collected the ancient testimonia. The Greeks rarely indicated precise duration in hours. I assume that the common generic statement *epi polu* must include anything from a few minutes to up to an hour or two. Most battles were decided essentially within an hour; mopping up, pursuit, the killing of stragglers and capture of prisoners could, of course, take much longer. I have watched well-conditioned students duel in full armor (ca 70 lbs/31.7 kg) under the early afternoon sun of late May (90°F/32°C); most are exhausted within minutes. Donlan and Thompson in their careful studies found it was impossible to re-create the 'mile-run' of Marathon; they concluded that men in armor could manage a speed of 5–6 mph for little over 200 yds (8–10 kmh over 182 m). See Delbrück 1975: 83–5 for a lengthy discussion over the problems of endurance for men on the move and weighted down by armor.

3. For this change in tactics and reduction in the panoply, see Snodgrass 1967: 93–4; Anderson 1970: 27–37; Hanson 1989: 57–8, and especially Chrimes 1949: 362–8.
4. Some of this reluctance (e.g. Courbin [in Vernant 1968: 90]) to admit this is well illustrated by Cartledge (1977: 20) who, like Pritchett and Latacz, seems willing to accept earlier phalanx tactics. At one point, for example, he rightly suggests: 'Salmon fails to do justice, it seems to me, to the fact that the Greeks *invented* the double-grip shield: why should it not have been with the phalanx in mind rather than the other way round?' Yet, on the same page he states: 'The hoplite shield was invented by c. 700. Hoplites properly so called (i.e. operating in phalanx formation) *followed* somewhere in the first quarter of the seventh century, the precise date varying naturally from state to state' (emphasis added). However, it seems improbable to me that the Greeks would have had specific tactics only 'in mind' or even 'in progress' and thus proceeded to manufacture precise equipment for a form of fighting which existed in theory only! Surely men must have already been phalanx fighters of some sort and thus created the items of the panoply through a process of trial and error to meet their own demonstrated needs, that is, to improve their battle efficacy in massed array.
5. Modern methods of procurement also reflect this sequence. The Pentagon usually publishes criteria for new weapons systems based on their own evolving particular tactical and strategic needs; the defense industry then develops technology that meets those military requirements. Reversals in the process are seen by the public as deliberate distortions, cynical attempts to sell new weapons that are not needed. True, on occasion, an innovative breakthrough (e.g. gunpowder, rifling) can sometimes suggest new tactical applications, but this is rarer, and it is usually a matter of modifying, rather than creating, tactics. (One can even here argue that musketry grew out of a general call to increase missile velocity and thus to penetrate fortifications and body armor.) For example, fighter aircraft in the First World War were developed in response to pilots who desired a new technology superior to the aerial exchange of revolver and rifle fire: battle in the air antedated the appearance of true fighter aircraft. No one would suggest that air combat grew out of the discovery of novel aerially mounted automatic weapons. Even though there is a 'chicken-or-egg' character to the dilemma, the same can be said of most weapon discoveries: they do not burst from the head of Zeus without some consideration of the battlefield.
6. For earlier use of the round shield, see P. Schauer, 'Der Rundschild der Bronze und Früher Eisenzeit,' *Jahrbuch des Römische Germanischen Zentralmuseums Mainz* (27) 1980: 196–246; Snodgrass 1964b: 37–68. For the breastplate, cf. Snodgrass 1964b: 72–90; 1967: 59–60; 1971: 33–50, and, more generally, cf. Garlan 1975: 124; Courbin (in Vernant) 1968: 89.
7. This view has been most cogently argued by Snodgrass 1965, following Nierhaus. See also W. Donlan, 'Archilochus, Strabo, and the Lelantine War,' *TAPA* 101 (1970) 137; Salmon 1977: 86–90 (who dates the phalanx earlier than Snodgrass's 650 BC). A modified version accepts the

gradual, incremental introduction of weapons, but postulates a closer relationship with phalanx tactics, the idea being that once the shield was known, the equipment mandated new tactics, cf. Garlan 1975: 123–4.

8. Lorimer first argued for the radical change in tactics based on the discovery of the *porpax* and *antilabe*. Both Cartledge (1977: 20) and, to a lesser extent, Greenhalgh (1973: 73), have supported this view, but with important additions and modifications. They stress (*contra* Snodgrass) the unsuitability of the hoplite shield for skirmishing and individual combat, and therefore believe the double-grip inevitably led around 700 BC to new tactics, some of which, according to Cartledge, were already 'in progress' or 'in mind.'
9. Although my concern here is not with these larger issues, I shall suggest briefly in the epilogue that, if there was a reform, it must be associated with equipment, not tactics, and thus probably was without wider social and political ramifications (ca 700 BC).
10. Van Wees (1986: 302) cf. especially Latacz (1977: 36–8). Most recent studies have questioned the certainty of either late or early dates for the phalanx. For example, Cartledge (1977: 20) points out: 'Arguments from visual and literary art are too insecure to decide the issue.' The problem in ascertaining an exact date lies in the intrinsic limitation of the contemporary genres, both pictorial and literary, which precludes any argument from silence (cf. Pritchett, *War* 4.72 n. 212). Quite simply, even if a vase-painter wished to portray a phalanx before 650 BC, he would not have yet had the technical capacity to do so (cf. Cartledge 1977: 21 n. 75; Salmon 1977: 91; Pritchett, *War* 4.41). In a rather different manner, Ahlberg (1971: 49ff), who presents dramatic visual evidence which often supports Latacz's and Pritchett's conclusions from Homer, likewise seems to suggest that the apparent soloists of early vase-painting are no proof at all for the absence of earlier mass formations. Her Late Geometric pictorial examples may reveal phalanx-like tactics, though in a convention not easily understandable to those (i.e. us moderns) unacquainted with the painters' peculiar techniques at this time. The same surely holds true of Homer and – only a generation or two later – the lyric poets. Both were 'working within the conventions of a tradition. But in this case the tradition was entirely epic and so singularly inappropriate for describing a new hoplite context' (Cartledge 1977: 25). Cf. Van Wees 1986: 286; J. Griffin, *Homer on Life and Death* (Oxford, 1980) 48; Latacz 1977: 45. Remember that even the dry, unheroic narrative descriptions of phalanx battle in Herodotus, Thucydides, and Xenophon often comprise anecdotes concerning just a few individuals, e.g. Eurytos and Aristodemos at Marathon, the 'old man' at Mantineia, or Sphodrias and his son at Leuktra.
11. Pritchett, *War* 4. 30; Latacz 1977: 48ff. Pritchett, like Latacz earlier, has made an exhaustive reexamination of the so-called 'phalanx' passages in the *Iliad*, and argues persuasively that they must represent massed attacks of some sort even if lacking precisely the organization and precision of the classical model. For a list of some of these lines, see Snodgrass 1964b: 176–7, who rejects them all. Latacz, though, who devoted an entire monograph to the subject and whose treatment of these passages has

superseded all earlier discussions, proved in 1977 that such references must illustrate mass formations. Indeed, he made the next logical assumption: how could there then be any subsequent hoplite reform in tactics (1977: 237–44)? Cf., too, Kromayer and Veith (1928: 23), Lammert (1921 – 'Schlachtordnung' col. 1625), G. S. Kirk (in Vernant 1968: 110), and especially A. Lang, *The World of Homer* (London, 1910) 51ff. For the idea that phalanxes also fought in the first Messenian War, see Detienne (in Vernant 1968: 139); Pritchett, *Topography* 5. 20–1.

12. The presence of occasional duelling with missile weapons need not rule out the general preference for massed conflict in Homer (e.g. Delbrück 1975: 59; Van Wees 1986: 286); Latacz (1977: 46–9) has demonstrated that references to the 'mass' (e.g. *plethus*) exist almost everywhere in the *Iliad* and are the rule rather than the exception; the rarer soloist passages receive greater detail and length because of the heroic quality of the epic genre. Nor can phalanx tactics be discounted in the *Iliad* because the hoplite panoply had not yet fully emerged. All kinds of arms and armor were used in massed attacks throughout Greek and Persian history (e.g. Xen. *An.* 1.8.9; 7.8.15, and, if we can believe the *Cyropaedia* on Persian practice, *Cyr.* 6.2.10; 6.3.23; 7.1.33). See Salmon (1977: 91): 'Uniformity of weapons and of methods may not yet have been thought vital for the phalanx: what mattered was its cohesion and the unflinching maintenance by the members of the group.' For a collection of examples where 'hoplites' employ a variety of weapons, see Pritchett, *Topography* 5.22–3; *War* 4.11–13. Consequently, scenes on early vases or in Homer which suggest soloists equipped with javelins and non-hoplite armor are not arguments against the presence of the phalanx. We must also keep in mind that while the term 'hoplite' nearly always suggests 'phalanx' tactics, the reverse is not always true. Phalanxes at various times and places could be composed – no doubt less successfully so – of variously armed warriors, but hoplite infantrymen – perhaps the most perfect of all phalanx fighters – rarely fought outside massed formation. Their use as *epibatai* (Krentz 1985a: 53) on ships was a special circumstance (ships offer far different 'terrain' than flat plains) and should not be construed as evidence of their suitability as soloists on land. The career of Demosthenes in Aitolia and Sphakteria and the rise of light-armed skirmishers assumes the unsuitability of hoplites outside the phalanx (e.g. cf. also Polyb. 9.15.7.ff.; Thuc. 4.129).
13. Cf. e.g. Cartledge 1977: 20 n. 73; Chrimes 1949: 361–2; Lorimer 1947: 107–8.
14. (1) The shield offered less protection for the right side, e.g. Thuc. 5.71.1; Xen. *Hell.* 4.4.11 (cf. Cartledge 1977: 20) and thus was 'shared' by two combatants along the line (Plut. *Mor.* 220A). (2) It also restricted maneuverability (Cartledge 1977: 20). Many (e.g. Snodgrass 1965: 85; Salmon 1975: 85 n. 6: Greenhalgh 1973: 73; Krentz 1985a: 60–1) fail to appreciate just how clumsy a 3 ft (ca 1 m) shield actually was, carried on the forearm by a man not much over 5 ft 6 ins (1.67 m) in height and wearing 50 lbs (22 kg) or so of other bronze armor on his head, back, and legs, holding an 8 ft (2.4 m), double-pointed spear. Cf. Hanson 1989: 66; Donlan and Thompson 1976: 341; Lorimer 1947: 76–7. Tyrtaios'

description (1.11.16), then, of a shield covering a man from shin to shoulder is probably not an exaggeration or proof of some pre-hoplite body shield, as is sometimes thought. After all, if the diameter of the hoplite shield was 3 ft (less than a metre), we can readily imagine only 2 ft 6 ins (76 cm) of unprotected flesh below and above the rim on a 5 ft 6 ins (1.67 m) crouching hoplite. See e.g. Greenhalgh 1973: figs 45, 50, 54, 67, 72. The lack of the *telamon* made protection for the back impossible, cf. Greenhalgh *ibid.* 73–5. Also, the expense and difficulty in construction was considerable. See H. Blyth, who examined carefully one of the few extant wood cores (currently in the Vatican Museum):

> Moreover, the skill with which the timber has been shaped, the care taken to adjust the thickness and control it over the cross-section, the neat fitting of the leather lining, and still more that of the bronze covering, all indicate experience which must have been built up in a long tradition – and must have commanded a high price. (1982: 14)

The frequent references in literature to enormous shield factories (e.g. those of Kephalos and Pasion) suggest a far more elaborate procedure (e.g. lathe work, glue, bronze and leather working) than the occasional, on the spot creation of flat wood or wicker shields (e.g. Xen. *Hell.* 2.4.25). For other references to the general unsuitability of hoplite equipment to individual skirmishing, cf. Holladay 1982: 94–5. Heavily protected spearmen with such awkward shields never appear as soloists in other cultures at other times. We can imagine what a disadvantage the 'hoplite' would be at in the Roman gladiatorial arena when matched against the Thracian, Retiarius, Samnite or Mirmillo, all of whom had either swords or two types of offensive weapons and, of course, much different body armor and shields.

15. I do not understand why the shield is often termed 'convex' by modern scholars; should we not approach discussion of the shape from the vantage point of the men who carried such equipment? The usual Greek adjective ***koile*** reflects this view and is translated as 'hollow' or 'concave'; ***kurte*** (convex), on the other hand, was rarely used by the Greeks in association with the shield.
16. Cf. Donlan and Thompson:

> It is significant to note that running the prescribed distance with the shield in chest high position required an average increase of 28% in energy expenditure for each subject . . . The hoplite shield, which appears to have weighed about sixteen pounds, ***could only be carried isometrically***, and the considerable energy expenditure required sharply limits the distance over which troops could sustain great effort. (1976: 341, emphasis added)

Cf. Ar. *Nub.* 987–9 for an ancient example of the complaints over the need to produce nearly a third more in 'energy expenditure.' This disadvantage brought about by radical concavity must be behind Asklepiodotos' opinion (*Tact.* 5) that the best Macedonian shield is one 'not too hollow'; otherwise, the shield, which hung from the neck by a strap, would be too bulky and could not fit conveniently close to the chest.

17. In literature, cf. Tyrt 11.24; Eur. *Tro.* 1196–200; and especially Arrian *Tact.* 16.13. A sampling of vase-paintings: Ducrey 1985: pls 2, 47, 62, 84, 85, 178, 187; Anderson 1970: pls 2A, 12. In general, see Connolly 1981: 54; Hanson 1989: 68–9. For references to the unusual bowl shape of the shield, cf. Plut. *Mor.* 241 F 16 (as a bier for a corpse); Thuc. 7.82.3 (as a collection dish for money); Aen. Tact. 37.7 (to rest on the ground and resonate sounds of enemy miners below). Remember, the conical hill at Argos was dubbed the *aspis*.
18. The recurring 'heresy' that there was no push or *othismos* has recently (and rightly) been rejected once more. See Holladay 1982; Anderson 1984; Hanson 1989: 171–84 and especially Pritchett, *War* 4.65–7.
19. Cf. Snodgrass 1964: 37–54. If we can believe Diodorus (23.3.1), the early Romans assumed that round shields were properly to be used with the phalanx, rectangular shapes with maniples.
20. Cf. Snodgrass 1964: 133. It may have been used occasionally in late Mycenaean times (e.g. Snodgrass 1967: 29).
21. For some preserved remains, cf. H. Weber, *Olympische Forschungen* (Berlin, 1944) 1.154–8, pls 63–8. Markle 1977: 325; G. M. A. Richter, 'Recent acquisitions by the Metropolitan Museum of Art' *AJA* 43 (1939) 194–201.
22. *Sauroter* and *sturax* are often used interchangeably. However, *sauroter* (used in epic, Ionic, and late Greek, e.g. Hom. *Il.* 10.153; Hdt. 7.41.8; Polyb. 6.25.6; 11.18.4; *AP* 6.110) seems to be the more precise term and, although it should mean 'lizarder' (?), might perhaps really be derived from the long, slender shape of the spike which tapered to a point at the end and thus resembled a lizard (*saura, sauros*) or, more likely, a lizard's tail. *Sturax*, on the other hand, is Attic (Xen. *Hell.* 6.2.19; Pl. *Lach.* 184) and probably originated from the resin-bearing tree of the same name, which sometimes could be used for javelins or spears (e.g. Strab. 12.7.3). Since *sturax* could refer to the shaft as well (Onas. 10.4), often the diminutive *sturakion* was properly used for the spike alone (e.g. Thuc. 2.4; Aen. Tact. 18.10). *Ouriachos* (cf. *oura* = tail) is a general term for butt or end, and is on occasion used specifically for the butt of the spear and perhaps also is to be identified with the hoplite butt-spike itself (e.g. Hom. *Il.* 2.443; *AP* 6.111; Hdt. 9.75). In Homer, the choice of either *ouriachos* or *sauroter* is apparently determined by solely metrical considerations.
23. This auxiliary use of the spike is, of course, ignored by Euripides since the point here is to show the legitimacy, if not the advantage, of the bow over the spear.
24. Snodgrass 1967: 56, 80.
25. G. M. A. Richter, *Catalog of the Greek Sculptures in the Metropolitan Museum of Art* (Cambridge, Mass., 1954), pl. 82; Anderson 1970: pl. 10 and Richter (*supra* n. 21) 195.
26. The nature of fighting and equipment in the Dark Ages is a difficult topic. The web of relative historicity in Homer – Mycenaean, Dark Age, or 750–700 BC – is difficult to unravel. Archaeological evidence such as burial finds are not representative of society as a whole but are often predicated on class considerations, and few Geometric vases contain clear pictures of

fighting. In any case, figure representations do not appear until the very end of the period (e.g. ca 800 BC). Nevertheless, there is a consensus that in the eleventh, tenth, and ninth centuries many warriors were equipped with non-metallic body armor, long swords, thrusting (and later) throwing spears, and flat, round, and rectangular shields. Most believe that these aristocratic fighters made some such frequent use of the horse, and fought in a highly mobile, fluid, and individual fashion. I do not know when phalanx tactics first emerged in Greece, nor how long such shock fighting had existed with traditional, duellist weapons within this general period. We can be sure only that the 'phalanx' did emerge at least before Homer and prior to the introduction of hoplite weapons.

27. Cf. Snodgrass 1967: 91–5; Anderson 1970: 20–4.
28. It seems less likely (as Snodgrass 1965: 122 suggests) that individual warriors, most often aristocrats, would first employ the hoplite panoply and then be joined (under compulsion?) by newer land-owners. Why would aristocrats originally design weaponry so ill-suited to skirmishing and so ideal for the uniformity of (as yet unknown) massed battle? Are we to believe a knight would 'suit up' in the panoply, dismount (so unlike his medieval cousin), and then stab away or cast with his spear in single combat on the ground against non-hoplites, with such liabilities as reduced vision, comfort, and mobility? Once he abandoned his horse, would he not be defenseless – as later experience teaches us – against quick, lightly clad (and poor) javelin-throwers or bowmen? And how might such equipment then find its way into the phalanx – as if its ideal application came only through accident or chance? Clearly such unusual arms and armor must have been designed in advance for a specific type of combat, which was growing increasingly codified, if not ritualistic.
29. Even recent works dedicated to the premise that modern technology can determine the very course of warfare acknowledge the frequent primacy of tactics and thus (as was nearly always true in the Ancient Greek world) the responsive, rather than causative, effect of new weapons. So, S. M. van Creveld in *Technology and War* (New York, 1989) concludes with the observation:

> In sum, since technology and war operate on a logic which is not only different but actually opposed, the conceptual framework that is useful, even vital, for dealing with the one should not be allowed to interfere with the other. In an age when military budgets, military attitudes, and what passes for military thought often seem centered on technological considerations and even obsessed by them, this distinction is of vital importance. In the words of a famous Hebrew proverb: 'The deed accomplishes, what thought began.'

Part III

THE ENVIRONMENT OF BATTLE

> Even in daytime those fighting do not perceive everything, indeed no one knows anything more than what is going on right about himself.
>
> Thucydides

4

THE KILLING ZONE

John Lazenby

No one alive today has ever experienced anything really like a hoplite battle. Contemporary accounts survive, at least one by an eye-witness, but they chiefly take a wide-angle view. There is no 'blow-by-blow' commentary. To try to understand what went on at the 'sharp end', we have to draw on many sources, including poets and dramatists, and the best we can hope to achieve is a composite picture, since no two battles were exactly alike.

There is, at least, no good reason to distrust such evidence. Tyrtaios, for example, despite legends such as that he was a lame Athenian schoolmaster (cf., for example, Paus. 4.15.6), was almost certainly a Spartan, and had probably seen action. He describes a king of Sparta, for example, as '*our* king Theopompos' (5.1), and includes himself among Spartan warriors when he cries 'in a moment *we* shall all be slogging it out together' (19.16). Aischylos is supposed to have fought at Marathon, where his brother was killed (Hdt. 6.114). Euripides, whose descriptions of battle are amongst the best to have survived, was a well-to-do Athenian,[1] and would probably have been required to serve as a hoplite or in the cavalry. If he was born on the day of Salamis, as tradition has it, he could have fought anywhere from Greece to Egypt between 460 and 446 BC, and would still have been liable for military service at the beginning of the Peloponnesian War. In any case, it is better to rely on writers who were at least alive when hoplites were the dominant force in Greek warfare, than on the earlier Homer, or later authors such as Polybios, Diodoros, or Plutarch. After all, the audiences of Aischylos and Euripides would have included many a hoplite, and Tyrtaios' war-songs were still being sung in Sparta in Plato's day (cf. *Leg*. 629a and 667).

Homer's *Iliad* probably contains the most vivid descriptions of fighting to have survived from antiquity, but it was almost certainly composed before the hoplite age, and although it does make occasional references to massed infantry fighting, it is principally concerned with individual duels, and the throwing-spear is the dominant weapon. As for later writers, the difficulty is that we can never be sure what to make of what they say. Clearly they sometimes drew on earlier sources, lost to us, some of which were contemporary with the hoplite age, but unless they specify which, doubts must remain. Warfare in Greece was profoundly transformed in the fourth century, with the advent of Philip of Macedonia, and although hoplites continued to fight for a century or more, they were increasingly replaced by Macedonian-style 'phalangites', armed in a different way (cf., for example, Plut. *Cleom.* 11.2), and accustomed to fight in a different way. Thus we cannot be sure that what Polybios, for example, or the tactical writers, Asklepiodotos, Arrian and Aelian, have to say, is relevant. What follows, then, is an attempt to reconstruct what it was like to take part in a hoplite battle, based on contemporary evidence.

We begin with the setting, which was usually a flat terrain. Hills, streams, marshes, the sea, and other features, often play some part, but are rarely, if ever, crucial. There is much truth in the remark Herodotos attributes to Mardonios (7.9β.1), that 'when the Greeks declare war on each other, they choose the best and smoothest place and go down and have their battle on that', though it is less true, as we shall see, that they suffered heavily as a result. The area would be enough to accommodate several thousand men, but probably not more than 50,000 at most, if Greek was fighting Greek. Thucydides, for example, evidently thought that First Mantineia was a big battle (5.74.1), yet it is doubtful whether more than about 20,000 hoplites took part, and at the Nemea, possibly the greatest hoplite battle ever fought, there were probably fewer than 50,000 (Lazenby 1985: 128–9, 136).

Since battles were usually fought in the summer, it would be hot and sunny – this was the point of Dienekes' reply to the defeatist who told him, before Thermopylai, that the Persian arrows would blot out the sun (Hdt. 7.226). Bad weather, even thunderstorms, rarely, if ever, interrupted proceedings (cf., for example, Thuc. 6.70.1), though Plutarch alleges that one such aided Timoleon's victory at the Krimisos (*Tim.* 28.1–3). Battles could be fought at other times of the year, for example the one between the Mantineians and Tegeates at Laodokeion in the winter of 423/2 BC (i.e. between October and March: Thuc. 4.134), but perhaps the only time conditions affected the issue was when snow drove the forces of the 'Thirty' away from

Phyle in the winter of 404/3 BC (Xen. *Hell.* 2.4.3).

Before battle, the hoplites would form up in their files, eight deep or more. The greatest depth recorded is the 'fifty shields' of the Thebans at Leuktra (Xen. *Hell.* 6.4.12), though the forces of the 'Thirty' also formed up fifty deep at Mounychia in 403 BC, when confined to a single road (Xen. *Hell.* 2.4.11). Probably in most armies men from the same localities served together – Lysias, for example, implies that in the Athenian army men from the same deme fought alongside each other (16.14). But in the Spartan army, by Xenophon's time, recruitment was no longer on a local basis. Sons, fathers and brothers did not necessarily even serve together in the same *morai* (cf. Xen. *Hell.* 4.5.10).[2] Nevertheless, the members of the smallest units, the *enomotiai*, presumably knew each other, since they only consisted of forty men, even at full strength, and on campaign probably only contained thirty-five men or fewer (cf., for example, for Leuktra, Xen. *Hell.* 6.4.12 and 17). Presumably, too, since the composition of an *enomotia* was based on age-groups, with the younger men in the front ranks, each man also knew his place.

One wonders, however, whether this was true of most armies. There is no evidence that there were units smaller than a *lochos* in national armies other than the Spartan,[3] and although the size of a *lochos* varied from state to state, and from time to time, they always seem to have contained several hundred men. Unless units of this size were broken down into smaller ones, it is difficult to believe that every man would have had a fixed position,[4] and one suspects that before a battle there was a certain amount of jostling as men found themselves a place. This may be part of the point of Brasidas' scornful remark (Thuc. 5.10.5) that movement of spears and heads was characteristic of troops who would not stand their ground.

If the battle was at all unexpected, men could still be putting on their armour as they took their positions, as happened before Second Mantineia (Xen. *Hell.* 7.5.22). In Euripides' *Heraclidae* (723–5), it is even suggested that the aged Iolaos should have someone carry his equipment to the battle-line, and in real battles, officers in particular may only have taken their shields from their soldier-servants at the last moment (cf. Xen. *Hell.* 4.8.39). If there was time to kill before the advance, men would stand with spears at the slope and shields leaning against their legs (cf., for example, Xen. *An.* 1.5.13, *Hell.* 2.4.12). Sometimes the pose was kept up to show contempt for an advancing enemy, if an anecdote about Chabrias is true (Diod. 15.32.5, Polyaenus 2.1.2). Spartans possibly sat while waiting, as seems to have been true of Plataia (cf. Hdt. 9.72.1), though there they were being subjected to fire from Persian archers rather than waiting to advance against other hoplites.

Many generals would take this opportunity to harangue their men, perhaps addressing them unit by unit, as Pagondas did before Delion, 'so that they did not all leave the line at once' (Thuc. 4.91), or walking along the ranks as Archidamos did before the 'Tearless Battle' (Xen. *Hell.* 7.1.30), presumably so that all could hear him. But the Spartans preferred to encourage each other, according to Thucydides (5.69.2), 'knowing that long practice in action is of more help than brief, well-rounded, verbal advice'. Generals and their staff would also be busy with the sacrifice, and perhaps having a drink of wine to steady their nerves, as Kleombrotos and his officers were before Leuktra (cf. Xen. *Hell.* 6.4.8), though it seems unlikely that wine was normally served out to all.

The signal for the advance was often given by trumpet (cf., for example, Thuc. 6.69.2; Eur. *Heracl.* 830–1), and the hoplites would move forward, initially, perhaps, with spears still at the slope (cf. Xen. *An.* 6.5.25). Men would sing the 'Paian' (e.g. Xen. *Hell.* 4.2.19), or, in the Spartan army, if Plutarch is right (*Lyc.* 22.2–3), a hymn to Castor. Most armies did not march in step, judging by Thucydides' emphasis that the Spartan army did, to the sound of pipes (5.70). At a further signal, down would come the spears (Xen. *An.* 6.5.25), or at least those of the first two or three ranks, and a good general hoped all would be lowered simultaneously for effect. 'Since there were many soldiers,' Iphikrates is supposed to have said on one occasion (Polyaenus 3.9.8), 'they were neither able to level spears nor to sing the paian together; when I ordered "level spears", there was more noise of teeth to be heard [presumably chattering!] than of weapons.' But if it worked, the result could be terrific. It is vividly captured by Plutarch (*Arist.* 18.2) in his description of the moment at Plataia, when 'in an instant the phalanx took on the look of a wild animal, bristling as it turns at bay'.

Armies sometimes advanced at the double (e.g. Thuc. 4.96.1; Xen. *Hell.* 4.3.17), and Thucydides' description of the slow advance of the Spartans at First Mantineia (5.70) implies that this was unusual. But one suspects that all hoplites started at a walk, and then, unless they were Spartans, broke into a double when they got near the enemy. Xenophon ordered his men to double when the first sling-stones rattled against their shields (*An.* 4.3.29), and it was probably usually when they came within missile-range that hoplites started to run. The slow approach of the Spartans was designed to preserve their formation. At the Nemea they are even said to have halted within 200 yds (180 m) of the enemy, to perform a final sacrifice to 'Artemis the Huntress' (Xen. *Hell.* 4.2.20), which would also have given them a chance to dress their line. This was clearly a matter of concern. At Kounaxa, when the line started to billow out, Xenophon and his comrades shouted to each other not to 'run races' (*An.* 1.8.19).

Often, too, Greeks raised a war-cry, evidently sounding something like '*eleleu*' (cf., for example, Xen. *An.* 1.8.18; Ar. *Av.* 364), and sometimes drummed spear on shield (Xen. *An.* 1.8.18). In Aischylos' *Seven Against Thebes* (385–6) there is even a reference to the fearful clangour of bronze bells, apparently fixed on the insides of shields! Aischylos also remarks on the dust raised by advancing troops, the 'voiceless herald of an army' (*Supp.* 180, *Sept.* 81–2), and Euripides likens the flashing of the bronze accoutrements to lightning (*Phoen.* 110–1).

Many battles, it appears, were virtually decided almost before they began, by the flight of one side or the other. As one of the characters in Euripides' *Bacchae* remarks, 'it is common for fear to strike with panic an army under arms and in its ranks, before the spears touch' (303–4). At First Mantineia the centre of the allied line, particularly those opposed to the 300 Spartan *hippeis*, broke and ran, 'the majority not waiting to come to grips' (*es cheiras*: Thuc. 5.72.4), and notoriously at the so-called 'Tearless Battle', 'only a few of the enemy waited for the Spartans to come within spear-range' (*eis doru*: Xen. *Hell.* 7.1.31). As Euripides again says, the test of a man's courage was not the bow, but 'to stand and look and outface the spear's swift stroke, keeping the line firm' (*HF* 162ff.) or, as Xenophon more succinctly puts it, castigating a coward, 'because he could not look the spears in the face, he did not want to serve' (*Symp.* 2.14).

Sometimes, too, at least one wing of a phalanx contrived, by luck or judgement, to avoid a head-on collision. Thucydides says (5.71.1) that all armies tended to edge to the right, as each man sought the protection of his neighbour's shield for the unguarded right half of his own body, and there was thus a tendency for each side to create an overlap on the right. Euripides refers to the stalemate situation which could result (*Supp.* 704–6), and this was, presumably, why the battle of Laodokeion was 'ambiguous' (Thuc. 4.134.1). At the Nemea, however, the Spartans appear to have deliberately exploited the tendency (Lazenby 1985: 139–40), and although the result was that the left was sacrificed, this may have seemed acceptable. The left consisted of allied troops, who would not lose too heavily if they beat a hasty retreat, and the right could then take the victorious enemy right in its shieldless flank, as it broke off pursuit and attempted to retire (Xen. *Hell.* 4.2.22).

If, however, phalanxes met head on and were prepared to fight it out, the gap between them would have closed rapidly until sometimes the opposing front ranks literally crashed together (e.g. Xen. *Hell.* 4.3.19). More often, one suspects, the advance of both phalanxes slowed as they got 'within spear-range', and the men in the front ranks probed with their spears, trying to stab their opposite numbers.

How were these initial thrusts normally delivered? The language Xenophon uses in the *Anabasis* (e.g. 1.2.17, 6.5.25) certainly seems to suggest that spears were lowered from the shoulder to the underarm position, below the waist, as the advance began (cf. Anderson 1970: 88–9). This would have had the advantages that there would, perhaps, have been less likelihood of accidentally wounding one's own comrades (Hanson 1989: 162), and that the thrust could then have been directed below the rims of enemy shields, at relatively unprotected parts of the body. But both Tyrtaios (19.12) and Kallinos (1.10) describe soldiers as carrying their spears aloft (*anaschomenos/oi*), and when Tyrtaios exhorts the Spartans to 'brandish the mighty spear in the right hand' (11.25), he can hardly be thinking of an underarm thrust.

It is true that the latter is sometimes depicted on vases, but where it is, the scenes are invariably duels between individuals. There does not seem to be any example of lines of hoplites advancing with spears levelled below the waist.[5] Admittedly, there are very few such scenes, in any case, but those that have survived, from the Chigi vase onwards,[6] invariably show hoplites carrying spears overarm. Similarly, although wounds to the lower part of the body, and to the legs, are mentioned (cf., for example, Tyrt. 10.25), it is not usually clear when they were inflicted. In one case where it is, when the Spartan prince, Archidamos, receives a wound through his thigh, right at the beginning of a fight, he is specifically said to be leading his men in column, two by two (Xen. *Hell.* 7.4.22–3). Assuming that he was on the right, the position normally occupied by a commander, the right side of his body would have been completely unprotected, and even an overarm thrust could have got him in the thigh.

It may be the case that advancing hoplites carried their spears in the underarm position, but it is unlikely (*pace* Hanson 1989: 162ff.) that they delivered their first thrusts underarm, and then changed grip in the melée. More likely they brought their spears to the overarm position, before they came 'within spear-range', though it is difficult to see how this was done. The change, it must be remembered, involves not just raising the spear, but also turning the hand round on the spear-shaft, since when a thrust is underarm, the thumb is towards the point, but when overarm, towards the butt.

The change-over could have been effected by sticking the spear in the ground, then picking it up again with the hand reversed. But this would have required a momentary halt – difficult when charging at the double, but perhaps possible for the Spartans, or any other troops who halted during the advance. Alternatively, a momentary shift of the spear to the left hand, gripping the strap or cord near the rim at the right of the shield, might have done the trick. More risky, but perhaps easier, would have been to lift the spear above the head, still with the underarm grip, then let it go for a moment, and catch it as it fell, with the grip reversed. Even lifting the spear from below the waist to above the shoulder would have been much easier if hoplites had not been standing shoulder to shoulder, let alone marching or running, and the difficulties would certainly have been compounded if the change was only made after battle had been joined. But somehow or other it seems to have been done.

With spears probably held high, then, hoplites in at least the front rank, possibly the front two, thrust downwards, aiming for the face (Eur. *Phoen.* 1385), and presumably the throat or shoulders, over the rim of the shield, or for the chest through shield and cuirass (cf., for example, Tyrt. 12.25–6, 19.21; Eur. *Heracl.* 738). There was, however, no loosening of the close-packed formation, at this point, as some have suggested (e.g. Cawkwell 1978: 150–3). Plato's *Laches* (182a–d) makes it clear that this only happened when one side or the other fled the field, and what would have been the point of each man seeking the protection of his right-hand neighbour's shield during the advance if they then parted company when battle was actually joined?

The only evidence that the hoplite phalanx was at all fluid are the occasional references by the poets, from Tyrtaios to Pindar, to 'fore-fighters' (*promachoi*), usually with the implication that this is where a brave man would seek to take his place. Thus Tyrtaios cries (11.4), 'let each man direct his shield straight to the fore-fighters', and Pindar (*Isthm.* 7.49–50) talks about the 'throng of fore-fighters' where the best men fought. However, there would, presumably, have been ample opportunities for hoplites to display either their courage by pressing forward, as men fell in front of them, or their faint-heartedness by holding back, and there is also a conventional note to what the poets say. It is noticeable that the historians do not use the word '*promachoi*'. When, for example, Thucydides or Xenophon want to talk about 'front-rank men', they use the word '*protostates/ai*' (e.g. Thuc. 5.71.1; Xen. *Cyr.* 3.3.57, 6.3.24; *LP* 11.5).

Euripides' description of the fight between Eteokles and Polyneikes (*Phoen.* 1382ff.), though a description of an imaginary duel, possibly allows us to glimpse something of the preliminary exchanges in a hoplite battle. The two antagonists keep their shields up, apparently eyeing each other through holes pierced in the rims of their shields (1386–7) – was this true, one wonders, of real battles? Then Eteokles turns his foot on a stone and exposes his thigh outside his shield. Immediately, Polyneikes thrusts and drives his spear through his brother's leg, but in so doing exposes his own shoulder to a counter-thrust.

It was, presumably, in such an encounter that the Spartan king, Kleombrotos, got his mortal wound in the opening moments of Leuktra (Xen. *Hell.*, 6.4.13). Eteokles and Polyneikes, however, survive this wounding, and go on to kill each other with swords (1404–13), and although they were heroes, it is alleged of the perfectly mortal Spartan, Kleonymos, that at Leuktra he fell three times, before finally being killed (Xen. *Hell.* 5.4.33), indicating that he was not yet shield to shield with the enemy. However, the Thessalian 'trick' which Eteokles finally uses to kill Polyneikes (*Phoen.* 1404–13), would not have been appropriate to a hoplite (*pace* Pritchett, *War* 4. 64). It involved taking a pace back, which would have been almost impossible for a man in the front rank of a phalanx (Hanson 1989: 167).

It was, perhaps, this preliminary stabbing and counter-stabbing that Tyrtaios had in mind when he talks about 'slogging it out' (*aloièseumen* – literally, 'we will be threshing': 19.16). Men probably still had breath to shout – Euripides, for example, imagines Athenians shouting 'Athens' and their opponents shouting for Argos (*Heracl.* 839). But the grimmest description of the sound of battle is Xenophon's of Second Koroneia (*Ages.* 2.12): 'There was no shouting, nor yet silence, but the kind of noise passion and battle are likely to produce.' Groans and screams (Tyrt. 19.20; Eur. *Heracl.* 833) no doubt mingled with the clash of spear on shield and of spear-shaft on spear-shaft. In Aischylos (*Sept.* 155) the 'spear-shaken air seethes', and in real battles indescribable confusion probably reigned. Thus in his account of the night attack on Epipolai, Thucydides says that even in daylight 'each man hardly knows anything except what is happening to himself' (7.44.1), and in Euripides' *Supplices* (846–7) Theseus says one question he will not ask, in case he is laughed at, is who met whom in the battle. It is significant that there was obviously no clear tradition about how even Epameinondas met his end (cf. Plut. *Ages.* 35.1; Paus. 8.11.5–6).

Far from this fighting bringing about any loosening of the phalanx, it was now that its cohesion mattered more than ever. At the beginning of the hoplite era, Tyrtaios adjures the Spartans to fight 'standing by one another' (10.15, 11.11), maintaining that 'fewer die' as a result (11.12), and that this was so is confirmed by Xenophon's description of a minor skirmish on Aigina in 388 BC (*Hell.* 5.1.12), and by many an occasion when hoplites in a difficult situation preserved themselves by maintaining their compact order (cf., for example, Thuc. 1.63.1, 3.108.3). As one of Plutarch's *Sayings of the Spartans* (*Mor.* 220a) puts it, a man carried a shield, unlike helmet and cuirass, 'for the sake of the whole line', and this was not just because of the protection one man's shield afforded to the man on his left, but because an unbroken shield-wall was virtually impregnable.

If we imagine what it would have been like to stand in the front line of a phalanx, swapping thrusts with enemy spearmen only a few feet away, we can understand why Euripides' Amphitryon argues (*HF* 191–2) that if a hoplite finds himself ranged alongside cowards, he may be killed by his neighbours' faintheartedness. Demosthenes puts the other side of the case when he says that no one who flees from a battle, ever blames himself, but the general, his neighbours and everyone else. But, as he goes on, 'they are none the less, of course, defeated by all who flee, for it was open to the man who blames the others, to stand, and if each man did this, they would win' (3.17). As Brasidas says, 'those who have no line, may not be ashamed to give ground under pressure. Advance or retreat having the same good repute among them, their courage is never tested' (Thuc. 4.126.5). For hoplites, leaving the line, even to challenge the enemy individually, as Aristodemos did at Plataia (Hdt. 9.71.3), was regarded as irresponsible folly, for, as Brasidas again puts it, 'independent action is always likely to give a man a good excuse for saving his own skin' (Thuc. 4. 126. 5).

Sometimes, it appears, this fighting went on until both sides had virtually wiped each other out. At the Nemea, for example, 'the men of Pellene being opposite the Thespiaians, they each fought and fell in their places' (Xen.*Hell.* 4.2.20). There may also sometimes have been a certain ebb and flow in the struggle. In the imaginary battle in the *Heracleidae*, for example, Euripides has his messenger describe how 'at first the thrust of the Argive spear broke us, then they gave back' (834–5), and Xenophon argues that at Leuktra the Spartans must have been winning initially, since otherwise they would not have been able to carry their king, still living, from the field (*Hell.* 6.4.13). This also shows that it was possible to get a wounded man to the rear, even in the thronging turmoil of a hoplite battle, though one suspects that an ordinary hoplite who fell stood less chance than a king of Sparta. Even the Spartan second-in-command on Sphakteria, Hippagretas, was left lying among the dead (Thuc. 4.38.1).

If neither side gave way in these preliminary exchanges, the pressure from the rear would sooner or later force the opposing front ranks to close right up to each other, shield to shield, and many sources mention the crash when this happened (Tyrt. 19.18; Aesch. *Sept.* 100, 103, 160; Eur. *Heracl.* 832, *Supp.* 699). Then the fighting would be as Euripides describes it in the second phase of his fictional battle, 'toe-to-toe, man to man' (*Heracl.* 836), or as Tyrtaios puts it, 'with foot set beside foot, pressing shield to shield, crest against crest, helmet against helmet, chest against chest' (11.31–2). Xenophon's description of the Spartans and Thebans at Second Koroneia, when 'crashing their shields together, they shoved, fought, slew and died' (*Hell.* 4.3.19), shows that the poets did not exaggerate.

At such close quarters, it is difficult to see how spears 6 ft (1.8 m) and more in length could have been of much use, though one could, perhaps, have aimed for the men in the second and third ranks. It has been suggested (Hanson 1989: 164) that most spears were broken at the first impact, and that swords were then used. But the evidence (e.g. Aesch. *Ag.* 64–6; Diod. 15.86.2) is not very good, and other passages (e.g. Hdt. 7.224.1; Eur. *Phoen.* 1382ff.) suggest that swords were only used after prolonged fighting. The spear was certainly the hoplite weapon *par excellence*. Archilochos' spear was his bread and wine and he drank leaning on it (2), and for Aischylos the typical Greek weapon, as opposed to the bow of the Persians, was the 'close-quarter spear' (*Pers.* 240). Euripides' Amphitryon, in his argument with Lykos over the respective merits of the hoplite and the archer (*HF* 159ff.), even declares that the former has only one means of defence – 'having broken his spear, he has no means of warding death from his body' (193–4). This was, strictly speaking, untrue, but when Xenophon says that after Second Koroneia you could see swords 'bared of their sheaths, some on the ground, some in a body, some still in the hand' (*Ages.* 2.14), does he not imply that you would normally have expected to see them still *in* their sheaths? This battle, it must be remembered, 'like no other of those in our time,' as Xenophon says (*Hell.* 4.3.16), consisted of two separate encounters, and, as a result, it is likely that more spears were broken than in normal battles.

There is another answer to how hoplites fought, once they were too close to the enemy to make effective use of their spears. Xenophon's description of the second encounter at Koroneia (*Hell.* 4.3.19) suggests that the opposing lines, having crashed into each other, shield to shield, literally started to shove, and shoving (*othismos*) evidently was a feature of many a battle. Herodotos, for example, says there was 'much shoving' over the body of Leonidas at Thermopylai (7.225.1) and that at Plataia the fighting was prolonged 'until they came to the shoving' (9.62.2); at Solygeia the Athenian and Karystian right wing 'with difficulty shoved the Corinthians back' (Thuc. 4.43.3); at Delion the engagement took the form of 'tough fighting and shoving of shields' (Thuc. 4.96.2); at Syracuse the Athenians and their Argive allies defeated both wings of the Syracusan army, by shoving (Thuc. 6.70.2), and at Leuktra, the Spartan right was 'shoved' back (Xen. *Hell.* 6.4.14).

But what form did this 'shoving' actually take? We do not really know, but it is possible that hoplites in the rear ranks literally put their shields against the backs of those in front and pushed (Hanson 1989: 174–5). Xenophon advocates that the best men should be placed in front and rear of a phalanx (*Mem.* 3.1.8) so that the worst men in the middle could be 'led by the former and *shoved* by the latter'. More directly, later writers talk about the men in the rear ranks of a Macedonian-style phalanx using the weight of their bodies to push those in front forwards (Polyb. 18.30.4; Asklep. 5.2; Arr. *Tact.* 12.10; Ael. *Tact.* 14.6), and it is arguable that this would be *a fortiori* true of a hoplite phalanx.

None of the earlier sources gives any clear indication how the 'shoving' was accomplished, but Thucydides, in saying of the Thebans at Delion that 'they followed up little by little as they shoved', makes it sound very like the inexorable 'heave' of a well-drilled pack on a rugby football field. The famous story of Epameinondas' cry for 'one pace more' at Leuktra (Polyaenus 2.3.2) also sounds like the kind of thing the leader of a rugby 'pack' might shout. The story is late and one wonders whether many of Epameinondas' men could have heard him, but Thucydides' account of Sphakteria implies that Spartans normally expected to hear orders, when he says (4.34.3) that they were unable to hear them there because of the shouting of the enemy. One suspects that commanders often did call for a supreme effort, and even if they could only be heard by those immediately around them, word could rapidly have been passed to the rest.

Of one thing we can be certain. Epameinondas would have been among his men. He was killed at Second Mantineia, and many another hoplite general also fell in battle – Pelopidas at Kynoskephalai (Plut. *Pel.* 32.7), Kleombrotos at Leuktra (Xen. *Hell.* 6.4.13), all three Athenian generals in a battle near Spartolos (Thuc. 2.79.7), Hippokrates at Delion (Thuc. 4.101.2), Kleon and Brasidas at Amphipolis (Thuc. 5.10.8–11), both Athenian generals at First Mantineia (Thuc. 5.74.3). There was sometimes criticism that generals took all the credit (cf. Eur. *Andr.* 693–8), but even an old cynic like Archilochos felt he could trust a commander who was 'short, bow-legged to look at, set squarely on his feet and full of heart' (114), and there was probably a natural camaraderie between hoplites and their commanders. After all, they belonged to the same class. Even in the Spartan army, men about to engage in or in the midst of a battle were not averse to shouting advice to their officers, king included (cf. Xen. *Hell.* 4.2.22; Thuc. 5.65.2).

It is evident, too, that the depth of a phalanx was significant from at least the time of Marathon onwards (cf. Hdt. 6.111.3). Thus Xenophon says (*Hell.* 4.2.13) that before the Nemea there was some discussion amongst Sparta's opponents about what depth to adopt. Later he implies that it was decided to form up sixteen deep, though in the event the Boiotians ignored the agreement, and made their phalanx 'really deep' (4.2.18) – perhaps twenty-five, as at Delion (Thuc. 4.93.4). Xenophon's remarks here may suggest that 'really deep' formations were defensive, but the significance of the depth of a phalanx was surely not just the defensive strength it imparted. When Epameinondas made his phalanx 'fifty shields deep' at Leuktra, he was not thinking in terms of defence, but of 'crushing the head of the snake' (Polyaenus 2.3.15).

It has also been suggested that the point of these 'really deep' phalanxes was to provide a reserve, which could be moved out to attack the flanks of an enemy phalanx, once its front was 'pinned' (Cawkwell 1978: 154–5). But there is no evidence that the rear ranks of a hoplite phalanx were ever used in this way, and there must be some other explanation for the importance attached to depth. The most probable is that it was thought that the deeper the phalanx, the more likely it was to be able to win the 'shoving' and literally smash through the enemy line. Thus, at Second Mantineia, Xenophon says (*Hell.* 7.5.23), Epameinondas used his phalanx, deepened just before the advance, 'like a trireme bows on'.

It may, finally, be of some significance that ancient authors occasionally imply that physical strength was a factor in winning hoplite battles. Herodotos, for example, remarks (9.62.3) that the Persians at Plataia were 'not inferior in spirit and strength' – it was only their lack of armour and expertise which let them down. Diodoros, too, several times alleges that the bodily strength of the Thebans gave them victory (12.70.3, 15.39.1, 87.1), and Plutarch even claims that their skill in wrestling helped to win Leuktra (*Mor.* 639f). This is treated seriously by some scholars (e.g. Pritchett, *War* 4.64), but it seems doubtful whether close-packed hoplites, with shields on their left arms and spears or swords in their right hands, could have wrestled with their opponents. When the Spartans were reduced to fighting with hands and teeth at Thermopylai (Hdt. 7.225.3), it was because all their weapons had gone, and similarly when the Persians tried to grab the Greeks' spears at Plataia (Hdt. 9.62.2), it was presumably because their own spears were too short (cf. Hdt. 7.211.2).

Physical strength would clearly have been important for the 'shoving', but in rugby football it is not necessarily the heaviest and strongest pack that wins – how the pressure is applied is also important. Hoplites needed to be strong, in any case, to stand up to prolonged fighting in the heat, burdened with heavy equipment. The way that men from Archilochos (5) onwards threw away their shields if they turned to run, shows that the shield was particularly burdensome, but the weight of hoplite equipment in general is often contrasted with that of other troops (e.g. Thuc. 3.98.2, 4.33.2). The physical exertion involved in hoplite fighting is perhaps most vividly brought out in a passage of Euripides (*Tro.* 1196ff.), where Hekuba draws attention to the stain on the rim of Hektor's shield, caused by the sweat from his face, 'as he endured the toils of battle'.

Even if the rear ranks did not literally push against those in front, they could have added 'weight' in the general sense that the greater the number of men pressing forward, the greater the force of the attack, and they would also have made it impossible for those in front to turn and run. This is a point made by the later writers Polybios, Arrian and Aelian (see p.97), and Xenophon's Cyrus orders the commander of his rear-guard bid his men watch for any shirking amongst those in front (*Cyr.* 6.3.27). Again there may have been a certain amount of ebb and flow at the shoving stage. Herodotos, for example, alleges that the Greeks flung the Persians back four times in the shoving over Leonidas' body (7.225.1), though this was not against hoplites. But, eventually, one side or the other would have had to give way, either because gaps opened in the line as men fell, or because of the sheer weight of their opponents' 'shove'. Often the collapse came in one section of the line and led to the flight of the rest. At Leuktra, for example, the Spartan left gave way when it saw the right 'shoved back' (Xen. *Hell.* 6.4.14). Epameinondas elevated into a principle the idea that if you could defeat one part of an army, the rest would give way, believing, Xenophon says, that 'it is very hard to find men willing to stand, when they see some of their own side in flight' (*Hell.* 7.5.24).

We might, perhaps, have expected to hear of the losers being knocked down and trampled underfoot as the victors surged forward, but possibly the disintegration was gradual. The rear ranks in the losing phalanx would have peeled off to run, and even the front ranks may have stayed on their feet, though the moment of disengagement would have been terribly dangerous. Perhaps they were helped by a momentary pause as the winners realized that the enemy line had given way and that shoving could give place to stabbing. We do hear of fugitives trampling each other in their desperation to get away, for example at First Mantineia (Thuc. 5.72.4), and the situation could be much worse if escape was difficult, as for the Athenians at the ford over the Assinaros (Thuc. 7.84.3). Xenophon has an appalling description of Argive fugitives trying to get away from Spartans between the 'long walls' of Corinth, in the Corinthian War (*Hell.* 4.4.11). They were penned up against one of the walls, and were trying to scramble up the steps leading on to it; some were even asphyxiated in the crush. A recent tragedy at a football match in England, in which ninety-five people were killed, is a terrible reminder of what such an incident would have been like.[7]

Undoubtedly the side that lost a hoplite battle tended to lose more heavily than the winners, and this was presumably because men who turned to flee, immediately exposed their backs. As Tyrtaios says, 'it's easy[8] to pierce the back of a fleeing man' (11.17–8). Often, too, as we have seen, they threw away their shields, so that even if they did turn at bay, they would have been at a serious disadvantage. It was in these situations that – according to Plato's *Laches* – weapons-drill finally came into its own. But not every retreating hoplite was a Sokrates, whose belligerent mien in the retreat from Delion, acted as an effective deterrent to anyone who thought of attacking him (Plato *Symp.* 221b). Often one imagines, once panic had set in, the mass of fugitives would have been more like the mob of Argives Xenophon describes, 'frightened, panic-stricken, presenting their unprotected sides, no one turning to fight, but all doing everything to assist their own slaughter' (*Hell.* 4.4.12). Even on a battlefield, parts of a defeated army could find themselves surrounded, as happened to the Thespiaians at Delion (Thuc. 4.96.3),[9] and once the winners' blood-lust was aroused, they might even slaughter some of their own men, in ignorance, as happened here. Xenophon says that the Spartans who had routed the Argives just described, thought their defenceless state was a gift from heaven.

But for all the horrors of such incidents, where figures are given, the losses suffered in hoplite battles actually seem to represent only a small percentage of those who had taken part. Thus the losses at Delion amounted to just over 7 per cent for the Boiotians and just over 14 per cent for the Athenians, if Thucydides' figures are reliable (4.93.3, 94.1, 101.2). Figures for other battles are less reliable, but in few, if any, do even the beaten side appear to have suffered more than the Athenians at Delion, and casualties amongst the winners seem sometimes to have been perhaps as low as 2 per cent.[10] Such figures pale in comparison with the appalling losses inflicted on the Romans, for example, at Trasimene and Cannae, where about 60 per cent of them may have been killed.

These were special cases, but part of the reason for the comparatively low losses in hoplite battles was that hoplites were not really suited to pursuit, and that although cavalry was frequently used instead, not all Greek states had cavalry, and those that did often had very few. Apart from the sheer weight of their equipment, hoplites who broke ranks to pursue, laid themselves open to counter-attack, and cavalry and light troops could also very easily find themselves in difficulties if beaten hoplites rallied. Thus it was no kind-heartedness which led the Spartans only to press the pursuit for a short distance, as Thucydides tells us was their custom (5.73.4), though they may also have felt it was not the 'done thing'.

However, even if losses in a hoplite battle were comparatively low, the nature of the fighting probably meant that the small area in which the decisive clash had taken place would have been a grim sight. We can probably discount some of the more lurid descriptions, for example Aischylos' talk of the 'clotted gore' lying on the soil at Plataia, and of the 'heaps of corpses bearing silent witness to the eyes of mortals to the third generation' (*Pers.* 816ff.), though Herodotos claims to have seen the skeletons of men killed at Pelousion during Kambyses' invasion of Egypt (3.12). Obviously, too, if fugitives were caught in a situation like the wretched Argives at Corinth, the slaughter would have been more than usually horrific. The heaps of corpses, Xenophon implies, looked like piles of corn, logs or stones (*Hell.* 4.4.12). But Xenophon's description of the battlefield at Koroneia, which he saw himself, is bad enough:

> When the battle was over, one could see, where they had crashed into each other, the earth stained red with blood, bodies of friends and foes lying with each other, shattered shields, broken spears, swords bare of sheaths, some on the ground, some in the body, some still in the hand.
>
> (*Ages.* 2.14)

The 254 skeletons, laid out in seven rows, around the site of the Lion of Chaironeia, assuming that they are the remains of men killed in the battle,[11] are a reminder that Xenophon's description of Koroneia is probably only too accurate.

At least when the fury died, Greeks usually behaved in a fairly decent manner. There was little exulting over fallen foes, indeed Agesilaos is said to have been saddened at the news that so many had fallen at the Nemea (Xen. *Ages.* 7.5), and Philip to have burst into tears at the sight of the dead members of the Sacred Band after Chaironeia (Plut. *Pel.* 18.5). Then, as now, survivors shook hands with their comrades (Xen. *Hell.* 7.2.9), and there was the usual boasting: 'Of the seven dead, whom we overtook on our feet,' sings Archilochos (101), 'we are the thousand slayers.' Sometimes men gathered round their generals to congratulate them (Xen. *Hell.* 4.3.18).

There are very few references to the care of wounded.[12] Xenophon's statement that the first Spartans wounded in the encounter with Iphikrates' peltasts near Corinth, were got away safely to Lechaion by the *hypaspistai* (*Hell.* 4.5.15), is a rare exception. More attention was obviously given to those of high rank. Agesilaos, for example, is said to have been severely wounded at Second Koroneia (Xen. *Ages.* 2.13), but clearly survived, and Plutarch claims that Pelopidas received seven wounds at First Mantineia (*Pel.* 4.5), though the story can hardly be true.[13] Philip of Macedonia certainly recovered from a series of horrific wounds (cf. Dem. 18.67). Herodotos' story of how the heroic Aiginetan marine, Pytheas, was patched up by the

Persians (7.181.2) suggests that this seemed most unusual to a Greek, and one suspects that enemy wounded left on the battlefield were either killed, or left to die. The enemy dead were stripped of their armour, which was then partly used to set up a trophy, or for subsequent dedication to the gods. But the corpses were almost invariably handed over for burial, once the defeated sent a herald requesting a truce for the purpose. The delay after Delion was for special reasons (Thuc. 4.97ff.), and Herodotos' evident disgust at the way Xerxes treated Leonidas' body (7.238), suggests that such behaviour was most un-Greek.

Prisoners are rarely mentioned, presumably because men who were not killed or too badly wounded, were usually able to escape. Some were certainly taken on occasion, for example, if escape was impossible, as at First Koroneia (Thuc. 1.113.2) and on Sphakteria (Thuc. 4.38.5). But the 2,000 Athenian prisoners Philip took at Chaironeia, twice as many as were killed (cf. Lycurg. fr. B 10.1, Demades 9), were quite unprecedented. Willingness to surrender, or at least to consider it, was indicated by holding out hands (Hdt. 7.233.1), or lowering shields and waving (Thuc. 4.38.1). Prisoners were usually returned at the end of the war, although they were sometimes enslaved, or, if they were generals, executed, as happened to the unfortunate Athenians in Sicily (Thuc. 7.85.2ff.).

How, then, were such battles won and lost? It is obvious from Plato's *Laches* that individual skills were not important, and Herodotos' Demaratos says that even Spartans fighting singly were merely 'second to none, though together they were the best of all men' (7.104.4). Thus at Plataia the personal courage of Persians, 'rushing out in ones and tens and in larger and smaller groups', was of no avail: 'they crashed into the Spartans and were destroyed' (Hdt. 9.62.3). Even the desperate courage of Aristodemos earned him no recognition from his fellow Spartans, since they considered he had been 'acting like a lunatic and *leaving the line*' (Hdt. 9.71.3). There was no place for such *virtuosi* in a hoplite line-of-battle.

Unit skills were, however, important, and here the Spartans clearly had an edge. As we have seen, their army was the only one to be articulated into manageable units, and the author of the *Constitution of the Lakedaimonians* attributed to Xenophon says that Spartan infantry tactics were thought to be too complicated for other troops, though he himself believed the reverse to be true (*LP* 11.5). Significantly, the one thing he did think was not easy to learn, except for those 'trained under the laws of Lykourgos', was 'to fight equally well with anyone one found, even if there was confusion' (*LP* 11.7). It was clearly this training in fighting together as units that enabled the Spartans to carry out complicated manoeuvres like the 'forward-bend' (*epikampe*), 'counter-march' (*exeligmos*), and 'back-wheel' (*anastrophe*): cf. Xen. *Hell.* 4.2.20, 4.3.18 and 6.5.18–19).

There was, however, a limit to the tactical skills that hoplites could display. The necessity to maintain cohesion made the phalanx an essentially unwieldy formation, and generals were not only untrained, but, as we have seen, in the thick of the fight. The most that even the best could usually hope to do was to set his army in motion according to a preconceived plan. The best of them all, Epameinondas,[14] apparently made no changes to his plan once the massed Theban phalanx started to roll at Leuktra: the Sacred Band's charge at the double was Pelopidas' idea, if Plutarch is right (*Pel.* 23.2). Similarly, at Second Mantineia, although Epameinondas increased the depth of his phalanx at the last moment, it was before the advance (Xen. *Hell.* 7.5.22). The Spartans sometimes tried altering their formation during the advance, or after battle had been joined, but each time it went disastrously wrong. At First Mantineia Agis was left with a hole in his line, through which the enemy poured to break his left (Thuc. 5.71.3–72.1);[15] on Corfu, Mnasippos' right was attacked and defeated while trying to carry out an *anastrophe* (Xen. *Hell.* 6.2.21); and at Leuktra Kleombrotos was possibly trying both an *anastrophe* and an *epikampe*, when the Sacred Band struck his line (Lazenby, 158–9).

Ultimately the single most important factor in a hoplite battle was undoubtedly what Napoleon thought, many centuries later, counted for three-quarters in war: morale.[16] We have already seen that on many occasions hoplites fled almost before a blow had been struck, and panic was easily communicated. Pindar (*Nem.* 9.62–3) says that even the sons of gods were not immune, and, as previously mentioned, it was Epameinondas' opinion that it was very hard to find men who would stand when they saw part of their own army in flight (Xen. *Hell.* 7.5.24). This was one of the reasons why the Spartans were so successful for so long. In effect their battles were 'three-quarters' won before they started, since their enemies feared to face them. As Plutarch says (*Pel.* 17.6), they were 'irresistible in spirit, and, because of their reputation, when they came to grips, terrifying to opponents, who themselves did not think that with equal forces they stood an equal chance with Spartiates'.

Morale, as Plutarch implies, works both ways: if you think you are going to win, you will gain in confidence; if your enemy thinks you are going to win, he will lose confidence. Spartans were supremely confident. On Sphakteria, for example, the 390 or so hoplites who remained, after their first guard-post had been overwhelmed, 'seeing an army approaching, formed up and advanced against the Athenian hoplites, *wanting to come to grips with them*' (Thuc. 4.33.1). One tends to forget that they were outnumbered by more than two to one by these hoplites alone (cf. Thuc. 4.31.1), to say nothing of some Messenian hoplites, 7,500 armed Athenian sailors, 800 archers and 800 peltasts (Thuc. 4.32.2)! Thucydides' description of the advance of the Spartan army at First Mantineia (5.69.2–70) gives a marvellous impression of soldiers who knew exactly what they had to do, and that they could do it.

This kind of confidence goes a long way towards explaining why many Greeks feared to face the Spartans. The mere sight of the *lambdas* displayed on their shields was enough to send a shiver down Kleon's spine, according to the comic poet, Eupolis (359 Kock), and Xenophon's story (*Hell.* 4.4.10) of the confident advance of a force of Argives against dismounted Spartan cavalry troopers who had borrowed shields bearing *sigmas* (for 'Sikyonians'), implies that the Argives would not have been nearly so confident, had they known that they were facing Spartans. Even the overwhelming numbers the Athenians had at Sphakteria did not prevent them going ashore 'obsessed by the idea that they were going against Spartans' (Thuc. 4.34.1).

What, then, motivated men in these encounters? Obviously their feelings were just as complex as those of men in more recent conflicts, and since we cannot question ancient Greeks, we must, in the end, confess that we shall never know what their motives were. Simple patriotism certainly played a part, and men were clearly concerned to defend their homes and loved ones. Then as now, too, even the aggressors often thought of themselves as engaged in what we would call a 'pre-emptive strike'. Thus, before Delion, the Athenian general, Hippokrates, declared that 'the battle will take place in their country but will be for our own' (Thuc. 4.95.2)!

Unlike the soldiers of modern armies, hoplites were not 'the nation in arms', in the sense that in most states, if not all, the poor were excluded because they could not afford to buy the relatively expensive equipment required. In Athens, for example, hoplite service was almost certainly impossible for the *thetes*, who formed, perhaps, 40 to 60 per cent of the population, at various times. It is true that the emergence of hoplites marks a break with the aristocratic past, and that the hoplite *ethos* differed from the aristocratic, as one can see by comparing Homer with Tyrtaios. But hoplites remained an elite, and the non-aristocrats among them probably adopted many aristocratic attitudes. It was not for nothing, after all, that Homer has been called the 'Bible' of the Greeks. Thucydides perhaps expresses the attitude of the hoplite class when he implies that the activities of 'stone-throwers, slingers and archers' before a battle, were of little or no importance (6.69.2), and his comment on the 120 Athenian hoplites who perished at the hands of Aitolian javelineers – 'these, so many and of the same age, were the best men from the city of Athens who perished in this war' (3.98.4) – seems to contain an added note of bitterness. Moreover, hoplites were 'the nation in arms', in another sense, in states where those who could not afford such service, were excluded from full civic rights.[17]

Thus, although men of the hoplite class were realists enough to know that war was a grim business – neither Homer nor Tyrtaios glosses over the horrors – they also retained sufficient of the aristocratic way of thinking to regard prowess in battle as glorious. 'This is the noblest virtue,' sings Tyrtaios (12.13), 'this the noblest prize among men', and he goes on to declare that if a brave man falls, his grave and his children and grandchildren are honoured, and if he survives, he is looked up to by young and old alike. This may just seem like a Spartan speaking, but Alkaios, too, said that 'to die in war is a noble thing' (400 Campbell), and even Thucydides' Perikles, who so poignantly expresses how death in battle is the end of all a man's hopes and fears (2.42.4), nevertheless maintains that such a death is the final confirmation of his worth (2.42.2).

Obviously there were pressures on a man not to play the coward, as there are now. They may have been strongest in Sparta, where cowardice not only caused a man to be shunned by his fellows (cf. Xen. *LP* 9.4–5; Plut. *Ages.* 30.2–4), but almost certainly led to his losing his civic rights (cf. Hdt. 7.231, Thuc. 5.34.2). Such men were called *tresantes* (tremblers) from Tyrtaios' day to Plutarch's (cf. Tyrt. 11.14; Plut. *Ages.* 30.2–4). But cowardice could also be an offence in Athens (cf., e.g., Andoc. 1.74; Lys. 14.11), and failure to perform one's military duties could lead to execution. The demagogue, Kleophon, for example, was condemned to death ostensibly on a charge of being 'absent without leave' (Lys. 13.12).

In the end, however, what modern research has shown about today's soldiers,[18] was probably also true of those of ancient Greece –

that it was mainly not wanting to 'let one's mates down' which kept them from shirking, though the evidence largely concerns the Spartans. Thus one suspects that the reason for the suicide of the sole Spartan survivor from the so-called 'Battle of the Champions' (Hdt. 1.82.8), was not just the fear that his mere survival might cast doubt on his courage, but also the thought of being left alive when all his comrades had perished. This may also partly explain why Eurytos insisted on being led into battle at Thermopylai, despite his ophthalmia – his fellow-sufferer, Aristodemos, lived to regret his decision not to join him – and why Pantites, though sent to Thessaly with a message, hanged himself when he returned to Sparta (Hdt. 7.229–32). Not letting others down was no doubt also partly what Tyrtaios had in mind when he exhorted the Spartans to fight 'standing by one another' (10.15, 11.11), and said that a soldier who encouraged his neighbour was 'a good man in war' (12.19). Xenophon's Cyrus, possibly thinking of the Spartans,[19] considered that those who messed together would be less likely to desert each other, and that there could be no stronger phalanx than one composed of friends (*Cyr.* 2.1.28, 7.1.30).

Athenaios even says that before battle the Spartans sacrificed to Eros, 'since safety lies in the love of those ranged alongside each other' (13.561e), and there can be no doubt that sometimes the feelings of hoplites for their comrades were homosexual, particularly in the Spartan and Theban armies (cf. Xen. *Symp.* 8.35; Plut. *Pel.* 18–19). The Sacred Band was supposed to have been composed of pairs of lovers (Plut. *Pel.* 18–19), which makes the skeletons at Chaironeia, if they are those of this elite force, all the more poignant.[20]

Ancient Greek armies, like more modern ones, no doubt contained their share of thugs and psychotics, and the Spartan way of life may have conditioned them to think of fighting as something normal, or even desirable. But the epitaph of those who fell at Thermopylai (Hdt. 7.228.2), is as poignant as anything ever said about war dead, and there is nothing of the berserker about the Spartan Anaxibios' remark to his soldiers, when he realized that he was trapped: 'Men, my duty is to die here, but you hurry to safety before the enemy closes' (Xen. *Hell.* 4.8.38). It is the impression one so often gets of ordinary men just doing their duty, which is so moving. Pindar, for example, says of a young man probably killed fighting for Thebes at Oinophyta: 'You breathed out the flower of your youth in the throng of fore-fighters, where the best kept up the struggle of battle with hopes forlorn' (*Isthm.* 7.48–50), and an Athenian who fought at the

Nemea, confessed in court that he did so 'not as one who did not think fighting the Lakedaimonians was a fearful thing' (Lys. 16.17).

But perhaps Simonides should have the final word. A friend of his, the Akarnanian seer, Megistias, was killed at Thermopylai. Before the last day, Herodotos tells us (7.219.1), 'on looking into the sacrifices, he declared the death coming would be with them at dawn', but although Leonidas urged him to go, he sent his only son away instead, and stayed to die with the Spartans he served (Hdt. 7.221). Simonides composed this epitaph for his friend:

> This is the memorial of famed Megistias, whom on a day the
> Medes slew, having crossed the Spercheios river.
> He was a seer, who all the time knowing well the fate
> approaching, had not the heart to desert the captains of Sparta.
>
> (Hdt. 7.228.3)

NOTES

Works referred to by author and date alone or with short title are cited in full in the Bibliography to this volume.

1. Euripides' mother, Kleito, was 'one of the very well born' (Philochoros *ap.* Suidas *s.v.* 'Euripides'), and as a boy he took part in rites in honour of Delian Apollo, in which only the 'first' participated (Theophrastos *ap.* Athenaios 10.424e). He was challenged to an *antidosis* (Arist. *Rh.* 3.15), and went on an embassy to Syracuse (op. cit. 2.6).
2. At Leuktra Sphodrias and his son, Kleonymos, were clearly serving together in the king's entourage for special reasons: cf. Xen., *Hell.* 5.4.25ff and 6.4.14.
3. I exclude forces like the Ten Thousand which could include *pentekostyes* and *enomotiai* (cf., e.g., *An.* 3.4.22), but which were probably modelled on the Spartan army: Xenophon's comrades included a number of Spartans.
4. Mantitheus' claim (Lys. 16.15) that he got himself posted in the front rank at the Nemea, does not necessarily prove that places were decided when the army was mobilized, any more than does Xenophon's view that the best men should be placed in the front and rear (*Mem.* 3.1.8).
5. The nearest I know is the scene on a seventh century aryballos from Thebes, possibly by the same artist as the Chigi vase, the 'Macmillan Painter': K. Friis Johansen, *Les Vases Sicyoniens* (Copenhagen, 1923), pl. XXXI, 1a, b and e (= Salmon, 88, fig. 3). But even in this scene only three of the twelve hoplites depicted are wielding their spears underarm.
6. For the Chigi vase see, for example, Erika Simon, *Die Griechischen Vasen* (Munich, 1976/81), pls 25, 26 and VII. Cf. also the aryballos from Rhodes, possibly again by the 'Macmillan Painter': Johansen (*supra* n. 5), pl. XXXII, 1a, b and d (= Salmon, 86, fig. 1).

7. See *The Sunday Times* 16 April 1989.
8. Reading *harpaleon* with Ahrens for the *argaleon* of the MSS, which seems to make less sense.
9. A grave-enclosure found near Thespiai last century may contain the remains of the Thespiaians killed at Delion: Kirchoff, *Studien zur Geschichte des griechischen Alphabets*[4] (Gütersloh, 1887), 141.
10. For numbers of casualties at First Mantineia, the Nemea, Second Koroneia and Leuktra, for example, see Lazenby, 1985: 128–9, 133–4, 136–8, 143, 143–4, 148, 152–3 and 160. Krentz (*GRBS* 26, 1985: 18) reckons that casualties averaged between 5 per cent for the winners and 14 per cent for the losers.
11. See W. K. Pritchett, 'Observations on Chaeronea', *AJA* 62 (1958), 310.
12. Scenes on vases sometimes show wounded heroes being tended, and presumably this also happened in real life: see, for instance, the cup by the Sosias painter, now in Berlin, showing Achilles bandaging Patroklos (Lazenby 1985: 35, pl. 4).
13. If Pelopidas took part in a battle at Mantineia, it must have been the first, since he was dead before the second. But Thucydides does not mention any Boiotians at First Mantineia, and if Pelopidas had taken part, he would presumably have had to be at least 20 years old, in which case he was 74 when killed at Kynoskephalai.
14. For a critical assessment of Epameinondas see Hanson 1988.
15. Despite W. J. Woodhouse, *King Agis of Sparta* (Oxford, 1933), 80–2, it is difficult to avoid the conclusion that 'someone had blundered'.
16. *Correspondance de Napoléon Ier*, xvii no. 14276 (Observations sur les affaires d'Espagne, Saint-Cloud, 27 août 1808).
17. It is significant that among the proposals of the Athenian revolutionaries in 411 BC, one was that only hoplites should 'share affairs' (cf. Thuc. 8.65.3, 97.1), and see in general Arist. *Pol.* 1279a 37ff., 1297b 1ff.
18. See, for example, S. L. A. Marshall, *Men Against Fire* (New York, 1947); John Keegan, *The Face of Battle* (London, 1976), 48, 53, 71–3.
19. By Xenophon's time the *phiditia* almost certainly had nothing to do with the organization of the army, as they may once have done (Lazenby 1985: 13): Xenophon may be harking back to an earlier, more ideal age.
20. See *supra* n. 11.

5

THE *SALPINX* IN GREEK WARFARE

Peter Krentz

In his tactical manual Arrian distinguishes three kinds of signal useful in war: verbal orders, visual signals, and *salpinx* calls (Arr. *Takt.* 27; cf. Asklep. *Takt.* 12.10 and Aelian *Takt.* 35.2). Verbal orders are the clearest, but 'the clash of arms, the exhortations shouted to one another, the cries of the wounded, the passing of the cavalry, the neighing of horses and the noise of the baggage-train' can make them inaudible. Fog, dust, the sun's glare, a snowstorm, rain, and overgrown or hilly ground obstruct visual signals. The *salpinx*, on the other hand, is good with regard to 'impediments from the air' (*ta ek tou aeros empodia*), that is, it can overcome both aural and visual obstacles. The peculiar conditions of classical Greek battle ought to have made the *salpinx* especially useful, for they only increased the difficulties mentioned by Arrian. Fought mostly during the dry summer season in small valleys ringed by mountains, hoplite battles were dusty and noisy. The widespread use of bronze armor made all blows loud (Tyrtaios 19.14–15 West). In foul weather the noise created by rain and hail hitting such armor made it difficult to hear verbal commands, as Timoleon's Carthaginian opponents discovered in Sicily (Plut. *Tim.* 28.4). Even in the best conditions the standard bronze helmets, with no openings for the ears and small ones for the eyes, must have made hearing extremely difficult, and restricted vision markedly. Lighter caps began to replace these helmets in the late fifth and fourth century, but the helmets did not disappear (Anderson 1970: 28–37). Nevertheless, in spite of these apparently favorable conditions for use, Greeks blew the *salpinx* before and after battles but rarely during a battle itself. I propose to explore what we know about this instrument and its uses, and then to discuss why the Greeks failed to use it more.[1]

Writing in the second century of our era, Pollux described the *salpinx* as 'in shape both straight and curved, made of bronze and iron, with a bone reed (*glotta*)' (4.85). Not all of this description applies to the classical Greek instrument, a narrow cylindrical tube leading to a bell (*kodon*). Both the tube and the bell were normally bronze: Bakchylides 18.3–4 (*chalkodon salpinx*) and Soph. *Aj.* 17 (*chalkostomon kodon*) refer to a bronze bell, while Bakchylides F4 (Snell) 35 (*chalkean salpingon*) and *CIG* 3765 (*chalkelatou salpingou*) mention a bronze *salpinx*. The Museum of Fine Arts in Boston, however, possesses a unique example with a cone-shaped bronze bell and a tube made of thirteen sections of ivory fitting into one another, and excavations on Cyprus have unearthed many fragments and two complete instruments made of clay.[2] The Boston *salpinx* is over 5 ft (1.57 m) long, rather longer than the instruments portrayed on vases, which appear to be 2 ft 6 ins – 4 ft (0.80–1.20 m). The bell, which led to Aristophanes' joke about a gnat's anus being like a *salpinx* (*Clouds* 166), made the *salpinx* more efficient at radiating sound waves at certain frequencies, sound more brilliant, and able to pass on more of the *salpinktes*' energy to the air.[3] On vase paintings the bell varies in shape from a ball to a bulb to a cone. Each shape must have had its own effect on the *salpinx*'s timbre.

The matter of the generator is more complex. Modern trumpets all have a 'lip-reed' generator, that is, a mouthpiece with the player's lips as the vibrating part. It appears the *salpinx* did not have much of a mouthpiece. The Boston example opens out slightly like a cone, and the Cypriot specimens and the few vase paintings that show this end of the *salpinx* also widen only slightly.[4] On the other hand, Pollux clearly describes the *salpinx* as a reed instrument.

Recently A. Bélis offered several arguments supporting Pollux:

(1) Simplicius (*In Phys.* 4.8) says the hydraulic organ used reeds of *salpinges* or *auloi.* Simplicius is correct that organs used reeds: other sources refer to the organ's *auloi* or *tibiae*, and Jean Perrot's standard work on the organ concludes that 'sets of reed pipes were widely used.'[5] Therefore Simplicius may also be correct in referring to a *salpinx* reed. (2) On vases *salpinktai* sometimes appear wearing the *phorbeia*, a leather band which passed in front of the mouth, around the cheeks and behind the head. Best known as an aid for playing the *aulos*, this *phorbeia* relieved the jaws' muscular tension and permitted continuous and powerful playing, as players breathed through their noses.[6] Its use by *salpinktai* makes most sense if the *salpinx*, like the *aulos*, was a reed instrument. (3) Excavators at Pompeii

found three circular bronze instruments, nearly 14 ft (4.20 m) long, with ivory bells. One had a mouthpiece, but the other two were reed instruments.

Bélis concludes that the Greeks had both a *salpinx* with a reed and one without.

This conclusion is not without difficulties. Since Pollux was describing Roman as well as Greek instruments, it is dangerous to apply what he says to the Greek *salpinx* without confirming evidence. The circular trumpets found at Pompeii are not good parallels to the straight Greek *salpinx*. Greek art shows no reed mouthpieces, and the *phorbeia* does not prove the existence of a reed: it might have been used with a 'lip-reed' *salpinx* requiring great force to blow because of its length and narrow diameter. Finally, bone is an unlikely material for a beating reed, which ought to be as flexible as possible. It therefore seems safer to conclude that the Greek *salpinx* was an early form of trumpet, and not a reed instrument. Certainly the *salpinx* blown on the battlefield was not a reed instrument, for reed instruments lack the necessary power. A clarinet or an oboe could not do much on a battlefield, but a trumpet or bugle is something else.

This *salpinx*, which Aristotle described as a 'melody without the lyre' (*Rhet.* 1408a), could probably play only the first harmonics, perhaps only four or five notes, at most eight or nine. In a 1939 test an Egyptian trumpet found in King Tutankhamen's tomb, 1 ft 6 ins (0.515 m) long, sounded only the first, second and third harmonics.[7] The longer Greek *salpinges* would have had a lower fundamental, and therefore could probably obtain more notes. Of course, as Curt Sachs observed, 'it is a grave error to confuse the potentiality of an instrument with the music it actually performed.'[8] Descriptions of the *salpinx*'s sound suggest the *salpinktes* may have played one or two notes as forcefully as possible.[9] Pollux describes its sound as shrill, booming, strong, violent, horrible, disordered, and warlike (4.85), and though he is describing Roman instruments as well as Greek, our earlier sources concur. Aischylos describes its sound as 'piercing' or 'shrill' (*diatoros*) and 'high-pitched' (*hypertonon, Eumenides* 567–8), and Aristotle says an elephant making a noise with its trunk sounded similar to a raucous *salpinx* (*Hist. anim.* 536b). Several sources agree that certain cities in Egypt refused to use the *salpinx* because it sounded like the braying of an ass.[10] Homer, therefore, uses an appropriate simile when he compares Achilleus' terrifying shout at the ditch to the *salpinx*'s conspicuous (*arizele*) sound (*Iliad* 18.219).

Above all the *salpinx* was loud. Homer uses the verb form to describe the clash of gods colliding on the battlefield (*Iliad* 21.388). Pollux claims that a *salpinktes* named Epistades could be heard fifty *stadia* (8.9 km.) away (4.88), and that it was difficult to approach Herodoros the Megarian when he was playing because he blew so hard (4.89). Perhaps more reliably, and certainly more amusingly, Alexander the Great's admiral Nearchos told how his men frightened away a threatening school of whales by shouting, banging on their shields and blowing their *salpinges* (Diod. 17.106.7; Arrian *Indica* 30.4–6; Curtius Rufus 10.1.11–12).

The *salpinx* served a variety of functions ranging from the solemn to the comic, the public to the private. Ps.-Aristotle says that revellers blew less hard in order to make the *salpinx* sound as soft as possible (*De audilibus* 803a). The *salpinktes* who began a drinking contest in Aristophanes (*Acharnians* 1001–3) and another who apparently signaled the start of a dance in armor,[11] we may imagine, blew softly.

Public performances, recorded more frequently in our sources, must have been more demanding. The *salpinx* sounded to begin the annual festival at Plataia (Plut. *Aristeid.* 21.3), as well as to indicate the final lap of horse races at Olympia. Pausanias (6.13.9) tells the story of a Korinthian mare which threw her rider but ran the course and, when she heard the *salpinx*, picked up her pace and finished first. From the fifth century in Boiotia and the fourth century at Olympia *salpinktai* had their own contests.[12] Pollux (4.88) says that *salpinges* summoned the competitors at competitions after Hermon, a comic actor, missed his call. By lot he was to perform after many others, so he left the theater in order to test his voice, and failed to hear the herald's summons when all those in front of him dropped out of the contest. At Argos a religious ceremony included the use of *salpinges* to summon Dionysos (Plut. *Mor.* 364F, 671E). In Aischylos' *Eumenides* a *salpinx* sounds to call the Athenians to assembly (566–70), a custom attested again more than a century later in Demosthenes' *On the Crown*, where Demosthenes describes the panic in Athens when news arrived that Philip II had seized Elateia: the *prytaneis* summoned the general and the *salpinktes* (169). Diodoros adds that the *salpinktai* blew all night long (16.84.3). The *salpinx* might also call for silence at great public occasions, such as when the Athenians said a prayer before departing for Sicily in 415 BC (Thuc. 6.32.1).

These references attest to the widespread use of the *salpinx* for various purposes, and explain why the orator Demades called the *salpinktes* the 'public rooster' (F31). Nevertheless the *salpinx*'s military role so overwhelmed all other uses that Aristophanes could have a character complain that peace would make his instrument worthless (*Peace* 1240–1). Perhaps, he hears, he could turn it into a stand for a *kottabos*-target, or a scale.

The *salpinx*'s combination of a piercing tone with a loud volume suited it to military use. Attested military uses in classical Greece include:

1. Summoning men to arms. Our earliest evidence comes from Bakchylides 18.1–10 (trans. Lattimore):

   King of Athens, the sacred city,
   lord of luxurious Ionians,
   what news of war is this that the *salpinx*'s
   bronze-belled braying call announces?
   Is it some enemy war captain
   overstriding our land's boundaries
   with his own host at heel?
   Is it robbers, whose ways are evil,
   overcoming our shepherds' resistance,
   driving our flocks away?

   Andokides (1.45) describes another military alert, declared during the panic surrounding the affair of the herms and the Eleusinian mysteries in 415 BC. The Boiotians were on the frontier, and the Council told the generals to proclaim that various citizens proceed to various places, and in particular the horsemen were to be summoned by *salpinx* to the Anakeion before nightfall. This passage suggests the Athenians had a separate *salpinx* call to gather the cavalry, and perhaps even calls indicating precise gathering places, though more likely the *salpinktes* stood at the Anakeion and blew for the horsemen until they reached him by following the sound. A third example comes from Sparta. During the earthquake of 465 BC King Archidamos saved the city by sounding the *salpinx* as if the enemy were attacking, in order to get the Spartans out of their homes.[13]
2. Sounding reveille. Plutarch (*Nikias* 9.2) says that the old saying, 'In peace not *salpinges* but roosters awaken sleeping men,' helped incline the Greeks to peace in 421 BC. Polybios (12.26.2) alters the emphasis slightly: 'In war *salpinges* awaken sleeping men, in peace the birds.' J. K. Anderson maintains that this saying can be explained without supposing a particular call for reveille (1965: 2), but such a call seems likely enough.

3. Summoning men to arm and form into line for battle. Aristotle describes what happens when the *salpinx* sounds in a military camp:

   > Each man hears the sound, and one picks up his shield, another puts on his breastplate, and a third his greaves or helmet or belt; one harnesses his horse, one mounts his chariot, one passes on the watchword; the *lochagos* goes to his *lochos*, the *taxiarchos* to his *taxis*, the horseman to the wing, the light-armed runs to his station; all is stirred by a single signal to a flurry of motion according to the ideas of the supreme commander.
   >
   > (*De mundo* 399a–b)

4. Calling for silence. Before the Sicilian expedition departed in 415 BC, a *salpinx* sounded to get everyone's attention for the public prayer (Thuc. 6.31.1). Later when Alkibiades and his men took Selymbria in 409 BC, the Athenian general had the *salpinx* signal for silence so he could have a herald tell the Selymbrians not to take up arms against the Athenians (Plut. *Alk.* 30.7). Similarly when Dion entered Syracuse he had the *salpinx* stop the crowd's noise so he could announce the liberation of the Syracusans (Plut. *Dion* 29.1). As Anderson (1965: 2) notes, however, there need not have been a special signal for silence. Any *salpinx* blast might have been effective, and even if the Athenians did have a special call, the Selymbrians are unlikely to have known what it was.
5. Sounding the charge (*to polemikon*). In its best attested use, the *salpinx* sounded to tell hoplites to lower their spears and charge, as Xenophon makes clear in a description of a parade-ground maneuver (*Anab.* 1.2.17) and later of an actual battle (*Anab.* 6.5.27): to impress the Queen of Cilicia at the close of a troop review, Kyros told the Greek generals 'to lower their arms and advance the whole phalanx. They passed these instructions on to the troops. When the *salpinx* sounded, they lowered their arms and went forward. Then they advanced more quickly and with a shout they were running toward the tents. Terror seized the barbarians, and the Queen fled on her covered carriage and the merchants abandoned their wares and fled, and the Greeks reached the tents with a laugh.' Similarly at the battle: 'The order had been given for spears to be held on the right shoulder, until the *salpinx* sounded; then they were to lower their spears to the attack position and advance steadily without running. . . . When the two

armies were close together the Greek peltasts ran towards the enemy before anyone had given the order. The enemy charged to meet them . . . and drove the peltasts back. But when the phalanx of hoplites approached, moving quickly, and at the same time the *salpinx* sounded and they sang the paian and then they shouted and lowered their spears, the enemy waited no longer, but fled.' At the battle of Syracuse in 415 BC the *salpinx* also sounded for the hoplites after the light-armed clashed (Thuc. 6.69.1).

Xenophon's *Anabasis* mentions the *salpinx* frequently for sounding the charge (see, in addition to 1.2.17 and 6.5.27, 3.4.4, 4.2.1, 8–9, 5.2.14, 7.4.16). Later sources mention it at a number of important battles: Himera in 480 BC (Diod. 11.22.2), Leuktra in 371 BC (Diod. 15.55.3), Mantineia in 362 BC (Diod. 15.85.3), Thebes in 335 BC (Diod. 17.11.3), and Timoleon's battle against the Syracusans (Plut. *Tim.* 27.10). The *salpinx* was obviously part of the standard battle description, and it appears even in fictitious scenes (Euripides, *Herakleidai* 831–2, *Phoen.* 1103, *Rhesos* 988–9).

Salpinktai also gave the signal to attack in naval battles, as is specifically attested for Salamis in 480 BC (Aischylos *Pers.* 396), Abydos in 411 BC (Diod. 13.45.8), Mytilene and Arginousai in 406 BC (Diod. 13.77.5, 99.1), Aigospotamoi in 405 (Plut. *Lys.* 11.2), and Aigina in 388 (Xen. *Hell.* 5.1.9). Vase painting supplies an illustration.[14]

6. Sounding the retreat (*to anakletikon*). Xenophon provides the best evidence when he describes how the generals of the hoplites used the *salpinx* to recall the peltasts who were pillaging Tiribazos' camp (*Anab.* 4.4.22). Xenophon himself took advantage of the distinct calls for 'charge' and 'retreat' to cross a river safely by having his troops retreat when the 'charge' was sounded (*Anab.* 4.3.29–32). Diodoros adds five other examples, both on land (Dionysios' siege of Motya in 397 BC [14.52.5] and battles between the Spartans and Thebans in 377, 369/8 and 362 BC [15.34.3, 65.4, 87.2]) and on sea (the battle of Mytilene in 406 BC [13.79.4]).[15]

For any other commands, the general had to issue orders in advance either by heralds or through subordinate officers, telling the troops to execute the orders when the *salpinx* sounded. A fictitious example occurs in Euripides' *Troiades* 1266–9, where the herald tells the Trojan captives to proceed directly to the ships when the *salpinx* sounds. Even for the above commands, the general had to issue separate orders if he wished to specify how a particular action was to be carried out, as Anderson (1965: 3–4) stresses with regard to Kleon's attempted withdrawal from Amphipolis in 422 BC (Thuc. 5.10.3–4).

In art the *salpinktes* often appears armed as a hoplite or serving among hoplites.[16] But archers[17] and peltasts[18] also serve as *salpinktai*. Moreover the *salpinx* gave cavalry signals. Xenophon mentions this usage during his account of cavalry displays (*Hipparch.* 3.12), and we see a cavalry *salpinktes* in a battle-scene on a red-figure vase.[19] This evidence raises the possibility of separate calls for different types of land troops, a possibility that we saw indicated earlier by the way horsemen were summoned in 415 BC (Andok. 1.45).

The *salpinx*, then, sounded alerts, wake-up calls, summons to arms, and calls for silence. It typically began a hoplite battle. Once the battle had begun, however, the *salpinx* did very little. Even the call for retreat appears only rarely. Why did the Greeks fail to codify a greater number of *salpinx* signals? The advantages seem obvious. The Romans certainly appreciated them. As Aristides Quintilianus says, Rome

> often rejects verbal orders as damaging if they should be discerned by those of the enemy speaking the same language and makes codes through music by playing the *salpinx* – a warlike and terrifying instrument – and appointing a specific melos for each command. When the attack was by line and the approach was by column, she set down special mele, and a different kind for retreat; and when the pivoting was to the left or to the right, again there were specific mele for each; and so she accomplishes every maneuver one after another by means of codes that are on the one hand unclear to the enemy and on the other hand both totally clear and easily recognized by the allies. For they do not hear these codes only in part, rather the whole corps follows a single sound.
>
> (62.6–19, trans. Mathiesen)

In Greek armies, by contrast, commanders issued these kinds of orders verbally. The evidence is especially clear for the Spartans. Xenophon says that the *enomotarchos* issued marching orders verbally (*logoi*, *Lak. Pol.* 11.6), and later adds that his men passed the orders along since the entire *enomotia* could not hear him (13.9). Presumably the Spartan king passed his orders down verbally through the *polemarchoi*, *lochagoi*, and *pentekonteres* who also received his orders after morning sacrifices (Xen. *Lak. Pol.* 13.4–5). At Sphakteria in 425 BC the Lakedaimonians found themselves at a loss because they could not hear commands owing to the enemy's loud shouting (Thuc. 4.34.3). Normally they could, as the instance of the old soldier calling out to King Agis at Mantineia suggests (Thuc. 5.65.2; cf. Xen. *Hell.* 4.2.22). Perhaps the most famous verbal command is Epameinondas' call at the battle of Leuktra: 'Give me one step, and we shall have the victory' (Polyain. 2.3.3). His cry might have been communicated more widely by some sort of visual signal, such as Polyainos says Iphikrates used to get one more step at a crucial moment (3.9.27), perhaps a simple helmet raised on a spear, such as Gorgias used to order his troops to turn around (Polyain. 2.5.2). Here we have an instance similar to Kleon at Amphipolis, with a signal given to initiate the fulfillment of instructions communicated verbally in advance. But the *salpinx* did not necessarily give the signal.

Various considerations may help explain the Greeks' limited use of the *salpinx*. First, hoplite battles lacked complex maneuvers; commanders made their plans in advance and then took their place in line, where, like other hoplites (Thuc. 7.44.1), they knew only what happened in their immediate vicinity. Second, hoplite battles lacked separate contingents or reserves; aside from the light-armed troops who fought before the main clash, the phalanx was the army, and it fought in unison. The Greeks had nothing like the Roman *triplex acies*. Third, all Greek hoplites spoke Greek. Lacking the foreign *auxilia* of Roman armies, the Greeks did not need a generic, understandable code such as the *salpinx* could provide. Finally, and I think most importantly, the scale of Greek engagements was much smaller than that of Roman combats. At Delion and Mantineia and Syracuse, for example, the greatest land battles of the Peloponnesian War, no side ever had more than about 10,000 hoplites. Even the Nemea River and Koroneia, the largest hoplite battles ever fought, involved less than 50,000 total troops. Most hoplite battles were much smaller. In smaller armies, direct verbal orders passed down through officers apparently worked tolerably well.

NOTES

I would like to thank Victor Hanson for inviting me to contribute to this volume and for helpful comments on an earlier draft; Darcy Kuronen of the Collection of Musical Instruments at the Museum of Fine Arts, Boston, for information about the Boston *salpinx*; Sharon Kazee, an oboist, and William Lawing, a trumpeter, for helpful discussions about reed instruments and trumpets.

1. I cite the following works by author's name and date: A. Reinach, 'Tuba,' DarSag 9.522–8; Maux, 'Salpinx,' *RE* Suppl. 2.1.2009–10; Daniel Paquette, *L'Instrument de musique dans la céramique de la Grèce antique* (Paris, 1984); Annie Bélis, 'La Phorbéia,' *BCH* 110 (1986) 205–18. On the military use of the *salpinx*, see J. K. Anderson, 'Cleon's orders at Amphipolis,' *JHS* 85 (1965) 1–5. For good general studies of the trumpet see Philip Bate, *The Trumpet and the Trombone* (2nd edn London, 1978) and Edward Tarr, *The Trumpet*, trans. S. E. Plank and Edward Tarr (Portland, 1988).
2. L. D. Caskey, 'Recent Acquisitions of the Museum of Fine Arts, Boston,' *AJA* 41 (1937) 525–7; M. J.Chavanne, *Salamine de Chrypre*, VI, *Les petits objets* (Lyon, 1975) 205–11 and plates 54–6. These clay *salpinges* may have been votive offerings rather than instruments intended for use.
3. Bate 1978: 16.
4. See Bélis 1986: 213 figs 12–14.
5. Jean Perrot, *The Organ from its Invention in the Hellenistic Period to the end of the Thirteenth Century*, trans. Norma Deane (London, 1971) 159.
6. Bélis 1986: 212.
7. Bate 1978: 96–7. For a detailed study see Hans Hickmann, *La trompette dans l'Égypte ancienne* (Cairo, 1946).
8. Sachs, *The History of Musical Instruments* (New York, 1940) 148.
9. If any *salpinges* were reed instruments, they could sound only a single note (or perhaps, by overblowing, two or three), since they had no holes with which to change the length of the air column, as reed instruments must do to achieve multiple notes.
10. Plut. *Mor.* 150F names Naukratis and Bousiris, while 362E mentions Lykopolis and Bousiris; Aelian *De Natura An.* 10.28 has Abydos, Lykopolis, and Bousiris. These sources may have in mind the Egyptian trumpet, which seems to have been about 2 ft (0.6 m) long, shorter than the Greek (Bate 1978: 96–8).
11. A black figure lekythos in the Walters Art Gallery (Baltimore) shows a *salpinktes* along with dancing hoplites (*ABV* 523 no. 9; see Lillian B. Lawler, *The Dance in Ancient Greece* (Seattle, 1964) 110 fig. 42. The standard article on the pyrrhic dance in art, J. -C. Poursat, 'Les Représentations de danse armée dans la céramique attique,' *BCH* 92 (1968) 550–615, misses this one). The *salpinx*'s limited musical capabilities suggest that it signalled the start of the dance rather than played accompaniment. I thank Steven Lonsdale for this reference.
12. Boiotia: *IG* VII. 419–20, 540 (*SEG* 19.335), 1667, 1760, 1773, 1776, 2448, 2727, 2871, 3195–7, 4147, 4151, 4164. According to Plut. *Mor.* 598D–E, *salpinktai* who happened to be present for the Herakles festival aided the liberation of Thebes in 378 BC. Olympia: Eusebius *Chron.* ad O1.96 [336–32] I 230 Migne; Paus. 5.22.1. Herodoros the Megarian, according to Pollux (4.89), won the contest seventeen times.
13. Plut. *Kimon* 16.5–6; see also Polyain. 1.41.3. This story shows that the Spartans did know and use the *salpinx*, in spite of the oft-repeated point that they marched into battle to the sound of the *aulos* (Athen. *Deipnosoph.* 626b, 627d; Paus. 3.17.5; Plut. *Lykourgos* 21, *Mor.* 1140C; Thuc. 5.70 attests the Spartans' use of the *aulos* when advancing into

battle, but does not deny their use of the *salpinx* for other purposes). Xenophon's account of the Lakedaimonian admiral Gorgopas sounding a naval attack with the *salpinx* confirms the Spartan *salpinx* (*Hell.* 5.1.9). Note also what Eudamidas, the son of Archidamos, said when he heard a philosopher speaking about generalship: 'The speech is admirable, but the speaker is untrustworthy, for he has never heard the *salpinx*' (Plut. *Mor.* 220E).

14. Paquette 1984: T8 (*CVA* Rome Capitole 2 pl. 9.2.1).
15. Plutarch tells a story about a Spartan who let his man go when the call for retreat sounded, even though he had his arm lifted to strike (*Mor.* 236E). But this tale is worthless since it is derived from that of Chrysantas in Xenophon's *Kyroupaideia*, where Kyros summons Chrysantas not by trumpet but by name (4.1.3, modified in Plut. *Comp. Pelop. and Marc.* 3.2).
16. For examples see Paquette 1984: T1, T4, T5, T6, T13 and T14 (*ABV* 294 no. 19; *ARV*^{2} 43 no. 74; *ARV*^{2} 43 no. 74; *ARV*^{2} 8 no. 9; *ARV*^{2} 30 no. 1; *RVAp* 1.36/11 pl. 9.1, respectively) and Bélis 1986: figs 17–19, 21 (*ARV*^{2} 62 no. 77; *ARV*^{2} 43 no. 74 and 55 no. 15; *ARV*^{2} 1628 add. to 135 no. 9; *ARV*^{2} 402 no. 17, respectively.)
17. Paquette 1984: T3 and T12 (*ABV* 294 no. 20 and 256 no. 21).
18. Paquette 1984: T2 and T7 (*ARV*^{2} 455 no. 8 and 70 no. 3).
19. Paquette 1984: T16 (Hellmut Sichtermann, *Griechische Vasen in Unteritalien aus der Sammlung Jatta in Ruvo* (Tübingen, 1966) 60 K 39).

6

THE GENERAL AS HOPLITE

Everett L. Wheeler

In the first confrontation of legion and phalanx King Pyrrhus of Epirus faced the Romans at Heracleia in 280 BC. The Epirote initiated contact by personally leading a cavalry charge. His gleaming, highly decorated armor immediately marked the king in a display of valor equal to his reputation. 'Most of all,' Plutarch says,

> while offering his prowess and physical presence to the contest and stoutly fending off opponents, he did not blur his power of calculation nor even lose his presence of mind. Rather he managed the battle, as though viewing it from afar, running from one spot to another and bolstering those seeming to be overpowered.[1]

Pyrrhus' penchant for heroics typified his career, a striving to equal the fame of his alleged ancestor Achilles, who from at least the late sixth century BC, if not from Homer's own time, symbolized the ideal warrior.[2] Yet Plutarch's description goes beyond the Achilles model in painting Pyrrhus as the ideal general: conspicuous armor, physical prowess in combat, but also the bolsterer of morale and the battlefield manager (cf. Polyb. 10.13.1–5). Pyrrhus showed mastery of the dual functions of generalship which had evolved from Homer's period through the fourth century – leadership in its most literal sense, the physical act of leading; and command, incorporating administration, management, analysis of situations, and oral directives, chiefly mental and verbal properties.[3]

The role of the general in the hoplite battle experience of Classical Greece is significant for the evolution of generalship – the transition from warrior chief to the general of Pyrrhus' mode. Scipio Africanus' reported quip that his mother produced a commander (*imperator*) not a warrior (*bellator*) illustrates the distinction, as does Iphicrates' remark that he was not a cavalryman, a hoplite, an archer, or a peltast, but one who knew how to command all these. Yet from a broader historical perspective many senior commanders continued to lead from the front until the second half of the seventeenth century, and Frederick the Great can be cited as the first general not to wear armor.[4]

The transition from warrior to general, however, far from being a minor military phenomenon, directly reflects the political, social, and economic developments converting a pre-state ('primitive') society to a state. Modifications in the nature and composition of armed forces corresponded to shifts in the relationship of armies to sovereign authority. The emergence of phalanx warfare among the Greeks did not alter invariable command functions, nor did major technological innovations revise the means of command. But improvements in military organization and, especially from the fifth century on, the growing complexities of war and coordination of diversified arms (e.g. the new significance of light infantry and cavalry) multiplied the need for command. Sophistication necessitated more supervision.[5]

Hyperbole about a dramatic shift to phalanx warfare (denied by some: see p. 127) demands caution. No one wiped the old slate of warrior values clean, but rather (as often) the new style accommodated remnants of the old. The chieftains of war bands investing Troy in the *Iliad* espoused a code of honor, whereby each strove to prove himself the best (*aristos*) in a display of martial excellence (*arete*). Valor in battle validated leadership of the group, and *arete* directly related to a warrior's *Risikobereitschaft*.[6] In this society respect among one's peers mattered, as did the glory (*kleos*) of an individual passed to future generations. Skill in combat proved a man's *arete*; death in battle assured *kleos* and fit the noble ideal (*kalon*). Thus a long life and peaceful death rated disdain in comparison to a short life made glorious by a noble death, which could even obliterate a previous existence of mediocrity. Needless to say, the Homeric warrior chief risked his life in the forefront of battle.[7]

The warrior code of the *Iliad* defined the Greek heroic ethos: an aristocracy of warrior princes in competition with each other for personal honor and eternal fame – both won in battle with great personal danger and without higher political goals. In apparent contrast, the hoplite phalanx emerged as the military representative of the polis. This mass infantry formation of files usually eight deep expanded the warrior function from the aristocracy to the middle class and by the fourth century at times also to the lower classes. Integrating aristocrats and shopkeepers, urban dwellers and farmers, the phalanx became (from one viewpoint) a conglomerate of 'interchangeable parts,' in which all put aside personal distinction for the common good of the state. Here was military democracy in action.[8]

The phalanx, however, brought with it a contradiction: although in appearance and practice it seemed a rejection of the earlier style of warfare (the masses, democracy, common good of the state *vs* individual heroes, aristocracy, an individual's *arete*), the ideology of the hoplite remained the heroic ethos of Homer. The Spartan poet Tyrtaeus (ca 650 BC) preached a transvaluation of Homeric *arete*, making death in the phalanx a hero's sacrifice which the polis would compensate with eternal fame.[9] Accordingly, the language of Athenian *epitaphioi* in the fifth and fourth centuries couched praise of the fallen in the epic glory of the individual hero, anchored in the aristocratic tradition but extending elite honors anonymously to all the slain. In such speeches Athens, the city of *arete*, became Achilles.[10] But this transvaluation of the heroic ethos did not constitute the only source of Homeric warrior values. Homer remained the basic text of aristocratic education, which the middle class also pursued, and presented numerous examples of heroic action as paradigms for emulation.[11] Even the 'new' education of fifth-century sophists exploited Homer as an encyclopedia of all knowledge, including military affairs. From this sophistic use of Homer arose in later periods a genre of Homeric *Tactica*, military handbooks deriving the authority of their advice and recommendations from Homeric citations.[12] The phalanx represented equality of risk, required coordinated group action, and functioned for the state; but in battle individual hoplites raised on a diet of Homer no doubt balanced fear with ideals of heroic glory when they sang the paean.[13]

In the transition from warrior chief to Hellenistic general, the Homeric hero of the forefront initially blended into the anonymous mass of equals in the phalanx, although retaining many of the old warrior values. In the fifth and especially the fourth centuries, however, the commander began to re-emerge, as the changing nature of Greek warfare demanded generals with cerebral skills as well as physical prowess. The final stage of the transition would come in the Hellenistic and Roman periods when the complexities of military organization produced a well-defined hierarchy of command (anticipated to some extent in Classical Sparta).[14] The roles of general (*strategos*) and the rank and file (*stratiotai*) became distinct (cf. already Xen., *Anab*. 3.1.37: 401 BC). Physical leadership in battle, often still attested (e.g. Pyrrhus at Heracleia), mattered less than the commander's presence (even if in the rear) and the functions of command. A general's personal daring could merit scorn – a sign of irresponsibility.

But apart from a commander's tactical and strategic functions, what were a general's duties? In a recent study of command Keegan discerns five basic categories: kinship – creation of a bond between commander and commanded; prescription – direct verbal contact between the general and his men; sanctions – a system of rewards and punishment; the imperative of action – strategic preparation and intelligence; and the imperative of example – the physical presence of the commander in battle and the sharing of risk. Any reader of Xenophon's *Cyropaedia* would recognize these categories in Cyrus' activities and admonitions. From another perspective the essence of command lies in the general's symbolizing authority in a way to motivate potentially indifferent or hostile soldiers and to counter psychological and real distance between the commander and the commanded – a view not significantly different from Xenophon's favorite doctrine of willing obedience.[15]

As the concern of this volume is the hoplite battle experience, we must restrict discussion chiefly to Keegan's fifth category, the imperative of example, for which Keegan offers three types of command style: generals who *always*, *sometimes*, or *never* enter battle. From this perspective the transition from Homeric warrior to phalanx commander to Hellenistic/Roman strategos represents a change from 'always' to 'sometimes.' The category of 'never' had but rare application in antiquity.

The problem is to determine when the shift from 'always' to 'sometimes' occurred. *Opinio communis* would date this change generally after 338 BC when distinct functions of strategos and stratiotes had evolved. The Homeric warrior converted to phalanx commander retained his role of physical leader in battle and stationed himself in the front ranks of the phalanx. Indeed, given the limited tactical maneuverability of the phalanx once battle was decided upon and the army was deployed as desired, the commander could do little to influence the outcome of battle and thus took his place in the ranks to aid the physical effort of combat. In this view the high fatality rates of generals and the types of wounds received confirm the commander's station in the front ranks.[16]

The *opinio communis*, however, would benefit from a healthy dose of criticism, for which the foregoing may serve as prolegomena. The transition from Homeric warrior to strategos, in which the age of the

Classical hoplite phalanx plays the central role, merits a more nuanced interpretation. Was the phalanx really so democratic in composition and operation, or did distinctions exist between commanders and commanded? Where did the general stand in the phalanx? Did he *always* participate in combat? My purpose is not to discredit the scenario of the *opinio communis* for phalanx battle but to demonstrate its weaknesses: how much of it rests on unequivocal evidence and how much is logical inference or conjecture?

Alexander the Great's exploits only marginally enter consideration, since he fought in the Macedonian tradition of cavalry as the predominant arm, and Philip II's reforms consolidating nearly two centuries of Greek military developments marked a new departure. Alexander's fondness for personal combat, his *to philokindynon* (Lucian, *Dial. Mort.* 12.5), would represent not a progression toward the battle manager but an anomaly, a retrogression to the warrior chief, prompted both by the demands of Macedonian kingship for strong personal leadership and by Alexander's own Homeric fixation with Achilles.[17]

Any assessment of the general's role in hoplite battle, however, immediately hits the stonewall of unyielding sources. Only Thucydides and Xenophon offer contemporary accounts by men of military experience, to be supplemented by secondary material in Diodorus Siculus, Plutarch, and others. No detailed account of a hoplite battle between rival phalanges exists before Thucydides' narrative of the Peloponnesian War,[18] and there is room to query both the frequency of formal pitched battles between Greek phalanges in the sixth and certainly the seventh centuries, and the number of the ritualistic aspects of hoplite battles, set within the prescribed but unwritten rules of war for the Greek in-group, which derive from romanticized notions about the Archaic Period of Panhellenists of the fourth century.[19] Even when details about pitched battles become more available in Xenophon and other sources for the fourth century, references to the battle role of generals or other officers are episodic at best. Furthermore, the contemporary sources largely derive from a period when Greek warfare underwent drastic changes and professionalism has already begun to infiltrate the phalanx, as seen in the rise of career officers, the use of mercenaries, and the establishment of elite units (*epilektoi*), often trained by professional drillmasters (*hoplomachoi*).[20] Thus the scanty and scattered sources complicate the task of disentangling a clear view of the general from the phalanx's 'interchangeable parts,' and the search for a 'typical' hoplite battle in its 'pure form' unadulterated by changing historical conditions is illusory. Only a composite picture is possible.

I

Given these caveats, examination of the general as hoplite should begin with the tradition of the warrior chief's combat leadership and the emergence of Greek massed infantry in phalanx formation.[21] Pre-state warfare (also called primitive warfare or submilitary combat) constituted an expansion of animal-hunting techniques to the human species – a connection still stressed by Xenophon and Plato.[22] War bands, in many cases representatives of a kin group, assembled with little obligation for individuals to participate, to remain in the venture once begun, or to obey orders from some chief, often only another warrior venerated for past success but without authority to discipline or to ensure obedience to commands. Apart from group motives for combat, such as tension release, revenge, or other causes (normally not economic), the individual saw war as a means of personal glory, recognition, and prestige – drives leading to tactical confusion and incompetence, as each fought for his own distinction. The venerated warrior who led the group could be marked by some token of authority, such as a special head-dress like that of the chief of a band seen in a Neolithic cave painting.[23]

To no surprise, many of these 'primitive' traits correspond to the warfare of the *Iliad* which, despite some Mycenaean heirlooms, surely reflects the combat characteristics of a pre-state society. Nestor urges organization of the war bands by tribes and phratries (i.e. real or mythical kin groups), a principle the Rhodians already followed,[24] and the Achaeans delight in ambush, a key feature of pre-state warfare.[25] A drive for *arete* and individual distinction motivates both the primitive and the Homeric warrior, who participates in or shirks battle at his own discretion, and even in combat jumps forward as a *promachos* or retreats to the war band without a sense for discipline or coordinated group action.[26] Particularly apt is comparison with Tacitus' description of German war chieftains who, without authority to punish, lead their war bands primarily by their own example of courage, even charging out in front of their group in battle.[27] Both the Homeric and the Germanic heroic societies display an egalitarianism among those who enjoy the privileges of the warrior function and offer an equal opportunity to all these to display their *arete/virtus*. Valor and social privileges are reciprocal.[28] An Homeric warrior may be *aristos* in counsel, physical form, or other respects, but excellence in combat rather than command skills or strategy was what counted most.[29]

The Homeric warrior chief's tactical function, however, tied to interpretation of the term *promachos*, is not entirely clear, for the issue involves the thorny problems of the hoplite phalanx's date of origin and the possibility of the hoplite phalanx in some form in Homer and Tyrtaeus, not to mention the need to distinguish military *Realien* from the selection of events for dramatic emphasis in Homeric epic. A full discussion of these matters lies beyond the scope of this chapter, but a few observations are pertinent.

Mass combat, certainly evident in the *Iliad*, does not necessarily indicate use of a phalanx in the sense of a mass infantry formation many ranks deep, composed of distinct subunits and obedient to definite commands and coordinated movement. Three schools of thought on the phalanx in Homer have emerged in recent years. Pritchett has revived the view of totally organized, disciplined armies at Troy with arguments based on analogies with ancient Near Eastern warfare and the accuracy of Homeric commentators. Accordingly, the *promachoi*, whose duels in *monomachia* the poet emphasizes, represent a forward echelon (company or battalion) from the main body, but mass combat decides the battles.[30] Latacz (1977) presents an intermediate position, whereby a phalanx of massed organized units (continuity of rows) exists, but a formation not identical to the Classical Greek phalanx. *Promachoi* constitute the first rank of this phalanx and their skirmishing and duels are preliminary to mass combat to decide the battle. Third, Van Wees rejects use of any sort of phalanx: Homer describes only chieftains (*basileis*) and their personal bands of *hetairoi*, who occasionally mass into unorganized dense throngs under conditions of battle.[31]

Although all three schools can be faulted in details, Latacz's view of a proto-phalanx (but not necessarily his scenario of Homeric battle) and Van Wees' notion of chieftains with their retinues correspond more closely to the stage of political and social development in the Greek world ca 750–700 BC than Pritchett's disciplined, organized armies, which assume a more advanced degree of state organization than sources for this period attest. Formations which lack control and evaporate immediately in battle, and chieftains who fight or shirk battle at their own whim resemble submilitary combat.[32] Denial of mass combat, however, is too extreme.[33] Moreover, all mass infantry formations do not signify a phalanx in its classical Greek sense: a single attack column of six files, each eleven men deep, as seen on the

Sumerian Stele of the Vultures (third millennium) need not indicate a phalanx, as Pritchett (*War* 4.8) presumes, nor does it fit the classical definition of a phalanx – a formation broader than it is deep (cf. n. 21 *supra*). Caesar refers to Helvetian and German formations as a phalanx, a term which Latin authors equated with the German *cuneus*, although the organizational structure of this formation (if it had one) is not precisely known.[34] By analogy with German practice, a proto-phalanx and retinues of individual leaders need not be contradictory (cf. Tac., *Ger.* 6.4).

Although concrete Homeric meanings for the terms *stix, phalanx, pyrgos*, and *oulamos* are probably beyond our knowledge, and certainly it has been too tempting to define them rigidly as fixed tactical/organizational units,[35] Homer does offer insight to rudimentary progress in Greek warfare. Apart from the *Iliad*'s problematic Catalogue of Ships, Nestor's advice to organize by tribes and phratries (*Il.* 2.362), Hector's division of the Trojan attack on the Achaean ships into five groups under subordinate chiefs (*hegemones: Il.* 12.86–7), and Achilles' distribution of the Myrmidons into five units likewise under *hegemones*, apparently subordinate to two *promachoi* (*Il.* 16.168–219) indicate a concern for organization, even if that organization is not maintained in combat. In the latter two cases the need to share the leadership of larger forces is also apparent. Such concerns surpassing the elementary chieftain – *hetairoi* model, it can be argued, may demonstrate the initial stage of progress from submilitary to military combat and the beginning of the transition to the classical phalanx.

Some change in the function of the war-band leader can also be discerned. In most cases the *basileis* arrange their forces before battle, exhort them, and physically lead. Comparison with Germanic practice shows that they may dash forward from the group (hence the term *promachos*), for they lead by example, which their *hetairoi* seek to emulate.[36] Personal exposure justified societal privileges, usually hereditary for Homeric chieftains, although *promachos* was not a title and the *basileis* did not yet have the monopoly on *arete* which Pindar claimed for the aristocracy of his day.[37] The retinues of chieftains probably consisted of both young nobles and men of lesser birth, who (by analogy with German practice) could win ennoblement through valor on the battlefield.[38]

Certainly fighting skill and bravado constituted the warrior chieftain's two most important functions in battle, but Hector offers at least one hint that larger considerations were beginning to enter the picture when, conspicuous in his shining armor during the initial Trojan attack on the Achaean ships, he is everywhere at once, now gleaming in the front ranks, then encouraging men in the rear. After Agamemnon drove the Trojans back to the Scaean Gate, Hector rallies the Trojans and leads the counter-attack to the ditch of the Achaean camp, where he reorganizes the Trojans into five assault divisions and is the first to enter the enemy camp.[39] This is not the behavior of a warrior chieftain but of a commander whose acts resemble those of Pyrrhus at Heracleia in his role as battle manager (cf. Plut., *Pyrrh.* 16.7–8). Indeed Hector, although like his peers covetous of personal honor, also fights for his family and his city, thus anticipating Tyrtaeus' transvaluation of the heroic warrior code for a political goal – the defense of his country.[40]

After Homer, details of the transition from warrior chieftain and *promachos* to phalanx commander are almost totally lost in the scanty primary sources for the seventh and sixth centuries – mainly fragments of poets, whose military information (although often firsthand) is subject to dispute. The material evidence of archaeology takes up some of the slack. Between ca 725 and ca 675 BC the elements of the hoplite panoply began to appear, most significantly the *hoplon*, a heavy shield ca 3 ft (almost a metre) in diameter, carried on the left arm by an armband and a hand grip and offering full protection only to the left side of the body. In open duels between individuals and particularly in retreat the *hoplon* provided less protection, but a closely spaced rank of men each covering his colleague's exposed right side (cf. Thuc. 5.71.1) presented a formidable obstacle.[41] Between ca 675 and ca 650 BC vase paintings begin to show rows of hoplites in combat, which some interpret as evidence for a true phalanx in action. Yet debate rages over a 'chicken-or-the-egg' problem: did hoplite armor perfect a formation already in use, did it immediately create a new style of battle, or was the phalanx the outcome of experimentation over time with a new type of armament?[42] If, as argued above, a proto-phalanx can be discerned in Homer and elements of a transition from pre-state to state warfare also appear, continuation of the process in the seventh century would be expected. Tyrtaeus, however, a most fragmentary but crucial primary source containing detailed combat data, scarcely confirms the view of a fully developed phalanx in the vase paintings.

Some doubt the presence of the true hoplite phalanx in Tyrtaeus (fl. probably ca 650 BC), but also in Callinus (fl. 700–650 BC), Mimnermus (fl. end of seventh century), and even Alcaeus (ca 620 to after 580 BC).[43] Certainly new elements appear: heavy infantry (*panoploi*) and light infantry without armor (*gymnetes*) have distinct functions. The latter skirmish with missiles under the protection of the fully armored or run forward from the main body of the *panoploi*, which seems reserved for close combat.[44] Furthermore, Tyrtaeus repeatedly emphasizes unified effort and maintaining formation; *promachos* now means a 'fighter in close combat,' not one in advance of the main body.[45] The fragments strongly imply a learning process, a lesson from Tyrtaeus the alleged 'schoolmaster' (cf. Paus. 4.15.6; schol. in Pl., *Leg*. 1.629A) – not just for inexperienced youth, but development of a new method of battle for all.

Tyrtaeus' *panoploi*, however, lack unified armament: some carry a full-body shield and others a smaller one, a diversity of equipment which corresponds to that in battle scenes on Late Geometric vases and which does not *per se* negate use of a phalanx.[46] More serious is fr. 11.35–8, where the most natural interpretation of the Greek indicates that the *gymnetes* are integrated alongside the hoplites, not deployed separately on the flanks or behind the heavy infantry.[47] Indeed, decisive against a fully developed phalanx in the seventh century is the total absence in both Tyrtaeus and the vase paintings of mutual support between men in files and any indication of the *othismos* – the great shoving match of the classical hoplite battle.[48] Tyrtaeus' references to shield-to-shield combat (e.g. 11.11–14, 29–34; 19.18–21 West) give no hint of mutual support within files. Likewise, the best representation of the 'phalanx' among the vase paintings, the Chigi vase of ca 650 BC or later, shows only a succession of parallel ranks with remarkable distance between them.[49]

Tyrtaeus' fragments, in comparison to Homeric battle, reveal a definite shift toward mass formation, close order of ranks (but not necessarily files), and a more sophisticated organization, but the classical hoplite phalanx has not yet evolved in the seventh century. With the spread of hoplite equipment throughout the Greek world and the re-emergence of the state, available manpower perhaps also increased, as the warrior function was extended beyond the aristocracy – that is, if theories of a connection between the rise of tyrants and the phalanx have any validity.[50] Nevertheless, the rate of progress in military development need not have been identical or even consistent in all areas. Fragments of Archilochus (680–40 BC) and Alcaeus indicate perhaps a more fluid, open style of warfare in the Aegean area than that of Tyrtaeus in the Peloponnese, and one which preserved the Homeric warrior's tenet that success in combat measured prestige and fame regardless of the means employed (Schwertfeger 1982: 262–4, 273–80). Even for the sixth century the occurrence of general mobilization by poleis for major battles can be questioned (Connor 1988: 6–7).

In contrast, Tyrtaeus' transvaluation of the heroic ethos emphasized another aspect of the Homeric warrior, the noble death in battle (esp. fr. 10 West), and had a more significant influence on the ethos of the hoplite and his commanding officer. The 'Spartan imperative' 'to conquer or die' could, at least by the late fourth century, be traced to Tyrtaeus.[51] A general's desire for a heroic death would be by no means limited to Spartans in the age of the hoplite phalanx.

During the phalanx's continued evolution in the seventh century specific references to the combat role of commanders vanish in the poverty of the contemporary sources. Logic dictates, however, that if the Homeric *promachos*, now in hoplite armor, yielded advanced skirmishing to the *gymnetes* and reserved himself for close combat, the place of distinction became the front rank of the ordered mass formation in Tyrtaeus. Social as well as military considerations shaped this development, for not only did this formation offer maximum benefit from the *hoplon*, but also the extended single line (however deep) permitted more participants to share simultaneously in the opportunity to display their *arete* and win glory than a line of individual units with intervals between them. Analogy with the Roman phalanx of the Servian constitution would also indicate placement in files according to birth and/or wealth, i.e. ability to equip oneself, with the richest and the hereditary aristocracy in the front rank.[52] In fact the names of some special units (*epilektoi*) in phalanges of the Classical Period, such as the *Heniochoi* and *Parabatai* (Charioteers and Chariot-fighters) at Thebes (a city known for its archaism) and units or social classes called *Hippeis* (cavalrymen but fighting as hoplites) at Sparta and Athens, could represent a tradition linked to the earliest days of the transitional phalanx, although membership in such units/classes in the fifth and fourth centuries was no longer a hereditary privilege.[53]

Nevertheless, placement of aristocrats in the first rank of the phalanx does not necessarily solve the problem of where the phalanx commander stood or what he did. Tyrtaeus and other archaic poets write from the perspective of the individual soldier and offer little explicitly about commanders. A later tradition making Tyrtaeus a general in the Second Messenian War lacks credibility, since Spartan armies before the fifth century always served under one of the two Spartan kings or a royal relative.[54]

Tyrtaeus' only direct reference to a commander, the lacunose fr. 19.11 West laconically states: 'we shall obey (our) leader(s)' (*peisometh' hegem*[*o*). Tyrtaeus may refer (depending on whether *hegemon* is restored in the singular or plural) to one or both Spartan kings, occasionally called *hegemones*,[55] but their place in the first rank of the phalanx is not so definite as often assumed (see pp.147–52). Restoration in the plural could alternatively indicate the file leaders (*protostatai*), who could be termed *archontes* (Xen., *Lac. Resp.* 11.5, cf. Thuc. 5.66.4). The latter view, of course, assumes (contrary to Tyrtaeus' evidence) both the existence of files and some form of the Spartan organization seen in Thucydides and Xenophon. Yet Spartan mobilization by *obai* and tribes, most probable in Tyrtaeus' day, in no way proves a fully developed phalanx in use.[56] Tyrtaeus' *hegem[o* is probably best taken as a reference to the Spartan king(s) and could signify another innovation – a definite command system quite unlike the Homeric *basileis* and their *hetairoi*, for Tyrtaeus' *hegemon* seems to require obedience.

A contemporary of Tyrtaeus offers a parallel development from his mercenary experience in the north Aegean. Archilochus (fr.114 West) states his preference for the 'down-to-earth' commander lacking pretensions and capable of empathy with his men, rather than the conceited officer fastidious about his personal appearance. From the standpoint of military literature Archilochus' contrast gives a prototype of the *miles gloriosus* and the first attempt to define the ideal general, here seen as the commander establishing kinship with his men – bridging the gap between commander and commanded (cf. Hanson 1989: 110–11). This fragment first attests the term 'strategos,' which then vanishes until Aeschylus about 150 years later (*LSJ*^{9} s.v.), although (less strictly) the word certainly became prominent in the late sixth century BC, the period of Cleisthenes' reforms at Athens. Indeed nothing guarantees that strategos in Archilochus denotes a 'general,' i.e. the highest ranking officer, rather than simply a commander of unspecified rank. Terminology for officers no doubt evolved over the centuries (cf. the terms *stratelates* and *anax*: Eur., *Supp.* 162, 688).

The novelty of the term 'strategos' requires examination, for which an anchor derives from the Athenian reform of 501/500 BC, creating a board of ten strategoi as tribal commanders, elected one from each Cleisthenic tribe.[57] This innovation should be viewed against the background of Greek constitutional development in the Archaic Period when, as the polis developed from monarchy, military command became institutionalized in civic magistrates, and only Sparta retained hereditary kings, a peculiar collegial monarchy with limited domestic powers but full command of field armies.

In the seventh century a magistrate called the polemarch first appears at Corinth, Sicyon, Athens, and probably also Sparta. The title implies military command and (except at Sparta) seems to indicate delegation of a king's military functions to a non-royal magistrate. Aristotle attributes the establishment of the post at Athens to the effeminacy of kings. Thus (in the Athenian tradition) Ion, the mythical eponymous founder of the Ionians and their customary four tribes, was summoned to become *stratarches* (polemarch). Although perhaps originally an *ad hoc* post, the polemarch became one of the annually selected nine archons by the second half of the seventh century.[58] In contrast, the Spartan polemarch remained strictly a military commander (eventually numbering six – each in command of a *mora*), the second level of field command, closely associated with the kings, and serving in the council of war.[59] Sources drawing upon Ephorus assert that Cypselus at Corinth (ca 657–25 BC) and Cleisthenes at Sicyon (ca 600–570 BC) were polemarchs before becoming tyrants – hence theories of a connection between tyrants and the phalanx – although no evidence of their military activity as polemarchs is known.[60]

Anachronistic and imprecise language in Herodotus and Aristotle impedes tracing the relationship between the office of polemarch and the term strategos at Athens between the seventh century and the polemarch's replacement in the top military command by the board of strategoi in the reforms of 487/6 BC.[61] Some believe the pre-Cleisthenic army consisted of contingents from the four tribes, each commanded by a strategos subordinate to the polemarch. These tribal leaders, probably not elected and imprecisely called phylarchs in Herodotus (5.69.2), were most likely tribal kings (*phylobasileis*).[62] To deny, however, that an Athenian army scarcely if ever mobilized before Cleisthenes' reforms seems, despite Peisistratid reliance on mercenaries, too extreme and renders the 'new' but inexperienced Athenian army's twin victories of ca. 506 BC over the Boeotians and Chalcidians too accidental.[63] Peisistratus' need to disarm the Athenian people, particularly those of the *asty*, points (contrary to Frost's (1984) arguments) in a different direction, and emphasizes the slow mobilization of the rural population which Cleisthenes' reforms attempted to correct.[64]

Certainty about the Cleisthenic title of the ten new tribal leaders (whether phylarch as Hdt. 5.69.2 or strategos as Arist., *Ath. Pol.* 22.2) is elusive, but Callimachus the polemarch still functioned as commander of the Athenian army at Marathon in 490 BC, where in the tradition of the king's military function he held the place of honor on the right flank.[65] Before the reforms of 487/6 BC the strategoi served as tribal commanders and consulted with the polemarch (cf. Hdt. 6.109–10). Taxiarchs, first attested in Aeschylus, were then created to replace the strategoi when they took over the polemarch's military function and *taxis* replaced *phyle* as the designation for the tribal contingents of hoplites. The existence of both taxiarchs and strategoi before 487/6 BC would involve an unnecessary duplication of function.[66]

Why did the term 'strategos' not attested since Archilochus become the name of the new Cleisthenic tribal commanders? A theory that strategos signified an *ad hoc* commander for campaigns outside Attica is attractive, but lacks detailed support: an Athenian strategos in the First Sacred War is as mythical as the war itself, and Peisistratus' *strategie* in the capture of Megarian Nisaea before 561/60 BC must surely be an anachronism for the post of polemarch.[67] Terminology for commanders was certainly in flux, if *stratarches* really was the original term for polemarch (Hdt. 8.44.2, cf. Arist., *Ath.Pol.* 3.2), and Archilochus (fr. 114 West), the only secure occurrence of strategos before the fifth century BC, probably refers to the commander of a mercenary band. Furthermore, if Cleisthenes' reforms aimed to eliminate aristocratic influence in Athenian government,[68] it is plausible that strategos was chosen to designate the ten new tribal commanders because this relatively obscure term lacked aristocratic taint.[69]

Emergence of the strategoi as a new civic magistracy at Athens in the late sixth and early fifth centuries corresponds to the date of the earliest attestations of the term 'hoplite' (Snodgrass 1964b:204). The twin subjects of this paper have at last achieved their initial union. Despite the absence of detailed accounts for pitched battles in the sixth century, a fully developed Athenian phalanx faced the Persians at Marathon with no hint in Herodotus (6.111–14, cf. 7.9β.1–2) that the formation was new. But the date of the Athenian phalanx's initial appearance should be queried.

Certainty on the matter is not possible. Reorganization of the

Athenian army in Cleisthenes' reforms may have perfected use of this formation, although the *Zeugitai* class at Athens, if indeed a term for middle-class hoplites, dates at latest from Solon's reforms in the early sixth century, and the *Zeugitai* possibly existed earlier.[70] Components of the army at Marathon were still *phylai* (not yet *taxeis*), and subtribal units, such as the *lochos* (under a *lochagos*) are first attested at Plataea. Plato, however, knew the term *trittyarches*, a subtribal officer who, like the term *trittyes*, could antedate Cleisthenes.[71] Despite the infrequency of references to subtribal units in the Athenian army, both the Cleisthenic and old Ionian tribes were too large to be the sole unit of military organization, and kin groups, the basis of the pre-Solonian constitution, must have also shaped army organization at some point, although as seen in Homer and Tyrtaeus, existence of subunits does not guarantee use of a true phalanx of the Classical Period.[72] Perhaps the best evidence comes from law, in which the state institutionalizes practice. Athenian military law on desertion, thought to derive from Solon, defined cowardice as refusal to serve (*astrateia*) and abandonment of one's rank in battle (*lipotaxia*). Punishment of desertion, which in the phalanx could prove disastrous for the whole army, must surely imply the fully developed phalanx in use. Unfortunately, Athenians of the late fifth and fourth centuries were inclined to attribute inaccurately all sorts of laws to Solon, but a law on desertion would fit the context of Cleisthenic military reforms.[73] At latest, the Cleisthenic Athenian army probably deployed as a classical phalanx.

Thus Marathon, the earliest Greek battle for which a reconstruction can be attempted (cf. n.18 *supra*), affords the first opportunity to study the general as hoplite in the classical phalanx. Herodotus' tactical account provides no explicit reference to the role of the commanders until after the rout of the Persians, when Callimachus the polemarch met a heroic death proving his *arete* in the assault on the Persian ships (perhaps an indication that he personally led the charge), and Stesilaus, one of the strategoi, also perished in this stage of the battle.[74] Both died, however, in the melée after the enemy's rout when the phalanx often had lost its pristine order of ranks (Pl., *Lach.* 182A–B). Of course Herodotus' language may be no more than a rhetorical eulogy of Callimachus, devoid of significance for where the polemarch/strategos stood in the phalanx. Parallels from later battles suggest that generals often were wounded or killed in the rout stage of a hoplite battle – therefore no support for a view that the commander *always* stood in the front rank.[75] Furthermore, despite the apparent double envelopment of the Persians who broke the Athenian center, the tradition on Marathon provides no hint that Callimachus, Miltiades, or anyone else in the role of battle manager planned this maneuver. Except for occasional heroics, the Homeric warrior would seem to have faded into the anonymity of the democratic phalanx.

II

The age of the fully developed hoplite phalanx extends to the battle of Chaeronea (338 BC). So far this study has traced chronologically the development of the phalanx and the combat role of its commander from a period of pre-state warrior chieftains in Homer to the institutionalized positions of Spartan king and Athenian strategos. The relative abundance of evidence for the fifth and fourth centuries now necessitates a more analytical approach to the transition from phalanx commander to the Hellenistic/Roman battle manager – essentially a change of emphasis from the warrior's physical leadership to the verbal and mental requirements of a commanding general. Although the term strategos rapidly spread throughout the Greek world in the fifth century,[76] the available primary sources (predominantly Athenian) permit a glance at the social and intellectual milieu of the transition at Athens, which probably applied in varying degrees to many other *poleis* of the fifth and fourth centuries.

It is important to emphasize the newness of the concept of the strategos. Initially the people's election of these magistrates mattered little, as aristocrats continued to dominate the strategic board (Themistocles being the only notable exception) until the death of Pericles. The generals as individuals continued to receive the lion's share of glory for military success from the Persian wars to the end of Cimon's ascendency (461 BC), when with the establishment of a public funeral for the war dead and its attendant *epitaphios logos* in 464 BC, anonymity of individuals' contributions and a collective glorification of the city became the norm.[77] This equal distribution of glory approximates to a new wave of democratic reforms from 462 BC on. Yet young aristocrats could be confident that their claim to innate *arete*, fortified by gymnastic training and equipped with instruction in Homer and archaic poets, provided them with 'the right stuff' for leadership, such as their fathers and grandfathers, the men of Marathon, had demonstrated.[78] An 'old oligarch' could boast that even in a democracy the people craved personally profitable magistracies, but were content to leave the important matters of generalship to the most capable men (Ps.-Xen., *Ath. Pol.* 1.3).

As the progress of Athenian democracy and imperialism converted the Delian League into Empire, the sophistic movement attempted to revolutionize education, turning knowledge into a collection of *technai*, Homer into an encyclopedia, and crafty rhetoric into the key to a political career. War itself became a *techne*, when first maintenance of the Empire, then the Peloponnesian War (431–04 BC) reinforced the military functions of Athenian strategoi (also the chief civil magistrates after 487/6 BC) and demanded increasing professionalism. Until his death in 429 BC Pericles the aristocrat, friend of sophists and skillful strategist, astutely guided Athenian democracy, but his death left a power vacuum in Athenian politics, exacerbating an issue probably already debated – who should be elected a strategos? How to define the good general?

In a sense the debate had raged since 501/500 BC, but conservatives first demonstrably raised military competence as a criterion for the strategos in response to high casualties after Cimon's ostracism (461 BC) and again in the 420s, when non-aristocratic demagogues began to manipulate the *ecclesia*.[79] The radical Cleon, however, could sling the same mud at the strategos Nicias for not actively supporting the Athenians at Pylos (425 BC): 'if our strategoi were men (*andres*)' (Thuc. 4.27.5). Euripides joined the debate in 422 BC, interspersing his *Suppliants* with aphorisms about the good general. Indeed the eulogies of the seven heroes who died at Thebes offer a composite description of the ideal general's traits of character, that is temperance, unselfishness, endurance of hardships, and devotion to the state.[80] Similarly, Thucydides turned the new genre of history into a textbook for strategoi (as both politicians and generals) to study – especially the models of Themistocles the astute general and Pericles the wise statesman.[81] Xenophon's Agesilaus and his fictitious Cyrus the Great, just as Isocrates' portrait of Timotheus (15.107–28), continued the concern for defining the good general into the fourth century.

As war became a *techne*, significant changes occurred. First, Achilles, the traditional ideal warrior, no longer satisfied the new complexities of generalship. The wily Odysseus emerged as an alternative model stressing intelligence, cleverness, and trickery instead of brute force and open confrontation. Themistocles, the master of stratagems, came to represent the first Odyssean general, whose trickery in war corresponded to the skillful craftiness of sophistic rhetoric.[82] Sophocles would indirectly discuss the ideal general in 409 BC with the contrast of Odysseus and Achilles as a major theme of the *Philoctetes*. Second, *techne* denoted a teachable skill. Hence generalship could be learned from Homer, lessons from *hoplomachoi*, or by digesting this skill from didactic handbooks, a genre the sophists developed.[83] Thucydides sought to teach strategoi their craft through the medium of history, but Xenophon in such works as the *Hipparchikos* and the *Cyropaedia* and Aeneas Tacticus in his *Strategika*, a military encyclopedia, founded the new genre of military theory.[84] Third, these changes affected not only strategoi but also the hoplites. Courage (*arete, andreia*) could now be taught as well as inherited, and excessive emphasis on bravery alone could be disastrous (Eur., *Supp*. 161–2). A basic tenet of the hoplite's ethos established by Tyrtaeus was being questioned.[85] Aristotle (*EN* 3.7.13–8.9) continued this discussion in his tripartite distinction of courage, whereby he rejected the new military trends: courage through fear and discipline and courage through the mercenary's professionalism were morally inferior to the citizen-hoplite's desire for honor and avoidance of cowardice – the shame culture which constituted the hoplite's Homeric inheritance.[86]

Definition of the good general, growing military professionalism, and the emergence of a new type of commander preferring intelligence to bravery, all form the background for the transition from phalanx general to the battle manager. Still another trend, however, also comes into play – the rise of great individuals, all commanders at one time or another, who resisted or refused to be bound within the restraints of the polis. Pausanias and Themistocles in the Persian wars, Alcibiades and, to a lesser extent, Brasidas and Lysander in the Peloponnesian War, the famous mercenary commanders of the fourth century, and the tyrants Dionysius I and Jason of Pherae mark stages in a progression toward military monarchy, often seen as a trend divorcing civil from military functions within the polis, and culminating in the greatest of all the 'great individuals,' Alexander the Great, and subsequently the apotheosis of the charismatic in Hellenistic ruler-cult.[87]

A few examples will suffice to demonstrate the growth of the general's personal importance. After Marathon Miltiades desired to claim sole credit for the victory by having his name inscribed on the depiction of the battle on the Stoa Poecile. The Athenians refused this honor, although they compromised by allowing Miltiades' figure a prominent place in the painting. Similarly, Pausanias had the tripod dedicated at Delphi from the Persian spoils at Plataea inscribed with a couplet attributing the victory to himself alone. The Spartans were outraged, erased the couplet, and added a list of all the Greek allies. A few years later, the Athenians also refused Cimon the privilege of inscribing his name on three stone herms set up in the Stoa of Hermae to commemorate his capture of Eion from the Persians. In all these cases victory was still believed to be the fruit of collective action, but a century later Iphicrates would be distinguished as the first strategos to have his own name instead of his city's inscribed on the spoils of war.[88]

Likewise the anonymity of individuals and the collective glory of the polis characteristic of the Athenian *epitaphios logos* yielded to a new prominence for generals in Hyperides' speech for the dead of the Lamian War (323–22 BC): a city could be praised for its policy and the dead for their *andreia*, but Leosthenes the strategos authored the policy and led the army as *hegemon*. Thus praise of Leosthenes denoted praise of his soldiers and praise of the victory was to honor the general and his men simultaneously, for the general's responsibility lies in good planning and ensuring that his army wins. For Hyperides *arete* belongs to the strategos alone.[89] The general of the hoplite phalanx has turned into the Hellenistic strategos.

If the general outline of the transition from Homeric warrior to battle manager is now clear, the details of that process in the age of the hoplite phalanx remain clouded. To view the problem schematically, the individualism of the Homeric warrior's physical leadership blended into the anonymous collective action of the phalanx, which as a group shared the laurels of *arete*. Subsequently the commander as an individual re-emerged, now to direct more than to participate in the group's action and once again to claim the most glory. It can be posited *a priori* that the warrior chieftain never lost his distinction within the group: his immersion into the phalanx and apparent obscurity are an illusion of scanty sources. Hanson (1989:107–16) has strongly argued, however, a view of 'the soldier's general' who inspired his men by becoming one of them and equally enduring the risk of personal combat. To what extent does the phalanx commander as a 'soldier's general' represent the true state of affairs, or is this simply an aspect of a general's 'mask of command'?

In the democratic phalanx of 'interchangeable parts' social distinctions had no place, since qualification to serve depended on the ability to furnish one's own equipment. Except for mercenaries, inclusion in the phalanx or relegation to the light infantry (*psiloi*, peltasts, archers, etc.) resolved the social question. Hoplites belonged to the middle or upper class until the fourth century (cf. Diod. 18.10.1) and usually had the means for their own servants to carry their equipment on campaign. In the Spartan army, where *perioikoi* could be hoplites, Spartiate could not be discerned from perioikic dead on the battlefield.[90] An officer class simply did not exist in classical Greek cities. By at least the late fifth century BC Spartan high commands were open to talent (e.g. Lysander), and Athenian strategoi and taxiarchs were annually determined posts: hoplites held these commands, then returned to non-officer positions (if not re-elected) the following year.[91]

Nevertheless, lack of an officer class did not mean that men in positions of command and authority were only distinguished by their physical place in the formation and did not wear special armor or clothing as a mark of rank (Anderson 1970:39–40). By the fourth century, if not the fifth, national uniforms became common, for example, the famous Spartan red tunics and cloaks or the white shields of the Argives. Similarly, family or clan emblems on shields known from archaic vase paintings gave way to lambda's on Spartan shields, Poseidon's trident on Mantineian, sigma's on Sicyonian, and mu's on those of the Messenians.[92] The level of available technology and practical experience also dictated a certain uniformity in the absence of 'government issue' equipment, but shield devices could remain a matter of personal preference – at times with disastrous results, as when the Athenians at Delium (424 BC) killed each other in the confusion of battle.[93] The type of helmet and/or crest may also at one time have differentiated friend from foe (cf. a Corinthian crater of ca 600 BC: Ducrey 1985:49 pl.28).

Officers did not necessarily wear more armor than their men (cf. Bugh 1986 (*supra* n. 53): 92 n. 41), but they were distinguished by differences in helmet/crest, clothing, and ornateness of armor. According to Thucydides the size of a Spartan army could be determined by applying a basic knowledge of their military organization to the view that the front rank of their phalanx offered. Thucydides implies that the individual subunits of the phalanx from *enomotia* to *lochos* were discernible to an observer. A distinction of subunits by spacing seems unlikely, given the phalanx's dependence on close continuity of files, so Thucydides must mean that commanders of at least some of these subunits were conspicuous by appearance in the front rank.[94] In fact a late archaic statuette shows a Spartan warrior wrapped in a military cloak and wearing a helmet with transverse (ear-to-ear) crest. This deviation from the normal front-to-back crest of Greek helmets and analogy with the transverse crests of Roman centurions would indicate an officer.[95] A peculiar, excessively plumed helmet seen on another Spartan statuette might also designate an officer (Sekunda 1986 (*supra* n. 93): 28). At Athens taxiarchs were known by their triple-plumed helmets and bright red clothing (whether tunics or cloaks is uncertain), and strategoi in the fourth century BC continued to wear Corinthian helmets as a sign of rank long after Phrygian helmets for hoplites of the rank and file came into vogue.[96]

Brilliantly shining and extremely ornate armor had characterized the Homeric warrior chieftains at Troy: Hector's conspicuous shining armor during the attack on the Achaean ships has been mentioned, and Achilles' equipment forged by Hephaestus (*Il.* 18.456–616, 19.367–91) merits note. Numerous examples attest that commanders of the fifth and fourth centuries continued this tradition, which Alexander, Pyrrhus, and other Hellenistic generals perpetuated. Nicias' elegant purple and gold shield was hung as a trophy in a Syracusan temple and Alcibiades' golden shield emblazoned by an Eros armed with a thunderbolt aroused conservative comment. Xenophon while with the Ten Thousand fastidiously prided himself on his armor. In Sicily Dionysius I had elaborate armor manufactured for his officers, cavalry, and personal bodyguard of mercenaries. Later Dion's brilliant armor also attracted attention.[97] Of course any wealthy citizen could equip himself with elaborate armor, but the sources emphasize that generals in particular were conspicuous by their dress and arms.[98]

Onasander's account of the ideal general (33.6) specifies that the strategos should be mounted, and the Hellenistic/Roman general usually would be on horseback during battle. Not until the fourth century BC, however, do references occur to a mounted general of infantry, but even these few are episodic. The mercenary general Clearchus occasionally rode a horse – not unusual, since his command included Thracian cavalry (Xen., *Anab.* 1.5.12–13). During the retreat of the Greeks after Cunaxa (401 BC), Xenophon relates that while mounted he tried to lead a sortie of peltasts and hoplites against the Persians, only to dismount after a hoplite's criticism for being on horseback (Xen., *Anab.* 3.4.46–9). In the *Cyropaedia* the young Cyrus fights the Assyrians in the Persian front ranks on foot, but immediately after the battle curiously he appears on a horse. At Thymbrara Cyrus definitely was mounted as commander of the cavalry on the right wing.[99]

Although evidence from mercenary practice in the Near East and the testimony of a didactic novel might be questionable for phalanx commanders on the Greek mainland, Xenophon implies that Agesilaus rode as well as marched on campaign, and Plutarch has him lead a cavalry charge against the Pharsalians at Mt Narthacium. Most problematic, however, is the contradiction of sources concerning Pelopidas' death at Cynocephalae (364 BC): in Plutarch he dies leading an infantry attack, while Nepos recounts a cavalry charge.[100] The mounted general became more or less a fixture from Macedonian influence in the second half of the fourth century, when cavalry became more than an auxiliary arm in battle. Thereafter battle management required the elevated view a horse provided and the speed to bolster morale at any threatened point on the battleline (cf. Polyaenus 6.4.1). Perhaps the episodic notices of mounted generals in the early fourth century anticipate another distinction of strategos from *stratiotai* yet to become customary.

Besides armor, arms, and (after 400 BC) occasionally a horse, the general surpassed other hoplites in pay and the proportion of booty he received. At Athens military pay, probably introduced about the same time as jury pay ca 462 BC, followed the principles of fifth-century democracy in opening the higher magistracies to all classes. Strategoi and hipparchs received a *per diem* wage, which wealthy aristocrats probably refused to draw. Campaign pay for taxiarchs and phylarchs tripled that of the simple hoplite and *lochagoi* received a double rate.[101] In mercenary service strategoi might get quadruple, and *lochagoi* double the pay of the rank and file.[102] If victorious, a general could expect to receive a superior amount of booty and even outright gifts from allies. After Plataea Pausanias was awarded perhaps ten times the amount distributed to other participants, and Spartan kings customarily (according to Phylarchus) claimed a third of all booty.[103] Gifts to victorious generals from their men and allies ranged from gold crowns and panoplies to the property of enemy commanders, but gifts to generals (whether before or after battle) could also lead to corruption or charges of treason and bribery.[104]

Generals, however, not only received greater rewards, but could also grant them (cf. Keegan's concept of sanctions *supra*). Agesilaus awarded prizes to motivate training, and Jason of Pherae promised mercenaries double, triple, or even quadruple pay for good performances. Iphicrates before battle encouraged his mercenaries with honors and a larger share of booty to those displaying the most valor as hoplites, cavalry, and peltasts.[105] The Homeric competition between warrior chieftains for each to prove himself the best fighter was perpetuated in the ethos of the hoplite whether mercenary or citizen. After battle, awards of *aristeia* to individuals and/or cities could be granted. The bonds of patriotism, friendship, and kinship which united citizen-hoplites competed with a drive for individual distinction and doing the most for one's city, including a desire to claim having killed the most of the enemy.[106] Yet the phalanx had replaced the fury (*lyssa*) of the Homeric warrior with *sophrosyne*: foolhardy daring could neither be tolerated nor rewarded with *aristeia*, as the Spartan Aristodamus at Plataea, and Isidas defending Sparta against Epaminondas discovered. Heroic death in battle had to be accepted without overtly seeking to be a kamikaze.[107]

Furthermore, officers as well as their men sought *aristeia*. In a skirmish with the Drilae near Trapezus, Xenophon notes that the *lochagoi* competed with *lochagoi* for distinction and junior officers with their superiors (*Anab*. 5.2.11, 13). Generals, too, contended for *aristeia* in battles from Salamis (480 BC) to the Granicus (334 BC).[108] Officers felt a greater drive for valor than the rank and file – the old obligation that privileges demanded greater exertion as recompense.[109]

A strategos' distinction from *stratiotai* in dress, arms, pay, and proportion of allotted booty undercuts the idealistic notion of the hoplite phalanx as an anonymous mass of equals sacrificing themselves for the glory of the polis – the general picture of Athenian *epitaphioi logoi* – especially since the agonistic spirit of Greek civilization maintained its vitality in the competition of hoplites and officers to prove themselves the best. Even the democratic basis of the phalanx at Athens comes into question from the realization that, except in a levy of the whole people (*pandemei*), levies by the taxiarchs before ca 375 BC aimed at drafting the best men available (even if they had previously served), rather than drawing the net of service indiscriminately among males of military age.[110] Nor is the anonymity of generals in *epitaphioi logoi* reflected in inscribed documents: the tribal casualty lists from the mid-fifth century to the time of Chaeronea (338 BC) show that generals killed in the line of duty were distinguished from other dead by inclusion of their office, and lists from the last years of the Peloponnesian War show designation of taxiarchs, a phrourarch, trierarchs, and a *mantis*.[111] Certainly the distinction of command also had its drawbacks: after the Syracusan debacle only the Athenian generals Nicias and Demosthenes were marked for immediate execution, while their hoplites were sold as slaves, died in the quarries, or saved themselves by reciting Euripides to their drama-starved captors.[112]

If the concept of the phalanx as a military form of democracy in action breaks down upon analysis, the fault lies not with Greek democracy but in the demands of war for a hierarchy of command. For the most part distinctions of strategos from *stratiotai* followed the pre-state tradition of the warrior chieftain, whose greater risks in battle justified social privileges and whose notable costume served the tactical function of easy recognition of the group leader in combat. Only commanders abusing this unwritten social contract encountered criticism. Archilochus' parody of his strategos (fr. 114 West) reflects a lack of confidence in an officer too fastidious and conceited to be trusted under combat stress. A hoplite's rebuke of Xenophon for being mounted in an infantry attack (*Anab.* 3.4.46–9) seems the common soldier's protest against officers enduring fewer hardships. Yet the other soldiers verbally and physically abused the protester. Furthermore, Aristophanes' lampoon of the taxiarch Lamachus, probably a displaced jab at Cleon, was intended not to ridicule officers but the war, symbolized by the officer's uniform, although calling Lamachus *mistharchides* ('a seeker of pay') may be an objection to higher pay for officers.[113] Outside the context of combat a Greek army could maintain the democratic functions of a polis, and even Spartan discipline permitted rank-and-file criticism of a commander's tactical decisions during battle.[114]

Proper observance of the social contract between general and men, however, produced the best *modus imperandi*. Plato's prescription for military service in his ideal Cretan city (*Leg.* 12.942A) listed obedience to leaders and collective action as the most efficient weapons for victory. Obedience and effective command method, as modern military commentators also stress, depend on establishing bonds between officers and men, removing psychological distance so as to motivate the commanded, that is the establishment of kinship. The general, an embodiment of power, regulates morale by his command style, whether keeping close to the rank and file's daily existence (the soldier's general), maintaining stern discipline, inspiring his army through personal bravery and tactical or strategic brilliance (*le grand chef*: cf. Plut., *Pel.* 2.2), or some combination of these.[115]

Xenophon (*Anab.* 3.1.37) advised that the general should be braver than others, plan for the good of his army, and set an example for enduring hardship. Agesilaus, Xenophon's model general, perhaps more than any other commander in the age of the hoplite phalanx, exemplified the principle of kinship in his 'mask of command.' His Spartan simplicity in dress, moderate consumption of food and drink, his indifference to heat and cold, his lack of sleep, and his delight in toils made him his men's equal but also their trusted leader by surpassing them in endurance.[116] Above all, Agesilaus strengthened his role as a soldier's general through accessibility and constant visibility (Xen., *Ages*. 9.1–2). Iphicrates also used kinship to inspire morale: when his men were ill-clothed and poorly fed on a winter campaign, he dressed in summer clothes and went barefoot (Polyaenus 3.9.34). Kinship became a common characteristic of great generals and a *topos* for Roman emperors in the *Historia Augusta*.[117] Yet even in the tolerance of hardships, as Cambyses tells the young Cyrus (Xen., *Cyr*. 1.6.25), the general and the private differ, for honor and the prominence of the general's every act lighten his burdens.

Whether the general built morale on kinship, as did Agesilaus and Iphicrates, or discipline like Clearchus (Xen., *Anab*. 2.6.7–15), the general and his army's morale became inextricably intertwined. Long before Napoleon, du Picq, or Foch, Xenophon recognized that morale counted for more than numbers[118] and a general's duty to bolster morale required his presence in battle, riding along his battleline sharing the danger, encouraging, praising, reproaching.[119] Indeed already by the fourth century (if not earlier) the general had become the single most important part of the army: an army was inoperative without its general – its metaphoric, spiritual, and physical head.[120]

Tactical repercussions ensued from this development. In an anecdote of Polyaenus probably related to the Leuctra campaign (371 BC), Epaminondas encouraged the Thebans by comparing the Spartans and their allies to a snake: if the Spartan head were crushed, the rest of the body was useless. Accordingly Epaminondas' fifty-man deep deployment against the Spartan right aimed at knocking out the Spartan king.[121] Some years before at Tegyra (375 BC), which Plutarch calls a prelude to Leuctra, the battle centered on the location of the commanders: Spartan morale collapsed with the loss of their two commanding polemarchs. Alexander the Great pursued a similar battle plan at Granicus, Issus, and Gaugamela, directing his own cavalry charge at the Persian commanders in the first case and at Darius III in the other two.[122] Given the usual placement of commanders on their respective right wings, a type of stratagem often called a *salubre mendacium* could be exploited: by shouting out to one's own troops and within hearing distance of the enemy that the opposing king or general had been killed, a commander could simultaneously further incite his own army and sow panic in the enemy ranks.[123] This stratagem could be effective, since a commander's death aggravated a tactical crisis or negated exploitation of victory: Cleombrotus' death at Leuctra precipitated a Spartan rout; Epaminondas' wound at Mantineia produced confusion in the victorious Thebans; and a Spartan attack on Olynthus collapsed after the death of the general Teleutias.[124]

As the general himself became the focal point of morale and hence a tactical objective for the enemy, it would be logical to expect that casualty rates for generals would increase. Moreover, if Xenophon is credible, officers had a greater drive for distinction and generals were expected to prove themselves braver than others.[125] The Homeric tradition of the warrior chieftain leading by his example of courage still flourished in the hoplite phalanx: generals, after all, also sought *aristeia*. Besides, except for Spartan kings, generals usually had previous experience as hoplites and would return to hoplite status after their term of office: Aristides and Themistocles served as hoplites at Marathon; Pericles, not yet a strategos, distinguished himself at Tanagra; Agesilaus before his kingship received hoplite training in the Spartan *agoge* and in old age fought in the ranks as a mercenary commander in Egypt; also Epaminondas and Pelopidas did hoplite duty at Mantineia (385 BC). Later, Pelopidas became leader of the Theban Sacred Band only when he missed appointment as a boeotarch (371 BC).[126]

Examples of valorous conduct by commanders abound. Brasidas' daring exploits as a local district commander at Methone (431 BC) and as a trierarch at Pylos (425 BC) mark stages in the advancement of his career. The Athenian strategos Lamachus died when he was cut off too boldly trying to exploit a Syracusan rout (414 BC). Chabrias fell leading an amphibious assault on Chios (357 BC) and Plutarch of Eretria charged at the head of his mercenaries at Tamynae (349 BC).[127] Battle scars were signs of reverence (Agesilaus) or a source of boasting (Chares).[128] Yet Homeric *lyssa* had not disappeared. Pyrrhus madly raged in battle against the Spartans who had killed his son Ptolemy. Pelopidas' grudge against Alexander of Pherae precipitated his death at Cynocephalae, and Teleutias' anger prompting his foolhardy demise at Olynthus aroused Xenophon's condemnation – emotions should not influence military decisions.[129]

Certainly generalship could be hazardous to health: defeated commanders usually died in battle; the victorious sometimes did; and few generals with repeated commands passed away through old age.[130] The scanty sources preclude, however, any possibility of quantifying casualty rates for generals to determine if they increased, declined, or remained stable in the fifth and fourth centuries BC.[131] Despite the logical assumption that rates would rise with the increased importance of generals, the transition of commanders from Homeric warrior chieftains to Hellenistic battle managers permits the hypothesis that rates declined, as the participation of generals in combat changed from the status of 'always' to 'sometimes.' For the commander of a hoplite phalanx, physical leadership in the tradition of the Homeric warrior continued to play an important role, as numerous cited examples attest. But leading a charge in a skirmish, rallying one's troops to pursue a routed foe, and a headlong sally in a burst of anger do not prove either that a general stationed himself in the front rank of the phalanx at the beginning of a formal pitched battle, or that kinship and morale explain the apparently high casualty rates for fifth- and fourth-century generals. The placement of officers within the phalanx as well as the circumstances and motives of commanders' deaths require closer examination.

Archaeological sources do not clarify these matters. The Nereid Monument of Xanthus in Lydia (ca 400 BC) bears a relief showing a row of charging hoplites, of which the figure in the center is taken to be an officer with his head turned to the right and his raised right army apparently gesturing.[132] Unfortunately, this figure is the only hoplite in the relief whose head and right arm are preserved. In the Spartan phalanx all the front-rank men (*protostatai*) were officers.[133] Thus, if a single row of hoplites in this relief is intended to represent a phalanx, all the figures could be officers and the better preserved central figure offers no indication of a strategos.

It is generally agreed that subordinate officers stood either at the head of files or somewhere within the body of the phalanx, although this rendered some files deeper than others. No geometric compulsion necessitated that all files, all *lochoi*, or all contingents in an army of independent allies observe the same depth, and blind files (i.e., an officer standing in the first rank of the phalanx, to the right of his unit, but without anyone behind him) did not exist.[134]

Nevertheless, even the detailed descriptions of a Hellenistic phalanx in the Stoic tacticians give no clue to the army commander's position.[135] Custom held that a Greek general commanded from the place of honor, the army's right wing, and a Spartan king could be either on the right between two *morai* or in the center of the line, as Agis at Mantineia.[136] These indications of battleline longitude omit reference to latitude: was the commander on the right or center in the front rank, somewhere within the body of the phalanx, or behind it? Once again, an argument must be pieced together from episodic anecdotes of what a general did or did not do in a particular situation. It can be hypothesized *a priori* that some commanders enjoyed and sought personal combat, while others did not. An exception can be found for any absolute interpretation. An argument, however, can be presented that generals of the fifth and fourth centuries BC did not stand in the front rank of the phalanx to begin a pitched battle and that motives other than morale and kinship contributed to commander fatalities, especially for defeated generals.

In his encomium of Agesilaus (6.1) Xenophon would appear to offer explicit testimony that generals always fought in the first rank of the phalanx: *proton heauton tatton*. But why should Xenophon exceptionally praise Agesilaus for his battle scars and front-line service, if such were typical of all generals? The real implication of the passage is that this conduct was not typical. Other evidence produces doubt of Agesilaus' frequency in the front rank. Plutarch (*Ages*. 26.2) gives no details of how Agesilaus was wounded in the Boeotian campaign of 378 BC. At Coronea (394 BC) Herippidas, commander of the mercenaries, led the charge from Agesilaus' sector of the battleline, and the Argives fled before the Spartans made contact. Agesilaus, who did not lead the mercenaries' charge, was nevertheless receiving garlands of victory from these men when the report came that the Thebans after routing Agesilaus' left were at his baggage train. Nothing so far indicates Agesilaus' participation in combat or front-line service.[137]

In the second stage of the battle Agesilaus countermarched his forces to face the Thebans head-on. A fierce struggle ensued, in which Agesilaus fighting with his bodyguard of fifty volunteers was wounded.[138] Plutarch emphasizes, however, that Agesilaus suffered his wound despite the efforts of his bodyguard to protect him. Hence the inference is justified that Agesilaus was close to, but not in the first rank of his phalanx.

This interpretation can be supported by other examples of Spartan kings. Agis at Mantineia was surrounded in the center of his battleline by the 300 *Hippeis* who routed the enemy center, but Thucydides says nothing of Agis himself joining in the combat. At Leuctra Cleombrotus also had the protection of the 300 *Hippeis* (or their equivalent as part of a *mora*).[139] Furthermore, there are several references to Spartans fighting in front of a Spartan king – additional proof that the king was not in the first line of the phalanx.[140] Indeed Xenophon (*Lac. Resp.* 11.6) recounts a special maneuver to protect the king, when fighting appears imminent. A lapse of over a century between royal Spartan deaths in battle (Leonidas at Thermopylae (480 BC) and Cleombrotus at Leuctra (371 BC)) would also suggest the absence of Spartan kings from the phalanx's front line (Lazenby 1985:160), although Thermopylae was not a conventional pitched battle (*parataxis*).

Agesilaus' wounding in the second stage of Coronea likewise corresponds to other evidence: generals were frequently killed or wounded not through presence on the front line in the initial clash of rival phalanges, but rather in the second stage of battle when a general too boldly attempted to exploit the rout of a beaten foe or tried to rally his own troops. Examples range from Callimachus at Marathon (490 BC) to Epaminondas at Mantineia (362 BC).[141] Casualties to strategoi would therefore correspond to du Picq's view that the greatest losses in ancient battles occurred after one side fled, and Hanson's thesis about certain types of wounds proving a general's place in the front rank needs some modification.[142]

A number of anecdotes relate commanders making tactical decisions at the beginning or in the middle of battles. These appear implausible for a general in the front rank of a phalanx when fighting for his life. At Oenophyta (457 BC) the Athenian strategos Myronidas employed a variant of the *salubre mendacium* stratagem: he first ordered his left to charge the Thebans, then ran to his right flank and shouted that they were victorious on the left. His ruse produced success. Daphaenus, a Syracusan general of the late fifth century, defeated a Carthaginian army with much the same trick.[143] At Delium (424 BC) when the Athenians were defeating the Boeotian left and the Thebans were winners on their right wing, Pagondas the Theban general ordered two squadrons of cavalry secretly to circumvent a hill and to surprise the victorious Athenian wing (Thuc. 4.96.5) – an impossible act for a man fighting in the forefront on his own right, while still gaging the action on the opposite flank. Nor could Alcibiades be fighting in the front when a messenger approached him with news of a Persian threat to his fleet (Front., *Strat.* 2.7.6). Although the silence of Plutarch, Xenophon, and Diodorus casts doubt on this incident's historicity, Herodotus (9.76.1) relates a similar story about Pausanias at Plataea. When the tide of battle had turned in the Greeks' favor and the Spartans were still engaged in slaughter, a female captive of the Persians succeeded in crossing the lines and approaching Pausanias. She did not find him personally engaged in combat, but rather directing the Greek effort (*horosa de panta ekeina dieponta Pausanien*) – presumably in the rear. Agis' last-minute attempt to adjust his left flank at Mantineia could also be cited, but Agis (as argued above, p.148) was not in the front row of the phalanx.[144] Certainly Iphicrates did not stand in the first rank of his troops when he deployed them in a plain with a ditch dug behind them to compel their bravery.[145]

Furthermore, the *sphagia*, a propitiatory blood sacrifice performed just before a formal pitched battle (*parataxis*), gives some indication of a general's location.[146] In theory the sacrifice occurred when both sides were present and deployed. The commander would perform the sacrifice, then raise the paean to begin battle. In practice, however, the *sphagia* often happened when the two battlelines were advancing or even already engaged (Pritchett, *War* 2. 73–4, 83). Even so, Pritchett insists that the sacrifice was made in the *metaichmion* (the no-man's land between the two armies) while the enemy watched, but this view is difficult to reconcile with reality.[147] At Plataea when Pausanias tried to gain favorable *sphagia* while his men endured Persian fire, Herodotus gives no hint that Pausanias was dodging Persian arrows.[148] Phocion (Plut., *Phoc.* 13.1–3) had the same problem at Tamynae: his sacrifices proved unfavorable until the enemy was actually storming the ramparts of his position. He was hardly stationed in front of his men. But then in the second stage of the battle he collected his scattered forces and led a charge.

No doubt some generals deployed their forces, harangued them, performed the *sphagia*, took a place in the front ranks, and began battle with the paean. Epaminondas probably stood in the forefront at Leuctra.[149] Others and particularly Spartan kings, however, as this survey of the evidence suggests, did not stand in the front rank when battle began, but could assume the moral and physical leadership of a Homeric chieftain at a crucial point, especially in the second stage of a hoplite battle when either one side fled or the ordered ranks of the rival phalanges dissolved into a melée of human carnage so graphically described by Hanson (1989:152–218).

But if all generals did not seek combat in the initial clash and the deaths and wounds of commanders seem to occur most frequently in a hoplite battle's second stage, then the general's kinship with his troops and his morale-boosting presence (not always in the first rank) do not necessarily explain the high fatality rates of generals – most of all for the losers. The collective action of the phalanx obscured the competitive nature of its 'interchangeable parts.' *Aristeia* awaited the most courageous survivors and the dead were guaranteed their eternal fame. As the spiritual descendants of Homeric chieftains, strategoi felt the burdens of the heroic ethos. Epaminondas said that the noblest (*kalliston*) death was in war (Plut., *Mor.* 192C). Some in the spirit of Heraclitus' dictum (fr.119D–K) felt that a man's character was his *daimon*: Agesilaus considered a quiet death for himself unworthy; Leonidas thought a glorious death nature's gift to *aristoi*.[150]

Moreover, death in battle provided an honorable departure for losers. In Onasander's view a defeated general should not desire to live, and no Spartan king survived a lost battle until Cleomenes III fled to Egypt after Sellasia (222 BC).[151] Some losers resorted to suicide, although this ultimate act gained more respectability in the Hellenistic period under Stoic influence.[152] At Athens strategoi who failed, even if not defeated in a major battle, faced exile, fines, or prosecution for bribery and treason.[153] Paches, who put down the revolt of Mytilene (427 BC), committed suicide at the audit of his generalship, and the Athenians condemned to death Lysicles, the strategos who survived Chaeronea.[154] As the Athenian siege of Syracuse (415–13 BC) dragged on without success, Nicias justifiably feared the consequences of returning to Athens (Thuc. 7.48.3–5).

Yet Greek punishment of unlucky generals was no worse than at Carthage, where the ignominy of defeat brought disgrace for the commander's family but exile or crucifixion for the general.[155] No wonder that the Spartan Anaxibius, the victim of his own carelessness and an ambush of Iphicrates, opportunely chose the noble (*kalon*) alternative – death in battle (Xen., *Hell.* 4.8.38). In contrast, Hasdrubal, killed at the Metaurus (207 BC), merited a fitting eulogy from Polybius (11.2) for taking the proper precautions but knowing his duty to die in defeat. Thus the frequent deaths of defeated generals often have little to do with their physical location within the phalanx at the start of battle or kinship with their men. Rather, failure demanded the ultimate sacrifice to avoid ignominy for the commander and to appease his city. Although defeated, the general could still claim a hero's status.

This survey of the transition from Homeric warrior chieftain to Hellenistic battle manager has traced the development of combat leadership in relationship to the evolution of the hoplite phalanx. The ethos of Homeric heroes continued to influence hoplite behavior even after the abandonment of pre-state warfare, and the presence of commanders in combat remained essential, although their physical leadership on the front line (at least initially in battle) did not always occur. Indeed the age of the hoplite phalanx witnessed a trend (exceptions considered) for commanders to avoid the front rank at the beginning of battle and to return to this traditional position of physical leadership only in a phalanx battle's second stage, when they led the pursuit of a beaten foe or, alternatively, either tried to stem a rout of their own forces or sought death to salvage their own reputations in defeat. To apply this to Keegan's categories of command style, the hoplite general already shows a tendency to participate personally in combat *sometimes*, but certainly not *always* in the same sense as a Homeric warrior chieftain.

Believers in a single scenario for the combat role of the strategos in a phalanx (i.e., the general was *always* in the front rank and *always* entered combat) will no doubt find these results disturbing. Some generals sought personal combat; others did not. Battle involves too many historical variables for a single scenario to satisfy all cases. The traditional scenario is a composite picture of direct evidence, logical inference, and conjecture, since no single ancient account of a phalanx battle provides all the details that we moderns wish to know, and (as suggested above pp. 125–6) a 'typical' hoplite battle is illusory. Certainly this study has not answered all questions of where the general was at every moment in battle: if he was not in the front rank, where was he? For all battles we simply do not know from direct and unequivocal evidence, although some cases suggest the rear and others indicate a position somewhere in the phalanx but behind the front rank. In ancient history a comprehensive, neat picture is not always possible, and there is value in recognizing the limits of the evidence. In fact, the *opinio communis* would often seem to exaggerate the extent to which one man fighting for his life in the front rank could control an army of hundreds or thousands and gage the course of a battle along an entire front sometimes hundreds of yards long. The role of battle manager did not exist from the beginning of the hoplite phalanx, but evolved over time. Some additional considerations remain to complete this account of the general as hoplite.

When the delimiting rules of Greek in-group warfare started to collapse, tactical considerations demanded that battles be managed as well as fought. Brains could now negate superior brawn. Supervision of combat required, apparently beginning at some point in the fourth century, the added mobility and visibility provided by a horse. The emerging significance of cavalry as an independent tactical arm and the prevalence of Macedonian influence from the time of Philip and Alexander guaranteed that Hellenistic army commanders would usually be mounted. Furthermore, the increasing importance of the general's person necessitated that he either did not enter battle or, if he had to, that he did so cautiously (cf. Garlan 1975:146–7). A general's rash personal daring, so the Hellenistic argument ran, could hurt his cause more if he were killed than a single man's contribution would aid victory.[156] Or, as Livy asserted in describing the duel of Junius Brutus and Arruns Tarquinius (2.6.8), *decorum est tum ipsis capessere pugnam ducibus* – implying that in his own time personal combat by commanders was improper. No doubt the 'Achilles complex' of the *philokindynos* Alexander influenced this shift in military theory, as criticism from the great Macedonian's contemporary Nearchus demonstrates (*FGrHist* 133 F 42.3 = Arr., *Anab*. 6.13.4). It is important, nevertheless, to emphasize – and it is confirmation of the trend in command style argued in this chapter – that this alleged Hellenistic idea already occurs at the end of the fifth century: Cyrus the Younger was strongly advised not to enter battle at Cunaxa in 401 BC.[157]

Cyrus refused to listen: a king must show that he is worthy of the kingdom he seeks to win.[158] A commander's personal bravado still mattered; generals on occasion still charged headlong to their doom. Homeric *arete*, however, also changed in the age of the hoplite phalanx. The *Iliad*'s chieftains were distinguished in arms and privileges – the benefits of superior *arete*. Tyrtaeus transvalued *arete* for the emerging phalanx of the nascent Greek city-state, but officers and especially strategoi still marked themselves by dress and, later, greater pay and booty. The democratic phalanx did not eliminate the gradation of leaders from followers: Xenophon (*Anab*. 3.1.37) testifies to their continued distinctness.

By the early fourth century even the criterion of heroic death differed for generals and rank and file. All types of battle deaths for generals were no longer equal. Surprised before the walls of Haliartus (395 BC) at the head of his army, Lysander suffered the inglorious death of a peltast or a scout, as did Hannibal's foil Claudius Marcellus, ambushed by Numidians in 208 BC.[159] Such deaths were improper for generals. The distinction of strategos from *stratiotai* became a permanent feature of antiquity in judging a general's personal daring.[160]

Even so, a general's personal, physical leadership was demanded in times of crisis. Two final examples will suffice. At the siege of Amida (AD 359), to boost the sagging morale of his army and although a Persian king was not obliged to enter battle, Sapor II led a charge *proeliatoris militis ritu* against the Roman garrison. Similarly, in one of history's most poignant instances of heroism, Brig.-Gen. Lewis A. Armistead commanding his brigade in Pickett's Charge (3 July 1863), initially drew his sword only as he broke the first Union line on Cemetery Ridge, placed his hat upon its point, and with his sword-tipped hat raised above his head charged to meet his maker against the second Union line. If the thesis of a recent book arguing the influence of the Celtic military tradition and Sir Walter Scott's novels on the American Southern aristocracy be accepted, then we gain some sense through a modern example of how the Homeric ideals of the warrior chieftain continued to affect the general as hoplite.[161]

NOTES

Works referred to by author alone or with short title or date are cited in full in the Bibliography to this volume.

1. Plut., *Pyrrh.* 16.7–8; on the importance of presence of mind (*phronein* in Plutarch, *echein noun* in Polybius) to generalship see Polyb. fr.63 B–W: 'Generals must have presence of mind and be daring – (properties) which indeed are most important for precarious and hazardous acts.' Cf. Polyb. 10.3.7.
2. Plut., *Pyrrh.* 1.2, 7.4; Just. 17.3. On Achilles see K. C. King, *Achilles: Paradigms of the War Hero from Homer to the Middle Ages* (Berkeley, 1987) 2–7, 58–66, 104.
3. Cf. van Creveld's definition of 'command,' understood as the modern C^3I (command, control, communications, intelligence): M. van Creveld, *Command in War* (Cambridge, Mass., 1985) 5–6. The general's duties as tactician and strategist lie beyond the scope of this chapter.
4. Scipio: Front., *Strat.* 4.7.4; Iphicrates: Plut., *Mor.* 187B; van Creveld (*supra* n. 3) 17. Battlefield duels between opposing commanders are attested as late as the Thirty Years' War: see Fuller 1958:152 n. 4.
5. A cursory discussion of the transition in John Keegan, *The Mask of Command* (New York, 1987) 122–4; also see Van Creveld (*supra* n. 3) 6, 9. Cf. H. H. Turney-High, *The Military: the Theory of Land Warfare as Behavioral Science* (West Hanover, 1981) 250–71.
6. *Risikobereitschaft* – readiness for risk. On the Homeric code see W. Jaeger, *Paedeia*, I (2nd edn, Oxford, 1945) 3–14; King (*supra* n. 2) 2–28; Keegan (*supra* n. 5) 123; on risk see Latacz 1977: 153–9.
7. Thuc. 2.42.3; Dion. Hal., *Ant. Rom.* 5.17.5–6; King (*supra* n. 2) 47; N. Loraux, *The Invention of Athens: the Funeral Oration in the Classical City*, tr. A. Sheridan (Cambridge, Mass., 1986) 52, 99.
8. M. Detienne, 'La phalange: problèmes et controverses,' in Vernant

1968:128–31, 140; P. Vidal-Naquet, 'La tradition de l'hoplite athénien,' in Vernant *ibid.*: 170–74. Cf. Plut., *Ages.* 26.4–5, *Mor.* 214A; Polyaenus 2.1.7. I owe this reference to Plutarch to Victor Hanson.

9. Tyrtaeus fr. 12 West; Hor., *Carm.* 3.2.13: *Dulce et decormest pro patria mori*; cf. Eur., *Tro.* 386–7; Cic., *Phil.* 14.31; Verg., *Aen.* 2.317; Jaeger (*supra* n. 6) 90–4; Detienne (*supra* n. 8) 129–31; C. W. Müller, "Der schöne Tod des Polisbürger oder 'Ehrevoll ist es, für das Vaterland zu sterben,'" *Gymnasium* 96 (1989) 317–40 (written without reference to Loraux's work).
10. Loraux (*supra* n. 7) 52; '*HEBE* et *ANDREIA*: deux versions de la mort du combattant athénien,' *AncSoc* 6 (1975) 30; 'Mourir devant Troie, tomber pour Athènes: De la gloire du héros à l'idée de la cité,' *Social Science Information* 17 (1978) 801–17.
11. Jaeger (*supra* n. 6) 32–4, 45–9, 185–6, 199–204, 216–18; H. I. Marrou, *A History of Education in Antiquity*, tr. G. Lamb (Madison, 1982) 3–13.
12. Ar., *Ran.* 1034–5; Pl., *Ion* 541B, *Lach.* 191A–B, *Rep.* 10.606E; Xen., *Symp.* 4.6; Isoc. 4.159; Strab. 1.2.3–4; Paus. 4.28.7–8; Jaeger (*supra* n. 6) 196; E. A. Havelock, *Preface to Plato* (Cambridge, Mass., 1963) 61–86; W. J. Verdenius, 'L'*Ion* de Plato,' *Mnemosyne* 11 (1943) 245–52. On the Homeric *Tactica* see Wheeler 1983: 17 n. 85, 18 n. 91 and '*Polla kena tou polemou*: the history of a greek proverb,' *GRBS* 29 (1988) 179–80.
13. Hanson (1989:25, 220–1, and *passim*) generally discounts the Homeric legacy of hoplite battle. Cf. my review in *Journal of Interdisciplinary History* 21 (1990) 122–5.
14. Thuc. 5.66.3–4, 68.3; Xen., *Lac. Resp.* 11.4–6; Kromayer and Veith 1928:35.
15. Keegan (*supra* n. 5) 315–38; R. A. Beaumont, 'Command method: a gap in military historiography,' *Naval War College Review* 31.3 (1979) 70–1. On willing obedience see Xen., *Cyr.* 1.1.3–5, 6.20–1; 3.1.37; 5.3.1–4; 7.1.41–5; R. Höistad, *Cynic Hero and Cynic King* (Uppsala, 1948) 78–86.
16. E. Lammert, 'Die geschichtliche Entwicklung der griechischen Taktik,' *NJb* (1899) 11; Delbrück (tr. Renfroe 1975) I, 232; Adcock 1957:6; Snodgrass 1967:62; Anderson 1970:70–1; Pritchett, *War* 2. 206; Garlan 1975:146; van Creveld (*supra* n. 3) 42; Keegan (*supra* n. 5) 119, 122–4, 331; P. Cartledge, *Agesilaus and the Crisis of Sparta* (Baltimore, 1987) 206; G. M. Paul, 'Two battles in Thucydides,' *EchMC1* 6 (1987) 307; on fatality rates and wounds see Hanson 1988:200–201 with n. 30 and 1989:107–8, 111–14, 162–4.
17. Cf. Delbrück (tr. Renfroe 1975) I, 232 on Alexander and the transition to battle manager. Delbrück's emphasis on the role of tactical reserves ignores that the idea of reserves began to develop in the late fifth century: see Wheeler 1983:2 n. 4. On Macedonian kingship see A. E. Samuel, 'Philip and Alexander as kings,' *AHR* 93 (1988) 1270–86; Alexander and Achilles: P. R. Hardie, '*Imago Mundi*: cosmological and ideological aspects of the shield of Achilles,' *JHS* 107 (1987) 25–31; P. A. Stadter, *Arrian of Nicomedia* (Chapel Hill, 1980) 74–6, cf. A. B. Bosworth, *Conquest and Empire: the reign of Alexander the Great* (Cambridge, 1988) 38–9. According to Onesicritus, Alexander slept with

the *Iliad* under his pillow: *FGrHist* 134 F 38 = Plut., *Alex.* 8.2. Keegan (*supra* n. 5) 122–3 and *passim* exaggerates Alexander's role as a religious leader in his position as warrior king.

18. Marathon and Plataea against supposed Persian hordes hardly qualify as 'typical', and the tradition about Marathon (despite detailed topographical investigations and the publication of at least one article on the battle nearly every year) is so steeped in Athenian propaganda as to be of questionable credibility. Cf. Theopompus, *FGrHist* 115 F 153.
19. Ritualistic aspects: Pritchett, *War* 4.1–7; Detienne, in Vernant 1968:124; cf. Connor 1988:3–27; on military myths about the Archaic Period see Schwertfeger 1982:253–80; Wheeler 1987: 157–82. Herodotus 7.9*β*.1–2 offers strong support that at least some aspects of the typical hoplite battle antedate the fifth century, although I surmise that a systematic survey of Greek military activity in the seventh and sixth centuries would conclude that few formal pitched battles (*parataxeis*) between Greek phalanges occurred. On the rules of Greek warfare see Lonis 1969; Garlan 1975:23–77; P. Karavites, *Capitulations and Greek Interstate Relations* (Hypomnemata 71: Göttingen, 1982) 13–26; J. de Romilly, 'Guerre et paix entre cités,' in Vernant 1968:207–20; on rules of war in general cf. E. L. Wheeler, 'The modern legality of Frontinus' stratagems,' *Militärgeschichtliche Mitteilungen* 44.1 (1988) 7–29 and J. Huizinga, *Homo Ludens* (New York, 1950) 11–12, 64–5, 89–100.
20. On the changes in Greek warfare see de Romilly (*supra* n. 19); Garlan 1974; Ferrill 1985:149–86 with my review in *Armed Forces and Society* 14 (1987) 156–8; Wheeler 1981:74–9; career officers: Lengauer 1979, cf. C. W. Fornara (1966) on the new position of *strategos autokrator* at Athens: *The Athenian Board of Generals from 501 to 404* (Historia Einzelschrift 16: Wiesbaden, 1971) 14, 64; mercenaries: Parke 1933; Best 1969; L. P. Marinovic, *Le mercenariat grec et la crise de la polis*, tr. J. and Y. Garlan (Paris, 1988); *epilektoi*: Detienne, in Vernant 1968:134–42; G. Hoffman, 'Les choisis: un ordre dans la cité grecque?' *Droit et Cultures* 9–10 (1985) 15–26; Lazenby 1985:54–6; N. Loraux, 'La "belle mort" spartiate,' *Ktema* 2 (1977) 117–18; Garlan 1989:149–50; L. Tritle, '*Epilektoi* at Athens,' *AncHistBull* 3 (1989) 54–9; cf. Hanson 1989:124; on the *hoplomachoi* see Wheeler 1983:1–9.
21. Contrary to modern usage, the term 'phalanx' in classical Greek does not denote a specific formation but either an arrangement of troops broader than it is deep or simply a 'battleline.' A battle formation in the sense of *Schlachtordnung* is *taxis* or *parataxis*: see Lammert 1938: 1631–5. Latin usage of 'phalanx' and the term in Greek writers of the Hellenistic and Roman periods can be more specific: cf. Wheeler 1979:303–18; B. Bar-Kochva, *Judas Maccabaeus: the Jewish struggle against the Seleucids* (Cambridge, 1989) 76 nn. 23–4, 432–7.
22. Xen., *Cyn.* 12; *Cyr.* 1.2.10, 6.28–9, 39–41; 7.5.62–4; 8.1.34–8; Pl., *Euthd.* 290B–D; Garlan (1989) 24–6; J. Aymard, *Essai sur les chasses romaines* (BEFAR 171: Paris, 1951) 470–2; cf. H. D. Dunn, 'The hunt as an image of love and war in classical literature' (Diss. U. Calif., Berkeley, 1980); Turney-High (*supra* n. 5) 21.
23. Turney-High (*supra* n. 5) 25–45, esp. 30, 34, and *Primitive Warfare: its*

Practice and Concepts, (2nd edn, Columbia, 1971) 61–90, 145–7; E. A.Thompson, *The Early Germans* (Oxford, 1965) 48–9, 56, 63–4; Neolithic painting: Ferrill 1985:21. For a full bibliography on pre-state warfare see R. B. Ferguson with L. E. Farragher, *The Anthropology of War: a Bibliography* (H. F. Guggenheim Foundation, Occasional Papers 1: New York, 1988). Keegan's scenario (*supra* n. 5, 8–10) for the evolution of the warrior chief from the hunting band leader need not be taken as universal.

24. *Il.* 2.362, 655, 668; Lammert/Lammert 1921:440. Van Wees (1986:296, 298 with n. 64, 299), overlooking the Rhodians, rejects any connection between Nestor's advice (*Il.* 2.362) and actual organization of the Achaean or Trojan war bands. Indeed he claims that kin groups never formed the basis of military organization in Greek history. This view ignores the anthropological data from comparable pre-state societies (cf. *supra* n. 23), denies the well-known connections between social and military organization (cf. the modern classic, S. Andreski, *Military Organization and Society* (Berkeley, 1971)), and seems contradictory to his own anthropological citation of the Philippine Tausug as a parallel to the retinues of Homeric chieftains. Although at Athens, the best documented polis, direct evidence is lacking and the relationship of clans and phratries to the organization of the pre-Cleisthenic army may be 'theoretical,' to reject all kin groups as a component of military organization is hypercritical. Cf. Frost 1984: 283–5, 293; P. Siewert, *Die Trittyen Attikas und die Heeresreform des Kleisthenes* (Vestigia 33: Munich, 1982) 156. For a belief in tribal organization of the early Spartan army (cf. Tyrtaeus fr. 19 West) see Cartledge (*supra* n. 16) 427–8, cf. Lazenby 1985:50–2, 70–2. Furthermore, Van Wees denies any possible regional or kin association in the five Trojan units which attack the Achaean ships (*Il.* 12.86ff), but comparative data would support a contrary view: the retinues of German war chiefs could be 'inter-tribal.' See Thompson (*supra* n. 23) 58.
25. See A. Arnaud, 'Quelques aspects des rapports de la ruse et de la guerre dans le monde grec du VIIIe au Ve siècle' (3rd Cycle Thesis: Paris, 1971) 28–31.
26. H. van Wees, 'Kings in combat: battles and heroes in the *Iliad*,' *CQ* 38 (1988) 13–22.
27. Tac., *Ger.* 7.1–2: *Reges ex nobilitate, duces ex virtute sumunt. . . . et duces exemplo potius quam imperio, si prompti, si conspicui, si ante aciem agant admiratione praesunt. ceterum neque animadvertere neque vincire, ne verberare quidem nisi sacerdotibus permissum . . . quodque praecipuum fortitudinis incitamentum est, non casus nec fortuita conglobatio turmam aut cuneum fecit sed familiae et propinquitates.* Cf. *Ger.* 13–14 and Thompson in n. 23 *supra.*
28. T. S.Burns, 'The Barbarians and the *Scriptores Historiae Augustae*,' in C. Deroux, ed., *Studies in Latin Literature and Roman History* (Collection Latomus 164: Brussels, 1979) I, 524–5; van Wees (*supra* n. 26) 18–22. Cf. Tac., *Ger.* 14–15.
29. King (*supra* n. 2) 3–4; van Wees (*supra* n. 26) 19–20.
30. Pritchett, *War* 4. 7–33; similar views in F. Albracht, *Kampf und*

Kampfschilderung bei Homer (Naumburg, 1886); A. Lang, *The World of Homer* (London, 1910) 54–59; Lammert/Lammert 1921:436–45; Lammert 1938:1625–7; Kromayer and Veith 1928:26; Detienne, in Vernant 1968:138 n. 101. Cf. Latacz 1977:26–44 for additional bibliography.

31. Van Wees 1986:285–303 and (*supra* n. 26) 1–24. Cf. Hanson 1989: 41; R. Leimbach, review of Latacz, *Gnomon* 52 (1980) 418–25: no coherent, unified picture of Homeric combat possible; Snodgrass 1964b:176–9: no phalanx in Homer.
32. Van Wees 1986:285–92 and (*supra* n. 26) 13–14.
33. Van Wees (*supra* n. 26) 10–11; cf. Latacz 1977:170–8.
34. Caes., *BG* 1.24.5, 5.2.4–5; cf. Liv. 32.17.11; G. Gundal, 'Der Keil in der germanischen Feldschlacht,' *Gymnasium* 50 (1939) 154–65; cf. Thompson (*supra* n. 23) 114.
35. Cf. Eust. ad *Il.* 4.250ff and Didymus schol. in *Il.* 3.136, where definite sizes are assigned to these units; Pritchett, *War* 4.22; Lammert/ Lammert 1921: 436–41; Lammert 1938:1626. That later Greeks (Polyb. 12.21.8; Diod. 16.3.2; Arist., fr. 152 Rose) conceived Homeric warfare in terms of the hoplite phalanx of their own time does not offer proof (so Pritchett, *War* 4. 24–5) that Homer described the hoplite phalanx. These later Greeks display the influence of the sophists' view of Homer the military expert; Aristotle's *Homeric Problems*, which included commentary on military questions (see Wheeler in n. 12 *supra*), and similar Peripatetic works in this genre probably originated some of the curious material in Eustathius and other commentators. Likewise, Xenophon's use of *hoplites* (the standard classical Greek term for a heavy infantryman) in reference to non-Greek heavy infantry does not prove the non-existence of a pre-hoplite phase of Greek warfare (so Pritchett, *War* 4.11). The word is not attested before the late sixth or early fifth century: Snodgrass 1964b:204.
36. Cf. Tac., *Ger.* 14.1: *Cum ventum in aciem, turpe principi virtute vinci, turpe comitatui virtutem principis non adaequare.* Van Wees ((*supra* n. 26) 5 with n. 18, 12 n. 40) correctly rejects Pritchett's concept of duels in Homeric battles and his view of the *promachoi* as a forward echelon unit (*War* 4. 21–6). *Monomachia* of commanders or champions, as Pritchett's own catalog of examples shows, generally occurs as a substitute for an engagement of all forces. The term *monomachia* in classical Greek and Hellenistic historians for the occasional confrontation of opposing generals is no doubt used to recall the heroic duels of epic, although the word *monomachia* and its variants do not occur before Herodotus: LSJ^9 svv.; Pritchett, *War* 4.19–20 nos. 13–14, 16–17.
37. See nn. 27–9 *supra.* Military service, the *impôt de sang*, remained an aristocratic argument for privileges until the French Revolution: A. Vagts, *A History of Militarism* (New York, 1959) 57. On Pindar see Jaeger (*supra* n. 6) 214–16. Latacz (1977:43–59) correctly argues that *promachos* and *promachesthai* do not indicate social rank. *Contra* Pritchett, *War* 4.26 n. 83; van Wees (*supra* n. 26) 18–22, although he concedes (21 nn. 68–9) that all *aristoi* in battle are not *basileis*.

38. Tac., *Ger.* 13.2: *insignis nobilitas aut magna patrum merita principis dignitatem etiam adulescentulis adsignant.*
39. *Il.* 11.61–6, 163–71, 284–99; 12.86–7, 437–71. Cf. Latacz 1977:175–8.
40. King (*supra* n. 2) 248 n. 11. Nestor's deployment of suspected cowards between reliable troops and his other tactical instructions at *Il.* 4.297–309 could also be cited as early evidence of battle management. The frequent citation of this passage in later sources indicates its use in Homeric *Tactica*: n. 12 *supra*; Xen., *Mem.* 3.1.8, *Cyr.* 7.5.5, cf. 3.3.41; Arist., fr. 152 Rose; Pyrrhus, *Tactica*, in Front., *Strat.* 2.3.21; Amm. 24.6.9.
41. On the hoplite panoply see Snodgrass 1964b: esp. 61–7 and 1967:53–5 on the *hoplon*; also Hanson 1989:55–88, esp. 63–71, and essays in Part II of this volume.
42. Perfection of the phalanx or sudden creation: Latacz 1977:237–8; Cartledge 1977:11–27; Lorimer 1947:76–138; cf. Salmon 1977:87–122; outcome of experimentation: Snodgrass 1965:110–22 and *Archaic Greece: the Age of Experiment* (London, 1980) 104–6. For Pritchett (*War* 4.7–44), who finds a disciplined fully organized phalanx in Homer, changes in Greek armor had no effect.
43. Snodgrass 1964b:179–83, 1965:116, 1967:61–7 and *supra* n. 42: 104–6; Latacz 1977:229–37 with M. L. West's review, *CR* 29 (1979) 135–6; van Wees (1986) 302; *contra* Pritchett, *War* 4.33–42; Cartledge 1977:11–27; Lazenby 1985:76–7 (apparently unaware of Latacz's book). Latacz 1977:233 denies use of the hoplite shield in Tyrtaeus, based on fr.11.23–4 West (the shield covers both shoulders, whereas the *hoplon* protected only one), but he places too much weight on a poetic plural.
44. Tyrtaeus (ed. West) fr.11.35–8, 19.1–9 with Pritchett, *War* 4. 38; *P. Oxy.* 3316.14; West (*supra* n. 43) 136; Kromayer and Veith 1928:80 n. 2.
45. Tyrtaeus (ed. West) 10–12, 19.10–17; Pritchett, *War* 4. 39–41. Tyrtaeus reported that Spartan lack of discipline necessitated deployment before a trench to prohibit flight: Arist., *EN* 3.8.5 with anon. schol. in 3.8.11 (*Comm. Arist. gr.* 20, ed. Heylbut). Pausanias' account of the battle of the Great Trench (4.17.6–9) omits this aspect of the struggle.
46. Tyrtaeus (ed. West) fr.10.21–25, 11.23–4; Pritchett, *War* 4. 41, 43 with n. 142. I remain unconvinced by Pritchett's ingenious attempt to rehabilitate Pausanias' account of the Messenian wars (often thought to reflect Messenian propaganda of 370 BC and later) through topographical study and arguments that Pausanias' narrative derives from Tyrtaeus: see *Topography* 5.1–68 and *War* 4.37–8, 41, 42 n. 135. Nor do I find compelling West's analysis of Tyrtaeus fr. 19: a change in perspective from marching to battle order occurs at 19.13. See West, *ZPE* 1 (1967) 174–6, followed by Pritchett, *War* 4.38, 41.
47. Snodgrass 1964b:181–2, 1967:61–7; *contra* Pritchett, *War* 4.40 n. 131. Cf. the insertion of files of *psiloi* between the hoplite files of the phalanx, called *parentaxis* in Asclep., *Tact.* 6.1 but *entaxis* in Ael., *Tact.* 31.3; Arr., *Tact.* 26.6. Lorimer (1947:127) has the *gymnetes* protect themselves with their own shields.
48. On *othismos* see Pritchett, *War* 4. 65–76, 91–2; Hanson 1989:28–9, 169–77. Hanson ibid., 173 takes Tyrtaeus 11.21–2 as an illustration of

othismos, but I see here no evidence of collective pushing by those behind the file leader, if files are meant at all. An attempt to argue that the phalanx was an open and not a closed formation is totally misguided: Cawkwell 1978:150–3 and 'Orthodoxy and hoplites,' *CQ* 39 (1989) 379–83 (the latter written without reference to Wheeler 1979, 1982, 1983; Krentz 1985a:50–61. *Contra* Holladay 1982:94–7; Anderson 1984:152).

49. Chigi vase: Lorimer 1947:81 fig. 2; H. Payne, *Neocorinthia* (Oxford, 1931) 32, 301 no. A–3; D. A. Amyx, *Corinthian Vase-Painting of the Archaic Period* (Berkeley, 1988) II, 369: a date of ca 640BC. Despite arguments concerning the technical inability of vase painters to depict a phalanx, a rigorous methodology requires evaluation of what the evidence actually shows, not what we conjecture a painter had in mind. Furthermore, Tyrtaeus (11.11–14 West) does refer to men in the rear, as Hanson (1989:168) notes, but just as on the Chigi vase no indication is given that the second rank directly supports the first. In fact, *laon opisso* could refer to those behind the first rank of the formation or even men behind the formation possibly guarding the army's camp. Comparison of the Spartan flutists at Mantineia in 418 BC (Thuc. 5.70, cf. Plut., *Lyc.* 22.2–3) with those seen on the Chigi Vase and a proto-Corinthian aryballos from Perachora (Lorimer 1947:93 fig. 7: ca 675 BC) is too facile. Although the classical Spartan and other Greek phalanges marched in step and one tradition (Ath. 14.630e) credits Tyrtaeus with the composition of marching songs (*enoplia*), except for these vase paintings flutists and drill or cadenced marching in Greek forces of the seventh century is not attested. The function of the flutists in these vase paintings cannot be to ensure keeping in step. Cf. Snodgrass (*supra* n. 42) 106 against Salmon 1977:87–122. Also see Wheeler 1982:232–3 with n. 51. According to Greenhalgh 1973 many hoplites rode horses to battle and dismounted to form the phalanx.

50. See Arist., *Pol.* 5.5.6–8; A. Andrewes, *The Greek Tyrants* (New York, 1963) 31–53, 66–77; Cartledge 1977:11–27 and *Sparta and Laconia: a Regional History 1300-362 BC* (London, 1979) 123–40; Salmon 1977 87–122; *contra* Snodgrass 1965:114–16, 120.

51. Lycurg., *Leoc.* 106–7; Polyaenus 1.17; Ath. 14.630e; cf. Hdt. 7.104.5, 9.48.1; Thuc. 4.40.1; Loraux (*supra* n. 20) 105–6. Lazenby (1985:83) sees this Spartan imperative as part of the 'Spartan mirage' – a myth created by the battle of Thermopylae.

52. Lammert 1899:10; cf. Wheeler 1979:305 with n. 7 on the Roman phalanx. The earliest epigraphical attestation of a soldier who died *en promachois* comes from the base of a sixth-century Attic *kouros*. This wealthy young Athenian (a poor family could not commission a *kouros*) possibly died in the front ranks at the battle of Pallene ca 540 BC. See Pritchett, *War* 4.88, cf. 39–41.

53. Thebes: Diod. 12.70.1; Lammert 1899:10 n. 1; Sparta: Lazenby 1985:11, 54–6; Athens: Arist., *Ath. Pol.* 7.3–4, cf. 4.3; Plut., *Sol.* 18.1–2; cf. Lammert 1899:2 n. 11. Aristotle (*Pol.* 4.3.3, 13.10–11, cf. 6.7.1–3) associated cavalry with the aristocracies of the Archaic period. On *epilektoi* see n. 20 *supra*. Diodorus' identification (probably from Ephorus) of the Theban *Heniochoi* and *Parabatai* with the 300 *epilektoi*,

the latter a phenomenon of the fifth and fourth centuries, would imply transfer of a traditional name to a new type of unit, and Diodorus' use of *proemachonto* would indicate deployment in the front ranks, not as an advanced unit (see Pritchett in n. 52 *supra*). Lazenby plausibly argues that the 300 Spartans at Thermopylae and at the *monomachia* for Thyreae are not the *Hippeis*, a royal escort of men under the age of 30, although the name implies a connection with cavalry in the distant past. Most recently, Bugh argues for the existence of Athenian cavalry before the fifth century (see Pollux, *Onom.* 8.108), but denies that Solon's classes called *Hippeis* and *Zeugitai* reflect a military function: see G. R. Bugh, *The Horsemen of Athens* (Princeton, 1988) 4–38. Not all his arguments are equally compelling. Cf. Rhodes (*infra* n. 57) 137–8.

54. Tyrtaeus as general: *Suda* s.v. Tyrtaios; Polyaenus 1.17; Diod. 8.37; Philochorus, *FGrHist* 328 F 216 = Ath. 14.630f; Callisthenes, *FGrHist* 124 F 24 = Strabo 8.4.10; Lycurg., *Leoc.* 106; Spartan kings: Hdt. 5.75.2 with How and Wells (*infra* n. 58) II, 41: Lazenby 1985:20. A second-century papyrus (copying Ephorus?) ascribes a military command to the famous ephor Chilon ca 556: *FGrHist* 105 F 1; Cartledge 1979 (*supra* n. 50):140, 158. Possible military activity of the lawgiver Lycurgus was debated in antiquity: see Wheeler 1983:16–17.
55. Xen., *Lac. Resp.* 11.9, cf. 13.6. Unlike Lazenby (1985:175 n. 7), I do not accept assignment of this work to a Ps.-Xenophon, as K. M. T. Chrimes, *The Respublica Lacedaimonicorum Ascribed to Xenophon* (Manchester, 1948) and *Ancient Sparta* (Manchester, 1949) App. VII.
56. Thuc. 5.66.2–4, 68; Xen., *Lac. Resp.* 11.4. The complex problems of Spartan military organization cannot be treated here. See A. Toynbee, *Some Problems in Greek History* (Oxford, 1969) 365–404; Anderson 1970:225–51; Lazenby 1985:4–10, 50–2, 66–80; T. J. Figueira, 'Population patterns in Late Archaic and Classical Sparta,' *TAPA* 116 (1986) 165–211; Cartledge (*supra* n. 16) 427–9.
57. Arist., *Ath. Pol.* 22.2; differing interpretations of this passage in P. J. Rhodes, *A Commentary on the Aristotelian Athenaion Politeia* (Oxford, 1981) 264–5; G. R. Stanton, 'The tribal reform of Kleisthenes the Alkmeonid,' *Chiron* 14 (1984) 15–16; Fornara (*supra* n. 20) 3–6; C. Hignett, *A History of the Athenian Constitution* (Oxford, 1952) 145–6, 169–70, 176.
58. Arist., *Ath. Pol.* 3.2, 41.2, cf. 4.2; Hdt. 8.44.2 (Ion = *stratarches*); W. W. How and J. Wells, *A Commentary on Herodotus* (Oxford, 1912) II, 249; Hignett (*supra* n. 57) 47–55; Rhodes (*supra* n. 57) 66–73, 100; Schaefer, 'Polemarchos 4,' *RE* Supplbd. 8 (1956) 1101–2.
59. Xen., *Lac. Resp.* 11.4; 13.1, 4, 9; Plut., *Lyc.* 12.3; Thuc. 5.66.3; schol. in Pl., *Phd.* 235D; Schaefer (*supra* n. 58) 1124–8, 1132.
60. Nicolaus of Damascus, *FGrHist* 90 F 57.5; anon., *FGrHist* 105 F 2; Schaefer (*supra* n. 58) 1121–2. Ephorus probably drew on the fourth-century tyrant of his own time as a model of interpreting archaic tyrants. On tyrants see n. 50 *supra*.
61. For the date of this reform I find Hignett (*supra* n. 57) 171–6 more convincing; opposing views summarized in Rhodes (*supra* n. 57) 264–5. The whole of *Ath. Pol.* 4 (Draco's constitution), where strategoi and

phylarchs are mentioned, is anachronistic: cf. Rhodes 109–12. It should also be noted that tyrants and magistrates in Sicily also were called strategoi in the fifth century, but it cannot be demonstrated that Sicilian use of the term antedates the Athenian reform of 501/500 BC. Cf. How and Wells (*supra* n. 58) II, 197; Hignett, 116–17.

62. Arist., *Ath. Pol.* 8.3, 41.2; W. Schwann, 'Strategos,' *RE* Supplbd. 6 (1935) 1071–2; Hignett (*supra* n. 57) 77; Fornara (*supra* n. 20) 6–7 with n. 17; Siewert (*supra* n. 24) 154. The analogy of phylarchs in Hdt. 5.69.2 with the tribal cavalry commanders in the fifth and fourth centuries (Arist., *Ath. Pol.* 61.5; Xen., *Mag.Eq.* 1.8.21–22, 25; 2.1.7; 3.6; 8.17–18) is false; nor can it be proved that the Athenian army was predominantly a cavalry force before the sixth century: see Fornara (*supra* n. 20) 1, 8 with rebuttal by Bugh (*supra* n. 53) 5 with n. 14; Rhodes (*supra* n. 57) 686. Schwann (1072) equates *phylobasileus* with *stratarches*, but the latter word in Aesch. fr.304 Mette, where it would indicate a phylarch, is textually uncertain. Pindar twice uses *stratarches* in a Trojan War context for the leader of the Ethiopians (*Pyth.* 6.31; *Isth.* 5.40), and in Hdt. 3.157.4 it denotes Zopyrus' appointment to high command by Darius I. Definition of the term outside Athens may have been fluid, but Ion was believed to have been a polemarch (*stratarches*): see n. 58 *supra*.

63. Frost (1984) 283–94; H. van Effenterre, 'Clisthène et les mesures de mobilisation,' *REG* 89 (1976) 1–4; Connor 1988:6–7.

64. Arist., *Ath. Pol.* 15.4–5; Polyaenus 1.21.2; Frost 1984:291; on Cleisthenes' mobilization scheme see Siewert (*supra* n. 24) 10–13, 141–5; *contra* Stanton (*supra* n. 57) 3–6.

65. Herodotus' account (6.109–10) is riddled with anachronisms: see Hignett (*supra* n. 57) 170–3; M. H. Jameson, 'Seniority in the Stratêgia,' *TAPA* 86 (1955) 79–81; How and Wells (*supra* n. 58) II, 357; Rhodes (*supra* n. 57) 264–5; Fornara (*supra* n. 20) 6–7, 72–3. The right flank as the place of honor: Eur., *Supp.* 656–8; Hdt. 6.111.1; 9.28.1, 46.1; Thuc. 5.71; Xen., *Hell.* 2.4.30, *Lac. Resp.* 11.9; Plut., *Mor.* 626D–E; cf. Lammert 1899: 18–19.

66. Hignett (*supra* n. 57) 176; F. Lammert, 'Taxiarchos' and 'Taxis,' *RE* 5A.1 (1934) 75, 85–7; earliest reference: Aesch. fr.304 (= Ath. 1.11d–e), 596 Mette, cf. Arist., *Ath. Pol.* 61.3; *taxis* = *phyle*: Thuc. 6.98.4. Rhodes (*supra* n. 57) 684–5 unconvincingly argues for taxiarchs before 487/6 BC based on the fourth-century Oath of Plataea.

67. *Ad hoc* command: see Rhodes (*supra* n. 57) 264; First Sacred War: Plut., *Sol.* 11.2; bibliography in Wheeler 1987: 172 with n. 69; Peisistratus: Hdt. 1.59.4; Arist., *Ath. Pol.* 22.3; Aen. Tact. 4.8–11; Front., *Strat.* 2.9.9; Just. 2.8.1–4; How and Wells (*supra* n. 58) I, 82; Schaefer (*supra* n. 58) 1122; Hignett (*supra* n. 57) 113. Given Herodotus' frequent anachronisms, his use of strategos for non-Athenian commanders of the seventh and sixth centuries does not prove widespread use of the term in the Archaic period, as N. G. L. Hammond thinks: 'Strategia and hegemonia in fifth-century Athens,' *CQ* 19 (1969) 113 with n. 2.

68. *Contra* Stanton (*supra* n. 57) 1–41: the reforms aimed at increasing Alcmaeonid influence.

69. Hignett (*supra* n. 57) 69; Fornara (*supra* n. 20) 3–6; H. T. Wade-Gery, *Essays in Greek History* (Oxford, 1958) 154.
70. Arist., *Ath. Pol.* 7.3; Plut., *Sol.* 18.2; Rhodes (*supra* n. 57) 137–8.
71. Plut., *Arist.* 5.3–5, *Mor.* 626D–E; Hdt. 6.111.1; subunits: Hdt. 9.21.3; Xen., *Mem.* 3.1.5, 4.1; Arist., *Ath. Pol.* 61.3; cf. Isae. 2.42; Kromayer and Veith 1928:49 with n. 3; Siewert (*supra* n. 24) 7 n. 42, 142–3; Lazenby 1985:193 n. 14; additional references in Rhodes (*supra* n. 57) 685, who doubts the existence of such units; trittyarch: Pl., *Rep.* 5.475A; cf. Arist., *Ath. Pol.* 8.3, 21.4.
72. The young aristocrat's death *en promachois* possibly at Pallene ca 540 BC (n. 52 *supra*) implies close combat, but is too vague to prove use of a fully developed phalanx. Nor does reference to *parataxis* in a second-century AD commentary on Alcaeus (*P. Oxy.* 2506, fr.98) prove anything about the late seventh or early sixth century, as Pritchett (*War* 4.36–7) argues. As noted (*supra* n. 21), *parataxis* does not denote 'phalanx.' This noun first appears in Thuc. 5.11.2 (cf. 5.9.4) and the initial occurrence of the verb *paratatto*, Hdt. 9.31.2, regards *Persian* deployment at Plataea.
73. Law on desertion: Aeschin., *In Ctes.* 175; Schwertfeger (1982) 264–5; Solon's laws: Hignett (*supra* n. 57) 17–27.
74. Hdt. 6.114; for Herodotus' *aner genomenos agathos* = *arete*, see Loraux (*supra* n. 7) 99.
75. Cf. Hanson 1989:114. Miltiades' prominence in the depiction of Marathon on the Stoa Poecile, where he is seen exhorting the Athenians before the battle, in no way proves his presence in the front rank for combat. Aeschines' obscure *protoi* (*In Ctes.* 186: mistranslated as 'in the front rank' in the Loeb edition) is clarified in Nep., *Milt.* 6.3–4: *Namque huic Miltiadi, quia Athenas totamque Graeciam liberarat, talis honos tributus est: in porticu, quae Poecile vocatur, cum pugna depingeretur Marathona, ut in decem praetorum numero primaeius imago poneretur isque hortaretur militis proeliumque committeret.* Callimachus also appeared in the painting: Paus. 1.15.3.
76. Cf. Hdt. 7.158.5: Gelon of Syracuse's demand to be strategos and *hegemon* of the Greek confederacy in 480 BC. Strategos here may be anachronistic, but in this context it denotes absolute authority to command, whereas the leader of an alliance of equals was a *hegemon*, as Pausanias at Plataea (cf. Thuc. 1.18.2) and Philip II and Alexander in the League of Corinth: see Cartledge 1979 (*supra* n. 50):202–3; Bosworth (*supra* n. 17) 189–90 with n. 5. On Sicilian strategoi see *supra* n. 61. Analysis of Pausanias' tactical and strategic functions at Plataea lies beyond the scope of this paper. It should be noted, however, that Pausanias styled himself *archegos* on the inscription he set up at Delphi (Thuc. 1.132.2; Plut., *Mor.* 873C), a word denoting more authority and power than the tamer nuance of *hegemon* in the Classical Period: cf. LSJ[9] s.vv. *Archegos* also appears in an incomplete line of the Themistocles Decree: Meiggs/Lewis 1969: no. 23 line 11.
77. Loraux (*supra* n. 7) 42–76; on the date see Pritchett, *War* 4.112–24.
78. Ar., *Nub.* 960–86; Thuc. 1.121.4, 123.1; Pl., *Lach.* 179C; Xen., *Mem.* 3.5.3, 9–11, 22.
79. After 461 BC: Arist., *Ath. Pol.* 26.1, cf. Ps.-Xen., *Ath. Pol.* 1.3; Rhodes

(*supra* n. 57) 323–8; 420s: Arist., *Ath. Pol.* 28; Ar., *Pax* 672–8; Xen., *Symp.* 2.14, cf. Ar., *Av.* 1553–64.

80. Eur., *Supp.* 161–2, 861–917.
81. Thuc. 1.138.3, 140–44; 2.60–5.
82. See Plut., *Them.* 2.4, *Mor.* 869F; E. L. Wheeler, *Stratagem and the Vocabulary of Military Trickery* (Mnemosyne Supp. 108: Leiden, 1988) 25–41, esp. 29 with n. 22, 33 with n. 44.
83. On Homer and the *hoplomachoi* see nn. 12, 20 *supra*; cf. Euripides' satire of sophistic military instruction: *Supp.* 902–8.
84. Wheeler 1981:74–9 and 1983:2–6. Bibliography on Aeneas in Wheeler 1983:8 n. 40 and (*supra* n. 12) 175 with n. 67.
85. See J. de Romilly, 'Réflexions sur le courage chez Thucydides et chez Platon,' *REG* 93 (1980) 307–23.
86. Arist., *EN* 3.8.3; cf. E. R. Dodds, *The Greeks and the Irrational* (Berkeley, 1971) 17–18; E. Sagen, *The Lust to Annihilate: a Psychoanalytic Study of Violence in Ancient Greek Culture* (New York, 1979) 75–80.
87. For a study of the trend from the standpoint of militarism see Lengauer 1979. Pritchett (*War* 2.4–116) disputes that a separation of civil and military functions occurred and documents, especially at Athens, continued civilian control of generals.
88. Miltiades: Aeschin., *In Ctes.* 186; Nep., *Milt.* 6.3–4; cf. n. 75 *supra*; Pausanias: Thuc. 1.132.2–3; Plut., *Mor.* 873C; cf. Meiggs and Lewis 1969: no. 27; Cimon: Aeschin., *In Ctes.* 183–6; Plut., *Cim.* 7–8.2; Iphicrates: *Suda* s.v.; Parke 1933: 74 n. 2. Cf. M. N. Tod, *A Selection of Greek Historical Inscriptions*, II (Oxford, 1948) no. 130 (*IG* VII 2462) for an apparent protest by one boeotarch and two others against Epaminondas' prominence after Leuctra.
89. Hyperides, *Epitaph.* 3, 14–15; Loraux (*supra* n. 7) 52, 111–13.
90. Plut., *Mor.* 193B; Paus. 9.13.11–12; Anderson 1970:39.
91. Anderson 1970:39–40; Hanson 1989:63, 110; on Spartan officers see Lazenby 1985:18–24. Keegan (*supra* n. 5) 125 believes an officer class existed at Sparta but not elsewhere.
92. Greeks did not develop the more intricate Roman system of identification of subunits and even individuals' names on the shields. See Veg. 2.18: *Sed ne milites aliquando in tumultu proelii a suis contubernalibus aberrarent, diversis cohortibus diversa in scutis signa pingebant, ut ipsi nominant, digmata, sicut etiam nunc moris est fieri. Praeterea in adverso scuto uniuscuiusque militis litteris erat nomen adscriptum, addito et ex qua esset cohorte quave centuria.*
93. Snodgrass 1967:67, 95–6, 137 n. 25; Anderson 1970:17–20, 39–40; Lazenby 1985:30 175 n.4; Ducrey 1985:52; N. Sekunda, *The Ancient Greeks: Armies of Classical Greece, 5th and 4th Centuries BC* (London, 1986) 3, 6, 8, 25–6, pl. A1, A3; on shield emblems see esp. L. Lacroix, 'Les "blazons" des villes grecques,' *EtArchClass* 1 (1955–6) 89–116. Hardie (*supra* n. 17) 12 discusses astrological symbols on shields.
94. *Pace* Kromayer (Kromayer and Veith 1928:83–4) intervals separated the subdivisions of the phalanx, but a supposed parallel with the deployment of Maurice of Nassau (early seventeenth century) is the

only evidence cited. Nevertheless, a battleline consisting of contingents from more than one polis probably did tolerate gaps between the respective phalanges of each city, since each polis' forces functioned as a distinct unit: cf. the battles of Mantineia (418 BC), Nemea (394 BC), and Coronea (394 BC). A battle-line of allied Greek cities should not be conceived as a continuous phalanx from flank to flank.

95. Thuc. 5.68.2–3; Lammert 1899:17; statuette: Lazenby 1985:33, pl. 3; Sekunda (*supra* n. 93) 3, 6, pl. A1; cf. Veg. 2.13: *Centuriones ... transversis cassidum cristis, ut facilius noscerentur, singulas iusserunt gubernare centurias*; G. Webster, *The Roman Imperial Army* (London, 1969) 132 with n. 4, 133, pl. IV.
96. Taxiarchs: Ar., *Pax* 1172–6, schol. in 241; *Ach.* 965; Kromayer and Veith 1928:51; Anderson 1970:40; strategoi: Sekunda (*supra* n. 93) 56. The shield apron of leather or cloth, doubtless an anti-missile device inspired by combat with Persians, appears on vase paintings of Asia Minor and the Greek mainland ca 550 BC to the early fourth century and was once thought the sign of an officer. Since file leaders do carry them, it cannot be denied that officers could be so equipped, but the shield apron would not necessarily distinguish an officer from a non-officer. See Anderson 1970:17 and, most recently, J. Eero, 'On the shield-apron in the ancient Greek panoply,' *AArch* 57 (1986) 1–25.
97. Arr., *Anab.* 1.14.4; Plut., *Alex.* 16.7, *Pyrrh.* 16.7, *Nic.* 28.5, *Alcib.* 16.1–2; Ath. 12.534e; Xen., *Anab.* 3.2.7, cf. Ael., *VH* 3.24; Diod. 14.43.2–3; Plut., *Dion* 28.3. Cf. Plut., *Demetr.* 21.3–4, Diod. 19.3.2.
98. Agesilaus, renowned for his simplicity of dress (Xen., *Ages.* 11.11), might appear an exception, but in his military role as Spartan king he did not renounce the customary royal Spartan practices. Plutarch (*Ages.* 19.4–6) shows only that he refused to adopt Persian customs, not that he lacked distinguishing armor. A general's spear (Plut., *Ages.* 19.6), unless ceremonial, would not have greatly differed from that of the rank-and-file hoplite. Cf. Hanson 1989:59.
99. Xen., *Cyr.* 3.3.61–2; 4.1.6; 7.1.20, 23, 26.
100. Agesilaus: Xen., *Ages.* 2.15; Plut., *Ages.* 16.5; Pelopidas: Plut., *Pel.* 32.5–7; Nep., *Pel.* 5.4. Diodorus (15.80.5) is vague on the matter. Buckler's reconstruction of the battle homogenizes the contradiction: Pelopidas first led a cavalry charge, then dismounted and died at the head of an infantry assault: J. Buckler, *The Theban Hegemony 371–362 BC* (Harvard Historical Studies 98: Cambridge, Mass., 1980) 176–80.
101. See J. A. O. Larsen, 'The *Acharnians* and the pay of taxiarchs,' *CP* 41 (1946) 91–8; Hignett (*supra* n. 57) 220; Bugh (*supra* n. 53) 53–4 denies that strategoi, hipparchs, and phylarchs received state pay, but cites no modern discussions of the question. Rates of pay for hoplites and rowers are discussed in Pritchett, *War* 1.3–29.
102. Xen., *Anab.* 7.6.1; Griffith 1935:295. Cf. Xen., *Anab.* 3.1.37.
103. Pausanias: Hdt. 9.81.2; cf. Pritchett *War* 1.83, *War* 2.289–90 with n. 56 on the amount; Spartan kings: Polyb. 2.62.1 (from Phylarchus); Pritchett, *War* 1.84, cf. 75–6; *War* 2.126. Little is known about the officer pay in the Spartan army (if it existed at all) except that the kings

received a double portion of food and drink: Hdt. 6.57.1; Xen., *Lac. Resp.* 15.4, *Ages.* 5.1. Cf. Arist., *Pol.* 3.14.3–4; Cartledge (*supra* n. 16) 105–6, 206.

104. See Pritchett, *War* 1.84; *War* 2.126–32, 276 n. 1.
105. Agesilaus: Xen., *Ages.* 1.25–6; *Hell.* 3.4.16, 4.2.5; Jason: Xen., *Hell.* 6.1.6; Iphicrates: Polyaenus 3.9.31. Cf. Xen., *Cyr.* 2.1.22–4.
106. Xen., *Ages.* 2.8 and esp. *Hiero* 2.15–16; cf. Hanson 1989: 119–21, 190–1. Evidence on the *aristeia* collected in Pritchett, *War* 2.276–90; *War* 3.57. A notable recent study of Roman military awards fails to consider Greek precedents: V. A. Maxfield, *The Military Decorations of the Roman Army* (Berkeley, 1981).
107. Hdt. 9.71.3–4; Plut., *Ages.* 34.6–8, *Pel.* 1.4; Loraux (*supra* n. 7) 99; *lyssa* vs *sophrosyne*: Detienne, in Vernant 1968:122.
108. Salamis: Hdt. 8.123.2; Plut., *Them.* 17.1, *Mor.* 871D; Granicus: Diod. 17.21.4. Cf. Caesar at Pharsalus: App., *BC* 2. 82.
109. Xen., *Mag. Eq.* 2.6, cf. *Anab.* 3.1.37, *Cyr.* 1.6.25.
110. See Andrewes 1981:1–3; Garlan 1989:148–9.
111. Meiggs and Lewis 1969: nos. 33 lines 5–6, 33, cf. lines 128–9 (*mantis*), lines 67–70; 48 line 4; D. W. Bradeen, *The Athenian Agora* XVIII: *Inscriptions: the Funerary Monuments* (Princeton, 1974) nos. 22 A line 34, C lines 152–3, 159; 23 A; 25. Cf. Bradeen 1969: 145–59.
112. Thuc. 7.86.2; Plut., *Nic.* 28.2, 4; 29.
113. Ar., *Ach.* 597, 1071–234; Larsen (*supra* n. 101) 96. The ridicule of a taxiarch at Ar., *Pax* 1172–90 likewise is aimed at the officer as a symbol of military service.
114. Thuc. 5.65.2; Xen., *Hell.* 4.2.22; on the army as a city see C. Mossé, 'Le rôle politique des armées dans le monde grec à l'époque classique,' in Vernant 1968: 221–9.
115. Keegan (*supra* n. 5) 316–17, cf. 329–38; Beaumont (*supra* n. 15) 70–1. A current example of kinship is the US Army's policy that even general officers wear combat fatigues as their daily uniform.
116. Xen., *Ages.* 5.1–4; 6.4–7; 7.2; 8.1–4, 6–8; 10.1–2; 11; cf. *Cyr.* 1.2.1; Hanson 1989:110–11; Cartledge (*supra* n. 16) 206–7.
117. E.g. Liv. 21.4.2–8 (Hannibal); Dio 68.23.1 (Trajan); *HA, Had.* 10.2–6; *Pesc. Nig.* 10.11.
118. Xen., *Anab.* 3.1.42; *Cyr.* 3.3.19. Cf. Keegan (*supra* n. 5) 122–3.
119. Onas, 33.6; Phil.Mech., *Syn. Mech.* 5.D.68–9 Garlan; cf. Front., *Strat.* 2.8.12–13.
120. See Xen., *Anab.* 3.2.29–30; Arist., *Metaph.* 11.10, 1075a12–15; Polyaenus 3.9.22; Plut., *Pel.* 2.1–2.
121. Polyaenus 2.3.15; Xen., *Hell.* 6.4.12.
122. Tegyra: Plut., *Pel.* 16.1, 17.3–4; Granicus: Arr., *Anab.* 1.15.3; Issus: Diod. 17.33.5; Curt. 3.11.7–11; Gaugamela: Arr., *Anab.* 3.14.2–3; Diod. 17.60.1–4; Plut., *Alex.* 33.3–8. Cf. Nep., *Epam.* 9.1.
123. Onas. 23; Front., *Strat.* 2.4.9 (cf. Plut., *Pyrrh.* 17.1–3), 2.4.10; Sall, *Iug.* 101.6–8. Although all known examples of this stratagem are Roman, Onasander's treatise is a compendium of Greek military thought (fourth century and Hellenistic) for Roman consumption. See D. Ambaglio, 'Il trattato "Sul Commandante" di Onasandro,' *Athenaeum*

59 (1981) 353–77.

124. See Hanson 1988:200–1 and 1989:112; Teleutias: Xen., *Hell.* 5.3.6. Cf. the death of the polemarchs at Tegyra (Plut., *Pel.* 17.3–4) and Nepos' account of Epaminondas' end at Mantineia (*Epam.* 9.1–2).
125. Xen., *Mag. Eq.* 2.6; *Anab.* 3.1.37.
126. Marathon: Plut., *Them.* 3.3, *Arist.* 5.3–5; Tanagra: Plut., *Per.* 10.1–2; see Fornara (*supra* n. 20) 46 on Pericles' status; Agesilaus: Plut., *Ages.* 1.1–3, 37.1, 39.3–4; Mantineia: Plut., *Pel.* 4.4–5, 20.2; cf. Nep., *Epam.* 7.1–2.
127. Brasidas: Thuc. 2.25.2, 4.11.2–4; Lamachus: Thuc. 6.101.6; Chabrias/Plutarch: Plut., *Phoc.* 6.1, 13.1.
128. Xen., *Ages.* 6.2; Plut., *Ages.* 36.2, *Pel.* 2.3, cf. *Mor.* 187C.
129. Plut., *Pyrrh.* 30.4–6, *Pel.* 32.5–7; Nep., *Pel.* 5.1–4; Xen., *Hell.* 5.3.6–7.
130. See Hanson 1988:201 n. 30 and 1989:113–15.
131. Paul (*supra* n. 16) 308 counts twenty-two generals or independent commanders killed in approximately eighty-three land battles in Thucydides. Casualty figures for generals are not treated in P. Krentz, *GRBS* (1985) 13–20. Casualty rates for generals need not be a function of the level of technology. To cite a modern example, the so-called first 'modern war,' the American Civil War (1861–5), is known for high casualties among general officers: 80 generals on each side were killed in battle and 123 Union and 135 Confederate generals received battle wounds. But the American Revolution (1775–83), fought at a lower technological level, produced a higher ratio of general to total fatalities, 1:499 – the highest of any American war, although only twelve American generals fell in battle. For the Civil War the ratios are 1:1729 (Union) and 1:932 (Confederate). See R. K. Brown, *Fallen in Battle: American General Officer Combat Fatalities from 1775* (New York, 1988) 164, 197.
132. Snodgrass 1967:62 and pl. 54; Hanson 1989:111; Anderson 1970:pl. 13b.
133. Xen., *Lac. Resp.* 11.5; cf. Thuc. 5.66.4; Asclep., *Tact.* 2.2–3; Ael., *Tact.* 5.1–5; Arr., *Tact.* 5.4–6.6.
134. Pritchett, *War* 1.134–43, esp. 142–3; Lammert/Lammert 1921:446–8. The argument for blind files, based on the obscure Xen., *Lac. Resp.* 13.9, dates from Köchly and Rüstow 1852:121 and Boucher 1912:301. See Anderson 1970:79 with n. 49, 99 with n. 18.
135. I do not share the pessimism of Pritchett (*War* 1.150 n. 35, 153–4) and Hanson (1989:11–12) on the value of these treatises. Terms such as *protostates* and *ouragos* occur in Thucydides (5.71.1) as well as Xenophon (*Lac. Resp.* 11.5; *Cyr.* 3.3.40), and the basic evolutions of drill probably changed little. Asclepiodotus (*Tact.* 2.2) was aware of differences between the classical and the Hellenistic phalanx: cf. Wheeler 1983:19. On the other hand, a credulous approach to the theoretical treatises can lead to absurdity: see Devine 1983:201–17 with the rebuttal by Buckler 1985:134–43.
136. See n. 65 *supra*; Xen., *Lac. Resp.* 13.6 with Buckler (*supra* n. 100) 63, followed by Lazenby 1985:29–30; *contra*, Anderson 1970:248; Agis: Thuc. 5.72.4. The Persian king also commanded from the center both for his own protection and to facilitate communications with both flanks: Xen., *Anab.* 1.8.22; Diod. 14.23.5; Arr., *Anab.* 3.11.5.

137. Xen., *Hell.* 4.3.15–18, *Ages.* 2.9–11; Plut., *Ages.* 18.1–2.
138. Plut., *Ages.* 18.3, cf. 19.1; Xen., *Hell.* 4.3.19–20, *Ages* 2.12–14.
139. Agis: Thuc. 5.72.4; Cleombrotus: Xen., *Hell.* 6.4.14; Buckler (*supra* n. 100) 63; cf. Anderson 1970: 201, 247–9, 322 n.43. The wounding of Cleombrotus possibly did not occur as early in the battle as Lazenby (1985:160) thinks; cf. Diod. 15.55.5; Xen., *Hell.* 6.4.13–14.
140. Xen., *Hell.* 6.4.13, 7.4.23; Plut., *Lyc.* 22.4.
141. Callimachus: Hdt. 6.113–14; Lycophron at Solygia (425 BC): Thuc. 4.44.2; Brasidas at Amphipolis (422 BC): Thuc. 5.10.8, 11; Laches and Nicostratus at Mantineia (418 BC) – probably trampled by their own men while trying to stop the rout: Thuc. 5.61.1, 72.4; Lamachus at Syracuse (414 BC): Thuc. 6.101.6; Pelopidas at Cynoscephalae (364 BC): see n. 100 *supra*; Epaminondas at Mantineia (362 BC): Plut., *Ages.* 35.1; Xen., *Hell.* 7.5.23–5; Diod. 15.86.3–87.1; Nep., *Epam.* 9.1.
142. See A. du Picq, *Battle Studies: Ancient and Modern Battle*, tr. J. N. Greely and R. G. Cotton (Harrisburg, 1947) 63–93; Hanson 1989:162–4, cf. 70. Hanson's argument for Epaminondas' wound is based on Diodorus' account, but Plutarch and Nepos (see n. 141 *supra*; cf. Paus. 8.11.5–10) tell different stories. Archidamus' wound at Cromnus (365 BC Xen., *Hell.* 7.4.23) occurs in a battle of encounter, not a pitched battle (*parataxis*). Brasidas' wound when a spear pierced his shield is associated with his death at Amphipolis by Anderson (1970:16–17) and Hanson (1989:70), but not by Plutarch (*Mor.* 190B, 219C, 548B), the sole source of this anecdote, or by Thucydides (5.10.8). The story could also be a corruption of Brasidas' wound at Pylos (Thuc. 4.12.1) or a later invention. Thucydides' account of Brasidas' headlong charge to surprise Cleon (Thuc. 5.10.6–8, cf. the cavalry duel of Brasidas and Cleon in Tzetz. in Ar., *Nub.* 549a) without reference to Brasidas' troops is a prime example of the general's name symbolizing the force under his command and does not necessarily indicate that Brasidas led the charge. A study of *hegeomai* and similar verbs in military contexts would probably support this view. Amphipolis, in any event, was a surprise, not a pitched battle. Finally, even Diodorus' highly rhetorical account of Epaminondas at Mantineia has the general come to the fore only after the battle has gone on a long time (15.86.4). Diodorus' source was Ephorus, and Polybius (12.25f.3–5) considered Ephorus' account of Mantineia full of errors. See Buckler (*supra* n. 100) 268–9, 321 n. 26.
143. Myronidas: Front., *Strat.* 2.4.11; Polyaenus 1.35.1; Thuc. 1.108.3; Daphaenus: Polyaenus 5.7. Anderson (1970:160) rejects the story about Myronidas apparently from its sole occurrence in late sources, but it is well known that Ephorus was the chief source of Polyaenus' first book and Frontinus used earlier Greek sources: see Wheeler (*supra* n. 12) 174 with n. 65 and (*supra* n. 82) 18. Of course the authority of Ephorus does not guarantee accuracy, but it does eliminate Anderson's view for rejection.
144. See Thuc. 5.71–3; cf. Anderson 1970:71–2.
145. Polyaenus 3.9.12; cf. Arist., *EN* 3.8.5; Onas. 32.1. The controversy over the position of the Theban Sacred Band at Leuctra and Pelopidas' role in the battle does not concern us, since Pelopidas in this battle was a

subordinate commander. I remain, however, unconvinced by the attacks on Anderson's view, since critics have not adequately addressed *inter alia* the parallel between Leuctra and Xenophon's battle of Thymbrara in the *Cyropaedia*. See Anderson 1970:165–220; *contra* Buckler (*supra* n. 100) 55–66 and 'Plutarch on Leuctra,' *SymbOslo* 55 (1980) 75–93; Lazenby 1985:155–62; C. J. Tuplin, 'The Leuctra Campaign: some outstanding problems,' *Klio* 69 (1987) 84–93; Hanson 1988:196–7. Polybius (12.25f.4) called Leuctra a simple battle!

146. Evidence collected in Pritchett, *War* 1.109–12; *War* 4.63, 73–4, 83–8.

147. Xenophon (*Lac. Resp.* 13.8) states that the enemy watches the sacrifice, but Plutarch (*Lyc.* 22.2) says only that the enemy is present. Pritchett (*War* 3.86) also emphasizes Thuc. 6.69.2 and Eur., *Heracl.* 672–3. The verb *propheron* in this passage of Thucydides need not mean 'carry in front of,' but rather could simply indicate 'offer' or 'present.' A scholiast on the passage (*emprosthen tes stratias esphagiazonto*) does not have independent value. Likewise, Euripides says only that the sacrifice was *taxeon hekas*, not necessarily in front of the army. Similarly, the general or Spartan king did begin the paean (evidence in *War* 1.106–7), although *exerchen* in Plut., *Lyc.* 22.2 offers no proof that the king was physically in front of his men. In some cases the commander could raise the paean and lead the charge, as Cyrus commanding the right wing cavalry at Thymbrara (Xen., *Cyr.* 7.1.25).

148. Hdt. 9.61.3, 72.1; cf. Pritchett, *War* 3.78.

149. Diod. 15.56.1–2; Polyaenus 2.3.2. At Chaeronea (338 BC) Diodorus (16.86.4) has Philip II in the front ranks, but in Polyaenus (4.2.2) he executed a feigned retreat. The depiction of Miltiades on the Stoa Poecile offers no conclusive evidence that he stood in the front rank at Marathon: see n. 75 *supra*.

150. Plut., *Ages.* 36.3, *Mor.* 225D; cf. *Cleom.* 31.1–2.

151. Onas. 33.5; Polyb. 2.69.10; Plut., *Cleom.* 28.5; Hanson 1988:201 n. 30, 1989:113. Cf. Polyb. 11.2.11; Plut., *Comp. Pel./Marc.* 3.2, *Mor.* 24D.

152. Evidence in Pritchett, *War* 2.32; cf. Plut., *Cleom.* 31; F. W. Walbank, *A Historical Commentary on Polybius*, I (Oxford, 1957) 287; cf. J. T. Roberts, *Accountability in Athenian Government* (Madison, 1982) 139–40.

153. Exile/fines: e.g. Thuc. 4.65.3, 5.26.5 (Thucydides, cf. 4.104.4–107.2); prosecution: Pritchett, *War* 2.4–33; Roberts (*supra* n. 152) passim.

154. Paches: Plut., *Nic.* 6.1–2, *Arist.* 26.3; cf. Thuc. 3.18.3–5, 27–8, 33–6, 49–50; Diod. 12.55; Front., *Strat.* 4.7.17; Polyaenus 3.2. Roberts (*supra* n. 152:136–41) doubts the historicity of Paches' suicide, but offers no alternative explanation of Paches' end or the origin of the story. C. J. Tuplin defends the story's historicity: 'Fathers and sons: *Ecclesiazusae* 644–45,' *GRBS* 23 (1982) 327–30.

155. Diod. 13.43.5; Polyb. 1.11.5. Romans later interpreted Carthaginian practice to mean that not only a general who suffered defeat but also one who planned poorly, even if victorious, was punished: see Val. Max. 2.7 ex. 1; J. Afric., *Cest.* 7.1.2; cf. Liv. 38.48.5; *De Vir. Ill.* 38.3.

156. Onas. 33; Phil. Mech., *Syn. Mech.* 5.D.20, 28, 68–9 Garlan; Polyb. 10.3.7, 13.1–5, 24.2–5, 32–3, 41.2; Plut., *Pel.* 1–2, *Comp. Pel./Marc.* 3.2–3;

Polyaenus 6.4.1; Lucian, *Dial. Mort.* 12.5.

157. Xen., *Anab.* 1.7.9. Later sources attribute this advice to Clearchus alone: Plut., *Artax.* 8.2; Polyaenus 2.2.3. Cf. Hanson 1989:111; Paul (*supra* n. 16) 307–8.
158. Diod. 14.23.5; Plut., *Artax.* 8.2–3.
159. Plut., *Lys.* 28.5 (cf. Xen., *Anab.* 3.5.18–19), *Comp. Lys./Sulla* 4.1–4, *Comp. Pel./Marc.* 2.3.
160. See Plut., *Pel.* 2.4; Nearchus, *FGrHist* 133 F 42.2 = Arr., *Anab.* 6.13.4; Polyb. 10.32.11; App., *Hann.* 50, *BC* 2.58.
161. Amm. 19.7.8; Fitzhugh Lee, *General Lee* (repr. Greenwich, Conn., 1961) 185–6. Cf. G. McWhiney and P. D. Jamieson, *Attack and Die: Civil War Military Tactics and the Southern Heritage* (University of Alabama, 1982).

Part IV

THE RULES OF THE GAME: HOPLITE TRADITION AND PRACTICE

The Greeks of old did not even choose
to defeat their enemies by deceit, thinking
that there was nothing glorious or even
secure unless one side killed those drawn
against them by fighting in open battle.

Polybius

7

HOPLITES AND OBSTACLES

Josiah Ober

INTRODUCTION

The long dominance of hoplite battle as the primary means of conflict resolution among the city-states of classical Greece is ironic. Hoplites were soldiers of the open plain. Because of their highly specialized equipment and phalanx formation, hoplites could do battle properly only in a wide, clear, flat space that was free of even minor obstacles. Yet as the most casual visitor is immediately aware, the geography of central and southern Greece is not defined by wide open plains, but rather by rugged mountains and deep ravines. The set forms of hoplite battle thus defy geomorphic logic. Common sense suggests that since Greece was a mountainous country, and the Greeks were (sometimes) rational men, the citizens of the city-states should have developed the arms, armor, and tactics suitable to mountain warfare. Yet, for most of the Classical Period, they failed to do so.[1]

A second irony is involved in the slow development of poliorcetic science in classical Greece. Greece is not only a land of mountains, but a land of stone – the limestone and marble bedrock is typically close to the surface of the ground, and makes ideal building material. Early Greek masons learned how to quarry and finish large stone blocks, and architects assembled these blocks into formidable walls. Stone walls could be made higher by adding superstructures of dried brick. Thus, from the Mycenean period onward, major Greek settlements were protected by massive and well-built circuits.[2] This being the case, we might expect that the classical Greeks would have developed effective forms of siegecraft – ways for warriors victorious on the field to get at the wives, children, and goods of their defeated opponents. Yet, once again, our commonsense expectations are confounded. Until the mid-fourth century BC, Greek poliorcetics remained rudimentary, and well-walled cities were usually secure from enemy attack.[3]

For most of the Archaic and Classical Periods neither the natural obstacles of mountain and ravine, nor the man-made obstacles represented by fortification walls had a place in the central moment of Greek warfare: the clash of the opposing phalanxes in the fair field. But those same obstacles loom in the background of the hoplite battle. Throughout the period of hoplite warfare, obstacles defined the action before and after the trial of the phalanxes. By the late fifth century, man-made obstacles and the exploitation of natural obstacles were becoming increasingly problematic features of the hoplite's experience of warfare. By the fourth century, natural obstacles were being systematically reinforced by man-made ones and this development led to the end of the traditional Greek way of war.

MOUNTAINS AND ROADS

The potential importance of obstacles in Greek warfare is linked to the physical structure of the polis. The territory of the city-state was often (although not always) delimited by mountain ranges, so that in order to go by land from one city-state to the other, it was frequently necessary to cross a mountain range. Since hoplite armies ordinarily travelled by land, rather than by sea, they often had to traverse mountains in order to invade the territory of a neighboring state (Ober 1985a: 111–29). If the war was against a more distant foe, several mountain ranges would have to be crossed (Hammond 1954). The mountains of central and southern Greece are very rugged, and they are characterized by deep gorges and dry-washes, the result of torrential seasonal runoff. Because of this morphology, it is not possible to cross the mountains just anywhere; only a few routes are available across any given range which avoid excessively steep slopes and gorges, and which take advantage of natural passes (Ober 1985a: 111).

Adding to the difficulty of the mountain obstacle was the fact that the hoplite army did not travel light. Hoplite arms and armor were much too hot and heavy to wear in the summer while marching across difficult terrain (Hanson 1989: 60–3). This meant that armor and weapons had to be transported, along with several weeks' rations, for each hoplite and his attendants.[4] Perhaps in some 'next-door-neighbor' campaigns, the baggage could be carried by the hoplites and their attendants alone. More often, however, baggage was hauled either on the backs of pack-animals or in ox-drawn carts. In either case, this meant a quantum leap in the size of the marching column, since at least some of the fodder for the pack/draft animals would also have to be carried along. Thus, even quite a small hoplite army – consisting of only a few hundred actual fighting men – would require a very significant baggage train.[5] Large bodies of men accompanied by pack-trains or wagons cannot make effective use of narrow shepherd paths. Carts, especially, must stick to roadways that maintain minimum tolerances in terms of grade, width, and switchback design. Thus, the hoplite army was restricted to established routes across the mountains and the ideal was always a route that had been built into a properly designed highway.

Modern topographers (e.g. Hammond, Pritchett, Vanderpool, and Van de Maele) have traced the routes of a number of quite well-built, pre-modern roads in the mountains of central and southern Greece.[6] Many of these roads are very impressive in their design and execution. Stretches of 'Edward Clarke's Road' to Marathon, the 'Road of the Towers' in the northwestern Megarid, and the 'Panakton Road' in north-central Attica were studied by surveying teams under my direction. We found that these roads maintain very steady grades across extraordinarily difficult terrain. The grade is maintained by the use of frequent and well-designed switchbacks; in some cases the roads are wide enough to accommodate cart traffic. In order to maintain a constant width, the road-builders cut deeply into bedrock on the uphill side, and built massive rubble-stone retaining walls on the downhill side. Uphill stone embankments across drainages ensured that seasonal flooding would not wash out the roadway. Road metal, probably in the form of packed broken rock, smoothed the surface of some sections of the highway.[7] The existence of wheel ruts (worn or cut grooves in the bedrock of the roadway) demonstrates that at least some ancient mountain roads were used by wheeled traffic.[8]

Pre-modern roads are usually difficult to date, but in some cases (e.g. the 'Road of the Towers' across the Megarid, the 'Koulouriotiko Monopati' across western Attica) the presence of datable classical remains (buildings or graves) along the line of the road confirms the hypothesis that the road was built in classical times. In sum, roads across mountainous borderlands were built in the Classical Period, and these roads could be used by hoplite armies.

It is worth asking the question, 'who built these classical roads – and why?' Some Greek roads display the same sort of architectural skills evident in the design of classical Greek temples and public buildings.[9] It is impossible to believe that they were simple improvements effected by local amateurs to facilitate everyday traffic on existing paths. Rather, they must have been surveyed, designed, and built by experts who possessed considerable engineering ability.[10] There is no evidence for the existence of large-scale overland trading companies in classical Greece that could harness the technical engineering skill or the manpower necessary to construct and maintain highways across international borders. As in the case of temples and other sophisticated structures, it is necessary to suppose that mountain roads were public projects, built by state authorities.

Why would a Greek polis undertake the expense of building a road – especially one across its own frontier? The obvious first guess might be to facilitate trade.[11] But in most cases this hypothesis seems unlikely. Overland trade between poleis was limited in volume, and was not typically a matter for state involvement. The reason for this state of affairs was not so much a cultural disinterest in trade, but rather the relative ease and much lower cost of water-borne shipping. Thus, most bulk trade in heavy goods went by sea, and there was relatively little economic incentive for building roads.[12]

The roads of classical Greece were not casual improvements by local residents, and were not built to link commercial markets. Rather, most of the classical roads across Greek mountain ranges are best explained as military highways – designed by military engineers and built and maintained with the labor of the armies that used them. The recognition that hoplite battles often required a long march across mountainous terrain, along with the assumption that roads across the mountainous borderlands between poleis were built and maintained by hoplite armies, adds to our understanding of the hoplite's experience of war.

The brief and bloody business of actual fighting was, for the offensive hoplite force, invariably preceded by a long, dusty, sweaty, thirsty hike. In most cases this hike would involve bivouacking in the field, perhaps under canvas, perhaps in the open. Rainstorms are rare in central Greece during the summer campaigning season, but when they do come they are torrential and would make the unsheltered hoplite's life very unpleasant.[13] Furthermore, when camping in the mountains, level terrain is often hard to find; it would sometimes have been necessary for each hoplite or group of hoplites to build a stone platform into the steep hillside on which to pitch tents or spread bedding. Food would have been carried along, but adequate water must have been a real problem. Hiking in the dry summer heat of central Greece requires drinking great quantities of water to maintain one's health and strength. The hoplites, their attendants and the pack/draught animals all required drinking water; the daily water requirements for even a small army would be tremendous. In some areas, it would not be easy to procure the required amounts, and thirst would then torment man and beast alike.[14]

The work of the march would not be limited to hiking and making camp. If it were necessary to build a roadway from scratch, the labor involved would be prodigious, but even maintenance roadwork could be tough and time-consuming. Rock-cutting with simple tools is very hard work. Hauling stone for building retaining walls is exhausting. And all this labor would be done under time pressure, since the campaigning season was short (Hanson 1989: 32–3). Some of the work might be done by attendants, but the need to get the road through surely required that the hoplites put their own backs into the chore. There is nothing incongruous about the image of free citizen and slave-attendant working side by side; Athenian citizens worked beside metics and slaves in other public building projects.[15]

In the context of hoplites as road-crews, it is important to remember that the hoplite soldier was, most typically, a citizen-farmer who ran his small plot by the sweat of his own brow and the labor of family members.[16] Most Greek farmers had to build and maintain fences, often these were of stone (Hanson 1983; 37–8). For a farmer, whose land included any hilly area, the business of hauling rock to build and maintain retaining walls was part of everyday life. Thus the grunt-work of roadbuilding would be a continuation of the labor performed by the citizen-soldier in his ordinary life, but with this exception: as a farmer he worked alone, or with his family and/or close neighbors. As a soldier he worked as part of a greater community of citizens, in a project that was likely to earn him no personal reward. The rough labor of road building and maintenance thus helped to integrate the everyday, private life of the individual citizen with the strange and frightening realm of military duty and self-sacrifice. Perhaps, then, the work of roadbuilding was reassuring to the Greek hoplite, despite the toll it took in arduous labor. The toilsome march across the borderland erected a bridge of familiar manual labor between the day-to-day existence of home and farm and the nightmare of the battlefield. The psychological bridge of common labor helped prepare the hoplite to meet his opponent.

The Greek soldier's work on the military highway not only provided a way into enemy territory, it represented the route home. If the battle resulted in victory for the invaders, the road might not seem so important; the homeward march would be orderly, even leisurely. But if the invaders were beaten in battle, the road he had built was the hoplite's lifeline. A good road out of enemy territory was the defeated soldier's best chance to make good his escape. The horror of defeat in battle would be doubled and trebled if the pursuing enemy were able to chase the beaten soldiers along narrow paths well known to the native, but strange to the invader.[17] Consider the situation of the defeated Athenian army in Aetolia in 426 BC. After the Athenians turned to run

> Many were killed after rushing down into dried-up water-courses from which there was no road up or in other parts of the battlefield where they lost their way. . . . The main body, however, took the wrong road and rushed into the forest, where there were no paths by which they could escape and which was set on fire by the enemy so that it burned all round them. Everything, in fact, which could happen in a flight happened to the Athenian army, and men perished by every form of death.
>
> (Thuc. 3.98.1–3, trans. Warner)

A well-built military highway, whose every switchback was familiar, represented the defeated army's best chance for effecting an orderly withdrawal from enemy territory. Thus, the product of his labor symbolized the hoplite's hope of returning home safely. During the hours the soldier worked as a member of a road-crew, he was buying insurance that could be cashed in when worse came to worst on the battlefield.

We can imagine, then, the hoplites in the invading army working quite cheerfully at their sweaty road-building labors, despite the heat, thirst, and discomforts of the marching camp. But what of the residents of the territory to which the road led? It is hard to suppose that the citizens of a neighboring state could be ignorant of the intentions of road-builders hacking their way through the mountains. Shepherds, beekeepers, or others who used the mountains in the summer would relay the report of the construction, even if formal watchposts had not been established.[18] Why, then, did the citizens of the threatened state not take preemptive action against the advancing invaders? When, occasionally, fifth-century Greek armies did occupy passes against their fellow Greeks, the defenders sometimes prevented the enemy from even attempting the crossing. Other pass-holders found that their uphill position made it easy to slaughter approaching hoplites with projectile weapons.[19]

Yet, despite its effectiveness, the tactical ploy of temporary occupation of mountain passes by Greek armies seems to have remained quite rare before the late fifth century. No city-state adopted a coherent strategy of blocking passes into the home territory until the fourth century (see p. 190). Why did Greeks allow a military highway to be constructed into their territory, in full knowledge that this road would allow their enemies easy access to their homelands, and an easy escape route even if the invaders were defeated? Of course, military roads were not one-way streets, and this year's defenders could be next year's invaders. Perhaps an element of optimistic calculation was sometimes involved in the decision: let our enemies do the work to build the invasion route that will in the long run do us more good and them more harm.[20]

But more to the point, blocking the road would have been a breach of the unwritten rules of hoplite combat. The goal of invader and invaded was ordinarily identical: to set up a decisive battle in the open plain, rather than to avoid battle by clever stratagems. The Greek military ethos no more allowed the ordinary hoplite army to ambush the invaders in the hills than the aristocratic code allowed an eighteenth-century duelist to consider bushwacking his opponent on the way to the duelling ground. In both cases the conflict was an affair of honor, fought according to established conventions, between moral (if not physical) equals (cf. Connor 1988).

The unwillingness of the invaded to take advantage of the natural obstacles that had to be overcome by invaders reveals the essentially agonistic nature of hoplite conflict: a form of warfare that could only be engaged in by men who had agreed (formally or informally) on the nature of weapons, armor, and formations that would be permitted to the field of honor. This agreement did not make the ensuing battle any less fierce or more 'civilized' – but it did permit the battle to take place, and contained the bloodshed within a few hours. The importance of natural obstacles also alerts us to the fragility of the hoplite *agon* as a system of warfare. As soon as defenders began to take advantage of difficult terrain in order to prevent the incursion of enemy forces, the entire system of hoplite-battle conflict resolution would be upset, and a new form of warfare would necessarily replace it. This, as we shall see, is what happened in the fourth century.

FORTIFICATIONS AND POLIORCETICS

Consideration of the second primary category of obstacles – man-made walls, ditches, and so on – further clarifies the context in which the hoplite battle took place. The fortification history of most archaic Greek cities remains obscure, but there is good evidence for a city wall at Athens by the mid-sixth century, and other major cities were probably walled by this period as well. Certainly by the fifth century, circuit walls were standard for a proper polis. The Spartans were the peculiar exception (as in many other areas) because they refused to wall their central settlements.[21] For most Greek cities, walls were an important symbol of autonomy and strength and might even be decorated with apotropaic symbols and relief carvings of gods to avert evil and protect the city. Walls could be constructed of solid stone, or with a stone socle topped by courses of mud-brick. In either case, the walls were erected wide and high, and were an efficient barrier against assault.[22]

Hoplite warriors were not, as a rule, effective assault troops. In the early to mid-fifth century the Athenians had a reputation as being better at it than most, but that reputation seems to be based on their destruction of the Persian camp after the battle of Plataea, hardly a typical assault action. There are relatively few reports of attempted (and fewer of successful) assaults on strongly fortified positions by hoplite armies before the period of the Peloponnesian War. Several campaigns during the Peloponnesian War itself demonstrated how poor hoplites were at capturing even small, seemingly vulnerable, and ill-manned fortified places.[23]

The inefficiency of hoplites as practitioners of poliorcetics cannot be laid to a generalized disinclination of ancient heavy infantry to assault walled positions. During the imperial period of Assyrian history (ca 800–600 BC), the Assyrian heavy infantryman time and again proved his ability to take strongly fortified cities. The Assyrians used projectile (especially arrow) barrages and battering-rams, along with scaling and mining techniques against major walled cities, with impressive results. Like that of the Assyrians, the Roman army was very good at siegecraft. There is no reason to suppose that towns of sixth- and fifth-century Greece were any better fortified than (e.g.) Phoenician cities of the eighth and seventh centuries or the Italian towns of the fifth, fourth, and third centuries.[24] If Assyrian and Roman infantrymen could take fortified positions by storm, what was wrong with Greek hoplites?

There were only three approaches to assaulting an ancient city wall: the attackers must go over, under, or through it. For a variety of reasons, both to do with arms and armor and to do with the ethos of Greek combat, none of these approaches was at all attractive to the hoplite warrior.

Going over the enemy's wall meant, for most classical Greek armies, using ladders.[25] Ladder assaults were considered to be at least theoretically possible by Aeschylus, who in *Seven Against Thebes* (466–7) describes the shield of Eteokles as depicting 'an armed man climbing the rungs of a ladder/towards the tower of his enemies, wishing to sack it.' One of the panels of the Xanthian Nereid Monument (ca 380 BC) depicts three hoplites (helmeted, carrying shields) ascending a ladder, under protection of covering fire from archers on the ground.[26] Ladders would have to be built by the besiegers with materials scavenged on the spot, or assembled from wooden components brought from home. In any event the ladders would be tall, narrow, flimsy, unstable, and flammable.

The city's defenders would be massed at the top of the wall (e.g. Euripides, *Phoinissai*, 1137–8), ready to make life as nasty as possible for those coming up the ladders. As soon as the assault ladders were in place, the defenders would attempt to throw them down – along with any hapless soldiers who might be clinging to them. Aeneas the Tactician (36, cf. Garlan 1974: 174–6 with fig. 2) describes a simple swinging rig that defenders could use to sweep ladders from their walls. The defenders on the wall above had gravity on their side, and could drop heavy stones on the enemy below. Furthermore, many city circuits were enfiladed by towers, meaning that defenders in the towers could get easy bowshots at the assault troops.[27] The hoplites scrabbling up the ladders could not, of course, fire back.

The ladder-climbing soldier had to haul himself, and approximately 70 lbs (31.7 kg) of armor and weaponry (Hanson, chapter 3 in this volume, n. 1) up the rungs. Hoplite armor, heavy and rigid, severely restricted its wearer's freedom of movement. His breastplate hampered the free upward extension of his arms; his legs were encased in constricting greaves. As a result, the climbing hoplite's movements were ill-coordinated; his progress up the ladder would necessarily be slow and clumsy. For a painfully long time he represented an easy, almost defenseless target to defenders on the walls above and on the towers to his sides,[28] who would hurl and shoot whatever was to hand at the attacker's head, back, shoulders, and arms: certainly stones, perhaps also javelins, arrows, and torches.[29]

Because of his defenseless position in relation to the threat from above, a strong helmet was essential to the ladder-climbing hoplite (cf. the helmeted hoplites on the Nereid Monument). The face-enclosing and neck-protecting Corinthian style helmet would offer a much greater degree of security against bombardment than would the lighter Boiotian helmet. Yet, the same heavy Corinthian helmet that might deflect missiles away from the hoplite's head and neck completely obscured his vision. At best, the Corinthian helmet allowed very constricted visibility to a man looking straight ahead (Hanson 1989: 71–2); it would be virtually impossible for the ladder climber in a Corinthian helmet to see up. Thus he climbed blind, through a hail of missiles that must have deafened him if they did not kill him, unsure even of where the top of the wall was, certain only in the knowledge that if he did live to get to the top, he would be at a terrible disadvantage.

The hoplite's shield was normally his best protection, but it would be worse than useless to him on the ladder. Unlike earlier models of shield, the hoplon lacked the strap that would allow it to be easily slung on the hoplite's back, although perhaps such a strap could be jerry-rigged.[30] But even if a strap were rigged up, the shield would be more bother than aid. The enemy was to the side (in the towers) and above, so the shield hung on his back would offer no protection from the former, and little from the latter. But it would add considerably to the weight he carried, and would tend to drag him backward and unbalance him on the ladder.

As he mounted the ladder the hoplite must have felt a terrifying sense of aloneness. His experience of proper, phalanx battle (hellish as it was) had always been as a member of a close-knit group, whose members were in constant physical contact with their fellows, both front to back and side to side. The hoplite on the ladder was essentially alone. There might be a man ahead of him or behind him (cf. the Nereid Monument frieze), but he had none of the usual comfort of being one of a mass of friendly comrades. And when (or if) he did achieve the top of the wall, he was surrounded by enemies. If he had brought his shield, he now had to unsling it, if he did not, he was an easy target. In any case there were no comrades by his side, no one to watch his back. His chances of survival were slim. There was little hope of striking an effective blow and no hope of retreat. In short, going up the ladder was suicidal, and death would come in a lonely, ugly way. The situation is graphically described by Euripides:

How am I to tell how Kapaneus went mad?
For grasping the rungs of the long ladder
He ascended and boasted thus
That not even the sacred fire of Zeus would
Hold him back from seizing the city and its lofty towers.
Calling out these things while being stoned,
He crept up having drawn up his body under his shield
Passing up the smooth rungs of the ladder.
Just as he reached the cornice of the wall
Zeus struck him with his bolt; the earth rang
So that all were terrified. From the ladder
He was hurled, his limbs spreading apart,
Hair towards heaven and blood to the earth.
His arms and legs like the wheel of Ixion
Spun; the fiery corpse fell to earth.

(Eur. *Phoinissai* 1172–86, trans. Childs, *City Reliefs*)[31]

A worn frieze from the Heroon at Trysa (ca 370 BC) depicts the likely aftermath of mounting the ladder: a hoplite falling head over heels through space, his round shield tumbling behind him, his ladder broken.[32] These artistic and literary references demonstrate that ladder assaults were conceivable, and were presumably actually attempted. But they leave little doubt as to why there is such scant evidence for hoplite armies resorting to the 'over the top' option.[33]

Going under the enemy wall meant digging beneath the wall in order to cause it to collapse. In many cases this was simply not an option, because the wall was constructed of stone blocks set on foundations cut into the bedrock (Lawrence 1979: 201–5). Only when the foundations of the wall were laid in fairly deep soil could undermining be attempted. Digging was hot, nasty work. Unlike rock cutting and hauling, tunneling was not the sort of labor that a peasant soldier would undertake as part of his normal agricultural round. Rather, mining was (especially for the Athenians, who gained much of their state revenue from the silver mines of south Attica) prototypically the work of the slave, and thus was regarded as labor beneath the dignity of the free citizen.[34] Not only was the work of tunneling uncomfortable and degrading, it was dangerous: tunnels that were inadequately shored up could collapse suddenly, burying the tunnelers alive.

As soon as the defenders realized that the besiegers were trying to undermine their walls, they would immediately enact counter-measures. They might detect the precise location of the enemy tunnel by placing the concave side of a shield on the ground, and using the shield to amplify the sounds of excavation (Hdt. 4.200). Once the defenders knew where the tunnel was heading, they could engage in counter-mining and so catch out the tunnel-diggers from above or below. The men in the tunnel would be without armor, unarmed (except for their picks and shovels), and completely unprepared for battle. Like moles dug out by a gardener, they would be slaughtered by the enemy without hope of striking a blow in their own defense. Little wonder, then, that there is no securely documented example of an early classical Greek assault based on mining.[35]

The third option, going through the wall, was also dangerous, but at least it allowed the hoplite the advantage of fighting, and dying if need be, in the company of his fellows and with his feet planted on the ground. Going through the wall, in the days before the invention of effective barrage-artillery (see p. 192) meant using battering rams to knock down a gate. There was not much hope of breaching the thick, double-faced and rubble-packed stone wall itself. The wooden gates were the weakpoint, and might be smashed open if the attackers could bring sufficient weight and forward momentum to bear in horizontally directed blows. The shaft of the ram would ordinarily be a tree-trunk, its head might be of bronze – perhaps decorated with rams' heads, as in an example dedicated at Olympia.[36] Only quite heavy battering rams would be effective, and, of course, the heavier the ram, the less offensive and defensive equipment the ramming crew could carry with them.

Greek military architects were well aware that the gate was the weakest part of any circuit; consequently they lavished considerable ingenuity on making gates difficult to approach and easy to defend.[37] Some simple gates were flanked by massive towers, from which the defenders could safely attack the rammers from above and from the sides. Often the right-side gate tower (thus on the attacker's left) was built bigger, so as to give the defenders an especially good shot at the attackers' vulnerable unshielded side (e.g. the Athenian fort of Rhamnous). Somewhat more sophisticated was the 'overlap' style of gate (e.g. Mantinea) which forced the attackers to approach the gate itself through a corridor flanked on both sides with extensions of the city walls, walls that would, of course, be lined with defenders.

But perhaps most diabolical, from the attackers' point of view, was the gate-courtyard (e.g. the Athenian Dipylon Gate). In attacking this style of gate, the invaders had first to break through an external gate, often defended by towers. If they succeeded in this, the attack troops entered a small courtyard. A second gate, at least as strongly built as the first, lay at the end of the courtyard. The courtyard was designed as a killing ground: the besiegers were now surrounded by defenders on the walls and towers above. Until they broke the second gate the invaders would be pounded by a barrage of missiles from all sides. Although the hoplite on a ramming crew had the comfort of his fellows at his side, and he might be protected by a mantlet of some sort (Lawrence 1979: 42), his chance of survival was not much greater than the ladder-climber's. Unless the defenders jumped down into the courtyard, the attacking hoplite had no way of returning the fire of his tormentors above. Indeed, since he had to use at least one arm to hold even a light ram, his choice must have been whether to carry a shield or a spear – a devilish choice between being unarmed (but for a sword), or undefended (but for body armor) if he succeeded in breaking through the second gate.

Even if the assault crew did manage to break into the city by any of the means discussed above, the battle was still far from won. The residential areas of Greek towns built before the early to mid-fifth century were seldom designed on an orthogonal street plan. Rather, most of the city was characterized by a hodge-podge of narrow, winding streets and dead-end alleys. The streets were fronted by houses which often featured conjoined walls.[38] Until they fought their way to the central agora (assuming they could find it), the intruders had no hope of forming a proper phalanx. Rather, they would find themselves in a running street fight, a form of warfare in which their heavy armor and unwieldy shields would be of little use. The ordinary rules of hoplite combat did not pertain in the case of intra-urban warfare. The defenders had the advantage of intimate knowledge of the streetplan, and could use that knowledge to set ambushes and booby-traps for the invaders. Furthermore, once the attackers were within the walls, persons who were ordinarily noncombatants would take an active part in the resistance. Women, children, old men, even slaves, could stand on the rooftops bombarding the invaders with a hail of stones and heavy rooftiles: the third-century general Pyrrhus died in a street fight, struck on the head by a rooftile hurled by an Argive woman (Plut. *Pyrrhus*, 34.1–3). All the horrors of the street fight were suffered by Theban troops who were introduced into Plataia in 431 BC:

> Twice or three times [the Theban hoplites] succeeded in beating off the assault, and all the while there was a tremendous uproar from the men who were attacking them, and shouting and yelling from the women and slaves on the roofs, who hurled down stones and tiles. . . . Finally they lost heart and turned and fled through the city, most of them having no idea, in the darkness and the mud . . . of which way to go in order to escape, while their pursuers knew quite well how to prevent them from escaping. The result was that most of them were destroyed . . . only a few of them got away . . . others were cut down here and there in different parts of the city . . . finally the . . . survivors wandering about in the city handed over their arms and surrendered unconditionally to the Plataians.
>
> (Thuc. 2.4. trans. Warner)

Furthermore, as the Theban survivors learned, the invaders could expect no mercy if their attack faltered – the town residents, driven to a frenzy of anger and fear by the incursion into the normally sacrosanct realm of the city, would massacre the intruders if given a chance (Thuc. 2.5.7).

The problems faced by the individual hoplite soldier in attempting any of the approaches to assault discussed above were horrendous. His chance of survival was slim, and his death would come in a fashion inappropriate to his ideals. No hope of a noble death with 'all wounds in the front.' No praiseworthy demise while holding the line, or breaking the enemy ranks. Instead, death would come from above, from the side, visited upon him by an enemy he could not reach. Almost any wound suffered in an assault would be fatal, since in the fray there was little hope of a wounded man being evacuated by his comrades. If killed, his body, pierced with humiliating wounds in side and back, and his armor would belong to the enemy. It is hardly surprising that descriptions of frontal assaults on fortified positions are rare in classical Greek texts.

In lieu of the assault, a besieging army might try two possible approaches to taking an enemy city. The easiest, and most likely to be successful, was finding a traitor to open a gate and introduce the invaders into the city under cover of darkness. A convenient traitor might not be easy to locate in a city fully at peace with itself. But in late fifth- and fourth-century Greece the rash of civil wars between oligarchs and democrats created significant numbers of men willing to let in an enemy who promised to support their political agenda.

Aeneas the Tactician, author of a mid-fourth-century treatise 'On the Defense of Fortified Positions,' spends relatively little time on defeating frontal assaults, but was obsessed with treason and its prevention. Aeneas, probably an experienced mercenary captain, saw internal subversion as considerably more dangerous than poliorcetic science.[39] Even if attackers were successfully smuggled in by a traitor, however, they still faced the horrors of the streetfight, as the Thebans learned in Plataia.

The other non-assault technique used to defeat the wall-obstacle was blockade-siege. This approach was only practicable for a very large army against a relatively small city. The sole way to ensure that supplies were not brought in to the besieged, while simultaneously containing the danger of counter-attacks from within the city, was to build a wall around the whole of the enemy's city. Counter-walling a huge circuit like that of classical Athens was obviously out of the question, since the attackers could never man the many miles of wall that would have been necessary. The building of a counter-wall was a major undertaking, and would require hauling great quantities of materials (especially timber) from far away.[40]

A full blockade-siege required a very large army, and one willing to serve continuously for a very long time. The enemy trapped within always enjoyed the advantage of internal lines of movement. Hidden from view behind their walls, the defenders could quickly mass their troops at a specific point just within the wall and sally out from a gate or postern. If the defenders did not have enough men permanently stationed in the threatened sector they would have a hard time containing the breakout. The besiegers' external lines of deployment (outside their makeshift wall) made it hard for them to concentrate troops against the sallying defenders.[41] These difficulties help to explain why it took a good part of the combined Theban–Peloponnesian army (Thuc. 2.78.1–2) two years to reduce Plataia, a small town (Thuc. 2.77.2) protected by only a few hundred men (Thuc. 2.78.3), and why many of the Plataians could succeed in effecting a night escape. Given the relatively small numbers of hoplites that could be fielded by the average Greek polis, and the requirement that most of them return to their farms after a short campaigning season, circumvallation strategies were not often a real option.[42]

The problems hoplite armies faced in undertaking either assaults or long-term sieges underline just how 'voluntary' hoplite battles really were. The warriors of the invaded state could always avoid battle simply by staying within their fortified enclave. The enemy could not get in without inordinate and dangerous efforts – efforts that they were reluctant to attempt. Furthermore, the amount of economic damage the invaders could inflict on agricultural resources was (at least until the fourth century) quite limited (Hanson 1983; Ober 1985a; 33–5). The defenders came out from behind their walls into the field of battle, not because they had to, but because they accepted a code of military behavior that made the risk of death in a short battle in the open field seem preferable to the protracted and indecisive struggle between inefficient attacker and unwilling defender. Greek hoplite warfare was carried out within a relatively homogeneous cultural matrix. Because Greek defenders 'played by the rules' and seldom locked themselves in, Greek attackers had little need of the tactics or the projectile weapons suited to siegecraft. There is an important contextual difference between early classical Greek warfare and Assyrian and Roman warfare. The Greeks developed their agonistic style of battle by fighting one another. Assyrians and Romans fought imperialistic campaigns against foreigners. The victims of Assyrian and Roman expansionism often saw in the defense of their walled towns their only hope for independence. Thus, unlike the Greeks, the Assyrians and Romans were constrained to develop effective assault tactics.

Once again, we are struck by the fragility of the Greek system of agonistic conflict resolution, a system of war that was more ritualistic than rational in its set forms (cf. Connor 1988). The danger was ever present that some clever, rationalistic strategist would see that breaking the rules could give his side a huge advantage against traditionalist opponents. What would happen if a major war broke out and one side refused to accept the challenge to battle? What if, furthermore, the other side was neither willing to attempt the difficulties of assault or siege, nor able to find a traitor to let them in? What if neither side were satisfied with the stalemate that resulted? This is the scenario for the Peloponnesian War.

END OF THE *AGON*

Thucydides' account makes it clear that Pericles' strategy at the time of the outbreak of the Peloponnesian War was based on the assumption that as long as the Athenians refused battle in Attica, the Peloponnesians could not win the war. Getting the Athenian citizen-peasants to agree to this strategy took some doing, since it meant putting farms at risk and contravening the unwritten rules of engagement, but Pericles' political and rhetorical skills were equal to the task (Ober 1985b). The resulting conflict was unlike any in previous Greek history.

The war was not characterized by hoplite battles. In the place of battles between phalanxes there were many other varieties of organized violence – naval skirmishes, sneak attacks, sieges, hit-and-run raids, atrocities against civilians, treason, assassination and double-dealing diplomacy, cold-blooded mass executions of prisoners of war, blockades and counter-blockades, ghastly civil conflicts. The total loss of life and destruction of property entailed in these various actions far exceeded the ordinary toll of hoplite battle. In the end, the Spartans won by adopting a campaign of economic coercion. The strategic plan included permanent occupation of the Athenian homeland and strangulation of Athenian trade routes. The Athenians, who had refused to fight the invader, were ultimately beaten by simple hunger (Ober 1985a: 35–7).

The external forms of hoplite battle survived the Peloponnesian War, but the code of military ethics that had stood in the place of a system of strategy and tactics did not. The fourth century was an age of rational strategic planning by both invaders and defenders. The result was a radical change in the role of obstacles in intra-Greek warfare.

Given the defensibility of passes against hoplite armies, the mountainous nature of inter-polis borderlands, and the dependence of hoplite armies on roads through rough terrain, blocking roads into the home territory was an obvious defensive strategy. Fourth-century writers on military theory, such as Xenophon, Plato, and Aristotle, discussed ways in which the rugged borderlands could best be defended against enemy incursions (Ober 1985a: 75–80). Theory and practice went hand in hand. Passes were now frequently guarded against invaders, often successfully. Athenian light-armed troops prevented a Spartan army from using the cart road through the Kaza Pass in 379 BC, and Boiotian troops held a pass on the Road of the Towers in 376 BC against another Spartan force (Ober 1985a: 204). When Thebes was preparing to invade Laconia after the battle of Leuctra, the Theban soldiers feared that Spartan territory would be difficult to break in to, due to the presence of garrisons (*phrourai*) at the passes (Xen. *Hell.* 6.5.24).

The natural difficulty of rough terrain could be enhanced by man-made obstacles. In some cases defenders built field walls and ditches to enclose vulnerable territory.[43] The ideal was to keep the enemy out of the homeland altogether; this might best be achieved by building and garrisoning permanent pass-forts. Early to mid-fourth century BC Greece saw a wave of border fortress building; the archaeological remains of sophisticated fourth-century systems of fortresses and watchtowers have been documented for the territory of Attica and Boiotia; other territories were probably similarly defended.[44]

Border fortification systems could be very effective in keeping out the enemy. With the exception of an abortive sneak raid by the Spartan Sphodrias in 378 BC, the territory of Attica remained inviolate from 403 to 322 BC, despite Athens' decidedly mixed success in land and sea fights outside of Attica during the same period. With the prevalence of strategies based on defense of fixed positions – whether border fortress, field walls, or central city – the day of the single, decisive battle seemed over. While great and important battles were still fought by fourth-century phalanxes (Koroneia, Leuktra, Mantinea, and Chaeronea) hoplite battle no longer dominated the polis citizen's experience of war.

The roles played by the ordinary Greek warrior were drastically altered and multiplied as the result of the century of revolutionary military change that began with the Peloponnesian war. Many hoplites were forced to go into mercenary service when their local economies were wrecked by the drawn-out indecisive warfare typical of the age (Ober 1985a: 45–50). No longer a citizen-soldier who occasionally fought side by side with his neighbors in defense of home and country, the mercenary was a professional who fought constantly for pay and plunder, beside men of diverse backgrounds, in the service of any one of dozens of city-states, or for the Persian king, an Egyptian dynast, or an ambitious satrap. Even if he fought only as a citizen of his polis, the fourth-century soldier could not be just a hoplite. In the fourth century the Athenians instituted formal weapon-training for their young men. These ephebes were taught to use hoplite equipment indeed, but also how to use javelins and catapults – weapons well suited to the defense of fortified positions (Aristot. *Ath. Pol.* 42; Ober 1985a: 90–5). The fourth-century Greek soldier faced not only the exertions of the march and terror of phalanx battle, but also the long, dull grind of garrison duty in fortress or isolated watchtower.

By the mid-fourth century BC the military center of gravity of the Greek world had shifted north, to Macedon. Philip II introduced, or adapted, a number of Greek strategic and tactical innovations, many of which were in the area of poliorcetics. His men were expected to carry their own food and gear, which allowed them to dispense with baggage trains. As a result, Macedonian troops could move fast, and could use paths unsuitable for the baggage-encumbered hoplite army. This maneuverability meant that Philip often arrived at key passes before he was expected; thus, for example, he was able to surprise and destroy a force of mercenaries at Phocian Elatea in 339 BC and set up the decisive battle of Chaeronea.[45]

Philip was a master of diplomatic chicanery, and sensibly preferred to take strong positions by the use of traitors when possible. But if he had to assault a fortified position, his men were ready to make the attempt. Unlike traditional hoplites, Philip's soldiers were full-time professionals. Unlike mercenaries, they fought beside trusted comrades, for king and country. They had the training, the experience, and the morale necessary to be superb assault troops. Philip's men proved themselves able to take major cities (e.g. Olynthus) by assault. Their success was not just a matter of morale and training, however. The many sling-bullets inscribed with Philip's name found in the archaeological excavations at Olynthus demonstrate that, like the Assyrians before them, the fourth-century Macedonians had learned the usefulness of projectile barrage in siegecraft.[46]

The problem of overcoming man-made obstacles led to technological advances which resulted in the development of the world's first efficient siege artillery. The non-torsion (crossbow style) catapult was invented in Syracuse in 399 BC, as an assault weapon (D.S. 14.41.4, with Marsden 1969: 48–56). But artillery technology was quickly adapted to the purposes of defenders. By the second quarter of the fourth century, fortress towers often incorporated specially designed catapult chambers (Ober 1987a). Catapults could also be adapted for use as field artillery. Philip suffered one of his rare defeats when his army was bombarded by Phocian troops using stone-throwing catapults in 353 BC (Polyaen. 2.38.2, Marsden 1969: 59–60).

Catapult artillery was a further threat to the traditions of hoplite battle. The bolts and stones thrown by catapults were deadly at longer ranges than javelins, sling-bullets, and arrows. Now, a man in full armor was defenseless against projectiles hurled from a machine hundreds of yards away, fired by a mere technician. Instead of a few moments of vulnerability to light projectiles during the last stage of the charge (Hanson 1989: 31), the hoplite now had to fear absolutely lethal projectiles any time he was within 200 or 300 yards (180 to 270 m) of the enemy force or the enemy wall. Little wonder then, that when the Spartan king Archidamus first saw a catapult demonstrated, he reportedly cried out in anguish 'Man's valor is no more' (Plut. *Mor.* 191E, 219A; cf. Garlan 1974: 172–3).

By about 340 BC Macedonian military engineers had made a major breakthrough in artillery technology – the development of the torsion (hair- or sinew-spring) catapult (Marsden 1969: 56–62). Torsion catapults were much more powerful than the old non-torsion models. Artillery capable of smashing even well-built stone walls now became a major factor in assaults. This new weapon paved the way for the great siege successes of Alexander the Great and the Diadochoi.[47] Few cities could hope to withstand storming by a Macedonian army, but the spectacular resistance of Rhodes to Demetrius Poliorcetes in 305 BC showed that there was still hope for defenders – and that hope led to a long era characterized by long, bloody, sieges. Josephus' description of the Roman siege of Jerusalem in the first century AD, with its graphic scenes of assault, counter-assault, constant artillery barrage, and endless, senseless killing, gives some idea of how urban residents experienced the new style of warfare.

From the late fifth century BC onward, obstacles would play a central part in actual combat, as well as in the stages of conflict before and after battle. The use of obstacles for strategic and operational advantage led to a style of warfare in which open battle was just another tactical ploy in a general's bag of tricks. The urge to fight the decisive battle could never be completely eliminated. Indeed, the improvements in siege techniques provided a practical incentive to the residents of an attacked city to take their chances in the fair field. But the days when an hour's battle could solve conflict between independent states for a year or a generation was past. The long, complex, and ugly western tradition of war as strategy, war as a profession, and war as a technological problem, had begun. With that strategic, professional, technological tradition the seeds were sown of wars that exterminated entire cultures and would come to threaten the extinction of the human race.

NOTES

I would like to thank Victor Hanson for his very helpful comments on earlier drafts of this chapter. The fieldwork discussed below was made possible by grants from the Research Office of Montana State University.

Works referred to by author alone or with short title or date are cited in full in the Bibliography to this volume.

1. For a review of the literature on this well-known problem, see Will 1975; Cartledge 1977: 18, 23–4; Holladay 1982: 97–9; Ober 1985a: 33–5, 191–2.

2. On history of Greek wall-building, see Winter 1971; Lawrence 1979.
3. Aymard 1967; Garlan 1974: 125–34, 145–7; P. B. Kern, 'Military technology and ethical values in ancient Greek warfare: the siege of Plataea,' *War and Society* 6.2 (1988) 1–20; Ober 1985a: 43–5, 207–18.
4. In the Athenian retreat from Syracuse in 413 BC, the hoplites exceptionally carried their own rations because of a lack of attendants and distrust of those they did have (Thuc. 7.75.5). Rations and attendants: D. Engels, *Alexander the Great and the Logistics of the Macedonian Army* (Berkeley, 1978), 123–30; Pritchett, *War* 1, 30–52.
5. Pack-animals and carts: Engels (*supra* n.4) *passim* (emphasizing pack-animals); N. G. L. Hammond, 'Army transport in the fifth and fourth centuries,' *GRBS* 24 (1983) 27–31 (emphasizing carts); Pritchett, *Topography* 3. 181–96; Engels (*supra* n.4) 12–24. My student, John MacLeod (Montana State University), points out in a paper based partly on personal experience and interviews with horse and mule packers that a significant percentage (in his experience one to three animals in twenty) will be lame or sore at any given time, and thus suggests that Engels' estimates of the number of pack animals needed by an army may be somewhat low.
6. Hammond 1954; Vanderpool 1978; Pritchett, *Topography* vols 3 (with bibliography of earlier work), 4, 5; Van de Maele 1987.
7. For a preliminary discussion see Ober 1982; Ober 1985a: 111–29, 181–8.
8. Wheel ruts are found, for example, on the Coastal Pass Road from Megara to Eleusis: Ober 1985a: 128. See Pritchett, *Topography* 3.167–81, for full discussion.
9. On which see, for example, J. J. Coulton, *The Ancient Greek Architects at Work* (Ithaca, 1982).
10. This is the opinion of John Slonaker, a civil engineer with extensive experience in road surveying, who worked with me on ancient Greek roads in 1983.
11. Cf. J. B. Salmon, Review of Pritchett, *Topography* 3 and 4, *CR* n.s. 35 (1985) 100–3, who suggests that the Hysiai–Tegea may have been built to facilitate metal imports into Tegean territory.
12. Cf. the remarks of K. Hopkins, 'Models, ships and staples,' in P. Garnsey and C. R. Whittaker, (eds) *Trade and Famine in Classical Antiquity*, Cambridge Philological Society Supp. 8 (Cambridge, 1983) 84–109. Hopkins attempts to bring a nuance to the argument against large-scale ancient trade in bulk goods, but concludes that even at the height of the Roman empire, most trade was short-haul, from farm or village to the nearest market-town. While challenging the universal validity of the famous comment of A. H. M. Jones (*The Later Roman Empire* 1964: 841) that 'it was cheaper to ship grain from one end of the Mediterranean to the other than to cart it 75 miles,' Hopkins acknowledges the relatively greater cost of land transport (104–5) noting that 'going over a mountain pass cost much more than going over level ground.'
13. Cf. Plut. *Tim.* 28; Thuc. 6.70; Dem. 50.23; Plato, *Resp.* 3.404; Xen. *Hell.* 4.5.3.
14. Cf. Thuc. 7.4.6 and esp. the ghastly scene described at 7.84 in which the Athenian army completely disintegrates when the thirsty hoplites

reached a river. The Vathychoria area on the Athenian–Megarian border, along the Road of the Towers, is a good example of an area without a ready water supply: Ober 1985a: 167; Ober 1987a: 592–3.

15. Co-workers: R. H. Randall, 'The Erechtheum workmen,' *AJA* 57 (1953) 199–210. On the question of the labor required to build a military highway, cf. Polybius (3.54–5) on Hannibal in the Alps. A usable road across the mountains already existed, but it was washed out in one section. Polybius claims that Hannibal spent one day rebuilding the 1.5-stade stretch so that it was usable for horses and pack-animals; three days to make it ready for elephants. Hannibal's men were working at top speed (he feared being caught by autumn storms) and Polybius emphasizes the greatness of the toil. It thus seems unlikely that this building rate would be exceeded by a classical Greek army. I would guess that a mile a week would be about as fast as Greek road-builders could hope to proceed through difficult terrain – but this is only a guess and many factors would affect the actual speed of building operations.
16. Hanson 1983; Ober 1985a: 20–3; E. M. Wood, *Peasant-Citizen and Slave: The Foundations of Athenian Democracy* (London, 1988).
17. Cf. the ease with which the Syracusans were able to use their knowledge of the roads, fords, and passes, to defeat the retreating Athenian army in 413 BC (Thuc. 7.73–85). Examples could easily be multiplied.
18. The raid by Spartan harmost Sphodrias into Attica in 378 BC was detected by rural residents: Xen. *Hell.* 5.4.21. The watchpost and border fortification system of Attica may have been elaborated in part as a reaction to this raid: Ober 1985a: 211–13.
19. Cf. the Syracusan destruction of the Athenian army in 413 BC, esp. Thuc. 7.78.5–7.79.2. For a list of examples, see G. E. M. de Ste Croix, *The Origins of the Peloponnesian War* (Ithaca, 1972), 190–5.
20. The issue of whether specific sections of given pass-roads were built by different state authorities must remain up in the air until more detailed studies of roads across borders have been carried out. It may turn out to be the case that there are polis-specific 'specifications' (cf. the detailed specifications on Athenian building contracts) as to grade and width; if so, a large enough corpus of measured roads could address the issue of who built a given road.
21. Athenian city wall: R. E. Wycherley, *The Stones of Athens* (Princeton, 1978), 7–25; on early city walls generally: Winter 1971: 54–8; Lawrence 1979: 30–7.
22. Decoration: wall of Thasos: C. Picard, *Etudes Thasiennes 8: Les portes sculptées* (Paris, 1962). Construction technique, and relative merits of stone and brick: Lawrence 1979: 208–20.
23. The Athenian reputation for skill at assaults: Thuc. 1.102.2. Rarity of assaults before and during the Peloponnesian War: Garlan 1974: 125–34. According to Plutarch (*Per.* 27–8, cf. Thuc. 1. 116–17), when besieging Samos in 440 BC, Pericles preferred to spend money and time (in a siege that lasted eight or nine months) rather than risk the lives of citizens by attempting an assault. Failed assaults on small fortifications during the Peloponnesian War: Oinoe (Thuc. 2.18–19), Plataia (Thuc. 2.75–8). The

Spartan disaster at Pylos in 425 BC was set up by their unwillingness to assault frontally even a makeshift fortification (Thuc. 3.3–41).

24. Assyrian siegecraft: Garlan 1974: 138 n. 5; Ferrill 1985: 74–6; Roman siegecraft: G. Webster, *The Roman Imperial Army*[3] (London, 1985) 239–54.
25. Cf. Lawrence 1979: 40. The Peloponnesian-Boiotian army at Plataia attempted to build a siege-ramp against the Plataian wall. This project took the entire army (assuming the text is correct) seventy days of 24-hour shifts to build, and ultimately failed (Thuc. 2.75–8). The experiment was not repeated by later Greek armies. Mobile siege-towers were apparently unknown in the Greek world before the Carthaginians used them at Selinus in 409 BC. The technology was adopted by Dionysius of Syracuse at Motya in 397 BC (Lawrence 1979: 42–3); by the mid-fourth century siege-towers were sufficiently well known to be mentioned by Aeneas Tacticus (32.8).
26. Frieze II, Block 872. See W. A. P. Childs, *The City Reliefs of Lycia* (Princeton, 1978), 22–31, esp. 27; fig. 11, P1. 10.2.
27. Towers: Winter 1971: 152–203; Lawrence 1979: 376–98.
28. When the Plataians broke out of their besieged city in winter 428/7 BC, they used ladders to get over the Spartan wall of circumvallation (Thuc. 3.20, 22–3). Notably, the Plataian troops were light-armed and they took the enemy by surprise: first up the ladders were twelve men armed only with daggers and wearing breastplates; next came more light-armed men carrying spears; shields were carried only by the men who came up in a third wave. Of course, this system would not work if the ladder assault had been contested.
29. Stone-throwing: Aeneas Tacticus 38.6. A frieze from the Heroon of Trysa (Interior West Wall, Blocks A 7/8, B 9 = Childs (*supra* n.26) pl. 14) illustrates defenders on walls and towers, hurling stones and javelins at defenders huddling beneath their shields at the foot of the wall. For a discussion of other artistic evidence (sixth-century François vase, fourth-century Nereid Monument), see Childs, (*supra* n. 26) 77. Use of stones, javelins, arrows, slings, and fire by defenders: Garlan 1974: 135–47, esp. 135–6; Lawrence 1979: 39–40.
30. Earlier shields with straps for hanging shield across the back: Greenhalgh 1973: 64–74; Snodgrass 1964b: 37–68. The hoplites depicted on the Nereid Monument are carrying their shields on their arms, as usual in combat, and climbing 'one-handed.'
31. On the vivid description of siegecraft in Euripides' play, see Y. Garlan, 'De la poliorcétique dans les "Phéniciennes" d'Euripide,' *REA* 68 (1966) 264–77.
32. Childs (*supra* n. 26), 31–6, 72–3, fig. 9, pl. 5.1.
33. Childs ibid., (68) notes that the motif of the city wall is little used in classical Greek art and that when walls are depicted, it is 'only in set mythological cycles and not in general battle contexts.'
34. Slaves in mining: S. Lauffer *Der Bergwerkssklaven von Laureion*, 2 vols (Wiesbaden, 1955–6).
35. The Plataian *defenders* undermined the Spartan ramp (Thuc. 2.76). Aeneas the Tactician (37) discusses the use of defensive counter-mines.

He also recommends ways that enemy miners can be killed by forcing smoke into their tunnels, or pestered by the introduction of bees and wasps! Mining and counter-mining were also common assault tactics in the Near Eastern tradition: Garlan 1974: 131–2, 143–5; Lawrence 1979: 41.

36. Olympia ram: Garlan 1974: 137–40 with pl. 2; Lawrence 1979: 42 (dating it to ca 440 BC). Use of rams in fifth-century Greek warfare: Kern, (*supra* n. 3), 10–11.
37. On gates: Winter 1971, 205–33; Lawrence 1979: 302–42; and especially the article by J.-P. Adam in S. Van de Maele (ed.), *Ancient Fortifications* (Amsterdam, forthcoming).
38. Early Greek town layout: L. Martin, *L'urbanisme dans la Grèce antique* (Paris, 1956), 75–96.
39. Aeneas on traitors: Garlan 1974: 179–83. Treason and concern with traitors generally in the late fifth century: L. A. Losada, *The Fifth Column in the Peloponnesian War, Mnemosyne* Suppl. 21 (Leiden, 1972).
40. Cf. Thuc. 2.75.1–2: timber for the ramp at Plataia; 2.78, 3.21: construction of the counter-wall at Plataia; Athenians at Syracuse: Thuc. 6.99.1.
41. The Peloponnesian/Boiotian force at Plataia had a special force of 300 men detailed to counter attempted sallies, but these proved ineffective in the event: Thuc. 3.22–3.
42. Campaigning season: Thuc. 2.57 notes that the longest occupation of Attica during the Archidamian War lasted not more than forty days; difficulties involved with circumvallation: Lawrence 1979: 41–2.
43. M. Munn, 'Agesilaos' Boiotian campaigns and the Theban stockade of 378–377 BC,' *Classical Antiquity* 6 (1987) 106–38.
44. Attica: Ober 1985a, Ober 1987b. The definitive publication of the fortification system of Boiotia by John Fossey is forthcoming. Surveys of the fortifications of the Corinthia and Aitolia by (respectively) G. Gauvin and J. Scholten are producing evidence for what may turn out to be fortified lines. Macedonia (where the fortifications are not easily dated): A. Rizakis, 'Une forteresse macédonienne dans l'Olympe,' *BCH* 110 (1986) 331–46.
45. Philip's military reforms: Cawkwell 1978: 150–65; G. T. Griffith, 'Philip as a general and the Macedonian Army,' in M. B. Hatzopoulos and L. D. Loukopoulos (eds) *Philip of Macedon*, (London, 1981) 58–78.
46. Philip's siegecraft: Cawkwell 1978: 160–3; Griffith (*supra* n. 45), 59, 62. Olynthus bullets: Lawrence 1979: 39. Garlan 1974: 202–11, sees Philip as inaugurating a new age of effective siegecraft. Philip's record as a besieger of cities was, however, far from perfect; cf. his failure at Byzantion and Perinthos in 340 BC.
47. Torsion artillery and its use in siegecraft: Marsden 1969: 16–24, 99–108, 116–17; cf. Ober 1987a: 570, 597–9.

8

SACRIFICE BEFORE BATTLE

Michael H. Jameson

> It is with the gods' help that wise
> commanders launch an attack,
> never against their wishes.
>
> (Euripides *Erechtheus* Fr. 352 (Nauck *TGF*^{2}))

For the Greeks no undertaking was without its appropriate ritual, giving assurance of approval or, at the least, the withholding of hostility on the part of the supernatural. In war, where human life, pride, and prosperity were uniquely at risk, ritual was so conspicuous that it became the paradigm for other human activities. So Xenophon has Socrates say 'You see men at war appeasing the gods before they engage in battle and asking by means of sacrifices and omens what they ought to do. Do you think we should propitiate the gods any the less when we come to engage in farming?' (*Oec.* 5.19–20). Indeed, every stage of the process that led up to a clash of hoplite phalanxes on the field of battle was marked by attention to the gods. Victor Hanson (1989), writing on the Greek way of war, has brought out vividly the grim reality of the fighting, but he chose not to treat there the supernatural dimension. The aim of this essay is to complete the picture, in colors that will perhaps seem no less lurid than those used to describe combat itself.[1]

For the earliest stages in the sequence of rites we look to the Spartans who offer the fullest examples of religious practice in warfare, though other cities certainly followed the same procedures, no doubt less rigidly and with their own distinctive practices. Once the Spartans had reached a decision on a campaign, the king, who was to lead the expedition, sacrificed in his house to Zeus Agetor ('Who leads out') and other gods associated with him. If the signs observed in this sacrifice were favorable, the 'fire-bearer' (*purphoros*) carried fire from the altar to the border of the land where the king sacrificed to Zeus and Athena and, if the signs once again permitted, crossed the border with the army.[2] When the army marched out it was accompanied by a flock of sacrificial sheep, led by goats (Paus. 9.13.4). These were the most common sacrificial victims and could keep up with the army in its march over the mountainous borders of Greece. Before crossing any river or the sea, sacrifices were made and favorable signs looked for in order to continue.

On the march sacrifices were performed frequently, perhaps every morning and certainly before every important undertaking such as building a fort (Xen. *Hell.* 4.7.7) or attacking a town (*ibid.* 3.1.17), but no more than three victims a day could be assayed (*ibid.* 6.4.16 and 19).[3] The advisability of meeting the enemy at any particular place and time was always verified through signs derived from sacrifice. When the two forces were drawn up and facing each other, a final sacrifice was made in front of the battle-line. As the lines advanced against each other, the chant known as the *paian* was raised, to the accompaniment – at least for the Spartans – of the shrill reed instrument, the *aulos* (Pritchett, *War* 1. 105–8). After victory, the winning side (no specific ritual is mentioned for the defeated) set up a trophy and performed thanksgiving and victory sacrifices to which might be joined athletic contests (Xen. *An.* 5.5.5, Arrian *An.* 5.29.1, 6.28.3, 7.14.1). The Spartans are said to have limited the victims at their victory celebrations to a single, symbolic rooster (Plut. *Ages.* 33, *Marc.* 22).

Clearly, we know a great deal about what was done but there is disagreement on its meaning. The ostensible purpose of all rites before victory was achieved was to obtain from the gods favorable signs (*kallierein*, from the phrase *kala ta hiera*) for the next step in the campaign. Modern commentators, after a period when sceptical rationalism prevailed, have tended to be impressed by the Greeks' faith, their strict adherence to the signals they received through sacrifices and the rarity of cases in which the gods' advice was ignored or proved false.[4] However, examples of successful action *contrary* to negative signs are not likely to be reported in our sources. Most often both sides began fighting in the belief that, as far as the gods were concerned, there were no obstacles to their success (cf. Diod. Sic. 15.85.1) and, since few engagements ended in a draw, one side was almost always doomed to disappointment. Our sources describe dramatic delays while waiting for the signs to be favorable, and the disastrous error of proceeding when the signs were unfavorable is noted (Xen. *Hell.* 4.8.36), but we are never given an explanation of defeat despite fair signs. The defeated survivors were left to explain to themselves why things went wrong, as are all participants in systems of prediction, and like other such systems this one appears to have remained unshaken, at least through the fourth century BC, notwithstanding what must have been a high percentage of failures.[5]

More meanings were certainly embedded in the ritual acts accompanying warfare than were articulated in the limited viewpoints of our various sources. As always in the study of classical life, we are to some extent the prisoners of our evidence. Some modern attempts to go beyond the explicit motives reported in ancient literature have been sweeping and striking. Thus, the armed force has been described as a consecrated band,[6] and the entire process from the decision for war through victory in battle has been compared to the chain of ritual actions in the performance of a single sacrifice.[7] In hesitating to embrace such bold formulations I would note that neither the nature of the evidence nor the analysis that has been made of it is sufficiently unambiguous that we can dispense with a study of details, and unfortunately even that must be partial. For instance, by limiting ourselves to what happened before the battle we omit the celebrations after the battle, which have been interpreted as a reintegration of the community, comparable to a sacrificial feast.

A point that has often been made is that the propitiation of the gods in addition to the seeking of omens of the outcome, is implicit in all the ritual (e.g. Lonis 1979: 109; Pritchett, *War* 3. 87–8). So the society embarking on war ensures its good relations with the city's gods and conforms to their wishes, moving forward only when the sacrificial signs permit. Normal sacrificial ritual predominates: as mentioned, the Spartan army's herd was mainly sheep, the most common victim for routine sacrifice (Paus. 9.13.4), and the Spartan kings received their usual perquisites of skins and chines of animals while on campaign (Hdt. 6.56).

Our prose sources, whether faithful or selective, pedestrian or imaginative, largely offer the social view of the rites of warfare; they show the relationship of the community and the army, as a community, to its gods. The darker forces that hover over the battlefield, the terror of death and the pain the fighters must confront, are out of sight. From poetry, however, we can see that they were an integral part of the conception of war. In the archaic *Shield of Heracles* there is a description of men fighting to defend a walled town:

> these . . . were engaged in battle: and behind them the dusky

> Fates (*Keres*), gnashing their white fangs, lowering, grim, bloody, and unapproachable, struggled for those who were falling, for they all were longing to drink dark blood. So soon as they caught a man overthrown or falling newly wounded, one of them would clasp her great claws about him, and his soul would go down to Hades and chilly Tartarus. And when they had satisfied their souls with human blood, they would cast that one behind them, and rush back again into the tumult and the fray.
>
> ([Hes.] *Scut.* 248–57)[8]

It is to the embodiment of fear, Phobos, that Theseus is said to have sacrificed before engaging the Amazons in battle (Plut. *Thes.* 27.3). So too, we are told, did Alexander before engaging Darius, as well as performing certain sacred rites not to be spoken of (Plut. *Alex.* 31. 3).

One of the ways in which we may hope to penetrate behind the screen presented by the prose sources is through the images and metaphors of poetry and through myths and fictionalized history that serve as etiologies and analogies to the rites. We need also to consider the evidence of artistic representation of ritual in which the selection and emphasis throw certain elements into relief. But our first and constant task is to pay heed to the vocabulary of Greek ritual, distinguishing its categories and observing apparent overlaps and contradictions. Differences of language and deviations in practice may correspond to genuine ambiguities and gradations in the meanings of the rites and may not be solely the result of fossilized survivals, later misunderstandings, or mere carelessness.

RITUAL DISTINCTIONS

Modern scholarship sees a major division in Greek ritual between the terms *hiera* and *sphagia*. The distinction, though it may not be as sharp as is sometimes claimed, is central to the discussion of military ritual. *Hiera*, in a sacrificial context, is used in both a broader sense, 'rites,' and in certain more restricted meanings, especially for parts of the sacrificial victim that are burnt on the altar or examined for signs, and for the signs that emerge from examination. The broader sense, 'rites,' covers a variety of practices including *sphagia*. The noun *sphagia* (usually used in this plural form) is cognate with the verb *sphazein* (or *sphattein*), 'to pierce the throat.'[9] This action, described by this verb, is the way almost all sacrificial victims are killed. From *sphagia* is formed another verb, *sphagiazesthai*, 'to perform *sphagia*.'

All the words from this root, it has been well said, make one think of blood.[10] *Sphagia*, like *hiera*, may denote either rites (in this case of more specialized character) or the signs obtained from the rites.

Schematically the relationships may be shown as follows:

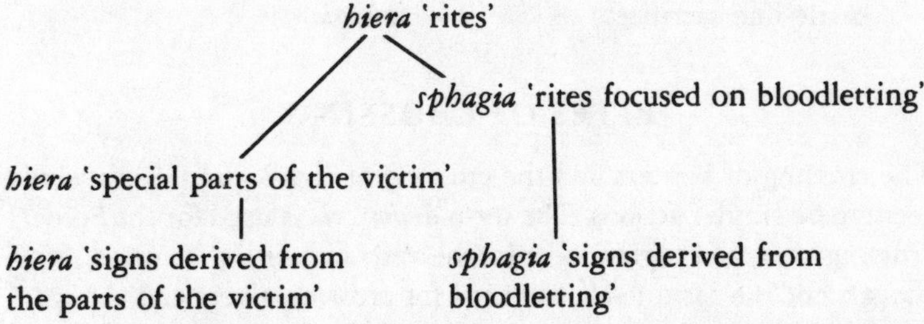

Sphagia and related words, with their focus on bloodletting, seem to be contrasted with normal sacrifice, commonly referred to by the most general verb for sacrifice, *thuein* (or *thuesthai*, in the middle voice) and implicit in the more particular meanings of *hiera*. In the course of a normal sacrifice signs are taken, specific parts are burnt on an altar and the flesh of the victim is available for human consumption.

For *sphagia*, however, a sacrificial fire is irrelevant, and therefore no altar is needed. Furthermore the flesh of the victim is not eaten by men. The concentration of the language of *sphagia* on the act of killing and the blood that spurts out from under the blade is in contrast with the subordination – not absence – of these aspects in normal sacrifice. (The act of killing there too can be referred to as *sphazein*.)

Sphagia is used in a number of situations such as oath-taking, some types of purification, certain rites for the dead or for heroes and the assuaging of winds (e.g., Xen. *An.* 4.5.4), as well as the crossing of rivers by an army and the final rite in front of the battle-lines. In all or most of these there appears to be an absence of the normal give-and-take between men and gods, while there is instead heightened tension among men, concentration on a single purpose and an awareness of the presence of disruptive, anti-social forces. These rites have been characterized as 'heilige Handlungen,' which may be freely rendered as 'powerful actions.'[11]

The terminology of both types of sacrifice is found in the ritual of warfare. Following the Spartan examples, on which we are best informed, the pattern can be outlined as follows:

at home, before departure:	normal
at borders:	normal
at rivers, at the sea:	*sphagia*
camp-ground sacrifice:	normal
battle-line sacrifice:	*sphagia*

RITES OF CROSSING

The crossing of borders and the crossing of rivers and the sea would seem to be similar actions. The term *diabateria* is used for the border-crossing rites, and cognate words (the verb *diabainein*, 'to cross,' etc.), though not the term itself, are used for crossing rivers and the sea.[12] But while the border rites are consistently spoken of as the object of the verbs *thuein* or *thuesthai*, that is as normal sacrifice (e.g. *Hell.* 3.5.7, 4.7.2, 5.4.47 etc.), and in one case Zeus and Athena are specified as the gods to whom the sacrifices are directed (Xen. *Rep. Lac.* 13.3), the crossing of rivers or the sea required favorable signs derived from *sphagia*, at least according to our earlier sources (Aesch. *Sept.* 377–9, Hdt. 6.76 and Xen. *An.* 4.3.17). By contrast, in Arrian's account of three crossings by Alexander the Great, the language is that of normal sacrifice, although Arrian, or rather his sources, knew of *sphagia* performed for Poseidon at sea (1.11.6) and when a fleet was about to sail (6.19.5), neither of which, however, are said to have produced signs.

The borders of a polis territory clearly constituted an important division between two kinds of space and were in some sense sacred. One may compare the expulsion of the homicide and polluted objects beyond the state's boundaries.[13] But borders were not usually thought of as having their own tutelary spirits. The Athenian ephebes took as witnesses to their oath various named gods who were followed by 'the borders (*horoi*) of the fatherland, the wheat, the barley, the vines, the olive trees, the fig trees.'[14] Though included among the *theoi* they are not personalized. Instead we hear of major gods, Apollo and Zeus, with the epithet *horios*, 'of the borders.'[15] While elsewhere simple ceremonies may have sufficed for appeasement of local forces, for the Spartans the regular transit of the army over the borders had resulted in normal sacrifice to verify the continued approval of two central figures of the polity, Zeus and Athena (cf. Plut. *Lyc.* 6.1), of whom Zeus at least had already received sacrifice from the king at home (Xen. *Rep. Lac.* 13.2–3).

In contrast to the shadowy conception of the borders as supernatural forces, river gods were widespread in Greece. Although there is only a single instance of a deity being named in connection with the crossing rites (the Spartan king Kleomenes supposes the river Erasinos protects the Argives when the *sphagia* are not favorable, Hdt. 6.76), well-delineated figures needed to be acknowledged when a crossing was made. Rivers and the sea had their distinctive mode of recognition. On the island of Mykonos, in an annual sacrifice for the river Acheloios, the throats of eight lambs were pierced (*s[phat]tet[ai]*) so that the blood would flow into the river while three other victims, a full-grown sheep and two lambs, were killed for him at an altar (Dittenberger *SIG*[3] 1024, lines 36–7). The same conspicuous use of blood is indicated for the sacrifice performed before crossing water (cf. Xen. *An.* 4.3.17 and, in an ostensibly Persian rite, Hdt. 7.113–14, the Magi slaughtering white horses at the river Strymon). In normal sacrifice the blood spurted over the altar or was caught in a vessel (e.g., *Od.* 3.444), but language and art did not call attention to this part of the procedure. *Sphagia* at rivers or the sea focused on the killing and the flowing of blood, liquid into liquid (at least when Greek rivers were true to their element and not dry gullies). Through this action signs of divine response were obtained that permitted or prevented the army's crossing.

Herodotus in his description of the sacrifice at the river Strymon speaks of the Magi as *pharmakeusantes*, 'having performed magical rites' (7.113–14), which seems to be a characterization of a foreign practice; such language never appears in descriptions of Greek versions of the rite. For an army making a potentially dangerous crossing in foreign territory neither the use of an altar for the burning of parts nor the meal that followed would usually have been feasible. But there was nothing about the nature of the god that prevented normal sacrifice as shown by the prescriptions on Mykonos, mentioned above, where the flow of blood into the river is combined with sacrifice at an altar and, presumably, consumption of the meat.[16] Normal sacrifice and *sphagia* were used for divination and unfavorable signs stopped the progress of an expedition. Herodotus, in both passages cited above, uses the term for signs obtained by normal sacrifice (*kallierein*). Xenophon, more precisely, speaks of the *sphagia* as being *kala*. The *sphagia* at rivers were, in effect, a more limited and concentrated version of normal sacrifice, dictated by the circumstances, the aims, and the nature of the supernatural force addressed.[17]

BATTLE-LINE SACRIFICE

After a routine of normal sacrifices on the march or in the camp ground, though these may have been compressed because of the circumstances (e.g. with the meal following the sacrifice omitted or postponed), came the final rite before the two armies clash, the 'battle-line sacrifice' consistently described in terms of *sphagia*. It might be performed when time was very short. Once, we are told, the enemy was 600 ft (182 m) away (Xen. *Hell.* 4.2.20), another time in sight, some two miles (3.2 km) distant (Xen. *Hell.* 6.5.8). The most circumstantial account is the only one in Thucydides, in his description of the first battle at Syracuse (415 BC):

> Nicias having thus exhorted his men led them at once to the charge. . . . On this occasion [the Syracusans] were compelled to make a hasty defence, for they never imagined the Athenians would begin the attack. Nevertheless they took up their arms and immediately went forward to meet them. For a while the throwers of stones, and slingers, and archers skirmished in front of the two armies, driving one another before them after the manner of light-armed troops. The soothsayers [*manteis*] brought out the customary victims [*sphagia . . . ta nomizomena*], and the trumpets sounded and called the infantry to the charge. The two armies advanced.
>
> (Thuc. 6.69.1–2)[18]

What was done in this short time, at an arbitrary location and in a charged atmosphere? A victim, of course, was killed and most of our references clearly state that signs were taken (e.g. Hdt. 6.112.1, before the charge at Marathon). In two cases, at least, the passage in Thucydides just cited and Xenophon *Anabasis* 6.5.7–8, the sacrificers are the seers, the *manteis*, whose only function was the interpretation of signs. This needs to be stressed because there has been a tendency to play down the divinatory function of the battle-line *sphagia*.[19] The taking of signs does not exhaust the meaning of the sacrifice but in the Classical Period at least we cannot suppose it was ever absent. Hesitation on this point has arisen, no doubt, from the difficulty in seeing what could be done about bad signs as the enemy bore down upon the front line. One is inclined to suppose that the signs were essentially confirmatory of what had already been decided by human judgment and the earlier *hiera* of camp-ground sacrifice, and were therefore simple and rarely known to fail.

How were the signs obtained? For the more leisurely *hiera* of normal sacrifice the victim was cut open, some innards – primarily the liver and the *splanchna* (kidneys, gall bladder, urinary bladder, perhaps the heart) were inspected for their appearance, and certain parts were put on the fire, where their behaviour and that of the fire itself were observed.[20] No prose source indicates unmistakably the method used before the battle-line and a single poetic passage is fraught with problems. Conceivably an expert *mantis* might be able to extricate very rapidly the essential parts from the victim without concerning himself with the butchery of the rest of the animal. In any case, it is generally agreed that no altar was constructed and no fire was lit. (The apparent exceptions, as we shall see, illustrate the difficulty of distinguishing the *sphagia* from the more normal sacrifices preceding them.) Instead, it is supposed that the way the animal fell and the way the blood flowed were the essential indications that were looked for. With the fall of the animals, we may compare Aeschylus *Suppliants* 450, 'omens must fall' (*dei . . . pesein khresteria*) and Polybius (22.4a) on the practice of all foreigners who, before going to war and risking danger, sacrifice (*sphagiazonta*) a horse and learn from its fall what is going to happen. These parallels are not compelling and the representations of this moment in art show the victim firmly held between the legs of the sacrificer (see Figure 1 (p. 218) and the accompanying discussion).

More probable is the observation of the flow of the blood. The very words used, invariably, *sphagia* and *sphagiazomai*, evoke blood. Euripides speaks of *sphagia* as 'streams of blood-loving earth' (*Suppl.* 174, reading *ges philaimatou roai*) and the *Keres* of the Pseudo-Hesiodic *Shield of Heracles* and Ares in the *Iliad* (22.267) drink blood, not of sacrificial victims, to be sure, but of fallen warriors. In effect, the *sphagia* narrow down to a single action and an observation – the killing of the victim with a stab into the neck and the observing of the flow of blood that results.

CAMP-GROUND AND BATTLE-LINE SACRIFICE

There is considerable functional equivalence between the battle-line *sphagia* and the normal sacrifices that came before them and were intended to find out whether the movement towards an engagement with the enemy should proceed. The dividing line between them may not always have been sharp. The linking of the two rites is clearest in the words of Xenophon. Just before the Battle of Cunaxa the Persian prince Cyrus announces to Xenophon, and asks that he pass on to the Greek troops, that both the *hiera* and the *sphagia* are good (*An.* 1.8.15). The distinction and the connection of the two become clear from the events of a single day described fully later in the *Anabasis*. Xenophon arises early and sacrifices for departure; the *hiera* are favorable with the first victim. On the completion of the rites, the seer Arexion observes a 'lucky eagle' (*aieton aision*) and bids Xenophon to lead on (6.5.2). Later that day the enemy is seen some two miles away. The seer performs *sphagia* and the *sphagia* are good with the first victim (6.5.8). Finally, when the troops hesitate to cross a gully, a dangerous maneuver for an army in line of march with the enemy nearby, Xenophon exhorts his men, concluding with the words: 'Men, the *hiera* are good for us, the birds are lucky and the *sphagia* are excellent. Let us go against those men. Now that they have had a good look at us, they must no longer enjoy their dining nor camp wherever they like' (6.5.21). The army then crosses the gully and engages the enemy successfully. All three prognostic items – *hiera*, the eagle and the *sphagia* – combine to strengthen the morale of the army and lead it to its engagement with the enemy.

Another example from Xenophon shows the close connection. On the previous day the *hiera* had proved unfavorable to leaving the camp. Through lack of victims they had had to buy and kill a cart ox (*An.* 6.4.22). Despite the lack of propitious signs one of the commanders, Neon, offered to lead a group of volunteers on a foraging expedition (6.4.23–4). Conceivably he and the 2,000 or so men who joined him thought that such an informal venture might be exempt from the need for good signs. His band was attacked and badly mauled by troops of the native people. When word reached Xenophon in camp, 'since the *hiera* had not proved favorable on that day, he took a cart ox, performed *sphagia* and rushed to help with all the soldiers under thirty years of age' (6.4.25). Note that the performance of *sphagia* here is explained by the failure of previous *hiera*. For him they had essentially the same function. Possibly, had the earlier sacrifice been successful he would not have paused for the *sphagia*. But, as his account of the *sphagia* the following day shows (success came with the *first* victim), the *sphagia* could not be counted on to succeed with every victim. One is left to speculate on what Xenophon would have done had the *sphagia* of the cart ox failed, and one may even wonder what the signs did in fact show – he does not tell us but leaves us to assume they were favorable.

But even in the descriptions of the scrupulous Xenophon there can be uncertainty as to which rite is meant. When the Spartan commander Derkylidas suddenly ran up against Persian forces he ordered his men into battle formation and he himself began to sacrifice (*ethueto*). The engagement did not in the end take place because Tissaphernes proposed a parley which Derkylidas accepted while observing: 'I have made ready to fight, as you can see' (Xen. *Hell.* 3.2.17–18). Everything points to battle-line *sphagia* (presumably the signs were good) but the word used is the more general term for sacrifice which could also refer to the seeking of *hiera* by means of normal sacrifice. Although Xenophon's account is circumstantial we would need more details to be quite sure which ritual was chosen on this occasion.

Contrasting usage is seen in the account of Mardonios' frustration before the Battle of Plataia in 479 BC when the *sphagia* performed by his Greek *mantis* would not come out as he wished (*katathumia*, Hdt. 9.45.2, cf. 41.4). These we may be fairly sure are not last-minute rites before the battle-line, but their purpose is so single-minded, directed only to moving to an engagement, that Herodotus uses the language of that final rite.[21]

The difference between Herodotus' language and understanding of the procedures and that of much later writers is instructive. According to his description of the preliminaries to the Battle of Plataia, the Tegeans and Spartans performed *sphagia* with the intention of engaging Mardonios and the army that faced them. The *sphagia* were not proving favorable to them (*ou . . . egineto ta sphagia khresta*) and many of them were killed and many more wounded by the arrows shot by Persian archers from behind a wall of wicker-work shields. Pausanias, the Spartan commander who would have been responsible for the rites, looked towards the local sanctuary of the goddess Hera and called upon her not to let them be disappointed of their hopes for victory. The Tegeans had already begun to advance – presumably their *sphagia* had proved favorable – and after Pausanias's prayer they turned favorable for the Lakedaimonians too (*thuomenoisi ta sphagia khresta*), and they advanced to victory (Hdt. 9.61.3–62.1). There is nothing anomalous in this account, not even the use of *thuesthai* here in the most general sense of 'sacrifice.'[22]

This incident when retold by Plutarch (*Aris.* 17–18) has been greatly elaborated. When the Lakedaimonians do not obtain *hiera kala*, they are explicitly ordered to ground their shields and not to defend themselves; they suffer stoically the attacks of cavalry as well as the rain of arrows. To delay a charge is one thing, not to defend oneself quite another, and we may doubt such a command was ever given. Plutarch also knows a version according to which a band of Lydians swoops down upon Pausanias, as he is sacrificing and praying (*thuonti kai kateukhomenoi*) a little away from the formation, and seizes and scatters the parts being burnt on the altar (so at least I understand *ta peri ten thusian*). They are repulsed by the Spartans with rods and whips. The details here are of normal sacrifice for *hiera*, not the battle-line *sphagia*. In fact, Plutarch says it is an etiology for a ceremony performed around an altar by ephebes at Sparta.[23] Plutarch goes on to describe the sacrifice of victim after victim and the prayer to Hera. No doubt Pausanias did sacrifice for *hiera* at some point before the battle but Plutarch's account has no authority for what happened at Plataia. It shows, however, that by his time at the latest the battle-line *sphagia* could be thought of in terms of normal sacrifice for *hiera*. Two rituals have been conflated, at the cost of clear visualization of what was done on the battlefield.

Another author of the second century of our era, Polyaenus, tells the story of a trick by the priestess of Thessalian Enodia, a Hekate figure, who in legendary times advised Knopos to deck out elaborately and then drug the largest and finest bull. The maddened bull breaks away, is captured by the enemy, the inhabitants of Erythrai in Asia Minor, who accept him as a good omen, sacrifice and feast on him and, thanks to the drugs they ingest, go mad and fall victim to the forces of Knopos when they attack (Polyaenus *Strat.* 8.43). The origin of the story has been traced by Walter Burkert to a type of scapegoat ritual found in Hittite and Sanskrit texts.[24] Polyaenus, however, has put the incident in the framework of Greek military ritual. The proximity to the enemy suggests *sphagia* while the elaborate treatment of the victim points to a normal sacrifice, such as is the 'sacrifice to get good omens' (*kallierein*), as does the feasting of the enemy, which is essential if the trick is to work and so indispensable for the story. Once again, distinctions are blurred, and for such a fantastic tale, developed around a different type of rite not apparently known in Greece, that is not surprising.

Our last example of the functional similarity of the two rites comes from tragedy. In a messenger's speech in Euripides' *Phoenissae* (1255–8), Eteokles and Polyneikes have been exhorting their troops. 'The seers slew (*esphazon*) sheep and marked the points of flame,/ its cleavages, any damp signs of evil,/ and that high shining which may have two meanings,/ a mark of victory or of the losing side.'[25] The messenger concludes with a plea to Iokaste to prevent the fighting.

The scholiasts on the lines quoted are exceptionally detailed in the information they give about the signs to be derived from sacrifice. Both the text and the scholia speak only of fire, which we have taken to be characteristic of the camp-ground sacrifice for *hiera*, but impractical and otherwise unattested for the final *sphagia*. While the word used for killing, *esphazon*, may suggest *sphagia*, and the urgency of the situation implies that fighting is about to break out, neither the language (*sphazo* is the word for piercing the throat in any type of sacrifice) nor the actions described are inconsistent with the preceding sacrifice for *hiera*. In fact, it might be thought that once the *sphagia* had been performed, nothing could prevent the battle, whatever their message. The poet, therefore, is probably not describing the very last rite before fighting begins, but the distinction in time and function is seen to be very close.

PROPITIATION OF THE GODS

Propitiation of the supernatural as well as divination is implicit in all these rites. But in most cases no divine addressee for prayers or recipient of the victim is mentioned. In Euripides' *Heraclidae* (399–400) the *sphagia* victims stand ready to be sacrificed (*temnesthai*, 'cut,' a word associated with powerful actions) to the appropriate (*hois khre*) gods, who are not further defined. In the realm of legend is Theseus' battle-line *sphagia* to Phobos (Plut. *Thes*. 27.3), but Alexander is also said to have addressed personified fear with *sphagia* and secret, magical rites (Plut. *Alex*. 31.3). Two human sacrifices in Attic tragedy are to Persephone, perhaps as Queen of the Dead (Eur. *Heracl.* 403–5, 489–90), and to Ares, but as the father of the Theban serpent rather than the god of war (Eur. *Phoen*. 933–4).

Though it has been guessed that the mercenaries of Xenophon's *Anabasis* would have prayed to Zeus Soter, and one might add Herakles (cf. Xen. *An*. 4.8.25), the only sure historical example of a specific addressee is Artemis Agrotera.[26] To her the Spartans customarily sacrificed a young she-goat as *sphagia*, in sight of the enemy and with the officiants and the whole army wearing crowns of foliage (Xen. *Hell.* 4.2.20, *Rep. Lac.* 13.8; Plut. *Lyc.* 22.4). The epithet Agrotera occurs once in Homer, coupled with the description 'mistress of wild beasts' (*potnia theron, Il.* 21.470–1). She was worshipped in the Peloponnese, Megara, and Athens, and a scattering of other cities.[27] But she was particularly associated with the Spartans (cf. Aristoph. *Lys*. 1262–4, Xen. *Hell.* 4.2.20), perhaps just because of their formal address to her before battle. At Aigeira in Akhaia she was associated with the use of goats to trick an attacking enemy (torches were tied to the goats' horns at night, Paus. 7.26. 3 and 11), a story that points to a military connection and a goat sacrifice. The epithet locates her in the uncultivated land outside of the settlement with its nearby cultivated fields.[28] The Greeks traced her epithet rather to *agra* or *agrai*, 'the hunt,' which took place in this zone. The Spartans also made a vow of a share of the prey to her and Apollo Agraios at the moment when hounds were let loose in the hunt (Xen. *Cyn.* 6.13; the same epithets at Megara, Paus. 1.41.3). She too appears at times as Agraia rather than Agrotera.

It is difficult at first sight to see the fighting of the developed hoplite phalanx having much in common with the hunting of hare (the most common game), deer, or even boar, unless we accept as a universal phenomenon the equation of hunting and warfare.[29] The nature of the territory the goddess frequents, the *agros*, seems more relevant than the hunt over which she presides. Despite the picture that we have for the Archaic and Classical Periods of warfare taking place on, and for, the best farmland (Hanson 1989: 4), it may be that when Artemis Agrotera gained her place in the rites of war either fighting took place in more marginal territory, or perhaps, rather, it was hoped that it could be confined to such territory.[30] This Artemis was the goddess of the wild, protectress of the wild animals and their haunts, but also the goddess of men in the wilderness with the distinctive dispositions and emotions they had when separated from the social world of the town. Commonly that situation is associated with the hunt and with the liminal condition of boys about to enter the adult world. The sacrifice to Artemis Agrotera shows that it was also the condition of men at war. Of the animals men had at their disposal for regular ritual, the goat, Artemis' favorite victim, was most at home in that marginal territory.[31]

Although Athenians thought of Artemis Agrotera as characteristically Spartan, the Athenians themselves had a long-lived cult of the goddess and a shrine just outside the city-walls. Her worship goes back to at least 490 BC and the Battle of Marathon, when a vow was made to her before the battle to sacrifice annually one goat for every enemy slain (fulfilled in practice by 500 instead of over 6,000 animals).[32] In the Hellenistic Period and in the second century AD ephebes under arms marched in her procession and participated in contests in her honor.[33] The shrine was located at Agrai ('the hunting lands'?) on the slopes of low hills on the far side of the Ilissos river from the town of Athens, where Artemis had first hunted when she came from Delos (Paus. 1.19.6). Symbolically it was wilderness in contrast to the town and the plowed fields of the plain.

Her military character was remembered not only by the arms born by the ephebes but by the fact that annually it was the polemarch who sacrificed to her along with Enyalios (= Ares, Pollux 8.21) and that her treasury in the late fifth century contained money derived from the ransom or sale of prisoners of war (*IG* I³, 383, lines 85–97 = *IG* I², 310, lines 220–4). Were these solely acts of recognition of her help in 490 BC or did she continue to take an active part in Athenian warfare, as the money from prisoners might suggest? Was she perhaps the normal addressee of battle-line *sphagia* for Athenians as well as Spartans? Against this is the silence about her in accounts of later Athenian fighting, in contrast to the Spartan associations recognized in Aristophanes. Furthermore, two Athenian representations of battle-line *sphagia* show unmistakably a ram as the victim, not a she-goat (Figure 1, p. 218, and the accompanying discussion).[34]

The location of her shrine may have bearing. The Athenian army mustered at the sanctuary of her brother Apollo, with the title Lykeios ('Wolfish,' an equally uncivil title), across the river on the plain some two stades (400 yds/365 m) due north.[35] Her shrine was in view of the troops assembled at the Lykeion, preparing to march out to Marathon. Eleven years later, Pausanias was said to have looked up to the Heraion at Plataia and prayed to Hera just before the *sphagia* proved favorable (Hdt.9.61.3–62.1). Artemis Agrotera may have been invoked in 490 BC, at a moment of unparalleled danger for Athens, in the course of a camp-ground sacrifice for *hiera* in the precinct of Apollo Lykeios. Even as the Spartan hunters vowed to share their prey with Artemis and Apollo, so the Athenians in effect vowed to dedicate to her all the men they killed by giving her an equal number of her favorite victims. Thereafter she may have had a role in war ritual that we cannot see but at the least she was remembered in an annual festival and by occasional dedications from the spoils of victory.

The battle-line *sphagia*, it is clear, could be thought of as addressed to supernatural figures. None the less, the predominant silence on their identity cannot be without significance, as is the absence of figures one might have expected to be named such as Ares and Athena. They lead the men setting out for the ambush on the Shield of Achilles (*Iliad* 18.516) and Ares and Athena Areia are among those who witness the oath of the ephebes of Athens (n. 14, *supra*). Ares receives the human sacrifice of Menoikeus in Euripides' *Phoenissae*, but explicitly in recompense for Kadmos' slaying of his serpent (933–4), though, to be sure, one might argue that at an earlier time an even more brutal war-god needed no excuse to demand blood. Some scholars have supposed that the figures addressed were unnamed, infernal gods, such as poetry conceives of as ranging over the battlefield (cf. [Hes.] *Scut*. 248–57; most recently, Pritchett, *War* 3. 87–8). Others have thought of Ge, the earth, who in the absence of an altar receives the blood that this rite emphasizes, or the local heroes in whose domain the fighting takes place.[36] Neither possibility would be inconsistent with the context and may well have been true at times, but instead of positing a single explanation, we might do better to suppose that the particular traditions and circumstances of the army and their commander, and the individual beliefs and feelings of the men, affected the choice and even the articulation of an addressee. To judge by the general lack of articulation, it looks as if what mattered at this juncture was the act itself.

SPHAGIA AS PURIFICATION

What, then, was the meaning of the act? 'Purification by placation' was proposed by Jane Harrison for *sphagia* in general and this has been applied, by analogy, to the battle-line *sphagia* by Pritchett who refers to carrying the dead victim around the targeted persons or place in purificatory rites.[37] There may have been a comparable action before battle. In Euripides' *Phoenissae* the *mantis* Amphiaraos is described as going into battle carrying the *sphagia* on his chariot, instead of bearing arrogant symbols on his shield (1209–12, cf. 174). Thucydides, in his description of the battle at Syracuse (6.69.2), says 'the seers brought forward (*proupheron*) the *sphagia*,' which is usually taken to mean that they brought live animals forward for sacrifice. But more likely it means that the dead animal or a critical part of the animal, such as the liver, was carried forward to show that the ceremony had been completed successfully. There is no mention of killing and of obtaining good signs. No sooner had the *sphagia* been brought forward than the hoplite ranks advanced. It seems that the killing had already been done.[38]

The dead animal has potency, certainly in Euripides' representation of Amphiaraos and probably for the Athenians at Syracuse, but the language of purification is absent from the rites of the battle field (the occasional purification of an army earlier or later is another matter, cf.

Pritchett, *War* 3. 196–202). Can the victim be seen as a scapegoat, an offering that takes upon itself the pollution of the army, as in the Hittite and Indic practices that have been compared to the story, discussed on p. 208 (and n. 24), of how the original inhabitants of Erythrai ate the poisoned bull sent among them? But for the Greeks we know of no comparable procedure before battle – the expulsion of the victim or its despatch to the enemy. Mythical and pseudo-historical examples of human sacrifices, all *sphagia* since their flesh is not to be eaten by the sacrificers, equally lack the language of pollution and purification and do not involve expulsion of victims from the community and toward the enemy. But a number of these are powerful, imagined conceptions of the situation before battle and may contribute to our understanding.[39]

HUMAN SACRIFICE

Phylarchus, the Hellenistic historian, wrote that at one time all the Greeks killed a human being before going out against the enemy (*FGrHist.* 81 F 80 = Porpyhry *De Abst.* 2.56). The mostly mythical examples on which such a statement was based were once thought to illustrate the evolution of civilization as mankind substituted animal for human sacrifice. More recently they have been examined as imaginative and symbolic expressions of human values and emotions in situations of great tension.[40] The most famous of the allegedly historical examples, the sacrifice of three Persian prisoners before the Battle of Salamis by Themistokles, has been shown to be unhistorical, which is not to say that human sacrifice before battle could not have happened since there are two instances of the killing of prisoners being put into a ritual context. Alexander the Great is said to have killed those suspected of his father's assassination at his father's tomb, in effect converting an execution into a sacrifice (Just. *Epit.* 11.2.1), and Messenian prisoners of war were killed at the grave of Philopoimen in the second century BC (Plut. *Philop.* 21). Both examples recall the killing of twelve Trojan captives at the pyre of Patroklos in the *Iliad* (23.175–6) and of Polyxena's death in Euripides' *Hecuba*. Here the imagined practices of legend have been made real.

If *sphagia* are powerful actions, nothing is more powerful than the piercing of a human throat so that the blood flows. Two contrasting types of human victim are found: (1) One of 'our own' community and, in the extreme forms favored by myth, of noble birth, a daughter or son of the king; (2) an enemy who can be slaughtered with less compunction, as in the two historical cases and the apocryphal story of Themistokles at Salamis; here is where we might expect but in fact fail to find the notion of the scapegoat. The stories of human sacrifice generally are concerned with serious threats to the community from plague or foreign invasion. Most often, as we shall see, these extraordinarily powerful sacrifices are not slotted precisely into the normal sequence of rites leading up to battle but bear on the overall emergency. They are, therefore, more revealing of general attitudes than of the specific meaning of particular rites.

Of the first type of victim Iphigeneia is the best-known example. The realistic correlate to her sacrifice is the *sphagia* performed for crossing water or to propitiate unfavorable winds. But the god who must be propitiated here is Artemis, not the powers of the sea or of the winds. In Aeschylus' treatment of the story in the *Agamemnon*, the reason for Artemis' anger as well as the immediate purpose of the sacrifice are left obscure, and the poet, by calling the sacrificers 'leaders who love battle' (230) and comparing the girl to a young she-goat (*khimaira*, 232), alludes to the battle-line *sphagia*.[41] At the end of Euripides' *Iphigenia in Aulis* (a part of the play whose authenticity is doubtful) Artemis is addressed as slayer of animals, that is the hunting goddess Agrotera (1570), and as the one who delights in human sacrifice (1524–5), an unmistakable reference to the Tauric Artemis of the same dramatist's *Iphigenia among the Taurians*.

The only explicit example of a human sacrifice serving as the battle-line *sphagia* is that of Marathos, the Arcadian, who because of some oracle offered himself for sacrifice (*sphagiasasthai*) before the battle-line (Plut. *Thes*. 32.5, citing the late fourth-century peripatetic philosopher, Dicaearchus). Marathos has accompanied the Tyndaridai on an invasion of Attica and through his death becomes the eponymous hero of the Attic deme of Marathon. Though we lack details the story seems to reflect the *aition* of how a foreigner gave his name to a part of Attica and thus became its protector, after dying – unusually – in the service of the invading army.[42]

The ritual correlates in other stories are less precise. Menoikeus, the son of Kreon, in Euripides' *Phoenissae* willingly accepts the death prescribed by Teiresias, fresh from success as a military *mantis* for the Athenians (852), and the commanders and generals concur (973). The context is military and the purpose is to save Thebes from the Seven. But he kills himself on a tower of the walls of Thebes (1090 ff.), not before the battle-line, and the blood he gives to the earth is in recompense for Ares' anger at Kadmos' slaughter of his serpent (933–4), not to Ares as the god of war.

Stories of the death of virgins of the highest birth were particularly popular in tragedy.[43] In Euripides' *Heraclidae*, when Aigisthos and the Argives invade Attica to destroy the children of Herakles, all sources of divination are consulted by the Athenian king and all agree that not bull nor calf but a virgin girl must be slaughtered for Persephone (Eur. *Phoen.* 403–5, cf. 489–90). Makaria, Herakles' daughter, offers herself; her request that she breathe her last in the hands of women, not men, is granted (565–74). This does not lead us to expect that she will be killed in front of the two armies. When later in the play there is a description of battle-line *sphagia* performed by *both* sides and without mention of Makaria one would see no allusion to human sacrifice if the text did not speak (literally) of 'the propitious killing of human throats.' Rather than seeing a very oblique reference to the girl's death that contradicts what we have been told earlier or accepting an interpretation that takes the animals here to be surrogates for humans, I find it more likely that there is a problem in the text.[44]

Of examples outside of drama, the story of the Boiotian Leuktrides is interesting because of the way it was developed and attached to an important historical event, the Theban victory over the Spartans at Leuktra in 371 BC. The battle took place near a sacred spot that was interpreted to be the grave of two maidens who had been raped by Spartans. The Theban general Pelopidas was said to have had a dream in which their father charged him with sacrificing (*sphagiasai*) a maiden to them if he wished to defeat the enemy. Fortunately a young filly strayed into the camp and was consigned to that fate by the seers.[45]

While these stories of the surrender and destruction for the gods of noble men and women are usually kept distinct from the specific rituals performed before battle, they can be taken to reflect the general atmosphere of a community in a crisis, such as characterized, to some degree, every battle and every siege. Two historical examples illustrate Greek views. The Spartan king Leonidas' death at Thermopylai in 480 BC was subsequently supported by oracles and interpreted as the necessary loss – we would say 'sacrifice' – which permitted the Greeks to defeat the Persians in the war.[46] Again, in 403 BC the *mantis* of the democratic Athenians fighting to regain the city from the tyranny of the Thirty is said to have advised no move by his fellow soldiers until one of them had been killed or wounded, after which he foresaw victory and his own death. When the enemy appeared he led the charge and was killed but his comrades won the battle (Xen. *Hell.* 2.4.18–19). It may have happened in just this way, or it may be that since the *mantis* was the first, or among the first, to be killed and since his comrades won, his death was taken to be the powerful surrender, i.e. 'sacrifice,' that brought about the successful outcome.

The second type of human victim is one of the enemy. Here we might expect to see the notion of a scapegoat and the expulsion of pollution at work, but that does not prove to be the case. The most notorious incident, that of Themistokles' sacrifice of three Persian captives before the Battle of Salamis in 480 BC, has often been accepted as historical and at first sight appears to fit the slot of *sphagia* before battle. Themistokles is sacrificing on the island of Salamis near the command ship in preparation for the naval engagement with the Persian fleet. Three handsome and splendidly dressed Persian prisoners, nephews of the Great King, are brought forward, at which point a bright flame shoots up from the *hiera* on the altar and a sneeze is heard on the right. The *mantis* urges Themistokles to sacrifice the Persians to Dionysos Omestes ('Raw-eater') to save the city and win victory. Themistokles is shocked but the crowd insists on the sacrifice (Plut. *Them.* 13.2–5, cf. *Arist.* 9.2, *Pelop.* 21.3). The story has been shown to be unhistorical because the prisoners were said to have been captured on the island of Psyttaleia, on which the Athenians landed only after the naval victory, and because the god who received the sacrifice was unknown in Athens but a local figure of Lesbos, the home of Plutarch's source, Phainias.[47]

The incident is omitted by Herodotus, though one could argue he did so because he was reluctant to attribute such barbarism to the Greeks at their moment of glory. But he does report that earlier that summer some Persians killed on the prow of their ship a comparably handsome Greek (*kallisteuon*) whose ship they had captured (7.180; the verbs are *sphazo* and *sphagiazomai*). They regarded him as a good omen, being their first captive and most handsome. The language and thinking are close to that of the Greek seer at Salamis, as reported by Phainias in Plutarch. It was common (not, as is sometimes said, a rule) in sacrifice to choose through a process of selection the finest victim (the *kallisteuon*) for sacrifice.[48] Here the finest victim serves also as a first-fruit offered to the gods, though that is not explicit in the language. The incident may be no more historical than the killing of the three noble Persians on Salamis since Herodotus is fond of commenting on the awful but fascinating strangeness of the Persians and other non-Greeks in ritual matters. But both are probably examples of sacrifice conceived of as offering a prize, a first-fruit, to the gods to gain their favor or to deflect their envy. The sheep and goats of armies or fleets on campaign are appropriate victims but they are not selected as the finest nor are they first-fruits. The stories say that the situation deserves the giving of a prize to the gods. The reality was the killing of the nearest domestic animal.

ART

Our last source of information is art. We concentrate on three examples of a warrior killing a ram, two from Attic red-figure vases of the fifth century BC, the third in a series of reliefs of the first half of the fourth century BC, from Lycia in Asia Minor but of Greek workmanship.[49] In the first (Figure 1), a warrior wearing a helmet but no armor, while holding the snout of a ram with his left hand and gripping its hindquarters between his knees, drives the point of a sword through the animal's neck. The blood begins to spurt both from the point at which the sword entered the neck and from its point of exit. The ram has been forced to its knees. The scene is entirely the act of sacrifice. In the second example the body of the sacrificer is missing. He straddles the ram whose body is flat on the ground and he pulls its head back by pushing down on its left horn. With his right hand he drives the sword into the animal's neck. The remains of the two bands of the calyx crater show, to the right of the sacrifice, two warriors armed with helmets and shields confronting each other with spears. In the lower band two men, one helmeted, the other wearing a cap, drag a bearded corpse. A youth carrying three spears and a shield faces them, his right hand on his head in a gesture of lamentation. In the third example, the relief shows a helmeted, beardless man wearing a short cape, and kneeling on a ram whose neck he grips between his thighs. With his left hand he pulls the victim's head back and in his right hand he holds up a sword to drive into its neck. To the right stands a bearded man, taken to be the commander of the besieged forces, wearing breastplate and helmet, holding up his shield with his left arm which rests on a spear while his right arm is raised in a gesture of prayer.

The last two examples certainly allude to heroic scenes of combat. The first is so narrowly focused that it is without context other than that of battle. But it is the most revealing in that it singles out the

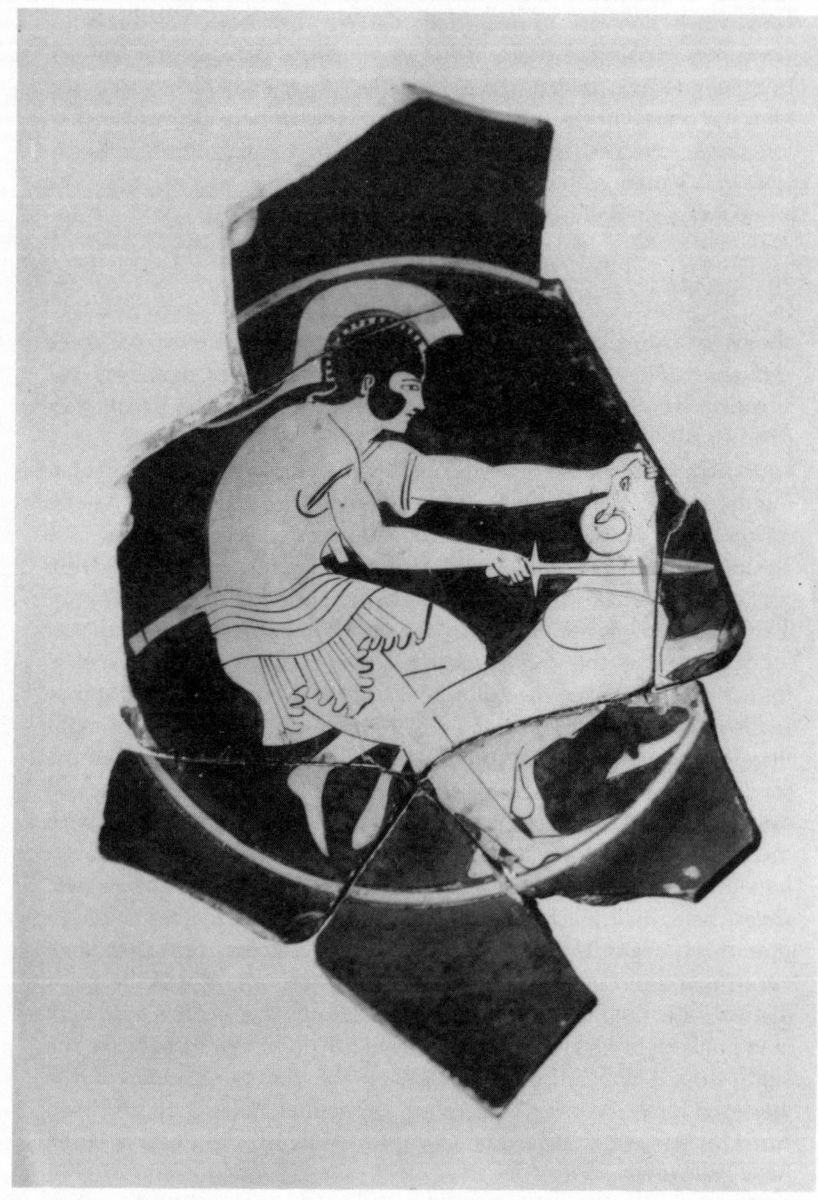

Figure 1 The sacrifice before battle (photograph: courtesy of the Cleveland Museum of Art, Dudley P. Allen Fund)

moment of performing *sphagia*, of driving the sword through the neck, as a self-contained scene. The absence from all these scenes of altar, fire, and the usual officiants and attendants seen in representations of sacrifice shows that this is the *sphagia* before battle. The sacrificer may be a *mantis* but he is also a member of the fighting force, since he wears a helmet and carries a sword. He kills with no special implement but the sword which he will shortly use in battle, and none of the paraphernalia of sacrifice, often lovingly depicted on Attic vases, is in sight. The depiction of the moment of killing the victim is in contrast to the usual representation of sacrifice. Aside from these scenes only the moment of killing a human victim is shown in Greek art, and that too was conceived of as a form of *sphagia*.[50] These scenes give us the essential message of battle-line *sphagia*. There are no signs of good omen, no symbol to represent the divinity addressed, not even the community of sacrificers though we know how concerned they were with this sacrifice. It is the act of killing, pure and simple, that matters at this moment.

CONCLUSIONS

The various types of formal killing of domestic animals, which we lump together and call sacrifice, were subject to a variety of meanings for the Greeks and were used in a wide range of contexts for diverse purposes. The actual context of any particular performance tended to limit its meanings. In warfare, the immediate aims of ritual seem especially clear. The stories told about remarkable sacrifices in the course of war and the imagery of poetry suggest how these sacrifices might be interpreted – as surrender of something of value to the home community to save the rest of the community, as passing on to the gods the first-fruits of success, and as the appeasing of dangerous powers. But how much of this impinged on the historically attested enactments? As the two armed forces move toward conflict the aims of ritual become narrower and more single-minded.

Ostensibly every step taken is approved by the gods through the signs they give in answer to inquiry. At the same time, proper acknowledgment of the role of the gods, of their power, is made through sacrifice, libation, and prayer. But the initiative is in the hands of men. The decision to go to war is taken by political institutions. It may be ratified by divination; or rather the timing, and thus also the place, for the decision's being put into effect are approved or delayed or, rarely, cancelled altogether by divination. So

Thucydides reports that a Spartan campaign was given up because the border-crossing sacrifices proved unfavorable (5.54.2, cf. 55.3 and 116.1). Had we more details we might well see that there had been disagreement about the advisability of the campaign or its timing, so that the failure to get the right signs at once was sufficient to reverse the decision. The religious and the pragmatic are so closely intertwined in this world that it would be futile for us to try to judge whether genuine religious feeling or practical considerations were at work. When a decision was firm or effectively inescapable, men continued sacrificing for the necessary omens until they were obtained or until the issue was moot, when the enemy was upon them. We do not need to believe that any Greek soldiers ever failed to defend themselves in this situation.[51]

The whole sequence of rites leading up to battle expressed what men desired, the ideal outcome being the collaboration of gods with men at every step. But the repeated sacrifices until the desired signs were received say more about the determination of the sacrificers than their willingness to govern their actions by divine guidance. Herodotus has Mardonios say, in effect, when the sacrifices do not come out as he desired (*katathumia*), 'To hell with trying to force (*biazesthai*) the *sphagia*' (Hdt. 9.45.2, 9.41.4). In the mouth of the foreigner is put a sceptical, ill-omened but recognizable description of what is being done.

At the last moment when the battle-line *sphagia* are performed, all aims culminate in and are subordinated to a single expressive action – the killing of the animal, which is immediately followed by the killing of men.[52] The spirit of the battlefield ritual has been caught by Albert Henrichs in his study of human sacrifice in Greek religion:

> the brutalizing experience of battle and impending doom . . . lies also at the root of the *sphagia* sacrifice as such in its regular animal form . . . men at the threshold of hand-to-hand combat sought unusual ritual remedies in an effort to cope with extraordinary psychological strain, and with the threat to their lives. Sinister and different, the *sphagia* anticipated the bloodshed of the battle and marked its ritual beginning.[53]

I have tried to clarify these unusual ritual remedies and to show that they are not in themselves distinctive but are sinister and different primarily because, as all activity accelerates to the clash of armed men, everything that is not essential gives way to the stark fact of the act of killing, not softened or veiled by the forms of normal sacrifice in a communal or familial environment.

It was the view of Alfred Loisy that in divinatory sacrifices the sacred action is a sign or representation of what is wanted, just as the portent is a sign of what is going to happen. Such sacrifices are in effect magical, designed to control and direct and not only to inquire. Loisy's knowledge of Greek practice was faulty and his further notion that magic is a confusion in the primitive mind now finds few adherents.[54] If, however, we think of such ritual as expressive action, it can be seen as representing simply what is desired and of serving to focus, while at the edge of the chaos of battle, on that goal.[55] The repeated sacrifices leading up to battle are in a sense magical, most clearly in the concentrated *sphagia* for crossing boundaries of water. At other times, the absence or vagueness of a divine recipient or addressee, the indifference to sacred places and instruments and to the disposal of the victim, are clearest in, if not limited to, the final *sphagia*. Divination is not abandoned; rather, the acts of killing and of divination are combined, their distinction collapsed. Battle was slaughter, 'us' killing 'them.' In the act of *sphagia* everything was reduced to a single action, a single stroke. Expressed fully, what the sacrificers said was: 'O gods! We destroy this life. We wish to kill and not be killed. Support us.' Put even more simply, it is an act and a wish: 'We kill. May we kill.'

NOTES

1. In addition to Connor 1988, Lonis 1979, and Pritchett, *War* 1 and *War* 3, cited in full in the Bibliography of this volume, essential contributions on the subject of the present essay are the following:
   Walter Burkert, *Homo Necans. The Anthropology of Ancient Greek Sacrifice and Myth* (Berkeley, 1983).
   Jean Casabona, *Recherches sur le vocabulaire des sacrifices en Grec des origines à la fin de l'époque classique* (Aix-en-Provence, 1966).
   S. Eitrem, 'Mantis und *Sphagia*,' *SymbOslo* 18 (1953) 9–29.
   Albert Henrichs, 'Human sacrifice in Greek religion: three case studies,' in Jean Rudhardt and Olivier Reverdin, eds, *Le sacrifice dans l'antiquité* (Vandoeuvres, 1980) 195–235.
   Arthur Darby Nock, 'The cult of heroes,' in *HThR* 37 (1944) 141–73 = *Essays on Religion and the Ancient World* II (Oxford, 1972) 575–602.
   Harald Popp, *Die Einwirkung von Vorzeichen, Opfern und Festen auf die Kriegführung der Griechen im 5. und 4. Jahrhundert v. Chr.* (Diss. Erlangen, 1957).
   Jean Rudhardt, *Notions fondamentales de la pensée religieuse et actes constitutifs du culte dans la Grèce classique* (Geneva, 1958).

Friedrich Schwenn, 'Der Krieg in der griechischen Religion' (part 2) *ArchRW* 21 (1922) 58–71.

Paul Stengel, *Opferbräuche der Griechen* (Berlin, 1910).

———, 'SPHAGIA,' *ArchRW* 13 (1910) 87–91.

Theodorus Szymanski, *Sacrificia Graecorum in bellis militaria* (Diss., University of Marburg, 1908). Virtually all the relevant passages are presented and discussed.

Ludwig Ziehen, *RE* 3A, 2 (1929) 1169–79, s.v. *Sphagia*.

2. Xen. *Rep. Lac.* 13.2–3, cf. Nic. Dam. *FGrH* 90 F 103 z 14, on the *purphoros*. The king also performed other sacrifices at the border, Xen. *Hell.* 3.4.3.
3. Szymanski op. cit. 76–7.
4. E.g. Lonis 1979: 102–3, and Popp op. cit. 39–73.
5. Lonis (1979: 102) sees the men who fought and died at Thermopylai as an exception to the rule that battle was not engaged unless the signs were favorable. In this case there was no alternative (Hdt. 7.219). True enough, but it was evident, after the fact, that neither human nor supernatural prognosis could have been anything but negative once the Greeks had been taken in the rear. The gods were not thought to have been mistaken about this glorious defeat. But who was to say what the signs had really shown? Pritchett (*War* 3.89–90) discusses the Greek acceptance of failure in terms of the unexpectedness of supernatural action.
6. Eitrem op. cit. 9.
7. Burkert op. cit. 46–8, 64–6, followed by Connor 1988: 22–3.
8. Translation by Hugh G. Evelyn-White, *Hesiod, the Homeric Hymns and Homerica* (Loeb Library, Cambridge, Mass., 1936). This passage and others are discussed by Eitrem op. cit. 16–18.
9. Representations in art of the actual killing of an animal are confined to *sphagia*, either the sacrifice before the battle-line or mythical human sacrifice (on the latter, cf. J.-L. Durand in M. Detienne and J.-P. Vernant, *The Cuisine of Sacrifice among the Greeks* (Chicago, 1989) 91). In the former a sword or knife is driven down into the neck of the victim (see Figure 1). This would seem to confirm the interpretation of Stengel op. cit. 92–102, 123–35 (who, however, uses illustrations of widely different dates and origins), and Ziehen op. cit. 1670; that *sphazein* refers to piercing, not cutting.
10. Stengel op. cit. 92. For the language of sacrifice, see Rudhardt op. cit. and Casabona op. cit. (overlapping categories discussed at 330–9).
11. Cf. Nock op. cit. 158 (but destruction of the body, included in his definition, is not relevant to military *sphagia*), M. H. Jameson, 'Sacrifice and ritual: Greece' in Michael Grant and Rachel Kitzinger, eds, *Civilization of the Ancient Mediterranean: Greece and Rome* (New York, 1988), vol. II, 973–5.
12. *Diabateria* are attested only for the Spartans and only by Xenophon, with the single exception of a reference to the legendary Herakleidai attacking Sparta (*huperbateria*, Polyaenus *Strat.* 1.10).
13. The testimonia for inanimate objects, D. M. MacDowell, *Athenian Homicide Law* (Manchester, England, 1963) 85–6.
14. M. N. Tod, *Greek Historical Inscriptions*, II (Oxford, 1948), no. 204, line

19, *SEG* XVI 140, P. Siewert, 'The ephebic oath in fifth-century Athens,' *JHS* 97 (1977) 103.

15. Apollo Horios, Paus. 2.35.2 (Hermion in the Peloponnese). Zeus Horios, H. Schwabl, 'Zeus,' *RE* Suppl. 15 (1978) 1469; in Attica he may have been concerned only with local boundaries.
16. It is not necessary to suppose with J. von Prott, *Leges Graecorum Sacrae*, Fasc. 1, *Fasti Sacri* (Leipzig, 1896) 18 that the animals killed at the river were thrown in and so unavailable for consumption.
17. In Alexander's campaigns as recorded by Arrian the language of normal sacrifice was used for all river crossings. It has been suggested that there had been a shift from understanding the rite as propitiation of a river god (by means of *sphagia*) to a normal sacrifice to higher gods with observation of signs of their approval (Szymanski op. cit., 31). Perhaps in foreign parts and in ignorance of the particular local god, the seers recommended consultation of familiar gods without the pouring of blood into the river. Arrian, incidentally, also reports two sacrifices, evidently of the normal type, *after* successful crossings, and for these he uses the term *diabateria*, earlier attested only for the sacrifice before crossing the borders of Lakonia (1.4.5, 5.8.2).
18. Trans. Jowett. As has been frequently pointed out, it is the massed advance of the hoplites that waits on the performance of *sphagia*. The light-armed are already engaged. But to conclude that *sphagia* were limited to pitched battle, *parataxis* (as does Pritchett, *War* 3.88–9) goes too far. Xenophon explicitly performs *sphagia* before racing to help a foraging party that has been set upon by natives (*An.* 6.4.25). Any serious fighting required *sphagia*. The fluid, tentative testing of the light-armed did not count.
19. So no less an authority than Pritchett, *War* 1.110 ('*Sphagia* were not necessarily, if at all, for divination purposes'), *War* 3.87. Delays resulting from unpropitious *sphagia* (Hdt. 9.61–2) and references to their coming out favorably with the *first* victim (Xen. *An.* 6.5.8) show unmistakably that signs were an essential feature of the rite. Pritchett understands the phrase, 'The *sphagia* are good (*kala*, or the like),' as 'merely to mean that the sacrifice went well' but then goes on to say that this 'could be deduced from many things, the flow of the blood etc' (*War* 1.113) which I would understand as a form of divination. It should be noted that references to the preceding sacrifices on the march or in the camp ground also often omit reference to the results (e.g. Xen. *An.* 4.6.13, *Hell.* 5.4.49). In his later study of the subject Pritchett lays stress on the very different methods of taking omens in the two rites (*War* 3.83). The difference, as I see it, lies in the stark simplicity of the *sphagia*. We can hardly suppose that whatever good or bad signs resulted from that killing would have been dismissed in a more leisurely and complex sacrifice. Rudhardt op. cit. 275 rightly sees *sphagia* as both propitiatory and mantic. Several scholars have suggested that the mantic function was not original but was added later, e.g. Szymanski op. cit. 89, Eitrem op. cit.

    The relationship of the seer (*mantis*) to the commander has been fully treated by Pritchett, *War* 1 and 3, and Lonis 1979. A seer had more specialized knowledge but a competent commander knew enough for most purposes. The sacrifices and the decisions based on them were the commander's responsibility. He may be spoken of as sacrificing without mention of his *mantis* just as any person may be who undertakes a sacrifice even though other persons perform the ritual acts.

20. Pritchett, *War* 3. 73–8. On the tail of cattle and the gall-bladder put on the fire, see M. H. Jameson, 'Sophocles *Antigone* 1005–1022. An illustration,' in Martin J. Cropp and Elaine Fantham, eds, *Greek Tragedy and its Heritage. Essays presented to Desmond Conacher* (1986) 59–65.
21. Two instances in Plutarch where the language is not precise: Phokion, while performing *sphagia*, might have been having no success with the *hiera (dusieron),* unless he was delaying for tactical reasons (*Phoc.* 13). Before the Battle of Salamis, Themistokles is said to have been engaged in *sphagia* when, on the arrival of three Persian prisoners of war, a large and conspicuous flame shot up from the *hiera (Them.* 13). The story, which will be considered shortly, is apocryphal and a fire is not surely attested for *sphagia* before land battles. On the question of the rituals preliminary to sea battles, see n. 47, *infra*.
22. An element of local piety has crept into the story. It seems that there had been a delay, for whatever reason, in the advance of the Lakedaimonian hoplites during which time Persian archery took its toll. Both the difficulty and the eventual success were later said to be religious in origin, and credit was given to the local goddess, Hera. The story requires that difficulties in the final sacrifice, *sphagia*, were credible.
23. It forms part of a well-known festival in the sanctuary of Artemis Orthia. Cf. Plut. *Mor.* 239C and M. P. Nilsson, *Griechische Feste von religiöser Bedeutung* (Leipzig, 1906) 190–6.
24. Walter Burkert, *Structure and History in Greek Mythology and Ritual* (Berkeley, 1979) 59–61.
25. Trans. by Elizabeth Wyckoff, in David Grene and Richmond Lattimore, eds, *The Complete Greek Tragedies*, vol. IV, *Euripides* (Chicago, 1959). These notoriously difficult lines have exercised ancient and modern commentators. Wyckoff (p. 456) regards them and most of the messenger speech in which they occur as spurious, and lines 1242–58 are deleted by Eduard Fraenkel, *SBBay* (1963) 60–3. But D. J. Mastronarde, ed, Euripides' *Phoenissae* (Teubner edn, 1988) regards lines 1255–8 as difficult to interpret and requiring emendation, but not spurious.
26. The Muses and Eros are mentioned as receiving sacrifices from the Spartans before warfare or battle – they sacrifice to the Muses before war (Plut. *Mor.* 458E), offer *sphagia* before dangers (*Mor.* 221A, cf. 238B) and the king makes preliminary sacrifices to them in battle (*Lyc.* 21.6). According to Athenaeus (13.561E) the Spartans make preliminary sacrifice to Eros in front of the battle-lines 'with the belief that salvation and victory depend on the friendship (*philia*) of the men in the battle line.' The latter is connected with the sacrifice of maidens before battle by Burkert op. cit. 65–6 and in *Greek Religion* (Cambridge, Mass., 1985) 267, cf. Connor 1988: 23–4. I do not fully understand the significance of the information nor the interpretations that have been offered.
27. See Lewis Farnell, *Cults of the Greek City-States* II (Oxford, 1896–1909)

431–4; Schwenn, op. cit. 62–7; no doubt more instances of her worship could now be added.

28. Pierre Chantraine *Dictionnaire étymologique de la langue grecque* (Paris, 1968–80), s.v. *agros*.
29. Cf. Burkert, op. cit. 46–8.
30. The poetic depiction of towns under siege (cf. Hom. *Il.* 18.509–40; [Hes.] *Scut.* 237–69) shows the failure for the defenders of fighting in the countryside, through being defeated or outwitted. In the Homeric passage the ambush of cattle and herdsmen by men from the besieged town is set in what could be described as the *agros* of the attackers.
31. Cf. Edward Kadletz, *Animal Sacrifice in Greek and Roman Religion* (Diss. University of Washington, 1976) 87–92.
32. The evidence together with a very useful note in P. J. Rhodes, *A Commentary on the Aristotelian Athenaion Politeia* (Oxford, 1981) 650. It is usually thought that the day of her festival, 6th Boedromion (or 6th Thargelion), was not the day of the battle but was the date of her festival even before Marathon. H. W. Parke suggested that it was 'the date on which the resolution was passed by the Athenian army [rather, the assembly] to set out from Athens, and the vow was made in anticipation of the battle,' *Festivals of the Athenians* (Ithaca, NY, 1977) 55. On the location and remains of her sanctuary, John Travlos, *Pictorial Dictionary of Ancient Athens* (London, 1971) 112–14.
33. Chrysis Pélékides, *Histoire de l'éphébie Attique* (Paris, 1962) 215–16.
34. E. Fraenkel, Aeschylus *Agamemnon* II (Oxford, 1950) 133, asserted that Athens (cf. Eitrem op. cit., 19) and several other Greek cities offered her battle-line *sphagia* but his citations do not show this to have been the case. Aristoph. *Eq.* 660–2 is an allusion to the vow.
35. On the sanctuary and its use, M. H. Jameson, 'Apollo Lykeios in Athens,' *Archaiognosia* (Athens) 1 (1980) 213–36. For the relationship between the two shrines, see Travlos (*supra* n. 31), fig. 379.
36. Cf. Ziehen op. cit. and Eitrem op. cit. Stengel op. cit. saw the *sphagia* as essentially apotropaic, to avert hostile spirits.
37. J. E. Harrison, *Prolegomena to the Study of Greek Religion* (Cambridge, England, 1980 3rd edn), 65; Pritchett, *War* 3.86.
38. The scholiast commented that the *sphagia* were performed in front of the army. One expects *phero* to refer to something that is carried with the arms, *ago* to refer to the bringing of animals. Cf. Eur. *Heracl.* 673 of the *sphagia* of both sides.
39. On human sacrifice, Friedrich Schwenn, *Die Menschenopfer bei den Griechen und Römern* (Berlin, 1915) and Henrichs op. cit.
40. See, especially, Henrichs op. cit.; Helene P. Foley, *Ritual Irony. Poetry and Sacrifice in Euripides* (Ithaca, NY, 1985).
41. In general, see Henrichs op. cit., 198–208. On the chorus's description of Iphigeneia's death in the *Agamemnon*, see Fraenkel (*supra* n. 34), 232 and K. J. Dover 'Some neglected aspects of Agamemnon's dilemma,' *JHS* 93 (1973) 58–69.
42. Dicaearchus, Fr. 66 in Fritz Wehrli, *Die Schule des Aristoteles* (Basle, 1944) with discussion on pp. 62–3. On the foreign origin of a number of tutelary heroes see François de Polignac, *La naissance de la cité grecque*

(Paris, 1984) 132–40.

43. Human sacrifices in story are reviewed by Friedrich Schwenn (*supra* n. 39), 121–39. Cf. Foley, op. cit. 65 and *passim*. On the death of virgins in particular, Henrichs op. cit., 195–208, and Burkert (*supra* n. 1) 65–7, who sees their killing as an element in the sexualization of war, sexually aggressive acts requiring restitution.
44. Cf. Pritchett, *War* 3.86, 'a surrogate – an animal in substitution for the human victim of earlier times.' Paley suggested reading *boteion*, 'sheep's,' for *broteion*, 'mortal.' Wilamowitz deleted lines 819–22, *Hermes* 17 (1882) 337 ff. Murray daggered the word *broteion*.
45. See Joseph Fontenrose, *The Delphic Oracle* (Berkeley, 1978) 146–8.
46. Hdt. 7.220.4, 239.1. Fontenrose (*supra* n. 45), 77–8 and 319, Q127.
47. Frank Frost, *Plutarch's Themistocles. A Historical Commentary* (Princeton, 1980) 150; Henrichs, op. cit. 208–24. Henrichs finds the language of the description correct up to the sacrifice of the Persians, at which point an unparalleled second sacrifice is added. It should be noted, however, that while Themistokles is engaged in *sphagia (sphagiazomenoi)* there are *hiera* burning in the fire, which we have not found surely attested for the battle-line sacrifice. There is a question whether the same rites were performed before a naval engagement as before hoplite battle. Xenophon is silent about the sacrifices before the Battle of Arginousai (406 BC) but Diodorus Siculus (13.97) has a melodramatic account of the head of the Spartan victim disappearing in the sea, which the seer interpreted to mean the death of the Spartan admiral, as indeed happened, and favorable *hiera* on the Athenian side being reported to the fleet while a dream of the Athenian commander of the day, Thrasyllos, that he and six other *strategoi* were playing the parts of the seven against Thebes in Euripides' *Phoenissae* in Athens, was not reported because the seer foretold that it meant their death. Normal sacrifice for *hiera* are indicated by the *eisiteria* before a naval expedition (to be distinguished from the rites performed on entering a public office). A seer is honored for having predicted Athenian victory in the Battle of Knidos (396 BC), as explained by Pritchett, *War* 3.63–7. We can safely assume that campground sacrifice for *hiera* was normal before a naval battle, as for all engagements, but it is unlikely that there was any equivalent of the final *sphagia* before the battle lines on land. Plutarch's *sphagiazomenoi* of Themistokles is vivid but probably not realistic.
48. e.g., SIG^3 1024, line 6, etc.; cf. Henrichs op. cit., 217, n. 2.
49. Example one (shown in Figure 1), five joining fragments of a red-figure cup, *CVA* Cleveland Museum of Art 26.242. Pl. 37.1, ca. 490–80 BC, cf. the Eucharides painter (Cedric G. Boulter); example two, a fragment of a red-figure calyx crater, formerly in the Bareiss Collection, now in the J. Paul Getty Museum, Malibu, California, *Greek Vases. Molly and Walter Bareiss Collection* (1983) N. 106, ca. 430 BC (Getty Museum number: 86.AE.213). The third example is the Heroon from Gjolbaschi-Trysa, now in Vienna. Fritz Eichler, *Die Reliefs der Heroon von Gjölbaschi-Trysa* (Vienna, 1950) Pl. 19 [upper left] and p. 62. A much larger series on coins and in reliefs of figures kneeling on a victim in this pose shows the goddess Nike or a hero. These too I believe represent military

sphagia; I hope to discuss them elsewhere. It should be noted that in all cases of this pose the head of the victim is pulled up, not down as has been claimed was necessary for *sphagia* as chthonic rites (e.g. Ziehen op. cit., 1670–1). What matters is where the blood flows.

50. See Durand, (*supra* n. 10) but my example (Fig. 1) is an exception to his rule. My second and third examples show that for representations of the battle-line *sphagia* whether the implement is or is not in the victim's neck does not matter.

51. When hoplites faced light-armed men their only defense, aside from trying to avoid missiles, was to advance. Agesilaos' hoplites suffered wounds at the hands of light-armed Akarnanians until the *sphagia* were completed whereupon they advanced against them (Xen. *Hell.* 4.6.10, and cf. *supra* n. 18). On the dilemmas of commanders forced to balance religious and military considerations, see K. J. Dover (*supra* n. 41) 62–7. There is an informative incident from peacetime Sparta. Early in the fourth century BC King Agesilaos at Sparta, while performing routine sacrifices in peacetime, received unfavorable signs from the *hiera* which pointed to a plot against the state (Xen. *Hell.* 3.3.4). After repeated sacrifices to 'apotropaic and saving' powers the king and his *mantis* were barely able to get favorable signs and so stop and resume their secular activities, which included investigations that led to the discovery of the source of subversion, a certain Kinadon and his associates. One might well speculate that the Spartan authorities wanted to move against a suspected danger and welcomed supernatural support for their views. The use of the apotropaic rites is a way of getting out of a situation that requires action by other means, comparable to turning off a smoke alarm while looking for the fire and putting it out.

52. Cf. 'the deadly activity that then continued in the human slaughter of battle,' Burkert, op. cit. 1983: 66.

53. Henrichs, op. cit., 215–16. Two minor points: first, Henrichs says that 'It is well known that *sphagia* required the wholesale slaughter of animals which took place on the battlefield. . . .' (Cf. Burkert op. cit., 66 'slaughtered in great numbers as the enemy looked on.') 'Wholesale' only if each victim failed to produce the right signs, and exposure to the enemy rarely permitted prolonged sacrifice and consultation. The number of victims as such is not part of the aim or the effect of the sacrifice. Second, although the sacrifice did mark the beginning of battle the language used of these rites does not, to my knowledge, employ the compounds of *archesthai*, 'to begin,' common elsewhere in sacrificial terminology. Cf. Rudhardt op. cit., 219–20.

54. Alfred Loisy, *Essai historique sur le sacrifice* (Paris, 1920) 259–60, criticized by Lonis 1979: 104, for some misconceptions of Greek practice.

55. Cf. the discussion of a much more complex ritual in Jonathan Z. Smith's essay, 'The Bare Facts of Ritual,' in his *Imagining Religion. From Babylon to Jonestown* (Chicago, 1982) 53–65. On the relation of magic to ritual (and of both to scientific thought), see S. J. Tambiah, 'The form and meaning of magical acts: a point of view,' in William A. Lessa and Evon Z. Vogt, eds, *Reader in Comparative Religion. An Anthropological Approach* (New York, 4th edn 1979), especially 358–62.

9

HOPLITES AND THE GODS: The Dedication of Captured Arms and Armour

A. H. Jackson

There could be few clearer proofs of victory than the arms and armour taken from the dead comrades of the routed enemy by the triumphant conqueror, nor any more abject confession of defeat than the enemy's request to be allowed to recover the corpses of those he had deserted in his flight. Proud and grateful thank-offerings made by victors to the gods who had helped them, from the best spoils to hand, are known from Homer to Hellenistic times as the studies of Rouse, Pritchett, and Lonis among others have shown.[1]

This chapter tries to relate a very important class of such dedications, collective ones made publicly on behalf of the whole community or army, to the prime form of combat between Greek states in Archaic and Classical times: hoplite battle, most recently and convincingly analysed by Hanson.[2] It is here argued that a city's existing dedications of armour, itself prestigious, would have developed and maintained its hoplites' pride and confidence and would, with such pre-battle ceremonies as sacrifices and vows of fresh spoils and other thank-offerings, have helped to increase their courage and discipline. Greatly valued then, old and new dedications would be on display at a city's temples for many years. Offerings would often be made at panhellenic sanctuaries as well, both to please the gods and to impress other Greeks, though at Olympia and some other shrines the spoils of Greeks seem to have been offered more and more rarely from the fifth century. This, it is argued, was not coincidence or due to changes in fashions and types of offering, but reflected growing unease at what was coming to seem brutal and out of place in panhellenic shrines, namely the commemoration of victories over fellow Greeks by means of armour and weapons stripped from the corpses of the slain.

CAPTURED ARMOUR AND WEAPONS AS VOTIVE OFFERINGS

Though arms and armour were never the only form that a thank-offering for victory might take, their own value and their associations with martial glory explain why they were often so used.

Their value in money explains why hoplites were normally drawn from the better-off. In Athens in the late sixth century a panoply could cost at least thirty drachmas. That was about what six fine oxen fit for sacrifice had cost in Solon's time and so probably was still a substantial sum (Meiggs and Lewis 14; Plut. *Sol.* 23.3). In fourth-century Thasos, panoplies fit for the state to honour its war orphans (so presumably of good quality) cost 300 drachmas, for which valuable assets like skilled slaves could be bought (Dem. 27.9).[3] Caricaturing arms merchants' greed, Aristophanes makes one ask 1,000 drachmas for a bronze cuirass (Ar. *Pax* 1210–64). From this exaggeration we might conclude that such equipment could cost several hundred drachmas, and Xenophon shows that some Athenians in his time did not even care if a cuirass fitted them properly, never mind what it cost, as long as it was decorated and gilded to their satisfaction (Xen. *Mem.* 3.10.9–15).

For armour, although usually businesslike in design, was almost always impressive to look at. Alcaeus' poem on the splendour of a great hall decked with armour shows how its fine appearance delighted Greeks of his time.[4] The gods too were thought to enjoy such spectacles, as shown by the Pythia's wistful tone in rejecting some fine Persian spoils (Paus. 10.14.5). It was to Delphi that Cnossos and Tylissos agreed to send the finest spoils they hoped to take, reserving the rest for the temple of Ares at Cnossos (Meiggs and Lewis 42 B lines 9–11). It is not surprising that some of the finest Greek armour known comes from sanctuary sites, notably Olympia.[5] Sometimes, to emphasize the choice quality of their gift, donors use the term ***akrothinion***, literally 'the top of the heap', or 'the pick of the crop'.[6] No dedicator would dare to offer less than the gods' due, for quite apart from the mockery of men, the displeasure of heaven was not to be risked (Hdt. 8.122; Soph. *Aj.* 172–81).

Apart from their cost and splendid appearance, arms and armour were valued for themselves. Cretans and Thebans took great pride in gifts of fine arms and armour, and Demetrius the Besieger's gift of 12,000 panoplies to Athens was a gesture of respect among other things (Strab. 10.4.16; Plut. *Mor.* 761 B; Plut. *Demetr.* 17). The panoplies that Athens' allies had to contribute at the Great Panathenaea illustrate the prestige they could enjoy (Meiggs and Lewis 69 line 57), as do Thasos' gifts to war orphans and Athens' to her ephebes (Arist. *Ath. Pol.* 42.4).

Armour and weapons won on the field of battle were even more honorific because victory and excellence in war were always admired. The right of Spartans who won Olympic victories to serve by their king in battle is one example of this (Plut. *Lyc.* 22). The glory that the spoils of battle brought to temples they adorned was appreciated even in the second century BC (*FGrH* III B no. 540 lines 7–8). Of all the panoply, shields and helmets were probably the most prized components. To lose one's shield in the battle-line endangered all, while to throw it away in flight meant disgrace, and therefore captured shields symbolized a glorious victory.[7] Those of very important people were greatly prized (Hom. *Il.* 8.191–3; Thuc. 4.12.1; Plut. *Nic.* 28.5; Diod. 15.87.6). The ordinary hoplite could not laugh off loss of a shield as sophisticated poets could.[8]

Helmets could look particularly impressive with their tall challenging crests and gleaming bronze. It has been well said that taking the slain enemy's armour was a substitute for head-hunting, of which Homer preserves a memory (e.g. *Il.* 17.38–40).[9] Though the Greeks of the Archaic Period and later hardly ever indulged in this practice, it was known to them among others (Hdt. 4.64–5 and 9.78–9), and some Greek troops could respond to it. Thus when Philopoemen not only slew and despoiled Machanidas of Sparta in 207 BC but also decapitated him, the sight delighted his men who fought with still more enthusiasm, according to Polybius (11.18.4–8). Perhaps unconsciously helmets were felt to be the least impersonal part of the panoply. But whatever the reasons for it, shields and helmets, complete or partly preserved, are among the commonest sorts of armour to be found so far at Olympia,[10] and most of these are probably products of the battlefield. For although soldiers and generals might dedicate their own equipment and huntsmen their spears, such dedications are not mentioned in the sources as often as captures in war, nor could they have been so productive.[11]

Thus captured armour and weapons could delight and glorify a god just as a gift of fine armour would please and honour a man, and dedicators could hope that for this they would in themselves attract the god's favour towards them in future. But to make that more certain it is likely that thank-offerings of spoils would be accompanied by prayers to that effect, especially for help in times of war, like those

Figure 2 Corinthian helmet nailed to stake (drawing: R. Clark)

actually inscribed on the Mantiklos Apollo and other votives.[12] It would be a very rash victor who did not take the opportunity to offer up the spoils of one success without praying for continued help in future battles. It is thought indeed on very good grounds that votive offerings were believed, and employed, to act while in a sanctuary as vehicles for or embodiments of the offertory prayers of their dedicators.[13] Thus, in a sense, once dedicated in the temples of friendly gods, the arms of a city's enemies could be turned against them.

In view of this belief it is remarkable that the pious Spartans are said by Plutarch not to have dedicated captured arms and armour (*Mor.* 224 B and F), and, as Pritchett has observed, no evidence clearly contradicts him.[14] In the two passages concerned, from the *Spartan Sayings*, first Cleomenes I and then Leotychidas II are asked to explain why Sparta did not make such dedications. Both reply, very unfairly it might seem, that since captured armour had belonged to cowards it was unfit to offer to the gods. (Leotychidas adds that it was unfit for the young to see, a remark considered on page 235.) This sweeping insult to all Sparta's opponents, as it appears at first sight to be, might condemn this doublet as part of the Sparta her Classical admirers liked to depict. But detached from the kings they are ascribed to, these words could quite plausibly have been said after battles when Sparta's enemies had fled before her hoplites in large numbers, such as Mantinea in 418 BC or the 'Tearless Battle' in 368 BC (Thuc. 5. 72–3; Xen. *Hell.* 7.1.28–32; Plut. *Ages.* 33.3–5). The true reason why Sparta did not dedicate spoils could have been her policy of taking as much as possible of the excitement out of battle and victory in the interests of unique and unshakable discipline in the phalanx, with its steady and orderly advance, its strictly limited pursuit and its austere victory sacrifices (Thuc. 5.70 and 73.4; Plut. *Ages.* 33.3–5). The Spartans thanked the gods for their help generously enough and prayed for their favour in future, but employed other kinds of thank-offering for the purpose (Meiggs and Lewis 36; Paus. 5.10.4 and 24.3; Xen. *Hell.* 4.3.21).

This Spartan exception proves the rule that, by other Greeks, offerings of spoils were valued very highly, and their dedication was an important part of the victory celebrations, as well as of the environment in which hoplites learned their role, a process now to be examined.

PREPARATION FOR WAR

Among the many experiences which for good or ill prepared each generation for their role as hoplites and for the ordeal of battle, the sight of the spoils of past victories at a city's temples and its countryside shrines could have had all the power of inspiration that highly indoctrinated elite units and proud and ancient regiments find in captured flags, cannon or silverware won by their predecessors. Indeed, they could have had still more power. In the phalanx, son followed father and set out to reach or surpass the standards set by past generations of kinsfolk as well as of fellow citizens, and the dedications symbolized those standards (Plut. *Lyc.*21.2; Thuc. 4. 95.3; Dem. 15.35). Further, they expressed a bond between men and gods which each generation could strengthen, if it were brave enough and deserved the help of the gods. What is more, the tacit (or perhaps sometimes explicit) indoctrination the spoils displayed could provide, could have become familiar to the sons of hoplites from their childhood upwards.

Spoils were often conspicuously displayed. Shields and other items might be fixed along the cornice, over the door or on the temple's doorposts (Eur. *Tro.* 571–6; *Andr.* 1122–3; *IT* 74–5; Paus. 2.21.4.; 6.19.13; 10.19.3), or they might be hung up inside on walls or even from roof timbers (Paus. 10.14.3; *IG* II^{2} 1469 B lines 67–8).[15] Unless the ground outside was solid rock, more might be nailed to posts around the temple, or be hung up in stoas (Paus. 1.15.4; Diod. 12.70.5).[16]

The roles of hoplites and of dedications would be learnt in childhood. By the age of 4 most boys would begin to learn what the panoplies hung up in the men's quarters or by the hearth were (Hdt. 1.34; Ar. *Ach.* 279). From that age or even earlier they would see and hear their parents praying and so come to believe in the gods (Pl. *Leg.* 887 D–E). Then, as they saw votive offerings in daily life, the first-fruits at harvest or the skin of a hunter's quarry hung up on a tree by a shrine in the country, they would come to believe in the power of votive offerings to influence the gods. From their fathers and others they would hear about enemies and battles, especially if they lived near a border disputed with a neighbouring city (Arist. *Pol.* 1330 A 20–3). In this process of learning what being a hoplite meant, the conspicuously displayed offerings of spoils at the temples, seen by many every day, and those within, seen when entering for prayer and on special occasions, would become quite comprehensible and very significant.[17] As prizes won by the gods' help and the courage of the hoplites from ever present and hostile neighbours, they would seem to entitle the hoplites to the respect they enjoyed compared with the less well-off, and to set a standard which their sons would hope to reach in the phalanx to which most of them would aspire to belong. All this could have been learnt well before the sons of the hoplites reached 10 years of age, indeed probably by the age of 7, which was when the real professionals in hoplite warfare, the Spartans, saw fit to remove their sons from the comparative normality of their early childhood and feed them into their own very much more intensive and effective system for producing hoplites.

The importance of the dedications of spoils for the young would-be hoplites may have lain partly in their dual character, belonging as they did to friendly gods from their point of entry to the temples onwards, but having originally been the arms and armour of deadly enemies. That hostility would still have been remembered. For Greek

Figure 3 Artist's impression of spoils displayed in a temple precinct (drawing: N. Farrell)

armour was of course designed to be at once efficient and impressive, as it seems to us in the tranquil environment of our museums. But to its owners and their enemies it was intended also to look as grim and menacing as modern weaponry and combat gear do today. Like much military headwear since then, the looming crests on helmets were meant to make their wearers look taller, to distract, challenge and startle the enemy in battle, as effectively (their wearers would hope) as Hector's scared Astyanax (Hom. *Il.* 6. 466–70). Shields till at least the fifth century BC commonly bore blazons intended to unsettle the enemy in the stress of battle, such as lions or evil-eyed gorgons, or dogs and birds that might tear his despoiled and unburied corpse (Chase 1902: 75–6 and 84–5). As for the weapons on display, the scarred limbs of the city's veterans and the graves of its war dead would prove to their relatives how lethal they had been.

But at the same time, and even more forcefully in the numinous surroundings of a temple, the dedications of spoils would make manifest and proclaim that with the help of the gods the arrogant violence of the enemy had been and could again be triumphantly crushed. The spoils, nailed or hung up still and silent within or impaled like battlefield trophies outside a temple of a god whose splendid and generous reward they were, showed, like all other votives of every sort, that in war as in peace the gods had answered the city's prayers, and that they might do so again. Of course it was not necessary to be an atheist to know that the gods did not always answer prayers (Cic. *Nat. D.* 3.89). But many remained optimistic that they might do so and even in the fourth century BC many were firm in their traditional beliefs (Pl. *Leg.* 887 C–D; 909 D–910 B: Xen. *Hell.* 3.4.18). It is very tempting to wonder if the Athenian ephebes on their tour of the temples were harangued on the great military treasures of Athens like the Persian spoils or the Spartan shields from Pylos (Arist. *Ath. Pol.* 42.3; Dio Chrys. *Or.* 2.36; Paus. 1.15.4) as well as others seen on service elsewhere, notably Demosthenes' spoils from Olpae (Thuc. 3.114.1).

There may be indirect evidence that some people approved of young hoplites and their younger brothers contemplating captured armour and weapons in temples for reasons like those already mentioned. In Plutarch's *Spartan Sayings* (*Mor.* 224 F) as remarked above, King Leotychidas II is made to say that as the property of cowards they were not fit for the young to see or for offering to the gods. Since they would not normally be seen except as dedications in temples, this seems to amount to a denial of the value of offerings in improving the young. Many of the practices criticized in the *Spartan Sayings* by stern Lacedaimonians were normal in other Greek states and this could mean that among the latter, it was commonly felt that the young benefited from admiring the thank-offerings of armour and weapons, won by their ancestors with the help of the gods, which their descendants might also hope for in trying to win more favours. That views on what the young should and should not see for the good of their military development were held and were argued over in the fourth century is at least suggested by Plato. He prescribes actual attendance as observers at battles for the Guardians' children (*Resp.* 466 E–467 E). If Leotychidas' opinion really originated after Mantinea in 418 BC or in the fourth century, this detail might have been inspired by debates on the military education of citizen young in an age when professional mercenaries were ever more important. Organized or not, such contemplation may have been encouraged, and it probably had some effect, if not in battles against Spartans.

To nobles like Alcaeus in the Archaic Period, the spectacle of the armour and weapons they saw as they feasted could serve as a spur to fulfil their warlike undertakings:

Brilliant the great hall shines
with bronze, its ceiling dressed overall for the War God
with gleaming helmets,
down from which their white horse-hair crests are nodding,
for warriors' heads
glorious adornment. Bronze set on hidden pegs
there shine suspended
greaves, a defence against the force of arrows.
New linen corslets
and hollow shields lie heaped about below,
with swords from Chalcis
and beside them lie many belts and tunics.
These we cannot forget
Ever since we first undertook this labour.[18]

To warriors less high-born but proud of the status their possession of arms gave them in the city, in Alcaeus' time and later, the spectacle of temples decorated within and outside with fine arms and armour could have been, for good or ill, a strong encouragement to fight when their city required them to do so, and one that would be all the more powerful for having begun to act on them from their childhood.

DEDICATIONS AND BATTLE

Others have analysed the main religious ceremonies that kept up the morale of hoplites as they marched out to war and were primed for battle.[19] Besides helping (as just indicated) to lay the deep foundations of that morale, the sight and memory of past dedications, together with the prospect of winning new spoils for the gods, could before, throughout and after battle have been of some help in keeping the hoplites' fighting spirit and discipline both up to equal strength and in balance with each other.

It is said that most of war is waiting, and, even if hoplites had to wait only hours between the muster and combat, the familiar displays at the temples of gods invoked to fight as their allies must often have prevented recurrent anxieties from wearing their nerves unduly. The report before Leuctra that Herakles' arms had disappeared from his temple, as if he were marching to join Epaminondas' Thebans and fight the Spartans with them, gives an idea of the encouragement that the temples of friendly gods could give (Ar. *Vesp.* 1081–5; Xen. *Hell.* 6.4.7). When inexperienced hoplites first saw the enemy phalanx, formidable in appearance and with its paean and war-cry, they could have been steadied by the memory of the lifeless and silent panoplies at home. This did not always work, at least against the Spartans. Thus, at Mantinea in 418 BC the Athenians, watching the unbroken and inexorable advance of the Spartans, did not all stand fast – despite the splendid memory of another less terrible Spartan shield line from Pylos in 425 BC adorning the Stoa Poikile, with its inspiring patriotic pictures (Thuc. 5.70–3; Paus. 1.15.4.). But where the odds were more favourable, such memories probably counted for more.

To win new spoils for further dedications would be one hope and ambition of hoplite armies, and that in itself should have raised its spirits and discipline. But this encouragement would have grown all the greater, if before the battle formal vows were pronounced to win and dedicate fresh spoils, along with other prayers and ceremonies performed when the army set out for war and combat. To judge from Thucydides' great portrait of the departure of the Athenian expedition to Sicily or Xenophon's of the Ten Thousand preparing for their perilous march to the Euxine, such ceremonies were solemn and moving occasions as thousands uttered prayers and sang paeans together (Thuc. 6.32; Xen. *An.* 3.2.9). If among the vows of other victory thank-offerings, a solemn collective vow of spoils in the name of the army or the citizens was pronounced, that would further strengthen the confidence and *esprit de corps* of the men. They would feel more secure both as a united body and as individuals under the championship and protection of the gods to whom spoils were vowed, and more sure of a share in the glory of a victory which their vow had made more certain. Just as such a vow would encourage them to unleash all their hatred, aggression and violence against the enemy, so its collective character would remind them of the need for the discipline, which could make the difference between victory and defeat. The many records attesting collective dedications of spoils and other booty may well be proof that such vows often were made before battles, and perhaps also proof of their value.

Further evidence for the content and character of vows of spoils, when they were made, can be found in Pritchett's study of military vows (*War* 3.230–7). He concludes that public vows of thank-offerings were commonly made before armies set out. To this, it may be added that offerings of captured arms and armour could have been included among them. They are not often directly mentioned, but this could well be because they need only have taken a few words to express and so historians busy with grander themes would omit them; even in Eteocles' prayer (see below) three lines at most are enough for them (Aesch. *Sept.* 277–8a). Historians very rarely mention specifically the indispensable animals routinely sacrificed on both sides before every hoplite battle (Hdt. 6.112.1; Thuc. 6.69.2; Xen. *Hell.* 4.2.20) because they normally produced favourable omens. A vow of spoils could equally have been part of the routine, as it would normally go with even fewer hitches than the usual animal sacrifice. When we do hear anything of them, it is when, as with Pausanias' disobliging animals at Plataea, the routine was somehow disturbed (Hdt. 9.61–2). Thus, we are told when Locri vowed one-ninth of the spoils, in order to outbid her enemy Croton, which had vowed the tenth of hers if she won the battle – which the pious Locrians in fact won (Just. *Epit.* 20.3).

Aeschylus as a tragedian, with purposes different from those of historians, has occasion in the *Seven against Thebes* (265–78a) to display the resolute and warlike Eteocles steadying the frightened Chorus and invoking the gods with a vow of thank-offerings in the event of victory. Despite its poetic language and some textual problems, we may take it that Aeschylus' Athenian audience would have recognized it as such a vow, and as a whole and in detail it can be defended as not too far removed from reality.

Now from the statues of the gods remove yourselves;
Better to beg the gods to fight as our allies!
When you have heard my prayers then in your turn you shall
Raise like a paean women's cheerful sacred song,
The Greeks' accustomed joyful chant at sacrifice
That heartens friends. So will you banish fear of war.

To all the gods I speak now that protect our state,
Who watch over its fields or guard its market-place;
Dirce's fountain I address and Ismenos' stream:
If we prove victors with our city saved from foes,
We shall with sacrificial sheep's blood stain their hearths
And shall kill bulls in honour of the gods. I vow
I shall plant trophies and the foes' apparel take
As spear-torn spoils for the pure houses of the gods,
And shall their temples with the foes' apparel crown.[20]

To speak of the gods as allies (line 266) is not an example of especially tragic language. Similar expressions are found in Selinus' victory inscription and in comedy (Meiggs and Lewis 38; Ar. *Vesp.* 1085). Eteocles' order to the Chorus to sing a song like a paean after he has prayed recalls the paeans that followed vows and prayers before other military enterprises (Thuc. 6.32; Xen. *An.* 3.2.9). To invoke all the guardian gods before attacking invaders is only natural, and paralleled by the equally comprehensive list of gods and goddesses and other beings protecting the state of Dreros, and by whom that city's young men swore perpetual hostility to Lyttos, in Hellenistic Crete (*SIG*[3] 527 lines 10–36). These gods of Thebes he promises to honour at their temples with sacrifices. The trophies, if they are the standard battlefield ones, are the instant thank-offering to Zeus normally set up as soon as the enemy had fled,[21] and the spoils are dedicated after the trophy and the sacrifices in a sequence which is perfectly natural. It is paralleled, so far as concerns the offering of spoils, by Jocasta's description of the trophies, sacrifices and dedications of spoils in Euripides' *Phoenissae* 571–6. It is unfortunate that lines 276 and 278a, and the second half of 277, are of very doubtful authority but the content of line 278, the offering of spoils, and its position at the end of the sequence, are beyond question. Even the idea of dedicating battle-damaged armour is not necessarily bombastic, for some armour found at Olympia and elsewhere shows what may well be battle-damage.[22] If there is any value in the references to 'foes' apparel', and if it means not armour but clothes,

Xenophon shows that in especially bitter battles, like those in civil war, tunics as well as armour were normally stripped from the dead enemy (Xen. *Hell.* 2.4.19). Eteocles might well seek this. We may in addition suppose that Aeschylus, like many in his audience, a hoplite and a veteran of Marathon, knew well – and meant to portray – vows like those he and they remembered, although in suitable language for a tragedy.

However their courage and discipline were fortified, by vows of collective thank-offerings, by Spartan discipline and flute music, or by several swigs of wine and decades of hating an arrogant and oppressive neighbour or hegemon, hoplites would need all the courage and discipline they could command. One danger was the creation of gaps in the shield-line, and one cause of this in the early days of phalanx warfare could well have been sorties by lone warriors who, ambitious for their own glory, might spring forth in the old way to challenge, kill and despoil an enemy champion thus terrifying his comrades (cf. Hom. *Il.* 11.91–121).[23] A city's nobles, inheriting a tradition of excelling in war and of asserting themselves whenever they could, produced more than one such individual, and the spoils they would especially seek would often be the fine arms of their social equals in the enemy phalanx. But if a collective vow of spoils (the best, of course) had been made beforehand in the interests of the gods, that would tactfully reduce the scope of these would-be champions and the danger they could cause to their comrades. The pattern of Hector's proposed duel with an Achaean champion, whose spoils he said he would dedicate to Apollo, could beneficially have been annexed from high-born individualists and extended over the phalanx as a whole.

Even in the close-pressed heat of battle, when willpower, morale and emotional energy could sometimes count as much as sheer physical strength, men might think of vows and utter prayers, some of particular sincerity then as now (Hdt. 9.61–2; Thuc. 7.71; Xen. *Cyr.* 7.1.35).[24] Thus perhaps finely equipped enemy hoplites in the first few ranks would get extra attention. Or if some close friend or kinsman fell dead or wounded, those around him might stand still firmer, or even push forward in front of him, for along with rage and grief they would want to save him and themselves from the shame, not just of losing his corpse and its armour to the spoilers, but of learning in defeat that his equipment was adorning the gloating enemy's temple (Xen. *Hell.* 6.4.13–14; Plut. *Ages.* 18.3; Paus. 9.16.5; Hdt. 5.95).

Once a battle seemed to be won, some might have the urge and the energy to get to such enemy dead as they could see and loot them, taking their armour and whatever other valuables they could find. Premature looting of this sort laid armies open to counterattacks, as Plato and Polybius remark (Pl. *Resp.* 469 C–470 A; Polyb. 10.17.1–5). Only training and firm discipline could prevent this. But since the finer armour was among the best loot on the battlefield, if it had been marked down for possible dedication, the pickings that were available instead might sometimes have seemed not worth hurrying to get to, and the phalanx might preserve its order and so deter the enemy from trying to win at the last minute. The Spartans are said by some sources to have forbidden any despoiling of enemy dead; Lycurgus is said to have held that the Spartans were better off poor but in their ranks (Plut. *Mor.* 228 F–229 A; Ael. *VH* 6.6). They are said by better sources to have collected the spoils of the battlefields as others did (Hdt. 1.82.5; Thuc. 5.74.2) but there may be no real contradiction. For helot attendants could have been used instead of hoplites, or the latter might have been permitted to fall out and collect the spoils after the enemy was reported far enough away (Hdt.9.80).

Thus, collective vows of spoils could sometimes have reinforced discipline and spurred the hoplites on even in battle itself, although their product, the dedications those same people had begun to understand since childhood, would probably have done more for their courage and discipline.

Like the battlefield trophy set up by the victor, the collection of the spoils was a proof of victory, just as the enemy's request for the bodies of his dead was an admission of defeat (Hdt. 1.82.6). The dedication of armour stripped from the enemy dead was in principle entirely acceptable and only what the enemy would have done if he had won. Furthermore, it had a respectable ancestry, since Hector in proposing a duel to settle the Trojan War quickly, undertakes to return his opponent's body to the Achaeans if he wins, but states clearly that he will dedicate the spoils at the temple of Apollo in Troy, to whom he vowed them if he won (*Il.* 7.81–90). This bargain was accepted, as in Greece after Homer's time, by losers in wars that were much controlled by convention, and in battles that were more like duels, such as the Battle of the Champions between 300 Spartans and 300 Argives ca 546 BC, the taking of armour and its dedication was the accepted custom.

But warfare and battles were not always so gentlemanly. In the *Iliad* to strip a dead opponent of his armour certainly inflicted shame on him and his runaway comrades, hence the bitter fights over fallen heroes (*Il.* 16.498–500). This feeling persisted in Archaic and Classical times (Thuc. 6.101.6–103.1; Xen. *Hell.* 6.4.13). As Xenophon shows, to leave a fallen enemy in his tunic was a conciliatory gesture, and so to remove it was to inflict shame as it was in the *Iliad* (Xen. *Hell.* 2.4.19; *Il.* 11.99–100; cf. *Il.* 2.258–64). Similarly, in Athens to beat up a fellow citizen and steal his cloak was an insult as well as an assault (Dem. 54.8–9).[25] In the bitter wars between Greeks of the fifth century and later, the stripping and return of the dead would often have little of the old-fashioned conventions and basic respect for the loser about it. In a similar way, in 420 BC Sparta regarded as folly Argos' proposal that if either side wished it, the ownership of a district each of them claimed should be decided by a pitched battle, much as the Battle of the Champions had been intended to decide it over a century before (Thuc. 5.41). After especially savage battles at all times and also (as in the Peloponnesian War and later) when battles were savage and desperate, the dedications of spoils set up by the victors in their own temples – and sometimes still in certain panhellenic sanctuaries – would have been hard to stomach for the defeated. They would doubtless feel like the Corinthian hoplites who fought a drawn battle with the Athenians in 458 BC, but left the field for the latter to set up a trophy, as if they had won. The Corinthians were then jeered at by their elders; they endured this for about twelve days and then marched back to the battlefield and set up a trophy of their own (Thuc. 1.105.4–6). The Spartans too found trophies set up by their few conquerors a bitter humiliation, and they must have felt as sour as the defeated Athenians must have been encouraged by the spoils of Pylos in the Agora when Athens surrendered to them in April 404 BC (Xen. *Hell.* 4.5.10; 6.4.14).

Sparta's charge that the spoils of her enemies were taken from cowards and so were unfit for the young to see or for dedication to the gods would, if it were current in the aftermath of victories like Mantinea, have some truth in it, as suggested here (Plut. *Mor.* 224 E). When a phalanx broke, many of the hoplites must have believed that the gods were against them, as well as their enemies. Some portion of any victor's haul would be equipment discarded in flight, especially when retreat took the losers over very rough ground, as the Athenians scrambling down from Epipolae at the cost of abandoning their shields vividly illustrated (Thuc. 7.45). Shields were the easiest armour to drop, and the most burdensome, and helmets could be untied and removed at a run. This may partly explain why helmets and shields are so common at Olympia, for to take greaves and corslets off would oblige the retreating hoplite to stop briefly. Whether the losers had really fled too soon or not, sneers from victors that they had done so would render the offerings from their spoils all the more galling to the defeated. Thus, although one of the goals and prizes of victory, dedications of arms and armour could help Greek hoplites to win some battles, they would also have helped to provoke fresh wars. Their irritant or inflammatory character may, as will be argued below, help to explain why from the fifth century some panhellenic sanctuaries appear to have ceased accepting spoils of battles between Greeks.

SPOILS TAKEN BY GREEKS FROM GREEKS

When the victorious army came home amid rejoicing and grief, relatives of the dead and dying might have seen in the blood-stained spoils some proof that the gods had granted vengeance for their menfolk. Certainly, captured armour and even arms with the blood of citizens on it were not regarded as polluted, unless they were the arms of the sacrilegious (Diod. 16. 60.3; Pl. *Resp.* 469 E–470 A).[26] To judge from Aeschylus, the dedication of the spoils could be the climax of triumphant thanksgiving celebrations (Aesch. *Sept.* 277–8a; Eur. *Phoen.* 571–6). Great glory and honour would be shed on all the hoplites who survived and on those whose families would still be in mourning, by this as by all the ceremonies. If the dedication was the fulfilment of a vow to the gods, that can only have increased its prestige and theirs, while if the vow, or decisions after victory, led to offerings at city and countryside shrines, that would help all the more to unite the state in triumph. When the mighty war-lord Pyrrhus of Epirus and his men died, trapped and butchered in the narrow streets of Argos in 272 BC, his shield adorned the temple of Demeter in the city, and his men's were doubtless proudly sent to shrines throughout the Argolid, like that of Enyalios near Mycenae (Paus. 2.21.4). Yet, even in the victors' own temples, the tone of votive verses and inscriptions rarely comes near the vulgar spite sometimes seen in jingoistic newspapers today. Some just name victor and vanquished, or point to the loser's *hybris* or boastfulness (Hdt. 5.77.4; Plut. *Tim.* 31.1; Paus. 1.13.3).[27] But there is nothing like the systematic hatred of the Teian Curses or the Oath of Dreros (Meiggs and Lewis 30; *SIG*[3] 527).

Because they mattered so much to the pride and prestige of cities and to their hopes of victories to come, displays might stay on show for centuries, like the Spartan shields from Pylos and those Thebes won from Leuctra, seen by Pausanias 500 years later (Paus. 1.15.4; 9.16.5). Only fire, earthquake, rebuilding, sheer overcrowding with votives, or finally intense political or diplomatic necessity could remove such valued prizes. Thus, it has been convincingly suggested that a spear captured by Athens from Lesbos and dedicated to the Dioscuri dates from 428/7 BC and was deliberately discarded when Lesbos joined the Second Athenian Confederacy fifty years later.[28] As if to show how serious a matter removal of military votives could be, when Cimon dedicated his bridle on the Acropolis in 480 BC and took a shield from the offerings in its place, he prayed to Athena (Plut. *Cim.* 5.2–3).

Just as offerings in victors' own temples might stay in their places for many years, so even after the Classical Period, Greek states continued to offer the gods dedications of spoils taken from their fellow Greeks, at least at sanctuaries that were, or were regarded as, their own. So Pyrrhus dedicated the spoils of Macedonians at Dodona, Argos those of Pyrrhus at her shrines, and the Aetolians had accumulated 15,000 panoplies or else individual arms and parts of armour at their sanctuary of Thermon by 218 BC, many no doubt the spoils of battle (Paus. 1.13.3; 2.21.4; Polyb. 2.2.8–11 and 5.8.8–9).

But in Hellenistic times there seem to be fewer examples than before of spoils taken from Greeks being dedicated even in their own temples.[29] This trend is anticipated at some panhellenic sanctuaries from various dates in the fifth century, and so it is worth examining more closely.

When famous and much-frequented panhellenic shrines accepted splendid spoils from pious and grateful victors, their own glory was increased and so too was the admiration or fear that other Greeks felt for the favoured dedicators. Proudly to flaunt their warlike triumphs, won by the help of Zeus at Olympia or Apollo of Delphi, before the eyes of tens of thousands from all over the Greek world at the great festivals was a coveted ambition.[30]

It is no wonder then that when Tegea and Mantinea each claimed the same drawn border battle as a victory in 423/2 BC, both sent spoils all the way to Delphi (Thuc. 4.134). Nor need an estimate that Olympia received about 100,000 helmets over the seventh and sixth centuries BC be thought seriously exaggerated.[31] Olympia could attract offerings from any battlefield in the Archaic Greek world, and Krentz has shown that the losers in hoplite battle might die in hundreds or even more.[32] Battles were not rare events among the Greek cities and to the victor's catch, runaways' shields and helmets might add an impressive supplement. Delphi, once the recipient of 2,000 shields from a battle at night, and just as renowned as Olympia, would not be far behind. Even Isthmia, celebrated only from the early sixth century, but centrally placed on land and sea routes, still has traces of 200 helmets and innumerable shields most from the hundred years down to the Persian invasion of 480–79 BC. Her annual takings might have been in scores rather than in Olympia's figures but could still have invited many to add to her displays.

Eager though victors were to advertise at panhellenic sanctuaries, their votive inscriptions seem generally restrained, some even omitting the loser's name and speaking just of 'the enemy', whether from fear of the gods or men, or else sheer preoccupation with their own glory.[33] Despite this sincere or overt restraint, donors would surely use all their influence and that of their guest-friends in Elis, Delphi or Corinth to get their offerings the finest positions in the shrines those states controlled. Themistocles sought a place for his Persian spoils within the hallowed temple at Delphi, where the god's own sacred arms were kept (Paus. 10.14.5; Hdt.8.37). At Isthmia too the Archaic temple's interior was probably crowded with armour by the time of the fire of ca 470 BC. Perhaps they were privileged, but the rock terrace on which the temple stands prevented many displays of panoplies outdoors on posts, unlike the flat ground of Olympia where such displays were so numerous. There, in the main part of the Sanctuary and even along the banks of the Archaic Stadium, pilgrims and spectators had fine spoils to marvel at from one side of Hellas to the other – when their eyes were not on the Olympic contestants.[34] To them there was no incongruity; such battles were a normal part of life, defeat bringing sorrow only to the loser and his friends. The splendour of the spoils, as of victory in battle or in the Games, would be what mattered, just as both spoils and Games were thought to please Zeus himself. Perhaps too in their duel-like quality, some early Greek battles – kept by custom well short of all-out war – were felt by many to be akin to the violent combat sports they loved to watch.[35]

As well as a conspicuous and honourable position for his offering, the donor would hope it would remain there for a long period. Isthmia may have allowed this, for so far no large deposits of armour buried before the fire of ca 470 BC have been found, so perhaps once accepted, displays stayed untouched. At Delphi the position is not clear, but at Olympia the outdoor displays were often dismantled after a few years and buried in wells or used to build up the banks of the Stadium.[36]

Perhaps this was done for practical reasons, when posts rotted, for instance, or to keep fresh offerings from cluttering the Sanctuary and the Stadium, but in at least one case politics may have been at work. A fine Oriental helmet captured by Athenians from the Persians was quite soon buried at a time when Spartan jealousy of Athens was strong.[37]

Whatever the reason for dismantling a display, it was not done casually, at least at Olympia. Much armour, particularly helmets, shows deliberate damage that can only have been done on dismantling. The nose- and or cheek-guards of helmets are often bent up or out, sometimes hiding their votive inscriptions – a clear sign that the damage was inflicted only at the end of their time of display. Much effort went into this. Somehow it must reflect the power the spoils had perhaps as vehicles of their donors' prayers. Perhaps the damage prevented possible interference with that role after they were discarded, rather as glasses are smashed after someone's health is drunk in them, as if to stop further toasts in them that might dilute the effect of the first one.[38]

What the frequent dismantling and damaging of dedications at Olympia certainly do not mean is that its authorities felt any unease at accepting spoils taken from Greeks by Greeks before the Persian invasion of 480–79 BC. But in the following decades signs of such uneasiness gradually accumulate. At Isthmia, for some time the headquarters of Greek resistance to Xerxes, the Archaic Temple, full of armour that was probably the spoils of wars between Greeks so convenient for the barbarians, was accidently burnt ca 470 BC. Its Classical successor built in the 460s has produced few traces so far of similar dedications. Perhaps to remind visitors of Isthmia's glorious role, Corinth discouraged such offerings there. At Olympia, Greek arms and armour seem to be less frequently offered from the mid-fifth century.[39] Taras' dedication from Thurii in the 430s is among the latest identified as the spoils of Greeks (Meiggs and Lewis: 57). By 420 BC the Spartans ridiculed Argos' proud attempt to revive duel-like battles (Thuc. 5.41), and the Peloponnesian and later Greek wars rarely resembled sporting contests.[40] Before 400 BC Elis refused to let King Agis of Sparta consult the oracle at Olympia as to a war against Greeks, as it never advised on such wars (Xen. *Hell.* 3.2.22). It is thus not surprising that it was to Delphi, not to Olympia (though it was nearer), that Tegea and Mantinea sent spoils from each other in 423 BC (Thuc. 4.134). Thereafter very few offerings of spoils taken from Greeks are reliably reported from Delphi, though Plato perhaps hints that the oracle might advise on the question (*Resp*. 469 E–470 A).

All this is just one of several similar responses to the awkward fact that when the Greeks had beaten off barbarian enemies at Salamis, Plataea, Himera and Cumae, they still so ferociously fought one another. Nor were the responses entirely futile. One of the consequences was the marked and significant decline in the practice of selling Greek cities into slavery on capture for more than a century after Alexander's sack of Thebes in 335 BC. The refusal of the three panhellenic sanctuaries to accept the spoils of Greeks is then probably not a mere matter of silence in the archaeological record. Nor need it be at all strongly influenced by changing fashions in votive offerings. It may be true that there was a decline in offerings of small objects including bronzes in the fifth century after the generosity of the Archaic Period.[41] But offerings of Greek spoils continued in Greek cities. The disasters of war and the horrors of hoplite battle, thrown into such sharp relief by more glorious events in the fifth century and by the eloquence of men like Gorgias and Lysias,[42] thus themselves contributed, through what came to seem to Greeks – at least when they were at Olympia – the lamentable and odious, even polluting spectacle of dedications from the battlefield, to a new perception of war. Certainly, some dedications stayed on display even at Olympia, and Dodona as well, as the temples of cities and federal leagues continued to welcome spoils (Paus. 6.19.4–5; 1.13.3; Polyb. 5.8.5–9). Certainly, the stone monuments and statues that jostle one another along the Sacred Way at Delphi and elsewhere were inspired by the same pride and jealousies that had filled the Archaic Stadium's banks with armour as fine to look at, almost, as the Games themselves, and monuments of stone could outlast bronze.[43] But just because cities and hoplites still needed the pride and encouragement that spoils from their rivals could give them in the face of battle, that is no reason to dismiss as an unlearnt lesson what some Greeks who looked at the spoils dedicated to the gods did see.

NOTES

Works referred to by author alone or with short title or date are cited in full in the Bibliography to this volume.

1. Rouse (1902), Pritchett, *War* 3, Lonis (1979). The term 'spoils' is used in the sense of captured arms and armour in this paper.
2. Hanson 1989. Dedications by soldiers and commanders, less common in the Archaic and Classical Periods are only cited for comparison; see esp. Pritchett, *War* 3 ch.7. On individual and phalanx, M. Detienne, 'La

phalange', in J. P. Vernant, ed. (1968) 119–42. No attempt is made in this chapter to explore the parallels between some Greek and Celtic practices in war; J.-L. Brunaux, *The Celtic Gauls* (London, 1988), ch. 10, is of special interest on these.

3. J. Pouilloux, *Recherches sur l'histoire et les cultes de Thasos* I (Paris, 1954) 371–9.
4. Alcaeus 167; D. L. Page, *Lyrica Graeca Selecta* (Oxford, 1968). An attempt at a translation is given on page 236.
5. Examples; A. Mallwitz and H. V. Herrmann, eds, *Die Funde aus Olympia* (Athens, 1980) pls. 50–73; H. Hoffmann and A. E. Raubitschek, *Early Cretan Armorers* (Mainz, 1972) pls. 1–47.
6. Rouse 1902: 54; Pritchett, *War* 3.240; Lonis 1979: 147–8; Lazzarini 1976: 93–5. This word's agricultural associations do not seem much exploited in votive texts to do with spoils, even though hoplites were often farmers or landowners on a grander scale fighting for disputed land in ranks as *zeugitai* (D. Whitehead, 'The archaic Athenian zeugitai', *CQ* 31.2 (1981) 282–6); cf. *Il.* 11.67–71, in line perhaps with the normally restrained tone of votive inscriptions.
7. Lonis 1979: 158–60.
8. Archilochus 1, D. L. Page, *Epigrammata Graeca* (Oxford, 1975); Alcaeus Hdt. 5.95.
9. M. I. Finley, *The World of Odysseus* (London, 1977) 119; E. Vermeule, *Aspects of Death in Early Greek Art and Poetry* (Berkeley, 1979), ch. 3.
10. H. Koenigs-Philipp, in Mallwitz and Herrmann (*supra* n.5), 88.
11. Pritchett, *War* 3, ch.7.
12. L. H. Jeffery, *Local Scripts of Archaic Greece* (Oxford, 1961) 90 and 94 n.1; 195–6 and 201 n.49; Paus. 5.24.3.
13. F. T. Van Straten, 'Gifts for the gods', in H. S. Versnel, *Faith Hope and Worship* (Leiden, 1981) 65–80 esp. 74; W. Burkert, *Greek Religion* (Oxford, 1985) 68–70, 92–5.
14. Pritchett, *War* 3. 292–3.
15. Simonides 19; Page (*supra* n.8).
16. Cf. Anderson 1970 pl. 1.
17. Votives in daily life, Rouse 1902: chs 2 and 6. Entry to temples, P. E. Corbett, 'Greek temples and Greek worshippers', *BICS* 17 (1970) 149–58.
18. Alcaeus 167, in Page (*supra* n.4).
19. Pritchett, *War* 3 esp. ch. 6; Lonis 1979 esp. chs 5 and 6.
20. The text used is that of G. O. Hutchinson, *Aeschylus. Septem contra Thebas* (Oxford, 1985).
21. Pritchett, *War* 2, ch. 23.
22. Kunze *OB* 6 (1958) pl. 44.1 (uninventoried); *OB* 7 (1961) pl. 35.1 (B5060); *OB* 8 (1967) pl. 78 (B353). Blyth 1977: 80–5 thinks serious damage from battle to armour at Olympia is rare. Also important discussion in C. Weiss, *CSCA* 10 (1977) 195–207.
23. Cf. Detienne (*supra* n.2).
24. M. Moynihan, *God on Our Side: The British Padre in World War I* (London, 1983) 17.
25. For discussion of the background, L. Bonfante, 'Nudity as a costume in Classical art', *AJA* 93 (1989) 543–70.

26. Cf. C. M. Parkes, *Bereavement: Studies of Grief in Adult Life*, (Harmondsworth, England, 1975), ch.6; R. Parker, *Miasma: Pollution and Purification in Early Greek Religion* (Oxford, 1983) 113.
27. Lazzarini 1976: 316–21 nos. 956, 973–5, 989. Argive dedication from Pyrrhus near Mycenae: G. E. Mylonas, *Praktika* 1965, 95–6.
28. J. McK. Camp II, 'A spear butt from the Lesbians', *Hesperia* 47 (1978) 192–5. Possibly the Spartan shield from Pylos buried by the early third century BC reflects some Athenian *rapprochement* with Sparta or pro-Spartan sabotage; T. L. Shear, *Hesperia* 6 (1937) 346–8.
29. Snodgrass 1967: 125.
30. P. de la Coste-Messelière, *Au Musée de Delphes, BEFAR* 138 (Paris, 1936):9–11.
31. A. M. Snodgrass, *Archaic Greece* (London, 1980) 131.
32. Krentz, 'Casualties in hoplite battles', *GRBS* 26 (1985) 13–20.
33. For example, Kunze, *OB* 8 (1967) 83–107. Also Lazzarini 1976: 316–23, esp. nos. 961a and b, 964–5, 967, 970–2, 976–80, 991, 994–6.
34. L. Drees, *Olympia, Gods, Artists and Athletes* (London, 1968) 88–91; H. V. Herrmann, *Olympia; Heiligtum und Wettkampfstätte* (Munich, 1972) 20–5; 106–12. Kunze and Schleif, *OB* 2 (1938) 5–27, 67; *OB* 3 (1941) 5–29; Kunze, *OB* 5 (1956) 11.
35. M. B. Poliakoff, *Combat Sports in the Ancient World* (London, 1987), esp. ch. 6.
36. Snodgrass 1967: 48–9. W. Gauer, *Ol. Forsch.* 8 (1975), esp. 213–43, notably 217 Well 81 (south-east area) and 219–20 Well 48 (south-east area), with Kunze, *OB* 8 (1967) 87 n.7 on the helmet B6081.
37. Kunze, *OB* 7 (1961) 129–37.
38. A. H. Jackson, 'Some deliberate damage to Archaic Greek helmets dedicated at Olympia', *Liverpool Classical Monthly* 8.2 (Feb. 1983) 22–7. The parallel with toasts was suggested by Prof. K. H. Jackson. Interesting similarities but not necessarily exact parallels appear in Celtic Gaul; J.-L. Brunaux and A. Rapin, *Gournay* II (Paris, 1988).
39. Gauer (*supra* n.36) 234–43.
40. Herrmann (*supra* n.34) 112.
41. H. G. G. Payne, *Perachora* I 93; W. Lamb, *BSA* 28 (1926–7) 106.
42. H. Diels and W. Kranz, *Die Fragmente der Vorsokratiker* II (Berlin, 1952) Gorgias 5b (Philostr. *VS* 1.9); Lys. 33.
43. For analysis of changes in types of offering at Olympia and Delphi and of differences between the two sanctuaries in relation to Panhellenic ideas, F. Felten, 'Weihungen in Olympia und Delphi' *AM* 97 (1982) 79–97.

Part V
EPILOGUE

Battle history . . . deserves a similar primacy over all other branches of military historiography. It is in fact the oldest historical form, its subject matter of commanding importance, and its treatment demands the most scrupulous historical care. For it is not through what armies *are* but what they *do* that the lives of nations and of individuals are changed. In either case, the engine of change is the same: the infliction of human suffering through violence. And the right to inflict suffering must always be purchased by, or at a risk of, combat – ultimately combat *corps à corps.*

John Keegan
The Face of Battle

THE FUTURE OF GREEK MILITARY HISTORY

Victor Davis Hanson

The intention of this small collection has been to advocate an alternative approach to the study of Greek warfare, one that eschews the traditional triad of strategy, tactics, and logistics to concentrate more on the experience of fighting. Because hoplite infantrymen of the Archaic and Classical Ages wore nearly identical equipment, often fought in almost equal numbers, and followed uniformly formal rules of engagement, which were usually without intricate maneuver and articulation, emphasis on the battle environment is particularly apt and, in fact, long overdue. More remains to be done – so much so that in the future the pragmatic concerns of hoplites will not be a footnote to more conventional studies; rather they will rightly become the central focus of Greek military history.

For example, it is still not clear how one phalanx engineered the defeat of its adversary, given such rough parity in technology, numbers, tactics, generalship, and terrain. Examination of hoplite battles from Marathon and Plataia to Delion, Haliartos, Leuktra and Mantineia may suggest that, in the majority of cases (the Spartans perhaps being only occasional exceptions), troops fighting on the defensive in their own territory usually repelled the invaders. Was classical hoplite battle then essentially protective and simply not designed for conquest or even attack beyond disputed borderlands? Unit morale – the real key to effective advance – was superb as long as citizen-farmers knew that each man fought to protect his own ground, not to harm, occupy, or even trespass on the farms of another.

In that general context, were the more subtle qualitative, national characteristics of particular hoplite armies (the discipline and professionalism of the Spartans; the bodily strength and combative skill of Theban hoplites; the emotionalism – characterized by reckless courage or abject despondency – of Athenian infantry; the similar unevenness and unpredictability of performance among Argive troops) less important than the knowledge that one fought on the ground of his fathers. Yet, such a 'home-court' advantage must not be discussed only in terms of *esprit de corps* when we keep in mind that hoplite killing-fields everywhere were nearly uniform, hoplite battle thus giving little opportunity to the defenders for manipulation of local terrain or indigenous populations.

Much, too, has been written about the frequency of hoplite battle. A systematic, inclusive list of *all* hoplite battles from 650 BC to Chaironeia (names, dates, combatants, outcome, etc.) is surely now needed – one that supplements traditional historical accounts through the use of (less certain) archaeological, epigraphical, and anecdotal literary evidence. Through such a *Catalogus Proeliorum Graecorum* we could obtain some rough estimate, not merely of the total time and numbers invested, but perhaps also of the casualties inflicted in land warfare during the history of the Greek city-states. While there have been some preliminary studies devoted to casualty ratios and the nature and incidence of wounds, no comprehensive account of war losses exists for the entire period of hoplite warfare.

Too much emphasis also has been placed on too few battles, for example, Marathon and Leuktra.[1] Others, such as Delion, Mantineia, and Koroneia, may tell us much more about what a hoplite battle was like. At Delion, for example we learn of the first appearance of a deepened phalanx, of a strange use of mounted reserves, of frightful accidental casualties, of bodies rotting in the sun for days, of a desperate, lengthy, and infamous Athenian retreat.

Were there also acknowledged arenas of battle? There seems to have been only a small, set number of suitable plains where hoplite armies traditionally agreed to meet in battle, a phenomenon which reinforces the ritualistic notion of Greek warfare. How else can we explain the repeated engagements, generation after generation, in the identical Argive, Corinthian, and Mantineian plains? Consider, too, the striking proximity of battle-sites in Boiotia – a veritable 'blood alley' of sorts – over a 200-year period; there, only a very few miles separate Plataia, Tanagra, Oinophyta, Delion, Haliartos, Koroneia, Leuktra, and Chaironeia.

On a more mundane level, the role of the middle and rear ranks of the phalanx is also poorly understood. Was it their task to push, to kill off at their feet enemy casualties, to prevent retreat, to replace the fallen, to deflect missiles, to aid their own wounded, to act as a reserve of sorts? What were the criteria – skill, courage, experience, age, size, class, status, armament, vote, lot, choice, random chance – which placed particular individuals or tribal contingents at particular slots in the phalanx? And what were the differing challenges and martial tasks inherent at these places, the front, middle, rear, and exposed right file?

In a wider sense, what led to the gradual transformation of classical hoplite warfare? Was it, as is so often argued, the steady decline – in a social and economic sense – of the free city-state and its landed hoplite class of amateurs, the diminishing importance of agriculture itself in the lives of the majority of the polis? Or was it the contagion of foreign military experience, the increasing frequency of battling against those with different equipment and strange notions about the nature and role of war and warrior in society? Or, did the formal rules of engagement ultimately become absurd, irrelevant to the hoplites who fought – men who saw no reason to cease fighting in defeat, when less than 20 percent of their own had fallen, men who simply found hoplite arms and armor anachronistic and expensive encumbrances? Or, finally, have we too often exaggerated such changes in battle of the fifth and fourth century BC, especially when we remember the classic hoplite collisions – Koroneia, Nemea, Leuktra, Mantineia, Chaironeia – rather than accompanying skirmishes or siegecraft, still remain a (even if not *the*) central focus in Greek warfare.

Such inquiry is not mere eccentricity. Knowledge about the Greek combat experience, its frequency and nature, can reveal much about the values of Greek society and the lives of many of its greatest thinkers: Tyrtaeus, Archilochus, Alcaeus, Aeschylus, Sophocles, Thucydides, Pericles, Socrates, Xenophon, Demosthenes and others. Far more importantly, battle history brings a much needed reality, a morality, to the whole time-honored notion of an 'art of warfare,' that obscene enough phrase which operational historians employ when investigating the 'science' of killing and maiming faceless mobs of humanity. In conclusion, we would do well when investigating Greek warfare simply to remember the words of Adlous Huxley:

> The language of strategy and politics is designed . . . to make it appear as though wars were not fought by individuals drilled to murder one another in cold blood and without provocation, but either by impersonal and therefore wholly nonnormal and impassable forces, or else by personified abstractions. . . . Accordingly, when we talk about war, we use a language which conceals or embellishes its reality. Ignoring the facts, so far as we possibly can, we imply that battles are not fought by soldiers,

but by things, principles, allegories, personified collectives, or (at the most human) by opposing commanders, pitched against one another in single combat. For the same reason, when we have to describe the processes and the results of war, we employ a rich variety of euphemisms. Even the most violently patriotic and militaristic are reluctant to call a spade by its own name.[2]

NOTES

1. W. K. Pritchett, for example, once remarked of scholarship concerning Leuktra that, "there are more reconstructions of Leuktra than any other Greek battle, and the end is not in sight" (*War* 4.54, n. 159); in this present volume (p. 156, n. 18) Everett L. Wheeler drew similar conclusions of Marathon: there is "publication of at least one article on the battle nearly every year".
2. Huxley, 'Words and behavior,' in *Collected Essays* (New York, 1958), 246–8.

BIBLIOGRAPHY

For the period 1918–39 there is a bibliography of Greek warfare in general by F. Lammert in *Jahresbericht über die Fortschritte der Klassischen Altertumswissenschaft* 274 (1941) 1–114; most recently, R. Lonis has done a similar study for the fifteen years between 1968 and 1983, 'La guerre en Grèce: 15 années de recherche 1968–1983' in *Révue des Etudes Grecques* 98 (1985) 321–79. The following titles refer to works cited in parentheses in the text. Abbreviations of periodicals follow those found in the *Oxford Classical Dictionary*.

Adam, J. P. *L'architecture militaire grecque* (Paris, 1982).

Adcock, F. E. *The Greek and Macedonian Art of War* (Berkeley and Los Angeles, 1957).

Ahlberg, G. *Fighting on Land and Sea in Greek Geometric Art* (Stockholm, 1971).

Anderson, J. K. *Ancient Greek Horsemanship* (Berkeley and Los Angeles, 1961).

——— 'Cleon's Orders at Amphipolis,' *JHS* 85 (1965) 1–5.

——— *Military Theory and Practice in the Age of Xenophon* (Berkeley and Los Angeles, 1970).

——— 'Hoplites and heresies: a note,' *JHS* 104 (1984) 152.

Andrewes, A. 'The hoplite katalogos,' in G. S. Shrimpton and D. J. McCargar (eds) *Classical Contributions: Studies in Honor of M. F. McGregor* (New York, 1981).

Arnould, D. *Guerre et paix dans la poésie greque* (New York, 1981).

Aymard, A. 'Remarques sur la poliorcétique grecque,' in *Etudes d'histoire ancienne* (Paris, 1967) 474–86.

Bar-Kochva, B. *The Seleucid Army: Organization and Tactics in the Great Campaigns* (Cambridge, England, 1975).

Best, J. G. P. *Thracian Peltasts and their Influence on Greek Warfare* (Groningen, 1969).

Blyth, P. H. 'The structure of a hoplite shield in the Museo Gregoriano Etrusco,' *Bolletino Dei Musei E Gallerie Pontifice* 3 (1982) 5–21.

Blyth, P. *The Effectiveness of Greek Armour Against Arrows in the Persian War* (Ph.D. University of Reading, 1977).

Borchhardt, J. *Homerische Helme* (Mainz, 1972).

Boucher, A. 'La tactique grecque à l'origine de l'histoire militaire,' *REG* 25 (1912) 300–12.

Bradeen, D. W. 'The Athenian casualty lists,' *CQ* 63 (1969) 145–59.

Brelich, A. 'Guerre Agoni e Culti nella Grecia arcaica,' *Antiquitas* 1.7 (1966) 9–21.

Buckler, J. 'Epameinondas and the *ΕΜΒΟΛΟΝ*,' *Phoenix* 39 (1985) 134–43.

Burford, A. 'Heavy transport in Classical Antiquity,' *Economic History Review* [2nd series] 13 (1960): 1–18.

Cartledge, P. 'Hoplites and heroes: Sparta's contribution to the technique of ancient warfare,' *JHS* 97: (1977) 11–23.

Cawkwell, G. L. *Philip of Macedon* (London, 1978).

Chase, G. H. 'The shield devices of the Greeks,' *HSCP* 13: (1902) 61–127.

Chrimes, K. M. T. *Ancient Sparta* (Manchester, England, 1949).

Connolly, P. *Greece and Rome at War* (London, 1981).

Connor, W. R. 'Early Greek land warfare as symbolic expression,' *Past and Present* 119 (1988) 3–27.

Couissin, P. *Les institutions militaires et navales* (Paris, 1932).

Curtius, E. 'Zur Geschichte des Wegebaus bei den Griechen,' Abb. *Akad. Wiss. Berlin*. (Berlin, 1854): 211–303.

Delbrück, H. *Geschichte der Kriegskunst im Rahmen der politischen Geschichte Vol. I, Das Altertum* (1900; new edn by K. Christ 1964) tr. W. Renfroe, *History of Warfare* Vol. I, (Westport, Conn., 1975).

Despotopoulos, T. 'Hê Odopoiia en Elladi,' *Technika Chronika* 17 (1940): 255–61, 329–39, 530–40.

Devine, A. M. '*ΕΜΒΟΛΟΝ*: a study in tactical terminology,' *Phoenix* 37 (1983) 201–17.

Dittenberger, W. *Sylloge Inscriptionum Graecarum* 3rd edn (Leipzig 1915–24).

Donlan, W. and Thompson, J. 'The charge at Marathon: Herodotus 6.112,' *CJ* 71 (1976) 339–43.

—— 'The charge at Marathon again,' *CW* 72 (1979) 419–20.

Droysen, H. 'Heerwesen und Kriegführung der Griechen,' in K. F. Herman, *Lehrbuch der griechischen Antiquitäten* II (2nd edn, Freiburg, 1889).

Ducrey, P. *Le traitement des prisonniers de guerre dans la Grèce antique* (Freiburg, 1968).

—— *Guerre et guerriers dans la Grèce antique*. (Paris, 1985) [tr. J. Lloyd, *Warfare in Ancient Greece*, (New York, 1986)].

Ferrill, A. 'Herodotus and the strategy and tactics of the invasion of Xerxes,' *American Historical Review* 72 (1966) 102–15.

—— *The Origins of War* (New York, 1985).

Fornara, C. W. 'The hoplite achievement at Psyttaleia,' *JHS* 96 (1966) 51–9.

Frazer, A. D. 'The myth of the phalanx scrimmage,' *CW* 36 (1942) 15–16.

Frost, F. 'The Athenian military before Cleisthenes,' *Historia* 33 (1984) 283–94.

Fuller, J. F. C. *The Generalship of Alexander the Great* (London, 1958).

—— *War in the Ancient World* [trans. Janet Lloyd (London, 1975)].

—— 'War and siegecraft,' *Cambridge Ancient History* 7.1 (Cambridge, England, 1984) 353–62.

——— *Guerre et économie en Grèce ancienne* (Paris, 1989).

Garlan, Y. 'Fortifications et histoire grecque,' in *Problèmes de la guerre* (Paris, 1968) 245–60.

——— 'La défense du territoire à l'époque classique,' in *Problèmes de la terre*, (Paris, 1973): 149–60.

——— *Recherches de poliorcétique grecque* (Paris, 1974).

Goodman, M. G. and Holladay, A. J. 'Religious scruples in ancient warfare,' *CQ* 36 (1986) 151–71.

Greenhalgh, P. A. L. *Early Greek Warfare: Horsemen and Chariots in the Homeric and Archaic Ages* (Cambridge, England, 1973).

Greger, M. *Schildformen und Schildschmuck bei den Griechen* (Berlin, 1908).

Gregoriandis, N. *L'art de la guerre d'Homère à Alexandre le Grand* (Paris, 1951).

Griffith, G. T. *The Mercenaries of the Hellenistic World* (Cambridge, England, 1935).

——— 'Peltasts and the origins of the Macedonian phalanx,' in *Ancient Macedonian Studies in Honor of Charles F. Edson* (Thessaloniki, 1981).

Grundy, G. B. *Thucydides and the History of his Age* (2 vols, 2nd edn, Oxford, 1911).

Hackett, J. H. (ed.) *A History of War in the Ancient World* (London, 1989).

Hagemann, A. *Griechische Panzerung* (Leipzig, 1919).

Hammond, N. G. L. 'The main road from Boeotia to the Peloponnese through the Northern Megarid,' *BSA* 49 (1954): 103–22.

——— 'Training in the use of the sarissa and its effect in battle,' *Antichthion* 14: (1980) 53–63.

Hanson, V. D. *Warfare and Agriculture in Classical Greece* (Pisa, 1983).

——— 'Epameinondas, the battle of Leuktra (371 BC) and the 'revolution' in Greek battle tactics,' *CA* 7.2 (1988) 190–207.

——— *The Western Way of War: Infantry Battle in Classical Greece* (New York, 1989).

Harmand, J. *La guerre antique* (Paris, 1973).

Hellström, P. 'A Corinthian bronze helmet,' *BMNE* 19 (1984) 49–56.

Hill, D. K. 'Early Italian Armor at Vassar College,' *AJA* 86 (1982) 589–91.

Hoffman, H. *Early Cretan Armorers* (Mainz, 1972).

Holladay, A. G. 'Hoplites and heresies,' *JHS* 102 (1982) 94–104.

Humble, R. *Warfare in the Ancient World* (London, 1980).

Jameson, M. H. 'The provisions for mobilization in the Decree of Themistokles,' *Historia* 12 (1963) 385–494.

Köchly, H. A. T. and Rüstow, W. *Geschichte des Griechischen Kriegswesen* (Arav, 1852).

Krentz, P. 'The nature of hoplite battle,' *CA* 4 (1985a) 50–61.

——— 'Casualties in hoplite battles,' *GRBS* 26 (1985b) 13–20.

Kromayer, J. and Veith, G. *Antike Schlachtfelder* vols 1–4 (1902–1924).

——— 'Heerwesen und Kriegführung der Griechen und Römer' in W. Otto (ed.) *Handbuch der Altertumswissenschaft* IV 3 (2nd edn, Munich, 1928).

Kukahn, E. *Der griechischen Helm* (Marburg, 1936).

Kunze, E. *V.-VIII. Berichte Uber die Ausgrabungen in Olympia* (Deutsches Archäologisches Institut, Berlin, 1956–67).

Kunze, E. and Schleif, H. *II.-III. Berichte Uber die Ausgrabungen in Olympia Jahrbuch des Deutschen Archäologischen Instituts* 53 (Berlin, 1938) and 56 (Berlin, 1941).

Lammert, F. 'Schild', 'Schlachtordnung' *RE* Ser. 2 Vol. 2A.1 (1921).

——— 'Synaspismos' *RE* Ser. 2 Vol. 4A.2 (1932).

——— 'Phalanx,' *RE* 19.2 (1938).

Latacz, J. *Kampfparänese, Kampfdarstellung und Kampfwirkichkeit in der Ilias, bei Kallinos und Tyrtaios (Zetemata* 66, Munich, 1977).

Lawrence, A. W. *Greek Aims in Fortification* (Oxford, 1979).

Lazenby, J. F. *The Spartan Army* (Warminster, England, 1985).

Lazzarini, M. L. 'Le formule delle dediche votive nella Grecia arcaica,' *Memorie della Classe di Scienze morale e storiche dell'Accademia dei Lincei*, 19 (Rome, 1976) 47–354.

Lengauer, W. *Greek Commanders in the 5th and 4th Centuries* BC*: Politics and Ideology, A Study of Militarism* (Varsovie, 1979).

Lippelt, O. *Die griechische Leichtbewaffneten bis auf Alexander dem Grossen* (Jena, 1910).

Lippold, G. *Griechische Schilde* (Berlin, 1909).

Lonis, R. 'Les usages de la guerre entre Grecs et Barbares' *Annales littéraires de l'Université de Bescançon* 104 (Paris, 1969).

——— 'Guerre et religion en Grèce à l'époque classique' *Annales Littéraires de l'Université de Besançon* 238 (Paris, 1979).

Lorimer, H. L. 'The hoplite phalanx,' *BSA* 42 (1947) 76–138.

——— *Homer and the Monuments* (London, 1950).

McCredie, J. R. 'Fortified military camps in Attica,' *Hesperia* Supplement 11 (Princeton, 1966).

McLeod, W. 'The Bowshot at Marathon,' *JHS* 90 (1970) 197–8.

McNicoll, A. 'Some developments in Hellenistic siege warfare with special reference to Asia Minor,' *Proceedings of the 10th International Congress of Classical Archaeology: 1973* I (3 vols, Ankara, 1978): 405–20.

Manti, P. A. 'The cavalry sarissa,' *AW* 8 (1983).

Markle, M. 'The Macedonian sarissa, spear, and related armor,' *AJA* 81: (1977) 323–30.

——— 'Use of the sarissa by Philip and Alexander of Macedon,' *AJA* 82: (1978) 483–97.

Marsden, F. W. *Greek and Roman Artillery* (2 vols Oxford, 1969, 1971).

Meiggs, R. and Lewis, D. M. *A Selection of Greek Historical Inscriptions to the End of the Fifth Century* BC (Oxford, 1988).

Nierhaus, R. 'Eine frühgriechische Kampfform,' *JdI* 53 (1938) 90–113.

Nilsoon, M. P. 'Die Hoplitentaktik und das Staatswesen,' *Klio* 22: (1929) 240–9.

Ober, J. 'Edward Clark's ancient road to Marathon, AD 1801' *Hesperia* 51: (1982) 453–8.

——— *Fortress Attica: Defense of the Athenian Land Frontier, 404–322* BC (Leiden, 1985a).

——— 'Thucydides, Pericles, and the strategy of defense,' in J. W. Eadie and J. Ober (eds) *The Craft of the Ancient Historian, Essays in Honor of Chester G. Starr*, Lanham, Maryland (1985b): 171–88.

——— 'Early artillery towers: Messenia, Boiotia, Attica, Megarid,' *American*

Journal of Archaeology 91 (1987a) 569–604.

——— 'Pottery and miscellaneous artifacts from fortified sites in northern and western Attica,' *Hesperia* 56 (1987b) 197–227.

Pélékidis, C. *Histoire de l'éphébie athénienne* (Paris, 1962).

Parke, H. W. *Greek Mercenary Soldiers* (Oxford, 1933).

Pritchett, W. K. *The Greek State at War*, vols 1–4 (Berkeley and Los Angeles, 1971–85).

——— *Studies in Ancient Greek Topography*, vols 1–6 (Berkeley and Los Angeles, 1971–89).

Podlecki, A. J. 'Three Greek soldier-poets: Archilochus, Alcaeus, Solon,' *CW* 63 (1969) 73–81.

Rahe, P. A. 'The military situation in Western Asia on the eve of Cunaxa,' *AJP* 101 (1980) 79–98.

Richter, G. M. A. 'Recent acquisitions of the Metropolitan Museum of Art,' *AJA* 43 (1939) 194–201.

Ridley, R. T. 'The hoplite as citizen: Athenian military institutions in their social context,' *AC* 48 (1979) 508–48.

Rolley, C. *Les Bronzes grecs* (Freiburg, 1983).

Rouse, W. H. D. *Greek Votive Offerings* (Cambridge, England, 1902).

Salmon, J. 'Political hoplites?' *JHS* 97 (1977) 87–122.

Schauer, P. 'Der Rundschild der Bronze- und frühen Eisenzeit,' *Jahrbuch des Romisch-Germanischen Zentralmuseums Mainz* 27 (1980) 196–247.

Schwertfeger, T. 'Der Shild des Archilochos,' *Chiron* 12 (1982) 253–80.

Scranton, R. L. *Greek Walls* (Cambridge, Mass., 1941).

Smith, G. 'Athenian casualty lists,' *CP* 14 (1918) 361–64.

Snodgrass, A. M. 'Carian armourers: the growth of a tradition,' *JHS* 84: (1964a) 107–18.

——— *Early Greek Armor and Weapons* (Edinburgh, 1964b).

——— 'The hoplite reform and history' *JHS* 85: (1965) 110–22.

——— *Arms and Armor of the Greeks* (Ithaca, NY, 1967).

——— 'The first European body-armour,' *Studies in Honour of C.F.C. Hawkes*, (London, 1971) 33–50.

Soedel, W. and V. Foley 'Ancient catapults,' *Scientific American* (March, 1979).

Tarn, W. W. *Hellenistic Military and Naval Developments* (Cambridge, England, 1930).

Van de Maele, Symphorien 'La route antique de Megare à Thèbes par le défilé du Kandili,' *BCH* 111: (1987) 191–205.

Van Wees, H. 'Leaders of men? Military organizations in the *Iliad*,' *CQ* 36 (1986) 285–303.

Vanderpool, E. 'Roads and forts in northwestern Attica,' *CSCA* 11 (1978): 227–45.

Vermeule, E. *Aspects of Death in Early Greek Art and Poetry* (Berkeley, 1979).

Vernant, J. P. (ed.) *Problèmes de la guerre en Grèce ancienne* (Paris, 1968).

Vidal-Naquet, P. and Lévêque, P. 'Epameinondas pythagoricien et le problème tactique de la droite et de la gauche,' *Historia* 9 (1960) 294–308.

Volkmann, J. 'Die Waffentechnik in ihrem Einfluss auf das soziale Leben der Antike,' in L. Wiese (ed.) *Die Entwicklung der Kriegswaffe und ihr Zusammenhang mit der Sozialordnung* (1953).

Vos, M. F. *Scythian Archers in Attic Vase Painting* (Groningen, 1963).
Wardman, A. E. 'Tactics and tradition of the Persian Wars,' *Historia* 8 (1959) 49–60.
Warry, J. *Warfare in the Ancient World* (New York, 1980).
Washington, H. S. 'Description of the site and walls of Plataia,' *AJA* 6 (1890) 452–62.
Watley, N. 'On the possibility of reconstructing Marathon and other ancient battles,' *JHS* 84 (1964) 119–39.
Westerman, W. L. 'On inland transportation and communication in antiquity,' *Political Science Quarterly* 43 (1928): 364–87.
Wheeler, E. L. 'The occasion of Arrian's *Tactica*,' *GRBS* 19 (1978) 351–66.
——— 'The legion as phalanx,' *Chiron.* 9 (1979) 303–18.
——— 'The origins of military theory in Ancient Greece and China,' *International Commission of Military History, Acta 5, Bucarest 1980* (Bucharest: Romanian Commission of Military History, 1981) 74–9.
——— 'Hoplomachia and Greek dances in arms,' *GRBS* 23 (1982) 223–33.
——— 'The hoplomachoi and Vegetius' Spartan drillmasters,' *Chiron* 13 (1983) 1–20.
——— 'Ephorus and the prohibition of missiles,' *TAPA* 117 (1987) 157–82.
Will, E. 'Le territoire, la ville, et la poliorcétique grecque' *RH* 253 (1975): 297–318.
Wilson, J. B. *Pylos 425 BC* (Warminster, England, 1979).
Winter, F. E. *Greek Fortifications* (Toronto, 1971).
Woodhouse, W. J. *The Campaign of Mantineia in 418 BC* (Oxford, 1918).

INDICES

I General Index

II Index and Glossary of Greek Military Terms Italicized in the Text

III Index of Ancient Authors Cited in the Text

INDEX III